THE MAKING OF THE MODERN NEAR EAST 1792–1923

A History of the Near East
General Editor: Professor P. M. Holt

★The Prophet and the Age of the Caliphates: the Islamic Near East from the sixth to the eleventh century
Hugh Kennedy

★The Age of the Crusades: the Near East from the eleventh century to 1517
P. M. Holt

The Rise of the Ottoman Empire 1300–1574
Colin Imber

The Decline of the Ottoman Empire 1574–1792
R. C. Repp

★The Making of the Modern Near East 1792–1923
M. E. Yapp

The Near East since the First World War
M. E. Yapp

Medieval Persia 1040–1797
D. O. Morgan

★ *Already published*

The Making of the Modern Near East

1792–1923

M. E. Yapp

Longman
London and New York

Longman Group UK Limited,
Longman House, Burnt Mill, Harlow,
Essex CM20 2JE, England
and Associated Companies throughout the world

Published in the United States of America
by Longman Inc., New York

First published 1987

British Library Cataloguing in Publication Data

Yapp, M. E.
The making of the modern Near East 1792–1923.
1. Middle East–Politics and government
I. Title
956 DS62.9

ISBN 0-582-01366-6 CSD
ISBN 0-582-49380-3 PPR

Library of Congress Cataloging-in-Publication Data

Yapp, Malcolm.
The making of the modern Near East, 1792–1923.

(A History of the Near East)
Bibliography: p.
Includes index.
1. Middle East – History – 1517–. I. Title.
II. Series.
DS62.4.Y35 1987 956′.01 87–2068
ISBN 0–582–01366–6
ISBN 0–582–49380–3 (pbk.)

Set in 10/12 Linotron 202 Bembo

Produced by Longman Singapore Publishers (Pte) Ltd.
Printed in Singapore.

Contents

List of Genealogical Tables and Maps

Note: Names, Titles, Dates and Currencies

NAMES AND TITLES

Near Eastern Muslim names commonly consisted of five elements: the personal name, the formal name, the patronymic, the group name and the honorific.

1. The personal name (*ism* or *ʿalam*), for example Aḥmed, ʿAlī, Ḥusayn and Muḥammad. Occasionally individuals were known by two personal names in combination, for example Muḥammad ʿAlī of Egypt. Another version of the personal name is the compound usually formed by the combination of ʿAbd (slave) with one of the so-called ninety-nine beautiful names of God, more precisely, attributes of God. Examples include the Ottoman sultans ʿAbd ül-ʿAzīz (Slave of the Powerful One), ʿAbd ül-Majīd (Slave of the Glorious One) and ʿAbd ül-Ḥamīd (Slave of the Praiseworthy One).
2. The formal name (*kunya*, usually denoting the relationship of the namebearer to another person, for example Abū (Father of) accompanied by the name of the other person. Thus, Abū'l-Qāsim = The father of Qāsim. Alternatively, the *kunya* may describe a metaphorical relationship, for example Abū'l-Faḍl (Father of merit), or a relationship to some familiar object with which the individual is associated, amounting in this usage to a nickname. Thus the Egyptian Jewish writer, James Sanua was known as Abū Naḍḍāra (Father of spectacles).
3. The patronymic (*nasab*) indicating the genealogy of the namebearer by listing the names of his ancestors, each name being preceded by the word *ibn* (son of), for example ʿAlī ibn Muḥammad (ʿAlī the son of Muḥammad). An alternative way of describing genealogy used in Persian and Turkish respectively is by the addition of the suffixes -zāda and -oghlu to the name of the father, for example Sulṭānzāda and Karaʿoṣmānoghlu.

4. The group name (*nisba*) often denoting the place of origin, for example al-Miṣrī (the Egyptian) or the occupation, for example al-Ṣayrafī (the banker or moneychanger).
5. The honorific (*laqab*) may be either a nickname or a title. An example of a nickname is to be found in the name by which a well-known Syrian Druze family is known, namely al-Aṭrash (the deaf). Titles were usually bestowed upon rulers, princes, soldiers and officers of state and were commonly compounds with *Dawla* (state), for example Nāṣir al-Dawla (Defender of the state), *Mulk* (kingdom), *Sultān* (ruler) or Islam. In Iran bureaucrats were commonly known by their titles or even by a title acquired at an earlier stage of their careers and indicating an office now relinquished. Thus the powerful minister, Mustawfī al-Mamālik (Accountant of the state), continued to be known by this title after he had ceased to be finance minister.

An individual might be known by names chosen from any of the above groups or by combinations of them. There was no direct equivalent of a surname until after the end of the period with which this book is concerned.

DATES

In this book only Christian dates (Gregorian calendar) have been provided. To find the Muslim (*Hijra*) date it is necessary to have recourse to a conversion table, for example W. Haig, *Comparative tables of Muhammadan and Christian dates*, London 1932, or G. S. P. Freeman-Grenville, *The Muslim and Christian calendars*, London 1963. During the nineteenth century for official purposes the Ottoman empire employed a modified calendar combining the solar year of the Julian calendar (with the Roman names of the months) and the Muslim era. The year began on 1 March and was known as *martiye* from the Turkish word for "March".

CURRENCIES

The basic unit of Ottoman currency at the beginning of the nineteenth century was the *kurush* (piastre). The severe depreciation of this coin led in 1844 to the introduction of the *lira* (pound) divided into 100 *kurush*. In 1881 a new gold pound (£0.90) was introduced divided into 100 new *kurush*. The principal coin in circulation was the silver *mejīdiye*, valued at 20 *kurush*. Various coins circulated in different parts of the empire and foreign coins were widely used, in Yemen the commonest coin was the Maria Theresa dollar. In Egypt in 1835 was introduced the piastre as a unit of account divided into 40 *paras*, the basic coin being the 20-piastre silver piece. In 1885 the Egyptian pound divided into 100 piastres was introduced. In Iran the principal coin was the *tūmān* (toman) which fell in value throughout the nineteenth century. Accounts were reckoned in the *dīnār*, a unit corresponding to one-ten-thousandth of a toman: 50 dīnārs = 1 *shāhī* and 20 *shāhīs* = 1 *kirānī* (kran) and 10 *kiranīs* = 1 toman. The *shāhī*, the *kirānī* and the toman were all represented by coins.

Preface

During the last twenty-five years I have taught the history of the Near East in the nineteenth and twentieth centuries to hundreds of undergraduate and postgraduate students. Many times I have assured myself that I would one day turn the experience of so many hours of reading, discussion and exposition to account by writing a general history of that period of the region's history. Whether I would have begun such a work without the special spur of circumstance I know not, and whether, had events been otherwise, I should have carried the project through to completion I strongly doubt, for the task was to prove more difficult than I had imagined. It so happened, however, that an unusual burden of administrative duties made it impossible for me to spend in libraries and archives the time which was required to finish the research upon which I was engaged and I was obliged to set that enterprise aside for a while and cast around for another topic which might satisfy my frustrated academic yearnings. It was at this fortunate moment that my old friend and former colleague, Peter Holt, invited me to write a volume in the Longman series on the history of the Near East which he had agreed to edit. For his invitation and for his help and advice with the writing of this book I am most grateful: the responsibility for its contents is, of course, mine alone. I am also grateful to those many students in whose company I have sharpened my ideas on the subject and to those many colleagues from whose work I have drawn inspiration and, probably, more than inspiration. I apologize to any of them from whom I may have unwittingly pillaged ideas, images or even phrases without acknowledgement: to pinch a good thing openly is an academic compliment but not to acknowledge its provenance is a serious impropriety, if not a worse sin.

Such merit as this book may have derives in large part from the long academic debate which I have held with the two groups mentioned above. Only those whose experience of teaching Near Eastern history extends over a considerable period can know how the subject has been carried forward by its practitioners in the second half of the twentieth century; where once one scraped to fill a bibliography there is now a real task of selection. It has been good to be part of that endeavour and it has been good also to stand back and to take stock of some of its results.

The principal difficulty which I encountered in writing this book was to combine the requirement for a straightforward, factual account of the modern history of the region, such as would be useful to students, with the desirability of providing an introduction to various ideas – some fairly well developed, others only half formed – about the nature of Near Eastern development during the period. My inclination towards the second possibility was strengthened by the opportunities for comparisons presented by the project. Looking at the results some readers may think the combination should not have been attempted and I confess that there were moments when I thought the same. But it seems to me now that the ideas have profited from the discipline of the factual narrative and that the narrative itself has been ventilated by the ideas and given a suitably provisional character. I do not know whether I can write received wisdom but I know I have never wanted to do so.

A similar, comforting rationalization has come to enfold my second difficulty which was to find the time to write the book. In the end most of it was written in various holiday homes in France. When I was a student I marvelled at the ingenuity of Henri Pirenne writing his history in a prison camp. Now, it seems to me to be the only way such a work could have been brought to a successful conclusion. Escape from libraries can be an intellectual liberation: deprived of his books even H. A. L. Fisher might have discovered some patterns in history. At all events I doubt if I would have picked my way through the Eastern Question without the help of the empty air of the high Pyrenees.

It is tempting to use a preface to seek to anticipate or even to disarm one's critics. Wise publishers like mine restrict writers to two pages and prevent them from offering a second book as an introduction to the first. Messrs Longman have served me well with patience, encouragement and help and I should not try their goodwill further. If they have a fault it is no more than a scepticism about the value of capital letters.

M. E. YAPP
St Albans–Normandy–Béarn–London
August 1984 to July 1986

CHAPTER ONE

Society, Economy and Politics in the Nineteenth-century Near East

INTRODUCTION

This first chapter will provide an outline of the main features of the social, economic and political condition of the Near East in 1800 and a sketch of the principal changes which took place during the course of the period down to 1923. Before embarking upon that task it will be helpful to say what is meant by the Near East.

The term "Near East" appeared towards the end of the nineteenth century, when it was used as a convenient expression to describe the Ottoman empire and the territories which had until recently formed part of it. The companion term "Middle East" appeared a few years later and was used to indicate the territories which extended from Iran to Tibet. These two terms were used in those senses down to the end of the First World War. The core of this study therefore is the political unit which Europeans called Turkey and which the Ottomans referred to as *mamalik-i ʿO̱smaniye* (the Ottoman lands) or *devlet-i ʿaliye* (the exalted state). In this book it will be referred to as the Ottoman empire.

The Ottoman empire in 1880 extended from Bosnia to Arabia and from the Zagros mountains to Algeria. However, it is not intended to devote equal attention to the whole of that territory but to concentrate on the central Ottoman lands. In 1800 Algeria, Tunisia and Libya were autonomous and only a brief account will be given of their fortunes. Little will be said also of the Sudan, which was independent in 1800 but conquered by Egypt in the nineteenth century; and Arabia will receive modest attention. The Balkan lands, which are usually referred to as Rumelia, although the term is not conterminous with the Balkan countries, were of great importance to the Ottomans and are given due prominence during the time they remained part of the empire. But as the Balkan states begin on their careers of autonomy little attention is given to their domestic affairs. The heart of the book is Anatolia, Greater Syria, Egypt and Iraq to which is added one area from outside the Near East, namely Iran, which, because of its size and because of the interest of comparing developments in Iran with those in more western areas, deserves inclusion. Finally, a few references are made to Turkestan in the east for the sake of comparison and completeness.

One major problem which besets any writer on the modern history of the Near East is what place to give to the activities of the European powers. To ignore their role is to distort the history of the Near East, yet to understand it fully requires a detailed consideration of purely European problems and space which is not available; and the effort distracts attention from the changes within the Near East which are the central concern of this book. Some compromise is essential but no compromise is likely to please.

SOCIETY

Writing at about the beginning of our period the Egyptian chronicler, al-Jabartī, described society in terms of five hierarchically arranged categories ranging from the Prophet Muḥammad to the masses. What is interesting about his arrangement is the criterion he used to determine the rank of each category, for he did not use wealth or birth or political power but instead applied the concept of justice (*ʿadl*). Social status is determined by the propensity of each group to behave justly. The concept is set out in the Ottoman Civil Code, the Mejelle: "The *ʿadl* person is one in whom good impulses prevail over bad." Of course, Muslims recognized that in this evil world social rank was not founded on justice but on power, but in stating the ideal Jabartī was also indicating that deviations were essentially impermanent; ultimately society must depend upon justice if there was to be stability. It is implicit also in his view that the just society was a Muslim society for only the believer had accepted the guidance which was necessary in order to behave with justice.

Another common view of the social order depicted it as related to the four elements. Society was composed of four classes: men of the pen, men of the sword, merchants and peasants. The classes were bound together in mutual dependence – the state rested on the military; the military on the peasants, the peasants on justice which was guaranteed by the *Sharīʿa* and the *Sharīʿa* required the support of the state.

It is useful to set out contemporary Near Eastern views of society in order to show how essentially anachronistic is the analysis which follows for modern analysis begins with the idea of describing the actual mechanisms of society in order to propound a view of the way it coheres or is organized.

To modern Western readers the term social organization suggests a pyramid wherein social classes are arrayed in a hierarchy according to wealth and status. That image will not do for the Near East in the early nineteenth century. According to one view there was no hierarchy but two distinct horizontal layers consisting of the rulers and the ruled. Applied to Near Eastern towns that scheme has some merit, but it fails when applied to the countryside for it overvalues the interest and influence of the rulers. The shadow of government certainly extended into the countryside, but it was there refracted through various prisms which themselves represent social groupings.

Another, valuable concept which has been applied to Near Eastern society is that of the mosaic. In this view Near Eastern society is seen as a mosaic of autonomous corporations existing side by side and not arranged in any particular order of eminence, or at least not an order accepted throughout the society. Government itself may be regarded as one such corporation and, like the others, defined partly by inheritance and partly by function – the provision of defence and some modest administrative services.

Birth was certainly the primary criterion which determined to which corporation within Near Eastern society an individual belonged. It was not impossible to achieve membership of another corporation, and in earlier periods a large part of the ruling group within the Ottoman empire was recruited by lifting children from one group and enrolling them among the rulers, but it was exceedingly difficult and it was an ambition which few cherished. In the nineteenth century the one substantial group which did not have its status determined by birth was the slaves. Slavery in the Near East chiefly involved the importation of pagan Blacks for domestic duties. White slaves were used primarily as soldiers or concubines but in the nineteenth century Circassian slaves were also employed, unusually, in agricultural work. Slavery was, however, also a door to the highest positions in the state: of twelve Ottoman grand viziers in the period 1785–1808 at least five were by origin the slaves of pashas. But for the most part people lived their lives within the group in which they were born and their children followed them in it.

The basic social group was the family. In the absence of any censuses or any system of registration we know regrettably little about the size of the Near Eastern family in 1800. It is usually assumed that the common pattern was that of the extended family and the isolated examples such as the Serbian *zadruga* which are recorded support that assumption.

The family was the basis of tribal organization. "Tribal" does not mean "nomadic" in the Near East; it is a much broader category, and may be regarded as a spectrum extending from settled peoples such as those in Syria who retained a memory or myth of Arab tribal descent, through settled tribes such as the Khazāʿil or Marsh Arabs of Iraq or the bedouin of the western provinces of Egypt through to the true pastoral nomads of Arabia. Even nomadism itself should be regarded as a spectrum rather than an absolute category for it embraced both those who confined their movements to the summer and cultivated grain or were sedentary stock-breeders in the winter and those aristocrats of central Arabia, the camel-herding tribes like the Ḥarb and the Shammar who looked down on those who merely herded sheep. It was the camel nomads who especially cherished their genealogies, but descent as well as occupation determined the status of all who retained a tribal identity. For them society was governed by categories such as the family, the segmentary lineage, the clan, the division, the group and the tribe (*qabīla*) itself, by traditional alliances, by an established hierarchy of tribal authority and by tribal obligations and customs, notably the blood feud. What proportion of the population of the Near East in 1800 may be classified as tribal is difficult to estimate, but the number would include most of the population of Arabia, half that of Iraq, a third of that of Iran and substantial proportions of the populations of Egypt, Syria and Anatolia, especially the eastern areas. Tribal groups also existed in the European provinces of the Ottoman empire, in Albania and Montenegro.

The category of peasant overlaps with that of tribesman but it embraces much more and peasants formed the largest socio-economic category in the Near East in 1800. Beyond the family the peasant looked to the village, which was the common focus of loyalty through much of the Near East and was a centre of economic as well as social life. The village created its own hierarchy, composed of the elders or heads of families who met in council under a village headman and took decisions affecting the village as a whole. The village was an enclosed community; a feature underlined by its appearance through most of the region. The description of an Egyptian village by Lady Duff Gordon in 1862 may convey something of the style:

The villages look like slight elevations in the mud banks cut into square shapes. The best houses have neither paint, whitewash, plaster, bricks nor windows, nor any visible roofs. They don't give one the notion of human dwellings at all at first, but soon the eye gets used to the absence of all that constitutes a house in Europe.[1]

Single-storey mud and timber constructions were the norm; apart from houses a Muslim village would have a few handicraft shops, a mosque and a Ṣūfī lodge. Christian villages would be similar with a church substituted for the mosque and Ṣūfī residence. Until the fashion of urban romanticism created the legend of the simple and deserving peasant, peasants were everywhere regarded with contempt in the Near East and held to be stupid and ignorant; civilization was an urban phenomenon and the countryside the realm of barbarism. Peasants were certainly illiterate, ignorant of the outside world and prone to superstition, although not necessarily more so than many town-dwellers: they were not, however, so submissive as they were often depicted to be and the history of the Near East contains many accounts of violent peasant uprisings against attempted impositions.

In the towns the focuses of social (and economic) life were the guild and the urban quarter, two institutions which tended to coincide. A quarter consisted of several narrow lanes with a single gated entrance which was closed at night. Within it were grouped the shops of people practising the same trade, who were usually organized in a guild. A guild was composed of apprentices, journeymen and masters and had elaborate regulations and ceremonies to control and celebrate passage from one grade to another. The guild masters formed a council and had a headman who represented the guild to outside bodies. Apart from its economic and governmental functions the guild also fulfilled social purposes, organizing parades, picnics, feasts and other ceremonies. Many, but not all, townspeople belonged to guilds; there was also a floating population of recent immigrants who were not absorbed into the guild structure and who constituted the element commonly described as the town riff-raff and who provided the muscle in the frequent urban riots. In addition, of course, the town was also a centre of government with the apparatus of bureaucrats and military garrison and of religion with a complement of religious teachers, lawyers, officials and students.

Cutting across the social divisions of the Near East described in the preceding paragraphs was the religious division. In 1800 the majority of the population of the Near East was Muslim: Turkestan, Iran and Arabia were almost wholly Muslim; a small Christian and Jewish minority lived in Iraq; a larger Christian minority (the Copts) lived in

Egypt together with a smaller Jewish community; most of the rest of North Africa was Muslim but with a substantial pagan element in the south; a sizeable Christian minority (over 10% of the population) lived in Greater Syria; another sizeable Christian minority of Greeks and Armenians lived in Anatolia; and there was a Christian majority of over two to one in Rumelia, the European provinces of the Ottoman empire. In Rumelia Muslims were especially the townspeople, with the exception of Bosnia, where there was a large class of Muslim landlords and free peasants, of Albania, where the rural areas contained a majority of Muslims, and of Macedonia, Bulgaria and Thrace, where there had been substantial Muslim settlement and conversion and there were many Muslim villages. There were no Muslim landholding in the principalities of Moldavia and Wallachia, where the Ottoman presence was confined to the fortress garrisons: in Serbia there was, apart from the garrisons, an urban Muslim population of about 20,000 composed of administrators, craftsmen and feudal landlords (*sipahis*): and in Greece about 65,000 Muslim landholders controlled about half the land of the future Greek state of 1830. By contrast, in Istanbul and the towns of the Asian provinces non-Muslims were represented disproportionately.

The Christian population of the Ottoman empire was divided into many sects but by far the largest group, concentrated especially in Rumelia, was the Greek Orthodox community. For organizational purposes the Greek Orthodox were divided into four patriarchates (Istanbul, Antioch, Jerusalem and Alexandria) of which the most important was that of Istanbul. For many purposes the Ottomans dealt with the Greek population through the patriarch in Istanbul, who was regarded as a high Ottoman official, entitled to a standard of two horsetails.

It is usually suggested that the Christian and Jewish communities of the Ottoman empire were organized in so-called *millets* and that the Ottoman government dealt with each *millet* through its hierarchical head. This did indeed become the practice during the nineteenth century, but in earlier periods the Ottomans commonly dealt with smaller groups (*ṭā'ifas*) of non-Muslims for most purposes and rarely used the term "*millet*" except in relation to the Muslim community. It is also suggested that all non-Muslims paid a special tax, the *jizye*, but in fact there was considerable discrimination between non-Muslim groups, depending upon age, status and services to the state and it has been calculated that no more than one-third of non-Muslims actually paid the tax.

In dealing with non-Muslims through their religious communities the Ottomans were also recognizing a social reality: religion was not merely a matter of church organization, worship and rites of passage but the religious communities also provided the two major social services of law and education. Personal law to the people of the Near East was the law of their religious community, and the authority of the religious community also penetrated other areas of civil law and occasionally even criminal law when cases involved members of the community alone. Such education as existed was provided almost entirely by the religious community through elementary schools attached to churches and through seminaries for higher education. Similarly with the Muslim community: although law was administered through the *qāḍī*'s court, education was provided through the mosque and the *madrasa*.

The Muslim community was far from uniform. In the first place it was divided into sects; Sunnī (the majority of Ottoman Muslims), Shīʿī (the majority of Iranian Muslims), and a variety of smaller sects mainly of Shīʿī origin. In the second place it was divided into what may be termed high Islam and popular Islam. High Islam was the religion of the *madrasa* and firmly rooted in the *Sharīʿa* and elaborated in the opinions of the most learned, the *muftīs* and (among Shīʿīs) the *mujtahids*. In the Ottoman empire, unlike other Muslim states, there existed by the late eighteenth century something approaching a Muslim hierarchy, led by the Shaykh al-Islām in Istanbul, to represent high Islam. Popular Islam was especially the Islam of the Ṣūfī orders which formed a major element in the social fabric of the Near East. A large proportion of the Muslim inhabitants of the Near East belonged to one or other of the many Ṣūfī orders which were extensive organizations owning property and providing a variety of social services for their adherents. Ṣūfī orders were of many types: some essentially religious, contemplative, literary organizations like the Naqshbandiyya and the Khalwatiyya in Istanbul; others were more like friendly societies, offering everyday services and appealing to the masses; many were distinctly heterodox like the Bektāshiyya; some had close links with particular guilds or professions; and some espoused the cause of social revolution. What is striking about the Ṣūfī orders is not only their diversity but their vigour. Far from being an old and decaying form of social organization they were entering, in the nineteenth century, a period of vigorous expansion when new orders were founded and older orders assumed novel aspects. The Ṣūfī shaykhs were powerful men in society.

Against that background it is possible to begin to sketch the social hierarchy of the Near East. At the top were those connected with government who comprised the military (almost entirely Muslim) and the bureaucracy (mainly Muslim but heavily penetrated with Christian and Jewish groups, for example the Copts, Armenians and Greeks who played a large part in financial administration in Egypt and the Ottoman empire as a whole). Without doubt this group enjoyed the greatest rewards. The second group was the religious establishment which included those claiming descent from the Prophet (the *sharīfs* and *sayyids*), those especially distinguished for their learning and the excellence of their behaviour, and those who held offices of importance, such as the imams of the leading mosques, the guardians of the great shrines, the principal *muftīs* and the members of the official Ottoman hierarchy. The existence of this hierarchy provided one link between government and religious groups. Another was provided by the existence of the *qāḍī*, a man with religious training who was a linchpin of administration throughout the Near East for he not only presided over a court but also discharged a host of administrative functions. The significance of the role of the ulema may be illustrated from the life of the Egyptian, Shaykh Muḥammad al-Mahdī (d. 1814) (curiously enough a Copt by origin who converted to Islam as a child) of whom al-Jabartī remarked that "he came to make the acquaintance of important people and through his good conduct with them, and the beauty of his words, he obtained much wealth".[2]

The third group was composed of the remainder of those outside government and consisted of merchants, peasants, tribesmen and townsmen, mainly the guildsmen. This was a large and heterogeneous group with considerable differences in manner and standard of life. In particular it is possible to distinguish a group which is usually described as notables (*aʿyān*) and which forms an essential bridge between government and the governed, representing the people to government. In no way should the notables be thought of as a species of middle class; their claim to consideration did not derive from their role in production or their professional status. They were in effect the people who had to be consulted by government because they were wealthy or because they had followers.

During the eighteenth century *aʿyān* was an official title but not an official post in the Ottoman empire. Many *aʿyān*, however, held an official post, namely that of *mütesellim*, by origin the agent sent to collect the revenues of a *sanjak* in the absence of the great dignitary to whom revenues were granted. These *aʿyān* became administrators of *sanjaks* and farmed the taxes thereof. Most of the Anatolian *derebeys* built their power in this way. But it would be wrong to restrict the term "notable" to this group for in functional terms it may usefully comprehend a much larger group.

The notables were diverse in origin and wealth. At the village level there were headmen. "The affairs of the Bulgarians", remarked an English traveller in 1829, "are referred in each village to a junta of old men, who may be considered, in the absence of the Turkish authority, as a sort of provincial government."[3] In Egypt, government could not have been carried on without the assistance of the *shaykh al-balad*. Among nomadic tribes the leader of each major division was also a notable. Large landowners such as the Anatolian *derebeys*, the Romanian boyars and the Bosnian begs were notables and able to defy government on occasion. So also did landowners and tribal leaders in Syria, some of whom were able to force from the Ottoman government incorporation within the formal governmental system. In the Peloponnesus the Council of Notables had the right of direct representation in Istanbul against the local government. In the towns the heads of guilds, of Ṣūfī orders and of *millets* all had followers and influence and had to be conciliated when, as was usually the case, they could not be coerced. In Aleppo and in Baghdad the head of the organization of the descendants of the Prophet, the Naqīb al-Ashrāf, was a man of substance.

Many writers have argued that wealth was the prime determinant of the notable. Baron de Tott wrote at the end of the eighteenth century that "the riches of some large landholders maintain, in the neighbourhood of Smyrna, a system of independence the progress of which increases every day. They rely principally on the power of money and this power is irresistible."[4] But money was decisive only if it bought followers; wealth alone was not a sufficient qualification. The Armenian *amiras* were the main bankers, controlled the mint and ran state industries in the Ottoman empire, but they had no direct political influence. Within the Armenian community, on the other hand, their power was considerable through their support of many institutions and they could achieve an indirect influence in that way. The same situation obtained with regard to many non-Muslim families which amassed great wealth in the service of Muslim rulers and who occupied major offices. Almost overnight they could be stripped of their offices and wealth and executed; they lacked the essential property of the notable, namely followers.

The Muslim ideal of a stable society, based on justice and composed of the four classical pillars – bureaucrats, soldiers, merchants and artisans, and peasants – bore little relation to the reality of Near Eastern society in 1800. Near Eastern society has been described as a block of flats in which the inhabitants met only in the corridors. It is right to emphasize the compartmentalized nature of the society but it is important also to understand the significance of the traffic in the corridors. Each compartment had its hierarchy and the leaders of those hierarchies transacted much business together. It was the people who bridged the compartments, *qāḍīs* and notables, who made the system work.

During the course of the nineteenth century Near Eastern society underwent a major transformation, the effect of which was to alter the character of the compartments and their relationship to each other. The causes of this transformation were, first, the growth in size of the compartment named government so that it squeezed all the others. In particular the extension of government control affected the position of the notables. A second factor was economic; increased competition and opportunity changed the relationship of peasant and landowner, altered the function of guilds and contributed to the decline of pastoralism. A third factor was intellectual; a new style of education and its extension contributed to the rise of a secularized intellectual class which challenged the position of the religious groups. The religious groups also lost most of their educational and legal functions.

It is even possible to detect a fall in the social status of some religious groups. In the eighteenth century a large proportion of holders of the post of shaykh al-Islām in Istanbul were the sons of former shaykhs: after 1839 not a single Shaykh al-Islām fell into the same category – all were of much lower social origins. In Iran, on the other hand, the great *mujtahids* continued to succeed their fathers.

For the non-Muslim *millets* the nineteenth century was a period of unparalleled advance. The patronage of Europe, the more rapid development of their educational systems and the opportunities created by the new ideas of secularism and equality led to their assuming a much larger role in the economy, in journalism and in government in the Near East. The *millets* were transformed into secular institutions and in some cases became the nucleus of separate states.

The changes are considerable and real, but what is more distinctive is how little Near Eastern society appeared to change. The changes were especially in the corridors; the compartments themselves proved remarkably enduring; their size changed and the furniture was moved but at the end of the period the Near East was still a society of compartments, no longer in equilibrium.

ECONOMICS

No reliable statistics for the population of the Near East in 1800 exist.

Formerly, historians employed the estimates of contemporary European travellers; more recently demographers have attempted to work backwards from later statistics. However, all calculations involve so many assumptions that they can never be more than enlightened guesses. Such guesses put the total population of the region in 1800 at a little over 30 million people, of which 6 million lived in Iran and nearly all of the remainder in the Ottoman empire. Of the Ottoman population, around 4.5 million lived in the three North African states of Algiers (3 million), Tunisia (1 million) and Libya (0.5 million). In Egypt were around 3.5 million people, in Iraq 1.25 million and in Greater Syria 1.75 million, made up of modern Syria 1.25 million and Lebanon and Palestine 0.25 million each. More heavily populated was Anatolia with around 6 million people, but the largest number of people (9.0 million) were in the European provinces of the Ottoman empire. This last total was made up of the Principalities 1.5 million (Wallachia 1 million and Moldavia 0.5 million), Greece (as formed in 1829) 0.75 million, Serbia (as in 1815) 0.4 million, Montenegro 0.1 million, Bosnia 0.75 million, Bulgaria 1.5 million, Macedonia (including Albania 1.2 million) and Rumelia proper, including Istanbul, 2.8 million. What the population of Arabia was is wholly unknown but the order of magnitude is in the region of 1 million.

Demographers are agreed that the population of the Near East had been falling for some time before 1800. To accept this proposition, however, does not mean that one should also accept the view that the region had once supported a very much larger population. It has been claimed, for example, that the population of ninth-century Iraq was 50 million and of fourteenth-century Egypt 14 million but the sources for such statements are wholly unreliable. While there is reason to suppose that the population of the Near East had been greater in the past there is no good reason to suppose that it had ever been substantially greater than it was in 1800. European travellers were often misled by the spectacle of the vast ruins which adjoined many Near Eastern cities and assumed that the population of the cities had once been much larger. But the nature of building materials, the movement of rivers, the blockage of canals, epidemics and political changes often led to the abandonment of one area and a movement to an adjacent location. An instructive example is provided by Cairo which consists of a succession of cities each constructed by a new dynasty which chose a site down river and upwind of the last site which was left to fall in ruins. By 1800 Cairo stretched from the old Byzantine city of al-Fusṭāṭ in the south to the Mamluk city in the north but at no one time had the whole area been fully inhabited. It is true, as comparisons of sixteenth-century Ottoman tax records with nineteenth-century observations have shown, that villages and small towns were occasionally abandoned in Palestine and elsewhere, but there is also evidence of increased economic activity leading to the foundation of new settlements in other areas during the same period. Another piece of so-called evidence relates to the rural population. In Iraq, it is argued, there are remains of water channels which demonstrate the previous existence of extensive irrigation schemes capable of supporting a substantial population. Both in Iraq and in Egypt, it is contended, changes in political organization led to failures to maintain these schemes and to a drastic fall in population. But it is not clear that the water channels were all irrigation channels and some appear to have been only flood-relief channels intended to protect cities like Baghdad from inundation.

To outside observers the Near East in 1800 appeared an empty land. They wrote of ruins, fertile lands uncultivated and a sparse population. Large parts of the European provinces, the most heavily populated part of the region are described as almost uninhabited: William Eton described the road from Belgrade to Istanbul as passing through a deserted countryside. The pashalik of Belgrade had a population density of only ten per square kilometre. Why was the population of the Near East not larger? Discussion has resolved around the four Malthusian checks of war, famine, disease and birth-control, and these provide a convenient framework for consideration of the question.

International war was a major problem in the border areas of the region. There were wars between the Ottomans and Iran which were fought in Iraq and Azerbaijan but most of the Ottoman Wars were fought on the European frontier of the empire. More important were the effects of endemic internal violence, the consequences of the conflicts between nomadic and settled people, the resistance offered by local groups to government demands, and faction fights. Insecurity, the destruction of crops and the flight of cultivators may account for much of the relative emptiness of the Near East. The eighteenth century saw a steady encroachment by nomadic peoples from Arabia on the settled areas of Syria and Iraq and of the bedouin on the Delta area of Egypt. Cultivation was abandoned in some areas, for example on the Tigris north of Baghdad. But one should be cautious about assuming that the relations of nomadic and settled peoples were always those of hostility deriving from competition for land. The relationship was much more complex; nomad and cultivator often lived in a symbiotic relationship. An economy dependent upon animal transport looked to nomads for supplies of camels and horses; much meat also came from nomads – Kurds brought around 25,000 sheep a year into Syria. The wool of sheep and goats was also an important product. Above all, nomads were major carriers of goods in the Near East. It is a question whether nomadic expansion caused a decline in cultivation or whether nomads entered upon lands already abandoned by cultivators.

There is ample evidence of the prevalence of famine and disease which were commonly sequential. Raymond, in his major study of eighteenth-century Cairo, lists six major famines in Egypt between 1687 and 1731 and further years of great scarcity between 1783 and 1792. In the 1784 famine al-Jabartī reports that the peasants came into the town and ate everything. Cannibalism was also reported. In Iraq eight famines are recorded during the period 1689–1801. Egypt and Iraq were perhaps especially vulnerable because of their dependence upon river water for cultivation but severe shortages were not unknown in the rainfall regions. Leaving aside the debilitating effect of endemic diseases there is much evidence concerning major epidemics of plague and cholera. Between 1689 and 1802 there were four outbreaks of plague in Baghdad; that of 1831 killed 50,000 in a single month according to a European missionary observer. Raymond records eight visitations of plague in Cairo in the seventeenth century and five in the eighteenth and estimates that some of the outbreaks may have killed between a third and a half of the population of the city. It is said that one-sixth of the population of Egypt died in the 1785 plague and a similar proportion in those of 1791 and 1834–5. In the Istanbul region in 1812 over 300,000 people were reported to have died in an outbreak of plague and the towns of Bucharest and Belgrade were each reported to have lost one-third of their populations. These figures, of course, were all estimates and mainly from towns. Deaths in the countryside, especially from epidemic diseases, may have been much less. Nevertheless, it is evident that contemporaries who observed the effects of these epidemics regarded them as major disasters.

Birth-control is a subject which has only recently been considered as an important factor in regulating the population of the pre-modern Near East. Basim Musallem, however, has produced evidence, albeit inconclusive, suggesting that Muslims made real efforts to regulate the size of their families. There are also indications of the use of abortion in western Anatolia in the late eighteenth century, but nothing which would show how widespread the practice was. Some nineteenth-century European observers, it is interesting to note, believed that the practices of the seclusion of women, the restriction of the size of Muslim families, polygamy and homosexuality would eventually cause the Ottoman Muslims to die out, but the population statistics show the impression of a declining Muslim population to be wholly inaccurate, and it is probable that the suggestion owed more to a dislike of the Turks and their institutions than anything else.

From this brief survey of a complicated and tantalizing subject it may be concluded that it is likely that the population of the Near East had fallen during the years before 1800, but that it had never been very much higher and that it was held in check not by pressure on the means of subsistence but by the effects of famine and disease preying upon a population made more vulnerable by internal insecurity. This lame and uncertain conclusion would hardly be worth setting out but for the circumstance that it is necessary to do so in order to highlight the major single change in the Near East during the period considered in this book, namely the increase in population. During the nineteenth century the Near East witnessed a demographic revolution. Down to 1914 the population increased at a rate of nearly 1 per cent per annum, probably more quickly during the second half of the period than during the first. This increase, I would argue, was quite unprecedented in the history of the region and the problems of feeding, clothing, housing and governing these extra people provided the major dynamic factor.

It is more difficult to account for this increase in population than to demonstrate that there was an increase. One reason was the reduction of the epidemic diseases; bubonic plague was no longer a major problem after the mid-nineteenth century and cholera reduced its toll after the last great attack of 1865 in Anatolia and Syria and of 1869 in Iran. Neither disease, however, was completely extinguished. Western medicine had some effect, chiefly in the cities, through the use of vaccination (replacing the older practice of inoculation) against smallpox, but its contribution was probably small for vaccination was virtually unknown in most of the countryside. More important were public health measures, notably the introduction of quarantine regulations, improved urban water supplies and better sewage disposal. Certainly, the effect of improvement was pronounced in the cities. In 1800 the towns of the Near East were death-traps, drawing in and killing people from the countryside; by 1914 they were more healthy than the rural areas. Famine was reduced by better communications which enabled food to be brought to regions where the harvest had failed. Probably most important of all, however, was the increased security throughout the region which was the consequence of the intervention of government to reduce the level of internal violence.

The increase in population was not accompanied by a substantial redistribution of the population between town and country. In 1800 the Near East was already more urbanized than most regions of the world, with something approaching 15 per cent of the population living in towns of over 10,000. Among these towns were Istanbul with 400,000 people, Cairo with over 200,000, Aleppo, Baghdad, Bursa, Edirne and Izmir each with more than 100,000, Bucharest 80,000, Damascus, Jassy, Tabriz and Tehran all with around 50,000. During the nineteenth and early twentieth centuries the urban population grew at about the same rate as the population as a whole; the only dramatic growths were registered by port cities linked with international trade, for example Alexandria, Beirut, Izmir and Salonika.

Among the rural population an alteration did take place in the balance between pastoral and agricultural pursuits. This change was most marked in the European provinces of the Ottoman empire where animal herding had been the occupation of a very large proportion of the population in 1800. During the nineteenth century there was a shift towards grain production; the oak forests of Serbia, which had supported so large a population of swine that Serbia was known as "The Land of Pigs", were burned down and farmers moved in; and Romania became a major grain producer. In Egypt also there was a substantial settlement of bedouin as the Delta region was irrigated and put under cotton; and the tide of nomadism was pushed back in Syria and Iraq. The great extension of cultivation was one of the most notable features throughout the Near East during the period 1800–1914, but calculations for Syria and Iraq show quite remarkable results: it is estimated that the cultivated area increased from about 125,000 *dunums* in the 1860s to about 1.6 million *dunums* (about 400,000 hectares) in 1913.

A second major change in the distribution of population concerned the religious composition of different areas. The loss of Ottoman authority in the European provinces was accompanied by a major emigration of Muslims to regions still under Muslim rule. In some cases they went voluntarily, in some cases they were expelled or refused permission to return after a temporary flight in wartime, and in some cases they fled to avoid the massacres which were the fate of many. They were joined by Muslim immigrants from Russia, especially from the Caucasus following the Russian conquest during the mid-nineteenth century, but also from other parts of Russia. Many Muslims moved more than once as the extent of Muslim authority in Europe diminished, until, by the end of the period, the great majority came to be concentrated in Eastern Thrace and Anatolia. Substantial pockets of Muslim people survived only in Albania, Bosnia, Bulgaria and Macedonia. At the same time the Christian population of areas which remained in Ottoman hands was very greatly reduced through forced and voluntary emigration and by murder and neglect.

The process of redistribution of populations reached a dramatic and brutal climax during the period from 1912 to 1923 which saw the Balkan Wars and the First World War. That period witnessed what has been described as a demographic disaster for the Near East; 20 per cent of the population of Anatolia died and another 10 per cent emigrated; 40 per cent of the Armenian, 25 per cent of the Greek and 18 per cent of the Muslim population died. In the same period 62 per cent of the Muslim population of the region conquered by the Balkan powers during the Balkan Wars had left that region and 27 per cent were dead.

The fine mosaic of religious communities living side by side which had been a feature of the Near East in 1800 was destroyed by 1923 in the northern part of the region; in the southern area the resolution of the problem was postponed until the second half of the twentieth century. The destruction of the mosaic was accomplished by violence and the threat of violence. The Greek uprising in 1821 began with a massacre of Muslims in Greece and with Muslim retaliation which included the hanging of the Greek patriarch in Istanbul. The cycle of violence continued throughout the century as governments sought to create demographic facts on the ground and at the popular level feelings of hatred and fear provoked massacre. Most people know the Eastern Question as an affair of diplomacy conducted in the chancelleries of Europe; in the Near East it was a bloody battle for land.

In 1800 the largest number of working people of the Near East were engaged in agriculture. The principal crops were cereals grown mainly for subsistence; wheat, barley and rice. There was also production for export in certain regions. In the late eighteenth century cotton was by far the most important export from Macedonia and Thessaly, and in that region maize was grown as an export crop. Cotton was also cultivated in many other regions. Silk was cultivated in several areas: the northern Iranian province of Gilan, the Bursa and Edirne areas of the central Ottoman lands and in Lebanon. Flax was produced in Egypt, tobacco in Latakia, coffee in Yemen and dates in parts of Arabia, notably in the Basra district of Lower Iraq. Fruits were also produced in the Mediterranean and exported from the Greek islands together with olives. Mocha coffee from Yemen was still prized.

During the course of the nineteenth and early twentieth centuries the area devoted to specialized crops increased. Most spectacular was the adoption of cotton as a major crop in Egypt and Turkestan, an event which completely transformed the economies of those countries. Cotton cultivation also flourished in other regions, for example Adana province in southern Anatolia and Khurasan in eastern Iran. Other cash crops which showed substantial increases included silk, tobacco, opium and sugar. It is true to say, however, that the Near East remained predominantly a cereal-producing area and this feature was accentuated by the decline of pastoralism, notably in south-east Europe. In 1909–10 between 80 and 90 per cent of Anatolia was still under cereals, cereal cultivation dominated Syria, and it was extending in Iraq.

The combined effect of the switch to cash crops and of population growth contributed to a change in one aspect of the Near East. In 1800 the region was self-sufficient in grain but that was no longer true in 1914. From about 1900 Egypt became a net importer of food: Turkestan also became dependent upon imports from Siberia, a dependence for which the region was to pay a heavy price in famine during the First World War when the transport system became overloaded by the demands of war and sufficient grain could not be brought in. Most surprising is the situation of the Ottoman empire. During the last quarter of the nineteenth century and the early twentieth century there was a steady increase of grain imports (allowing for the considerable fluctuations from year to year) and in 1910–11 the Ottomans imported twice as much cereal in value as was exported; during the last five years before the First World War average imports were of the order of £4 million a year. No doubt this circumstance was largely attributable to the demands of Istanbul and the fact that it was cheaper to supply that city from foreign sources than to use domestic grain, but the overall impression of the change in the Near Eastern agricultural economy is confirmed by these figures.

In 1800 agriculture throughout the region was dependent upon rainfall, or upon local irrigation systems by which water was drawn off from the adjacent river or spring by such means as the basin irrigation characteristic of Egypt or the underground channels found in Iran, Iraq and parts of Arabia. The development of major irrigation systems, involving the construction of barrages for storage and elaborate canal systems for the distribution of water, was a feature of the nineteenth and twentieth centuries and was concentrated especially in the cotton-producing regions of Egypt and Turkestan.

Cultivation in 1800 was carried on through crop sharing, according to which the product was shared between landlord and tenant in proportions dependent upon their inputs of land, labour, seed, implements (including animals for ploughing, etc.) and water. In much of the area the village community was the basic economic unit with its three characteristics of village lands held in common and periodically redistributed among the peasants, collective responsibility for payment of taxes and other dues and shared responsibility for providing labour for public works. In some areas individual proprietorship was more common, for example western Anatolia, Lower Egypt and part of Syria.

Serfdom, that is the binding of the peasant to the land, was not the norm, although not uncommon either. There were few landless labourers in 1800.

Either individually or collectively peasants had rights in land: normally the right to cultivate land during their lifetime and to pass it to their descendants, occasionally to alienate it temporarily and always to take their share of the crop fixed according to their contribution to the factors of production. Peasants also had obligations: to pay what was due, sometimes to perform labour services on the landlord's farm or on government property although their labour services were less onerous than in the Habsburg lands. Commonly, peasants paid their dues in kind but in some areas there was an increasing practice of demanding cash, a circumstance which obliged the peasant to cultivate marketable crops. By the end of the eighteenth century cash payments were usual in Lower Egypt, although still rare in Upper Egypt.

Cultivation was carried on by peasant cultivators with simple implements, usually wooden tools. Fertilizers were rarely used and two years fallow out of three was the common practice. The principal crops were cereals grown for human and animal feed and were consumed locally, mostly by the peasant and his family. In Egypt the peasant did not normally consume his own wheat, however; instead he sold it and ate cheaper grains including maize and millet (including dura (sorghum)). The remainder of the produce went either as payments in kind to the landlord or was sold to provide money to buy goods or pay taxes. The extent to which such sales were possible varied from region to region. Produce was usually sold in a local market; exceptionally, it was disposed of in a regional market – Istanbul consumed produce drawn from distant regions – or in international trade. Cultivators also reared animals for dairy products, meat, used in cultivation or sale, like the 200,000 Serbian pigs exported each year to Austria.

The largest part of the Near East, that is the whole of the north and hilly areas in the south, was dependent upon rainfall and a dry year could reduce the crop to a quarter of that harvested in a good year. In the few areas of irrigated agriculture mainly in the south and east of the region, notably Egypt, Iraq, Iran and Turkestan, floods or low rivers could produce the same effect. Egypt employed basin irrigation by which the land was flooded in August and sown in the autumn with a winter crop (wheat, barley, peas or beans). Summer crops such as rice, sugar, indigo, cotton and millet were produced by irrigation, using primitive lifting gear on the banks of the river.

Finally, villages carried on some industrial activity. Apart from the provision of local services, such as that of blacksmith, they produced handicrafts for their own use or for sale. In some areas such industrial activity was a major feature of village life, notably in southern Bulgaria and Thessaly and will be described below. For the most part, however, industrial activity was on a small scale. But one should not underestimate its importance anywhere in the traditional Near East. It is calculated that under basin irrigation in Egypt about 150 days a year were required for the tasks of cultivation, leaving a substantial time available for handicrafts even without reckoning on the labour of women and children. It is interesting to observe that the advent of perennial irrigation during the nineteenth century increased the time required for cultivation to about 250 days a year, drastically reducing the time which could be devoted to handicrafts.

The story of relations between peasant and landlord is a complicated one. It begins with the outstanding fact that land was the major source of wealth, and that in one way or another the great majority of people and institutions had to live off it and therefore claimed a share in the produce of land. The principal institution was the state and from the point of view of the state (and of Islamic law) there were three types of land: *milk*, *waqf* and *mīrī*.

Milk land was the nearest Near Eastern equivalent to freehold land and could be inherited, purchased and sold. *Milk* land was principally urban land or gardens in the vicinity of towns. Although the category included much of the most valuable building and agricultural land it formed only a very small part of the total stock of land and can be disregarded for the purpose of most of the following comments.

A *waqf* is a charitable endowment in which the revenues from a specified property are set aside for a charitable purpose, for example the maintenance of a mosque or shrine, school or college, road, bridge or caravanserai. The property involved might not be land, but given that land was the major source of wealth it usually was. Quite considerable amounts of land were held under *waqf* grants for the benefit of great institutions, for example the important Shīʿī shrines of Iraq. There is an obvious comparison to be made with the form of tenure in medieval Europe known as mortmain. Also, like many modern trusts, in practice the creation of *waqfs* was an activity carried on not only in the interest of charity but also to avoid making payments to the state; the *waqf* contract could be drawn up so as to ensure that a substantial part of the revenues went to the administrators of the *waqf*. In this way a family might escape paying the share which belonged to the state (or pay at a low rate) by naming itself as the hereditary administrator. Religious families especially benefited from this device. By the end of the eighteenth century one-fifth of arable land in Egypt was *waqf*. *Waqf* land was both rural and urban.

More than 90 per cent of all land was *mīrī* land, that is it was land which was liable to pay a certain proportion (usually one-tenth but it could be as high as a third) of its produce to the state. Nearly all *mīrī* land was rural land which could be either waste land, pasture land or arable. Waste land was a very extensive category and paid nothing: pasture land could be either nomad pasture or, more commonly, consisted of the pastures around villages used for the villagers' animals: arable land was the principal source of payments, although the tithe on agricultural produce was usually matched by a levy of one-fortieth on herds.

The state was, in theory, by far the biggest landlord in so far as that term is applicable to the Near East. But the state lacked the machinery to collect directly from the cultivators and therefore usually granted its share of the produce to individuals in return for services. Some of this land was granted to bureaucrats but most went in return for military service, because war was the principal activity of the state. Some land was not granted in this way but was held back as imperial estates and the revenues were collected directly by paid officials or tax farmers. In most of the Ottoman lands – most of Rumelia and Anatolia, much of Syria and Iraq, but not in Egypt – the state's revenues were allocated to horsemen (*sipahis*) in return for specified military services. The holdings were known by various names but the basic unit was the *timar*. A similar situation prevailed in Iran. The timariots or their equivalents became, in effect landlords, dealing with the cultivators or their representatives directly or through their agents. One says "in effect" because there is a necessary simplification in this outline. What we have been talking about is the fate of the state's share of the produce and have disregarded the possibility that other people had claims on the produce, that is, that there were other landlords. Because we do not know enough about the actual situation and because we believe it to be so we tend to treat the timariot as the only landlord of the lands of which a part of the revenue (and a farm of his own) was assigned to him.

This system began to break down as early as the seventeenth century, if not even earlier, although it was an unconscionably long time in dying. The system, however, came to serve neither the new interests of the state nor the interests of the timariot. One great puzzle of modern Near East history is what exactly replaced it in the different parts of the region and with what effect. As far as we can determine it was replaced by a variety of systems including an extension of *waqf* ownership (which need concern us no further), the *chiftlik* system and the *iltizām* system.

The *chiftlik* (Bosnian *agalik* and *beglik*) apparently became the predominant form of landholding in the European provinces of the Ottoman empire and extended into Anatolia. About the nature of the *chiftlik* controversy rages. It was a heritable, disposable estate. According to the Marxist interpretation, which has inevitably become widespread owing to the extensive work done on the subject by Balkan historians in recent years, it was a large-scale agricultural unit worked with wage-labour and sharecroppers producing for the market and forming a transitional stage between feudalism and capitalism. Other researchers have disputed this proposition and asserted that *chiftliks* of this description were rare and tended to be concentrated in areas near large cities and producing for the urban market, for example in the Istanbul–Edirne region, or were located in regions of high specialization such as in the cotton region of Macedonia or in Adana. The great majority of *chiftliks*, it is argued by the opponents of the Marxists, were small *chiftliks*, worked without wage-labour by a single family. Without more research one cannot say which view is correct, but in favour of the second view is the circumstance that big landlordism did not become the norm in the region. In most of Rumelia and Anatolia small peasant proprietors tended to predominate; the major exceptions were in eastern Anatolia and in Romania, which became areas of big estates. However, in part, this circumstance may be the result of the subsequent displacement of Muslim landlords, as in Bulgaria.

The *iltizām*, which was most common in the Arab provinces of the Ottoman empire, was a tax farm. In crude terms the right to collect the state's share of the produce was sold to the highest bidder, although the matter was rarely so simple as this statement suggests for local influence was often important. Frequently, the governor of a province would take a farm of the taxes for his own province (raising a loan from the Armenian bankers in Istanbul to finance the transaction) and would sublet the tax farms. In some cases, for example in Afghanistan in 1840, the chief minister would become the farmer of all the taxes of the state. During the course of time many *iltizāms* were also converted into heritable, disposable estates. Tax farming remained the mainstay of the Ottoman tax system throughout the nineteenth century, but landholding was subject to major modifications as a consequence of state action and economic forces. Unlike the situation in Rumelia and Anatolia, in the Arab provinces the norm became the great estate and a sharecropping peasantry.

It has been frequently argued that the change from *timar* to *chiftlik* and *iltizām* was greatly to the detriment of the peasantry. It has been contended that under the well-regulated *timar* system the peasant's rights were protected but that under the *chiftlik* and *iltizām* systems he was exposed, without protection, to rapacious, profiteering landlords. Some doubt has already been cast upon the merits of this argument in relation to the *chiftliks*, but the truth is that there is very little evidence, other than general statements and isolated examples, either for the view that the peasant was well off under the *sipahi* or that he was badly off under his successors. Opinions of different European travellers could be cited on either side and there is no evidence that discontent, measured by peasant uprisings, was greater under one system than another.

Local conditions were all important. The peasant needed protection and capital and the landlord needed labour and a regular income to cultivate his lands and to meet government demands. Ruthless exploitation served neither landlord nor peasant. In the first half of the nineteenth century the existence of much uncultivated land meant that peasants who were badly treated could pack up and leave, confident that they could find a more congenial landlord elsewhere. Alternatively, the peasant could go to the mountains and take up the life of a shepherd, cultivator or bandit. Such men were the Greek klephts, the Serbian haiduks and the Bulgarian haiduts. Eric Hobsbawm has suggested that these characters, whom he terms social bandits, appeared only at a time when traditional agriculture broke down and was replaced by capitalist farming but this suggestion cannot be a complete explanation; the klepht and his colleagues were not a new phenomenon and they were associated less with regions in which new types of farming were coming into existence than with the proximity of wild and mountainous territory. During the latter part of the nineteenth century the situation began to change due to the increase of population, the strengthening of the power of the notables under the 1858 Ottoman land law and the pressure on land in some areas, notably in Egypt. In this period and in some regions one observes the emergence of big landlords and landless agricultural labourers. But this deterioration in rural conditions was partly offset by the increased value of the produce and by the development of another safety-valve for discontented peasants, namely movement to the cities where the decline of the guild system allowed more flexibility of employment.

The greater part of industrial activity was carried on in towns. As mentioned above, there were exceptions of which an outstanding early example is the agricultural co-operative at Ambelakia in Thessaly which produced spun red cotton and exported it all over Europe. The co-operative was very successful for a period of several years at the end of the eighteenth and beginning of the nineteenth century, but eventually collapsed in anarchy assisted by foreign competition. Industrial activity also spread from certain towns in the Balkans to neighbouring villages which specialized in different stages of production. Such activities were a feature of the region around Plovdiv (Philippopolis) in Thessaly which specialized in the production of *ʿabā*, the coarse woollen cloth widely used throughout the Near East and bought in particular by the Ottoman government to clothe its soldiers. Another town, Sliven, also concentrated on *ʿabā* production and made a great deal of money through contracts to provide the new Ottoman army of the 1820s with uniforms. The *ʿabā* industry was one of considerable and continuing importance through the nineteenth century and the demand for wool stimulated sheep production throughout the Balkan mountains. But, essentially, the *ʿabā* industry was town-based and controlled and merely involved the surrounding villages. A similar development took place in other parts of the Near East, for example in Turkestan where the villages around Bukhara were drawn into the textile and carpet industries.

Industry in the city was predominantly handicraft industry carried on by workers organized in guilds. The number of guilds in cities was very large; Raymond calculates that there were at least seventy-four craft guilds in Cairo in 1801. The most prominent crafts were various forms of food processing, for example bakers, millers, butchers, who were the largest groups in cities and tended to be the aristocrats among guilds; crafts connected with construction (another very large group) including masons and carpenters; crafts linked to transport such as boatmen and porters, who often formed the lowest ranking group in the social hierarchy of the guilds; and those involved in manufacture, including textile workers, metalworkers, leather-workers and workers in wood. Enterprises were small and commonly consisted of a master, an apprentice and two journeymen working in the master's house. In some cases, for example in textiles, a series of processes carried on in such enterprises would be organized by an entrepreneur. Such men could become very wealthy, for example, the property of Mihalaka Gümüsrgedan, whose family began as *ʿabā* merchants in Plovdiv, was valued in 1880, shortly before his death, at £20,000. Characteristically, however, only small amounts of capital were employed in any single enterprise. Large enterprises, whether conducted in a single establishment or through connected processes carried on by small manufacturers, were usually linked to government demands; good examples are the manufacture of gunpowder and the construction of ships. In every town a large number of guildsmen were concerned with supplying government demands, including the needs of the garrison. How far they also supplied the requirements of the surrounding countryside is a matter of dispute. Some writers have tended to stress the interdependence of town and country; others to argue that the two were basically self-contained, that rural areas met their own simple needs for manufactures and that cities, apart from drawing food supplies from the country, worked primarily for themselves. This latter view sees the cities as essentially parasitic. It is not possible to discuss the issue further; one may only remark that regional variations were very considerable and raise the possibility that in some areas one may need to consider a triangular relationship of village, small town and city.

The social functions of the guilds have already been mentioned. They had other functions both economic and administrative. Their principal function was to act as an administrative link between government and the urban population, their leaders were to represent government to townspeople and townspeople to government. In most areas they had fiscal duties in the collection of taxes for government. The guilds also performed judicial functions in the arbitration of disputes between their members. In some towns, for example Serres and Damascus, there existed individuals who held sway over all guildsmen, and such powerful men could adjudicate disputes all through the artisan population. The economic functions of the guilds were concerned with the control of quality (including the superintendence of weights and measures, a duty which properly belonged to the *qāḍī*), the fixing of prices and wages, the purchase of raw materials, the supply and distribution of goods and the control of entry to the craft. This last important function gave guilds the possibility of protecting their own monopoly and of policing demarcation lines between their work and that of other guilds. This function or privilege was difficult to protect against pressure from new immigrants to the towns, and in the Rumelian provinces in the nineteenth century there came to be acute differences between entrenched Muslim guildsmen and new Christian Slav immigrants from the countryside. In the long run the guilds were dependent upon government, which had the power to recognize a new guild, although governments were reluctant to do so in case there followed a loss of quality or social unrest.

The guild system continued throughout the nineteenth century in most areas of the Near East but the guilds lost most of their functions, particularly the economic functions. Their survival was due especially to their usefulness to government as replacements for bureaucrats, but as bureaucracies developed their administrative functions also disappeared and with them, finally, the guilds. Down to the end of the eighteenth century the guilds had been largely the preserve of the Muslim population, which was everywhere dominant in the towns, but during the course of the nineteenth century Christians began to enter the guilds or, more commonly, form their own guilds and obtain recognition. In Istanbul in 1870 of 133,000 guildsmen 13,000 were Christian. The Christian guilds, as they became more powerful, tended to become more independent of the Ottoman authorities, more closely linked with their churches and more concerned with relations with Europeans. But the inroads which non-Muslims made into the guild system in no way reflects the full extent of their inroads into the economy; in 1800 the guild system had been more or less synonymous with industry in the Near East: by 1900 most industry was outside the guild system and was dominated by non-Muslims.

Transport in the Near East in 1800 was largely by animal carriage. A few regions benefited from use of the sea: the Mediterranean coastlands, where Greek sailors held sway, and the Red Sea and Persian Gulf which were the home of Arab seamen. There were also rivers, navigable in places, notably the Danube, the Nile, the Tigris and Euphrates. Throughout most of the area land transport afforded the only means of communication and, in the absence of roads which could sustain wheeled traffic, the usual mode of transport was by pack animal – horse, donkey and camel.

The capacity of animal transport should not be underestimated. The Sudan Darfur caravan which brought ivory, hides, skins, gum, ostrich feathers, gold dust and natron to Cairo, numbered 5,000 camels in 1800, a figure which may represent over 1,000 tonnes of goods. The Sudan caravan was so large because of the peculiar requirements of the route; elsewhere it was common to find more frequent, smaller caravans but the total quantities of goods involved were still significant; the Trebizond–Tabriz traffic employed 15,000 animals on three journeys a year moving 25,000 tonnes of goods. Nevertheless, animal transport remained slow, expensive and dangerous with the consequence that bulk goods rarely figured in long-distance trade by land; when such goods were moved, like grain to Istanbul or timber to Egypt, it was usually by sea. The Saharan salt caravans provided one of the few exceptions. Accordingly, most trade was local trade and long-distance trade was mainly restricted to goods with a high value to weight ratio or to those, like animals and slaves, which provided their own transport.

The nineteenth century saw the development of several new modes of communication. Chronologically, the first important development was that of steam navigation on the rivers of the region; steamboats were employed on the Danube in the 1820s, on the Nile, the Euphrates and the Tigris in the 1830s and on other rivers, notably the regular service on the Karun river in Iran opened in 1888. Steamboats pulling barges provided a much faster and more economic system than did sailing-boats. Subsequently, steamboats also came to be used extensively on sea routes around the Near East, although the high cost of transport by steam meant that in the early years the use of steam vessels was confined to mails, passengers and high-priced goods; the bulk of trade continued to be moved by sail. By the second half of the century, however, steam vessels were beginning to take over the bulk trade as well and their use was greatly enhanced by the opening of the Suez Canal in 1869.

The most characteristic transport system of the nineteenth century was the railway which played an increasingly important role in the Near East from the second half of the nineteenth century. As early as 1834 that enterprising modernizer, Muḥammad ʿAlī of Egypt, planned a line linking Cairo and Suez, although it was not built until 1858 when it became part of a line linking Alexandria with Suez via Cairo. Thereafter there was considerable railway construction in Egypt; by 1905 there were 3,000 kilometres of state railways and 1,400 kilometres of narrow-gauge private railways. In the Ottoman empire railway construction began after the Crimean War with lines built to open up the Danube valley, and in 1868 a concession was awarded for a railway to link Istanbul with the European system in Vienna, although for political reasons this line was not completed until 1888. In 1866 the first railway in Anatolia was opened to bring goods to Izmir from its hinterland, and towards the end of the century lines were constructed in Syria with French capital to link the main towns together. From Damascus the line was extended southwards to Medina (1903–8) by the Hijaz railway, which was built to serve the interests of the pilgrims but which also had strategic importance. The Hijaz railway was the only railway in Arabia.

The best-known railway in the Near East was the Baghdad railway, principally because of the diplomatic arguments which accompanied its construction. In 1893 a line from Scutari, the town facing Istanbul across the Bosporus, to Ankara was completed with extensions to other towns in Anatolia. In 1903 a concession was given for a further line from Konya to Baghdad and in 1903 for an extension to Basra. The Baghdad railway was still uncompleted in 1914. It was also planned that the system should be extended eastwards from Baghdad to Tehran via Khaniqin, but this line was not built and Iran remained with no significant railway development other than a short extension of the Russian system from Julfa to Tabriz for which a concession was given in 1913. Eastern Iran did, however, benefit from the development of railways in Turkestan; between 1881 and 1888 the Transcaspian railway was built to link the Caspian Sea with Samarkand and this line, running close to the Iranian frontier, offered opportunities to producers in Khurasan. The lack of railway development in Iran must be regarded as a major factor in the slow rate of change in Iran during the nineteenth and early twentieth centuries as compared with the Ottoman empire and Egypt; no other system of transport in the nineteenth century could provide for the speedy movement of large numbers of troops or large quantities of goods, two essential features of political and economic modernization.

The development of roads fit for wheeled traffic was a slow process in the Near East, and over the area as a whole had made little progress by 1914. Little was done anywhere before the 1890s when efforts were made to improve the roads of Anatolia and to construct a Russian-built road network in northern Iran, linking Tehran with the Caspian Sea and Qazvin. In Lower Egypt at the same time a road system was built under British supervision. The only notable road built in an earlier period was the French-managed Beirut–Damascus road, constructed between 1859 and 1863, which had a considerable effect on the economy of the Syrian interior. As a result of poor road development the Near East was ill-equipped to take advantage of the advent of motor-driven, wheeled traffic in the years before the First World War.

The growth of sea-borne trade and the arrival of large ocean-going steamships in the second half of the nineteenth century led to the growth of port facilities. The principal developments took place at Alexandria, the main cotton port of Egypt, but, after the opening of the Suez Canal, Port Said and Suez were also developed as modern ports. On the Syrian coast the great new port was at Beirut, constructed with French capital between 1890 and 1895. Further north, Izmir, the principal export centre of the Ottoman empire, was modernized in 1875, and Istanbul, the largest import centre, in 1901, the same year as Salonika. Elsewhere, there was little development; Aden became a major port but served not south-west Arabia but the movement of vessels between Suez and the East and the regional trade of the western Indian Ocean. Apart from some modest innovations at Abadan just before 1914 there were no important changes in the Persian Gulf, a circumstance which meant that Iran was again severely handicapped in her economic development by having no southern port which could handle a large quantity of goods.

In 1800 information travelled in the Near East no faster than the Tatar post could carry it. The Tatar post, carried by specialized messengers changing horses (or dromedaries) at special post-stations, could achieve remarkably fast speeds, but it was often slowed by its use for the carriage of parcels of valuable goods. The situation was transformed by the arrival of the telegraph in the second half of the nineteenth century.

Construction began in the Ottoman lands in 1855 with a line from Istanbul to Edirne and was quickly extended to link with the European telegraph system. From the European point of view it was important to build lines in the Near East in order to link Europe to European possessions and interests further east: from the point of view of the Ottoman government the telegraph was a valuable system of internal communication which could ensure tighter control by Istanbul over provincial governments. As the British ambassador in the 1870s, Sir Charles Eliot, put the matter: the telegraph is "the most powerful instrument for a despot who wishes to control his own officials".[5] Under this dual enthusiasm the telegraph system spread rapidly. The Iranian government quickly overcame its original suspicions and in 1864 a telegraph line linking Baghdad to Bushir through Tehran and other major Iranian towns was completed. The 1860s also saw the development of the Egyptian telegraph system. Modern postal services were also introduced in the Near East, beginning in 1834 with the inauguration of the Ottoman post although this was unsuccessful and for a long time foreign post offices were preferred. And, finally, the development of newspapers ensured a wider circulation of information. The first newspapers established in Egypt and the Ottoman empire in 1829–30 were official papers intended for the publication of regulations and proclamations. Newspapers in Western European languages, Greek and other languages appeared soon after, but it was not until the 1860s that newspapers in Ottoman Turkish carrying a variety of news began to appear. Similarly, it was the 1870s which was the great age of the development of Egyptian Arabic journalism principally in the hands of Lebanese Christian immigrants; by the end of the nineteenth century Egypt had a substantial free press capable of reporting and discussing a wide range of issues. Iran, as usual, lagged behind and it was not until after the constitutional revolution of 1906 that Iranian newspapers began to appear in numbers.

The nineteenth-century communications revolution in the Near East had three main consequences. First, it had the effect of increasing government control over its territories and its own officials. At the same time the development of newspapers provided an arena which was exploited by critics of government. Second, the pattern of development, by concentrating on links with ports and therefore with the world economy, tended to import a new imbalance into the economic development of the region by promoting the advance of particular regions and fostering the growth of crops for which export markets existed. Third, it tended to break down the isolation of different parts of the region, to promote specialization and exchange, to reduce the incidence of famine and to foster a change of outlook, a movement towards a recognition of membership of larger communities.

Trade in the Near East in 1800 may be classified in three groups: local, regional and international. We have no statistics for local trade but there is every reason to believe that it was the largest in bulk and value. It was conducted by small merchants or directly by producers and it was usually managed through barter. Nor do we have any reliable or comprehensive statistics for regional trade, that is, the exchange of commodities within the Near East. Partly this trade was conducted by direct exchange, for example the trade between Egypt and the Sudan, or that between Egypt and Syria; partly it consisted of the regular provisioning of great cities like Istanbul; and partly it was carried on through fairs, particularly in Anatolia and Rumelia. International trade was conducted between the Near Eastern region and Europe on the one side and the East on the other. There is reason to believe that until the end of the eighteenth century imports of cloth, spices and other goods from the East Indies may have been more important than the European trade to the Near East as a whole and certainly more important to the areas fed through the Red Sea and the Persian Gulf. Raymond calculated that Egyptian trade at the end of the eighteenth century (excluding local trade) was divided as follows: 45 per cent with other parts of the Ottoman empire; 35 per cent with the Red Sea; and only 14 per cent with Europe. The European trade was conducted by four routes: through the Caspian and through the Black Sea with Russia, via the Balkan land frontier with Austria, and via the Mediterranean with western Europe. We have little information about the absolute size of these trades. The Caspian trade was primarily in raw silk from northern Iran; the Black Sea trade developed after 1774 but really became important only after 1792 in the hands of Greek merchants sailing under the Russian flag; and the Austrian trade was heavily weighted in favour of the Ottoman lands – in 1779 it was estimated that exports to Austria exceeded imports by five to one. Most information is available concerning the Mediterranean trade. The dominant European country through most of the eighteenth century was France. As a consequence of the Revolutionary Wars and the Industrial Revolution Britain came to predominate in all the Mediterranean trade, a situation which was to persist throughout the nineteenth century, although French trade, especially in the middle of the century, was substantial.

The first obvious change in trade during the nineteenth century was its growth. Egyptian trade increased by 4 per cent per annum, Ottoman by 2.5 per cent and Iranian by about the same. These figures may be compared with an average figure for world trade of 3.5 per cent per annum, suggesting that the Near East was near or perhaps slightly below the world average. The increase of trade was certainly well above the increase of population and the increase of gross national product, suggesting that exchange became relatively much more important to the people of the Near East. The defect of these statistics, however, is that they are based primarily on the figures for international trade and take insufficient account of regional exchanges and none of local trade.

The second major change in trade patterns during the nineteenth century was the greatly enhanced importance of trade with Europe relative to regional trade and trade with the East and Africa. By the end of the nineteenth century it is claimed 90 per cent of Near Eastern trade was with Europe and the United States and the Eastern trade was little more than a trickle, although this claim is probably exaggerated and undervalues the importance of the trade of Iran, Iraq and Arabia with India. Britain was the leading trading partner but France and Austria also played a prominent role in the first half of the nineteenth century, and Germany, Russia and Italy in the latter part of the nineteenth and the first years of the twentieth century. Russia, in particular, continued to enjoy a favoured position in the northern Iranian market, in 1913 Russia took 70 per cent of Iran's exports and supplied over half of her imports. By 1914 Britain was still the leading trading partner of the Ottoman empire, but its share of Ottoman imports had fallen to 19 per cent and of exports to 22 per cent. With Egypt the corresponding figures are 31 and 43 per cent respectively.

A third variety of change concerns the character of the trade of the Near East. In 1800 the Near East conducted a mixed trade with Europe exporting raw materials, foodstuffs and manufactured goods and importing a similar mix. Turkestan, for example, exported more manufactured goods to Russia than were imported. By the end of the period the Near East exported almost only food and raw materials and imported manufactured goods together with some food, notably grain, sugar, coffee and tea; shortly before the First World War the last three commodities amounted to 30 per cent of the imports of Iran and 10 per cent of those of the Ottomans. The largest single item of imports, however, was cotton textiles which amounted to about 30 per cent of imports into the Near East between 1840 and 1914. Near Eastern exports to Europe were varied but were easily led by raw cotton which formed the major export from Egypt (90% in 1914) and from Turkestan. Cotton was also an important item in exports from the Ottoman empire and from Iran (19% in the period 1911–13). Another major export item was raw silk which accounted for one-quarter of Syria's export. In Iran in the mid-nineteenth century raw silk had amounted to one-third of exports but silkworm disease in the later nineteenth century greatly reduced silk production in the Caspian provinces. Dried fruits, tobacco, opium, wool and cereals also figured prominently in Near Eastern exports. The main cause of this change in the character of the Near Eastern trade was the Industrial Revolution in Europe which gave European industry a clear advantage over that of other areas of the world; other factors included the reduction in transport costs and the creation of favourable conditions for trade through such arrangements as the 1838 Anglo–Ottoman treaty which set tariffs on imported goods at a low level. It should be remarked, however, that the looming significance of Europe in the trade of the Near East was not matched by a similar importance of Near Eastern trade to Europe; for every European country Near Eastern trade accounted for only a small proportion of total trade.

The nineteenth and early twentieth centuries also saw a considerable flow of capital from Europe to the Near East. By 1914 the Near East owed Europe about £500 million, of which half was owed by governments and the rest was accounted for by private investment. The great part of this borrowing occurred in the Ottoman empire and Egypt. Ottoman borrowing began in 1854 and by 1875, when the Ottomans could no longer pay the interest on their debt, amounted to £242 million plus an unknown floating debt. Egypt began with short-term borrowing and contracted her first loan in 1860. When Egypt went bankrupt in 1876 she owed £100 million. In 1880 Egypt and in 1881 the Ottoman empire came to settlements with their creditors by which the principal of their debts and the rate of interest were reduced. Both were obliged to accept some form of international supervision over their finances; Egypt through the Caisse de la Dette and the Ottomans through the Ottoman Public Debt Administration. The arrangements did permit the two countries to resume borrowing, however, and between 1881 and 1914 the Ottomans borrowed £T166 million, paying off at the same time a similar amount of old debt. The burden of debt remained considerable. To service her debt cost Egypt half her revenues and 30 per cent of her export earnings between 1880 and 1914. By comparison Iran's public debt was derisory; her first loan was contracted in 1892 and by 1914 her total debt amounted to only £6.8 million. Measured in per capita terms this amount was insignificant and the circumstances that its servicing required 25 per cent of government revenue and nearly 7 per cent of export earnings merely indicates how small was the government share in the economy and how tiny was Iran's trade. The figures provide further confirmation of Iran's slow development and suggest an additional reason for her backwardness.

Private European investment in the Near East began at the same time as public investment but the greatest period of private investment came in and after the 1890s, compared with the 1860s which saw the peak of public borrowing. Most private investment went into public utilities linked to the export economy. The largest item was railways; over half of all private investment in the Ottoman empire was in railways. Other items included roads, port works and banking. In Egypt foreign companies also invested in land. Private investment in the Ottoman empire in 1914 amounted to £T181.5 million and in Egypt £E100.2 million of which £E92 million was in foreign hands.

The principal European investor in public debt was France; by 1914 France held 60 per cent of the Ottoman public debt compared with 20 per cent held by Germany and 14 per cent by Britain; France was also the largest private investor in the Near East; in 1914 France had 45 per cent of private foreign investment in the Ottoman empire, Germany 25 per cent and Britain 16 per cent; and in Egypt the corresponding figures were France 50 per cent and Britain 33 per cent. Russian investment was insignificant. To France the Near East was important in investment terms but to other countries it was of much less importance; in particular, to Britain with her world-wide spread of investments the Near East was small beer.

What effect did this investment have on the Near East? In the Ottoman empire and in Egypt it helped to finance the process of modernization, notably in military and railway development, and thereby to enlarge the power of government and increase gross national product enabling the two countries to sustain the increase in population and even improve the standard of living of the people. A comparison with the condition of Iran in 1914 shows some of the effects of investment. On the other hand it is certainly arguable that the Ottomans and Egyptians achieved this result very inefficiently. Over the whole period 1854–1914 Ottoman public borrowing amounted to about £T400 million of which they actually received about two-thirds. Nearly half of Ottoman borrowing was to liquidate past debts, 6 per cent went on the army and 5 per cent to cover budget deficits. Private borrowing gave rather better value for money and it may well be that increased export earnings through private investment paid for the extra charge of interest on the balance of payments although this can be no more than a guess. Nevertheless, by 1914 the Ottoman empire was burdened with a heavy requirement for debt repayment. The situation of Egypt was similar although probably Egypt acquired more economic infrastructure for her money.

It is claimed that in consequence of their borrowings the Ottomans, Egypt and Iran all suffered a loss of effective sovereignty by being obliged to permit foreign countries to exercise some control over their financial arrangements. This claim seems exaggerated. The Ottoman Public Debt Administration was an Ottoman institution which, on the whole, made life easier for the Ottomans and does not seem to have prevented them from doing any important thing which they desired. The Caisse de la Dette acted in Egypt in a fashion less advantageous to Egypt, insisting on tying up revenues which could have been used more profitably to finance further investment, especially in irrigation. Egypt, of course, suffered a more considerable loss of sovereignty because of the British occupation in 1882, but although Egypt's indebtedness contributed to this event it was not the proximate cause. In Iran the Russian loan condition that she should have a veto on railway construction in Iran was certainly damaging to Iran, but it is arguable that Russia did not need the extra power given by the loan condition; if she had not wanted railways in Iran no country was likely to build them against Russian opposition. On the whole, leaving aside the question of the occupation of Egypt, it does not seem that the countries concerned lost any major advantage through being obliged to make concessions to their creditors.

The statistics of foreign trade and investment, together with other evidence, have been used as the basis of a theory that during the nineteenth century Near Eastern handicraft industry was ruined by European competition and that the period saw the development of a colonial economy in the Near East, that is, one in which economic activity in the Near East centred round the production of food and raw materials for the use of Europe and that for manufactured goods the Near East relied upon imports from Europe. The theory, of course, is one which has been used much more generally to describe the economic relations of Europe with most of the rest of the world during the same period; the Near East is only one case, and a minor one, within the world picture and there is no doubt that the application of the model to the Near East owes much to the circumstance that it had been developed already, on the basis of greater evidence, in relation to India. It should also be noted that the extent to which the model justly describes the Indian situation has been questioned in recent years. Some general remarks about the Near Eastern situation will be appropriate here.

First, as noted above, the statistics undoubtedly show a large rise in imports of European manufactured goods and especially textiles. They also indicate, however, a substantial increase in the population. The first question to ask is whether European manufacturers, in addition to supplying the new market, also broke into the existing market and thereby injured the traditional producers. The answer appears to be yes, at least in the earlier period: Roger Owen has calculated that in 1842 alone enough British cloth (to say nothing of that of other suppliers) was imported into the Arab Near East to provide 3.6 metres for every inhabitant. More information about the whole region and period is required as well as information about consumption patterns, but there is certainly prima-facie evidence for supposing that cotton textiles were affected.

A second type of evidence commonly used is the reports of European consuls. Their reports consistently indicate substantial damage to handicrafts, especially cotton textiles. It has to be said, however, that their reports are often contradictory. For example, the consuls C. B. Henry and John Macgregor claimed that in Aleppo in 1838 there were 4,000 looms employing 4,800 people. Writing at about the same time the Russian consul, K. M. Barzili, stated that there were only 1,000 looms and said that this figure represented a fall from a previous total of 10,000 looms. If one pursues consuls' reports through the nineteenth century one can discover continual reports of falling numbers of looms, but the actual numbers cited do not always show a fall and in 1911 Consul Weakley estimated that there were still 10,000 looms in Aleppo, the same figure as Barzili's original peak of nearly a century earlier. It has been suggested that consuls were so sure that handicrafts must decline that they tried to show that it was already happening. Further, it is the consular reports from the coastal regions most exposed to European competition that suggest the most notable decline of handicrafts; in the interior handicrafts held up through the early nineteenth century and when reports of their decline appeared the reason was often competition from factories elsewhere in the Near East. Better communications not only aided European manufacturers but they also assisted the more efficient Near Eastern producers. In some remote areas of Anatolia handlooms continued to operate up to the First World War. In Iran handicraft production was also substantial in the early twentieth century. It should be remembered that a decisive point with domestic producers is leisure; if time is available they will work for almost nothing.

Within the cotton textile industry it was producers engaged in spinning who suffered the most. The situation of weavers varied: some went under, especially producers of cheaper cloths, but others, producing for a specialized market, could survive and prosper using imported threads.

Other handicraft industries suffered less than cotton textiles. Woollen handicrafts, especially the *ʿabā* industry in Bulgaria, performed well as also did silk in some areas. Copper, earthenware and leather provide other examples; shoemaking remained a purely handicraft industry in Anatolia and supplied almost the whole of local demand; Adipazar had 350 workshops producing 500,000 pairs of shoes a year. In Iran an old handicraft industry, carpet-making, underwent a spectacular expansion in the later nineteenth century by producing for export. By 1914 hand-made carpets accounted for one-eighth of Iran's exports.

When handicrafts declined it was often the consequence of local factory production and not of European competition. From the 1830s onwards modern processes were adopted for the spinning of raw silk in Bursa; in 1846 there were two factories with 120 reels and, by 1872, 75 with 3,520 reels employing 5,415 people, nearly all of them Armenians or Greeks. At the same time the output of finished silk products declined. In Lebanon, on the other hand, the output of silk goods increased after the adoption of Jacquard looms by weavers who used European thread. The ambitious attempt of Muḥammad ʿAlī to establish factory production of textiles in Egypt, failed completely, but some large-scale industries were established in Egypt by 1914 including the Filature Nationale d'Alexandrie which produced 7–8 million metres of cloth annually. In Iran there were disappointments when efforts were made to establish modern factory industries at the end of the nineteenth century. In these failures foreign competition was certainly a factor but so were under-capitalization, bad management and an unskilled labour force.

Finally, in considering Near Eastern industry as a whole it is important to remember that two of the largest industrial activities in terms of numbers employed, namely food processing and construction, were relatively unaffected by European competition and may well have reaped some advantages from the closer contact with Europe through the processing of foodstuffs for export, for example the sugar factories established in Egypt, and through construction work financed by European investment, notably in connection with railway development. Several cement factories were established during the period. New extractive industries were also established, notably coal-mining in northern Anatolia, and that this development was partly the consequence of the new demands of factory industry and the railways. The oil industry developed during the second half of the nineteenth century and Romania and Baku became important centres of world production.

South of the Black Sea oil was still insignificant in 1914. Production had begun in Iran in 1909 and the Abadan refinery commenced operations only in 1912.

To sum up, the new economic relationship with Europe had an important effect upon Near Eastern industry, but it is one which cannot be described simply in terms of the model of the colonial economy. Many, although not all, textile handicraft industries declined during the period and some were almost extinguished. In this process the competition of European manufacturers was a significant factor, especially in the earlier period. There was, however, some development of factory industry in the Near East and the decline of handicrafts also owed something to competition from this source. To some extent Near Eastern factory industry was assisted by the European connection, but for the most part its development was restricted by European competition. Outside the field of textiles, and especially cotton textiles, the picture is notably different, however, and much more varied. During the nineteenth century Near Eastern industry went through a period of drastic reorganization; by 1914 it was still in the throes of that development and an accurate picture must take account of a great diversity of conditions from industry to industry and from region to region.

POLITICS

The two leading characteristics of Near Eastern government in 1880 were its diversity and its minimality. Near Eastern government was an armed bazaar in which a variety of groups bargained with each other, reinforcing their bids with force or the threat of force.

It is unnecessary to say much about the diversity of government. Near Eastern society was composed, it has been noted, of various groups whose relationship to each other was like that of pieces in a mosaic. Governments recognized the existence of these groups and dealt with them in different ways. There was no assumption that society was composed of numbers of individuals who should be treated in a uniform fashion; rather different groups had different rights and interests and required to be governed in different ways. Non-Muslims were different from Muslims, they were second-class citizens who were not liable to military service, who paid special taxes and who suffered certain restrictions on their liberty, for example in the height of their houses or the style of their clothes. Notables were different from peasants and enjoyed privileges which recognized their superior position. Tribesmen were observed to have their own modes of settling disputes among themselves and were allowed to enjoy them. And foreigners were granted special privileges in regard to justice and manner of life. Not only did Near Eastern governments recognize that different categories of their citizens required different treatment but they also provided a variety of forms of government. Within the Ottoman empire were provinces and districts, but it should not be supposed that the government of one province or one district was like another or that it was thought appropriate that it should be so. A number of forms of government were thought to be suitable and these were adapted to suit the convenience of all concerned.

Minimal government implied that the state took only a small proportion of the gross national product in taxation and in return offered only a very limited range of services: principally, defence, some public works (roads, bridges, caravanserais, mosques and madrasas – although these were supplied principally by private institutions) and criminal justice. Most of the services offered by modern governments were supplied in the Near East of 1800 by non-governmental bodies – the family, the tribe, the village, the guild and the religious community. As the total quantum of governmental power was so limited the distribution of power between the various components of government was, at least as far as the great majority of citizens was concerned, of much less significance than would have been in a case in a different type of polity. To that small group of people who were directly concerned with government the matter was quite different, of course; to them the division of the insignificant spoils of government was a business of the utmost consequence and their struggles were conducted with a ferocity worthy of a greater prize. To Europeans also the distribution of that small quantum of political power was of absorbing interest, and as so much of our evidence about the Near East derives from European sources or from sources linked to government it follows that we tend to imbibe a false impression of the centrality of politics.

To Europeans the circumstance that so much power resided in the hands of bodies other than the central government signified the decay of the state. Europeans, however, reasoned from the premiss that political power should be monopolized by central government and this assumption was not that of the Near East. The Near Eastern view of government was conditioned by ideology and circumstance. By its careful regulation of the duties of the believer Islam left little scope for the state other than to uphold the system of rules contained in the *Sharīʿa*. The absence of communications and the presence of large, armed, tribal populations also provided practical restraints upon the power of government.

Given that Near Eastern governments were unable or unwilling to undertake the extraordinary tasks of coercion which would have been required in order to monopolize power they were obliged to bargain with their citizens. The elements which constituted the official hierarchy fitted into the system of bargaining. The authority of an Ottoman provincial governor depended upon a balance between Istanbul and local groups. A governor unacceptable to local élites would be left powerless like many an Ottoman pasha of Egypt, shut up in the citadel of Cairo while the Mamluk factions fought for power outside. Better for Istanbul to choose a man of local substance who might pay the tribute in return for being left to enjoy his local autonomy, reward his followers and make his own arrangements with his local rivals. Such men as Sulaymān the Great, the Mamluk pasha of Baghdad, who appeared to Europeans as an almost independent potentate, to Istanbul seemed to be a good steady payer who kept his troublesome province quiet and looked after the border. Near Eastern government depended not on right and force, blood and iron but on the nuances of bargaining among those whose control of resources of men and money demanded that they should be consulted. Modest coercion or the threat of coercion was a part of bargaining; an outright struggle for mastery took place only rarely and usually when the process of bargaining had completely broken down. One of the many titles of the Shah of Iran was Supreme Arbiter.

To many readers brought up on the legend of oriental despotism this picture of Near Eastern government may seem strange and some further comment is required. The notion of oriental despotism embodies two distinct propositions. The first proposition is that the peculiarity of much oriental government is that it involves provision of massive capital investment in flood control and irrigation works in order to tame and harness the great rivers of Asia. This circumstance is alleged to require an extraordinary control over resources by Asian governments, control on a scale wholly unfamiliar to the West. Such governments are called, by the elaborator of this theory, Karl Wittvogel, hydraulic despotisms. The theory was developed in relation to China but has been applied to the Near East with particular reference to the rivers of Egypt and Iraq. The theory has little merit when applied to the Near East of 1800: no state maintained major river works, the distribution of population indicated the predominance of the rainfall economies of the north and not those of Egypt and Iraq; and the main centres of political power lay in the north of the region.

The second proposition is that traditional Near Eastern government was unrestrained and rested on force rather than on law; the characteristic symbol of Near Eastern government, it is suggested, is the tower of skulls. There are two errors in this proposition. First, Near Eastern governments were not unrestrained by law; Muslim rulers were bound by the *Sharīʿa* and although the *Sharīʿa* says very little about the duties of rulers it says a very great deal about the rights and obligations of the believer and, by implication, restricts the authority of government within very narrow limits. The duty of the Muslim ruler is primarily to ensure that Muslims can live as good Muslims are supposed to live and to protect *dhimmīs* living under Muslim rule. Second, although it is true that Near Eastern governments often disregarded the *Sharīʿa*, as other rulers disregard written constitutions, and acted in a brutal, tyrannical and arbitrary fashion, arbitrary government is not the same as strong government. States may maltreat or murder their citizens when they can catch them but first they must catch them. In general, the less likely they are to catch them the more brutally they are prone to treat them when they do apprehend them on the principle that severity may compensate in deterrent terms for infrequency. The conduct of a government in its own capital city is little guide to its practice in more remote areas. The oriental despot is an arbitrary or whimsical ruler, but he is not a powerful ruler in the sense that he is head of a government which closely regulates the lives of its citizens.

It may be argued that while it could be true that the concept of minimal government fits the Near East in 1800 this is not true of earlier periods. Discussion of that question lies outside the scope of this book and an answer cannot even be attempted here. But the question is relevant in the sense that in this book it is claimed that what happened to Near Eastern political systems during the nineteenth century was unprecedented and flowed from a novel enhancement of the role of government. If the role of government was merely being restored to a past position it would be necessary to revise one's view of that whole process of change. It is fair to say, therefore, that it is my contention that, although there were periods when Near Eastern government was stronger than it was in 1800, for example the Ottoman government had more authority in the sixteenth century than it had in the eighteenth, Near Eastern government had never been so very different as to change the basic character of the political system. The nineteenth-century revolution in government was wholly novel.

In what did the nineteenth-century revolution of government consist? It involved government becoming more uniform and more extensive. The notion of uniformity was embodied in the Ottoman reform movement through the doctrine of Ottomanism – that all Ottoman citizens were equal, had equal rights and obligations and should be governed in the same way. This ideal was never realized and it is evident that many people found aspects of it repugnant, but much was done to translate the doctrine into practice by the establishment of uniform state systems of administration, education and law, by removing the disabilities suffered by non-Muslims and enforcing on them the same obligations as Muslims, and by a constant effort to bring tribal and foreign populations under the control of the Ottoman state. In particular the Ottomans sought to control the independence of the notables; the very notion of a notable was inimical to the idea of Ottomanism.

The extension of the power of the state may be demonstrated in a variety of ways, some of which will be discussed in later chapters in relation to particular regions, but one broad measure is that mentioned above, namely the ratio of tax revenue to gross national product. Of course we have no statistics of any value for the size of the gross national product in 1800, and those for the early twentieth century are to be used only with the utmost caution. But we can get some idea of the very small take of government if we bear in mind that the main contributor to the national product was agriculture and we note that in Egypt at the end of the eighteenth century the people of Cairo (although they represented only 7% of the population) paid as much to the state in taxes as did all the rural areas put together. This is not to say that the countryside did not pay taxes but that the taxes did not reach the state, or, to be more precise, the Cairo government. From the viewpoint of Istanbul all that was asked of any of the provinces was that they paid their way and remitted a modest tribute to Istanbul; often they did not pay the tribute. Again, the largest part of government revenues came from the tax on land and animals, but it was estimated in the early nineteenth century that only about one-tenth of the amount collected reached the central government; the rest went into the pockets of officials and notables. The situation in Iran was similar and the government sought to make up some of its losses by bargaining with its officials who were expected to make annual presents to the monarch, in effect to surrender a share of the revenues they had misappropriated.

The available figures indicate a rise in the total revenues of the Ottoman empire from about £T3 million in the early 1800s to £T29.2 million in 1913, a sum taken from a much smaller area and from a total population not much larger than in 1800 and representing about 10 per cent of the gross national product. It is quite impossible to believe that the gross national product increased by 1,000 per cent in that period and the only reasonable conclusion is that the figures measure a great increase of government power. Figures for Egypt indicate an increase from £E1.2 million in 1798 to £E17.7 million in 1913, representing about 15 per cent of gross national product. In the case of Egypt the population had increased by between three and four times in that period and the gross national product probably by a larger amount, but there is still a considerable margin which measures the increased impact of government on the lives of the people. Iran, however, presents a very different picture. Its revenues increased from about £1.25 million in 1836 to £4 million in 1913. This increase was greater than the increase in population and probably greater than the increase in gross national product, but the increase in government power was small and the amount of power which government had was still tiny by this measure, probably not more than about 2 per cent of gross national product. Once again one observes the very slow pace of modernization in Iran.

Several other measures could be applied to Near Eastern government in the nineteenth century, all of which would tend to bear out the claim that there was a major growth in the power of the state. These measures would include that of function and it could be shown that government took over functions, such as education or the provision of legal services, which were formerly performed by non-governmental agencies as well as greatly enlarging the scope of its existing function of defence. Towards the end of the period there was even some assumption of economic functions by the Ottoman government, while in Egypt economic tasks were undertaken early in the nineteenth century. Another measure relates to the size of the bureaucracy, military and civil. Although in theory the size of such an establishment is no index of power yet the extension of the bureaucracy down to far lower levels of decision-making shows that the capacity was there, and a study of the transactions of government at these petty levels indicates that government decisions had an effect even at the grass roots.

The causes of this transformation of government are to be found especially in the decision to adopt European-style military forces, in the new economic opportunities, in the development of communications and in increased demand for government services from a larger and more ambitious population. The causes will not be discussed further here; rather it will be more useful to sketch in some of the political consequences of the enlargement of government power.

A larger share of the gross national product for government meant a smaller share for others. Those others had three possibilities: they could contest the claims of government, they could accept a reduced status or they could endeavour to join government and to try to reshape it to fit their particular wants. Each of these responses was tried by different groups during the nineteenth century and their success or failure depended upon a variety of circumstances.

In remote areas such as central Arabia, the Yemen, the hinterland of Oman, the Zagros and Kurdish mountains, the Jebel Druze, in the remoter areas of the Sudan and Libya the encroachment of government was resisted with violent movements of protest commonly justified in religious terms. Often these movements succeeded for some time in postponing the imposition of government authority but the tendency was to make some compromise in the end. And it is also notable that the very act of resistance tended to promote government by requiring the protesters to organize and collect their resources. Thus the Mahdiyya in the Sudan developed into a species of state with an apparatus of administration comparable to that which it had rejected when supplied by Egypt.

In most of the European provinces of the Ottoman empire the protest took the form of nationalist movements which aimed at achieving first an autonomous status and eventually complete independence from the Ottoman empire. It is no accident that these movements enunciated their protest in nationalist terms. The pressure of government was felt especially in the area of employment and those who spoke Slav languages, Greek or Romanian, were at an increasing disadvantage as long as the language of government was conducted in Ottoman Turkish. Under a government conducted in their own language their hopes of jobs would be greater. So long as government did little or nothing and the society was illiterate the language of government was a matter of relative indifference, but when increasing government forms were imposed on a society in which literacy was spreading the language of government became a matter of great importance to the class of students and intellectuals who played so large a part in Balkan revolutionary movements and who articulated the goals. National revolution was not only a matter of romance; it was also a question of jobs. This is not to say that Near Eastern Christian protest began with language: on the contrary it began with religion, supplemented by economics, among an illiterate people. It was in the articulation of its goals and its subsequent direction that the nationalists of language played the dominant role.

A similar response is observable in the last part of the nineteenth century and during the early twentieth century among the peoples of the Asian provinces of the Ottoman empire, the Armenians, the Arabs and the Turks themselves. The causes were fundamentally similar although the effects among the Muslims were different. Peoples with rising expectations found themselves squeezed by government and they put forward new formulas for the arrangement of governmental power.

Another response to the extension of governmental power was the demand for greater participation in government decisions through democratic process. Constitutionalism in the Near East was slow to grow and early constitutions appear as boons granted by rulers to their subjects, as devices for controlling one group or another and as diplomatic weapons for use against European demands. There is also in the early constitutionalist movements a powerful element of the desire of bureaucrats, more conscious of their professional status, to limit the power of an arbitrary ruler. Yet from the 1860s and the 1870s there is also a wider demand based upon a recognition that new forms of government are required in consequence of the enlargement of governmental power and the destruction of older institutions which had acted as buffers against the power of government within society. This is the theme of the Young Ottomans in the Ottoman empire and it is clearly enunciated in the writings of the Umma Party in Egypt after 1906. During the early years of the twentieth century constitutions came into operation in all the major states of the Near East.

The response of the majority of the people of the Near East to the enlargement of governmental powers was often to accept and welcome it. A strong government was a protection against the tyranny of local officials, the usurpations of notables and the raids of tribes. True, people might pay more to government but they paid less to a host of predators. The most hated feature of the enlargement of government power was conscription and there was constant opposition to its application to villages. But it was more and more difficult to avoid the long arm of government and in Egypt and in many areas of the Ottoman empire people reorganized their lives to fit in with its demands and to take advantage of its services – its schools, courts and its protection. In Iran, however, the continuing response of many people was to avoid government; the heart of the Iranian constitutional revolution was a desire to reduce the power of government.

The last feature of the Near Eastern political revolution in the nineteenth century which will be discussed here is the secularization of politics. In 1800 government in the Near East was Muslim government based on the *Sharīʿa*. That situation was tolerable so long as government kept its distance; as government grew it was obliged to present itself in a more secular garb. Further, government encroached upon areas formerly left to the religious communities, Muslim and non-Muslim. As functions passed under the state they were secularized so that, one by one and slowly and reluctantly, the great institutions of the state were divorced from religion and the religious dignitaries who had formerly played so large a part in government were excluded from its operation. The effect was to turn religion into a private activity divorced from the activities of the state. Broadly speaking this was the situation in the Ottoman empire and Egypt; in Iran the position was very different because there the religious leaders led the opposition to government and introduced into the constitution a major position for themselves.

The varieties of Muslim and Christian reactions to this situation are discussed at various places in this book, but here one may note that there were three main reactions during the period down to 1923: by the majority of the orthodox leaders to fight a rearguard action but eventually to accept the change; by some groups in isolated areas to mount a violent resistance to secularization or innovation in the name of a pristine undefiled Islam; and by some intellectuals to try to find a compromise between the claims of Islam and those of the secular state; the remarkable achievement of these Islamic modernists will be considered in due course.

Lastly, there was a change in the concept of international relations in the Near East. The European notion is that international relations are conducted between states through their duly appointed agents and that states are the only bodies legally competent to conduct those relations. The states of the traditional Near East made no such clear distinctions; the boundary line between domestic and international relations was blurred; for example, relations with border tribes involving dealing between provincial governors of neighbouring states were not seen as necessarily involving the rulers of states unless they chose to become involved. It was not merely that the provincial governor was given discretionary powers to act on his own border – that is a European rationalization of the situation – rather he was the responsible official, it was his job to act and there was no clear distinction between his dealings with tribes, merchants or other states.

Europeans found it difficult to grasp this situation and regarded having to deal with provincial rulers as attempts to fob them off. They sought to deal directly with the head of state and to embody the results of their dealings in formal interstate treaties. Over many years they were successful in imposing their concept of international relations upon the states of the Near East. For the Ottomans the process began as far back as the seventeenth century when they were obliged to sign the European-style Treaty of Zsitva Torok in 1606 and to give up their former habit of putting their international agreements in the form of commands sent to provincial governors. But the Ottomans did not abandon their older practices completely. Ottoman governors continued to act as the competent authority in what would be considered international relations, often in their dealings with Europeans and invariably in their relations with Asian states. It is interesting to observe the other side of the blurred division; throughout the nineteenth century the Ottoman government dealt with its non-Muslim citizens through the Ministry of Foreign Affairs. In Iran the new system was not introduced until the nineteenth century. The first so-called Anglo-Iranian treaty of 1800 consisted of no more than the habitual orders issued by the shah to his officers, although it is true that this treaty was negotiated with a subordinate body, namely the English East India Company. The first European-style treaty signed by Iran was the Treaty of Finkenstein with France in 1807.

The traditional Near Eastern system reflected a different concept of government in which authority over men mattered more than authority over territory and in which power was dispersed among many groups within the same polity. Europeans could only interpret this concept as a decayed form of a political organism with which they were more familiar. They bent their efforts towards obliging the Near East to conform to their own notions of how states should behave, and in doing so contributed to the disappearance of the old system and its replacement by a state system which resembled that of Europe. Near Eastern states came gradually to accept the new roles designated for them and to conform to the European system of rules for international relations although, as late comers to the scene, they found themselves at a disadvantage in playing the new game of diplomacy. But the adoption of the new state personality caused much confusion. The Eastern Question was about the integrity and independence of the Ottoman empire. Europeans understood this famous phrase to refer to the territory and the form of government of a state; to many Ottomans it related to the preservation of the nature of the state, which involved the universal claims of Islam and the legitimacy of the Ottoman sultan.

The European pressure upon the Near East had a decisive effect upon the state structure of the Near East. Throughout the nineteenth century it was Europe which determined the emerging shape of the Balkan states which gradually separated from the Ottoman empire; and between 1914 and 1923 Europe completely reshaped the Near East. The principle of self-determination which was introduced into the Near East, even attenuated as it was by the interests and ambitions of the European powers and the resistance of Near Eastern people, had a revolutionary impact upon the region.

NOTES

1. Lady Duff-Gordon, *Letters from Egypt, 1862–1869*, London 1969, 56.
2. ʿAbd al-Raḥmān al-Jabartī, *ʿAjāʾib al-āthār fiʾl-tarājim waʾl akhbār*, IV, Cairo 1879/80, 233. (Quoted Afaf Lutfi as-Sayyid Marsot, "The wealth of the Ulema in late eighteenth century Cairo", in T. Naff and R. Owen (eds), *Studies in eighteenth century Islamic history*, Carbondale, Ill. 1977, 207.)
3. Major George Keppel, *Narrative of a journey across the Balcan*, I, London 1831, 307.
4. *Mémoires du Baron de Tott sur les Turcs et les Tartars*, II, Paris 1785, 244. The English translation of this work (*Memoirs of the Baron de Tott*, II, London 1785, 366) translates "plusieurs grands propriétaires" as "several individuals" and misses the association with land. Recent research suggests that de Tott exaggerated the importance of commerce in wealth formation.
5. Odysseus [Sir Charles Eliot], *Turkey in Europe*, London 1900, 158.

CHAPTER TWO

The Eastern Question

THE INTERESTS OF THE GREAT POWERS AT THE END OF THE EIGHTEENTH CENTURY

During the sixteenth and seventeenth centuries Habsburg Austria had been the principal European opponent of the Ottoman empire, at first on the defensive as the main barrier to the progress of Ottoman arms into central Europe and latterly on the offensive. At the Treaty of Karlowitz (1699) Austria wrested substantial territories from Ottoman control and made even greater gains at Passarowitz (1718). During the remainder of the eighteenth century Austria was unable to sustain this offensive because of her preoccupation with the threat from Prussia in central Europe. The gains of Passarowitz were lost at Belgrade (1739); Austria took no part in the Russo-Ottoman War of 1768–74 (although she took advantage of Ottoman helplessness in 1774 to seize the Bukovina); and she was dragged reluctantly into the Russo-Ottoman War of 1787–92 on the coat-tails of Russia and withdrew prematurely in 1791 (Treaty of Sistova) gaining only the Banat as compensation for her meagre efforts. By this time Austria had come to fear the growing threat from Russia in the Balkans, but could do little to oppose Russia lest she should drive that power into the arms of Prussia; instead Austria was obliged to endure an uneasy co-operation with Russia, even including a vague plan in 1782 to partition the European provinces of the Ottoman empire between the two powers. Nevertheless, it was plain that the Ottoman Balkans would become a major area of competition between Austria and Russia in the future.

During the eighteenth century it was Russia which emerged as the principal European antagonist of the Ottomans. Two factors are prominent in Russian involvement with the Ottomans: a religious factor deriving from Russian sympathies with the Orthodox Christians of the

Balkans (and a vague Russian claim to protect them was admitted by the Ottomans in 1774); and a strategic factor arising from the Russian advance to the Black Sea. The long process of Slav colonization of the former Turkish pasture lands north of the Black Sea constitutes one of the major transformations of European history and it provided the base for the successful campaigns of the modernized Russian army which gave Russia a foothold on the Black Sea in 1774. The establishment of Russia on the Black Sea had two consequences: it permitted the development of the economy of the Ukraine and it created the Straits problem. So long as the Black Sea was an Ottoman lake passage through the Straits of the Bosporus and the Dardanelles was a purely Ottoman matter but once another power became located on the Black Sea then the rules which governed the passage of vessels through the Straits became a matter of international concern. After 1774 there commenced the long search for a regime which would satisfy the very different interests of those states which claimed an interest in the passage of the Straits.

The eighteenth century saw a number of Russo-Ottoman wars beginning with the premature effort of Peter the Great to force his path into the south. The great Russian breakthrough came during the war of 1768–74, when the khanate of the Crimea was separated from the Ottoman empire (and was annexed to Russia in 1783), and the Russian frontier was planted on the River Bug. The Ottoman effort to recover the Crimea in 1787–92 ended in failure and in the concession to Russia of a frontier on the Dniester by the Treaty of Jassy (1792). During this period Russia also opened contacts in a new direction, namely Transcaucasia; the links established with the Christian princes of Georgia marked the establishment of the first foothold south of the Caucasus range apart from an abortive venture by Peter the Great. Russian claims in Transcaucasia threatened the interests not only of the Ottomans but also those of the rulers of Iran.

The newcomer to the Eastern Question was Britain. This is not to say that Britain had no interest before the end of the eighteenth century but that that interest was slight, consisting of a modest concern with trade with the Levant (which amounted to about 1% of total British foreign trade) and a negative political objective – that her Continental allies should not become so immersed in Ottoman affairs that their freedom of movement in Europe became impaired. Britain's closer involvement with the East in the late eighteenth century arose from her acquisition of valuable territories in India, which created two new points of concern: the preservation of speedy and safe overland communications between Britain and India through the Near East and the safeguarding of her trade with the Persian Gulf region. Questions of trade and communications also directed the attention of the Government of India towards Egypt, where the Levant Company possessed a minor trading interest. A Levant Company merchant, George Baldwin, was appointed to superintend the passage of mails through Egypt, and Baldwin promptly became a source of recommendations for a more active British policy in Egypt, at first for the sake of trade and communications and subsequently for political reasons connected with possible threats from France. But Baldwin failed to persuade his government to retain the Egyptian consulate in 1794. Baldwin's career is significant, however, because he was one of the first of many British agents in the Near East who attempted to justify their existence and enlarge their importance by painting strategic and other alluring fancies for their superiors.

One should not exaggerate the strength of these new British concerns with the Near East. Some writers have held that as early as the Ochakov crisis of 1790–2 the Indian connection had come to dominate British policy in the Near East and the Younger Pitt's demand, in March 1791, that Russia should surrender Ochakov to the Ottomans and his request for a vote of money to wage war for that end shows a concern with resisting Russian expansion, upholding the integrity of the Ottoman empire and safeguarding the routes to India. The contention is wrong: Pitt was only concerned to conciliate Prussia, Britain's principal Continental ally at that time. In Parliament the government rested its defence of its actions on the need to preserve the balance of power in Europe. Outside Parliament some references were made to the need to protect India and of these the Whig spokesman, Charles Grey, remarked: "It is thus that history, geography and all the principles of common sense and common observation were violated for the purpose of finding some pretext for this useless armament."[1] Far from seeing Russia as a threat most Englishmen believed that state to be a natural ally. Russia could take the Black Sea and the Balkans, said Charles James Fox, and no British interest would be affected. As for the Ottomans: "What", inquired Edmund Burke, "had these worse than savages to do with the powers of Europe?"[2]

France was the oldest European ally of the Ottomans. Since the sixteenth century the Ottoman alliance had been for France a convenient device for diverting Habsburg attention from Western Europe. In the eighteenth century France was concerned that Russia might destroy this useful ally as she had already largely contributed to the demise of another French buffer in the East, namely Poland. France had also some concern with trade with the Ottoman empire which amounted to about

5 per cent of total French trade in 1780. But behind the continued French commitment to the maintenance of the Ottoman empire one can discern the emerging shadow of an alternative policy to be implemented if the old policy should no longer work and the Ottoman empire should collapse and be partitioned among the European powers. In that event France should seek compensation for herself and that compensation should include Egypt. This policy found favour with merchants interested in the Mediterranean trade and with some diplomats, but other French statesmen wanted no part of it, seeing Egypt as a wasteful diversion from the true centre of French interests which was on the Rhine. In fact it made little difference which policy France espoused in the years before 1789 because the collapse of government finances left her in no condition to do much about either. The debate about policy alternatives, however, helped to pave the way for Bonaparte's famous expedition to Egypt in 1798.

THE NEAR EAST DURING THE REVOLUTIONARY AND NAPOLEONIC WARS

Bonaparte and the Near East

The expedition of Bonaparte to Egypt in 1798 is a key event in the development of the Eastern Question, comparable, in its momentous consequences, to the Treaty of Küchük Kaynarja of 1774. What the expedition seems to indicate is that the traditional French policy towards the Ottoman empire, which had been followed since the outbreak of the French Revolution in 1789, had now been abandoned and the alternative policy of partition adopted. This view is mistaken: France had not abandoned the Ottomans, who it was thought would accept the displacement of their rebellious Mamluk vassals in Egypt by France.

A second view of Bonaparte's expedition, namely that it was principally intended to threaten the British possessions in India, is also mistaken. The notion of a French threat to India via Egypt had been discussed at intervals since 1777. The threat had two aspects: first, merely by being in Egypt France could command Britain's overland communications with the subcontinent and provoke hostility towards Britain among the Indian princes; and second, Egypt could be employed as a base for an actual French invasion of India whether conducted overland through the Near East or by sea. Either form of the threat could have the effect of diverting British resources away from Europe and other theatres of war in order to protect India, about the value of which to Britain Frenchmen held an exaggerated view. In the Directory's instructions to Bonaparte only the first aspect of the threat to India was mentioned and, whatever Bonaparte or his apologists said later, there is no evidence that in 1798–9 he contemplated a direct invasion of India. Only the first form of the threat is therefore relevant, but even so the notion that France could achieve any purpose commensurate with the effort which the occupation of Egypt would require is one which needs some further comment. In 1798 it was plain that Britain could be defeated only through a cross-Channel invasion, and an invasion was what the Directors wanted. To Bonaparte such an enterprise was too hazardous. He believed the best opportunities for France lay in Mediterranean expansion but the Directors could be persuaded to support such a strategy only if it were presented as part of the war against Britain. In this circumstance lies the explanation of the emphasis placed upon the relation of the Egyptian expedition to the war against Britain.

Bonaparte left Toulon on 19 May 1798, took Malta from the Knights of St John, landed at Alexandria on 1 July, defeated the Mamluks on 21 July and occupied Cairo. Then followed a series of disasters. On 2 August Nelson's destruction of the French fleet at the battle of the Nile severed Bonaparte's communications with France; and the Ottomans, far from accepting French explanations of the attack upon one of their possessions, declared war on France in September 1798 and in January 1799 signed a triple alliance against France with Russia and Britain. The Directors, who did not want Bonaparte back in France, offered him three choices: to stay in Egypt, to march on India or to advance on Istanbul. Bonaparte set off into Syria, but was checked at Acre in May 1799 and returned to Egypt where he abandoned his army and sailed back to France. The French possessions in the Mediterranean – Malta and the Ionian Islands – fell to Allied forces and in October 1801 the French army in Egypt surrendered to a British expeditionary force. The war was ended at Amiens in May 1802. The uneasy alliance of Russia, Britain and the Ottomans had already collapsed. That the French expedition to Egypt had produced an alliance between two such enemies as Russia and the Ottomans is in itself evidence of the impact of that event. The Ottomans regarded Russia as their natural enemy and continued to fear Russian designs in Transcaucasia and the Romanian Principalities; and many Russians would have preferred to join France in a partition of the Ottoman empire than to unite themselves with Britain in its defence.

Following the Peace of Amiens there was a period when France and Russia sought to strengthen their positions in the Mediterranean and the Ottoman empire, and after renewal of the European struggle Russia formed new alliances with Britain and the Ottomans in 1805. But after her decisive victory at Austerlitz on 2 December 1805 and the acquisition of the Austrian possessions on the Dalmatian coast, the initiative lay with France. Again she had a choice of policies towards the Ottoman empire: to arrange a partition of the Ottoman empire and build up Austria as her principal buffer against Russia or to uphold the traditional policy of employing the Ottomans as the buffer. Napoleon chose the traditional policy and in 1806 sent his emissary, Sebastiani, to Istanbul to negotiate an alliance with the Ottomans against Russia, an agreement which was to form part of what was to be a triple alliance including Iran. "The unwavering aim of my policy", wrote Napoleon, "is to make a triple alliance of Myself, the Porte and Persia, aimed directly or by implication against Russia . . . I do not want to partition the empire of Constantinople; if they offered me threequarters I would not take it."[3]

Napoleon's strategy contemplated that the Ottomans, supported by the French army in Dalmatia, would guard the right flank of the French advance into central and eastern Europe. With the inclusion of Iran the flank would be extended eastwards to the Caucasus and a basis would also be laid for the renewal of the French threat to India.

Napoleon's alliance system came into being in 1806–7. The Ottomans declared war on Russia at the end of 1806 and on 4 May 1807 a treaty of alliance was signed with Iran at Finkenstein according to which France would assist Iran to recover Georgia, annexed by Russia in 1801, and Iran would declare war on Britain and give facilities to a French army marching on India. A French diplomatic and military mission under General Gardane was sent to Iran.

Having carefully constructed his eastern alliances, Napoleon promptly destroyed their whole *raison d'être* when he made peace with Russia on 7 July 1807 at Tilsit. The Ottoman alliance was abandoned on the excuse of the deposition of Sultan Selīm III on 29 May 1807, and the Iranian alliance emasculated; Gardane was now ordered to assist Iran to make peace with Russia, not war, and the alliance was to operate against Britain alone. Since Iran had no quarrel with Britain and was solely interested in obtaining military assistance against Russia, the end of the Iranian alliance was only a matter of time. Instead of the eastern alliance against Russia Napoleon entered into a series of fantastic discussions with Russia about a joint invasion of India and a partition of the

Ottoman empire. Almost certainly none of his proposals was serious and the discussions were intended only to buy time.

For all their dramatic appearance there was very little substance to Napoleon's eastern schemes either in 1798 or in 1807. In both cases they were essentially diversionary; the centre of French ambition remained in Europe and, as in the past, the Ottoman empire was drawn into French schemes so as to create opportunities for the realization of those ambitions. It is not in a change in French policy but in the reaction of Russia and especially of Britain that the revolution in the Eastern Question took place.

Russia and the Near East

Fear of French intervention hastened the development of Russian designs in the Near East. The annexation of Georgia was a major event in widening Russian involvement because it brought Russia into contention not only with the Ottomans over the possession of lands on the Ottoman frontier in eastern Asia Minor but also with Iran. In defence of the Georgian territories Russia pressed outwards to extend her control into Transcaucasia, pushing round the eastern shore of the Black Sea into the tangled mountains of Armenia in search of a defensible frontier, and advancing down the western shore of the Caspian into Azerbaijan and Iranian Armenia towards a stable frontier on the River Aras. The war with Iran which began in 1804 continued until the Treaty of Gulistan in 1813, but Russia remained dissatisfied with the results and disputes over the frontier led to a second war from 1826 to 1828 when, by the Treaty of Turkmanchay, Russia gained the coveted Aras frontier and acquired Iranian Armenia.

The war with the Ottomans over eastern Asia Minor became part of the larger struggle in Europe which centred on the fate of the Romanian Principalities. It was the Russian invasion of the Principalities on 23 November 1806, an event brought on by fears of the growth of French influence in the empire, which precipitated the Russo-Ottoman War of 1806–12 which was concluded by the Treaty of Bucharest. In the end it was the French attack on Russia which saved the Principalities for the Ottomans; at Bucharest the Russians retained most of Bessarabia but reluctantly surrendered the Principalities in return for a peace which enabled them to concentrate their forces against the greater French threat. But the long struggle had had its effect upon the Balkans; not only the ambitions for independence of the people of the Principalities but also those of the Serbs and Greeks had been aroused.

Britain and the Near East

The most significant change which was wrought by French activities in the East was that which took place in British perceptions of the region. It is important to emphasize that all Britons did not take the same view. As with France and Russia, one can detect at least two distinct British attitudes to the East during the Revolutionary and Napoleonic struggle. These two views were clearly displayed in the British reaction to Bonaparte's invasion of Egypt. To Pitt and to most of his colleagues it was an occasion for relief that the French had gone somewhere where they could do little damage to Britain and that the danger of a French attack on Britain herself or on Ireland was averted. They had no fear for India; for them the centre of the struggle with France was in Europe and, although in the following years more Britons came to see the possibility of a French threat to India through the Near East, this aspect of the struggle with France never rivalled the contest in Europe. To a small group of men, led by Henry Dundas, the minister responsible for India, the French threat to India was very real. Dundas feared a direct French invasion of India and he was the main supporter of a major British offensive in the Mediterranean to drive the French from Egypt. In 1801 he got his way, but Britain did not replace France in Egypt which was evacuated in March 1803.

Before the 1801 expedition to Egypt Dundas had adopted some interim measures to meet what he saw as the French danger to India, by actions in the Red Sea and Iraq. To the Red Sea he sent a naval expedition, backed by troops from India, to deny the Red Sea to France. In the course of this operation contacts were opened with the Sharif of Mecca and with Yemen, and Aden was temporarily occupied from September 1799 until March 1800. To Baghdad he sent a political resident. Hitherto British interests in Iraq had been purely commercial and based on Basra. Now Britain was to deal directly with the pasha at Baghdad and encourage him to resist any French movement. In these actions in the Red Sea and Iraq Britain departed from her former policy of dealing with the governors of Ottoman territories only through the Porte and entered into direct political negotiations with them. She was to do the same thing in Egypt. Although nothing came of these dealings at the time – the Red Sea operations were closed down in 1802 and the agent at Baghdad achieved nothing and was expelled in 1806 – they set a precedent for British relations with the Ottoman territories in the future.

The outbreak of war between Russia and the Ottomans at the end of 1806 obliged Britain to re-examine her priorities in the Near East. Her decision was entirely in favour of her alliance with Russia. She had no great interest in the Ottoman empire or in the eastern Mediterranean and certainly no wish for a partition of the Ottoman empire. But she needed Russian troops in central Europe to stem the French advance, especially after the collapse of Austria. As in 1915 it was thought that the best way to ensure that Russia would concentrate all her force in central Europe was to deliver a knock-out blow against the Ottoman empire. Such a blow was attempted by the naval expedition to Istanbul under Admiral Duckworth in February 1807 and it failed. The only other British operation in the region involved an expedition to Egypt to prevent the return of France to that country but this adventure also ended in defeat, this time at the hands of the Ottoman governor, Muḥammad ʿAlī, at Rosetta and Egypt was evacuated in September 1807. Britain had had enough of an Ottoman war which she had never sought and hoped that she might make peace in company with Russia. But when Russia made a separate peace with France at Tilsit Britain made peace with the Ottomans without her in January 1809 (Peace of the Dardanelles). The Ottomans were of no great interest to Britain one way or another; her relations with the empire were subordinated to the struggle with France and to her relations with Russia and Austria.

During the Revolutionary and Napoleonic Wars Britain also developed an interest in the regions which lay to the east of the Ottoman empire. In these regions British policy was shaped not only by the state of European affairs but by local problems of the government of the East India Company in India. Briefly, the British Indian government was engaged in a struggle for mastery with the Indian states and was handicapped in that struggle by the unwillingness of the authorities in London to countenance any expansion of the company's Indian territories or the creation of any system of alliances which might contribute to war in India. To the British authorities in India the alleged French threat to India was, in many ways, a great convenience for it was the one factor which would induce the London government to sanction war and alliances in India. On the excuse of their supposed links with France the British Indian government destroyed a number of Indian rulers or brought them under British control. Beyond India itself the British Indian government also sought arrangements with the rulers of Muscat, Iran and Afghanistan to exclude French influence. To what extent these arrangements were sought with sincerity and to what extent they were merely intended to facilitate the extension of British power in India is arguable; arrangements made with Iran in 1798–1800 appear to belong to the latter category; the initiatives of 1808 to the former.

In 1798–1800 agreements were made with Iran which provided for Iranian assistance to control Afghanistan and to exclude France, as well as for improved trade between Iran and British India. This agreement was subsequently allowed to lapse but a new agreement was sought in 1808–9 when news was received of French contacts with Iran which led to the 1807 Franco-Iranian alliance. There were then sharp fears in London and Calcutta of a French invasion. As has been remarked already the Tilsit agreement between Russia and France ultimately destroyed the basis of the Franco-Ottoman alliance, and in February 1809 Britain was able to displace France in Tehran and make her own alliance with Iran. That alliance, however, had a fundamental flaw: Britain expected it to operate against France but Iran thought it should work against Russia. Britain had no interest in assisting Iran against Russia, especially after Napoleon's invasion of Russia in 1812 had restored the Anglo-Russian alliance so much desired by British statesmen. Britain's main contribution was to help to persuade Iran to accept the Russian terms at Gulistan in 1813. Efforts were made to modify the alliance so as to bridge the difference between Britain and Iran but the definitive treaty signed in 1814 soon broke down. Britain failed to assist Iran against Russia in 1826–8 and the alliance was then so amended as to drain it of all utility to Iran.

The Iranian alliance was the most enduring of the various arrangements made by Britain in the eastern part of the Near East during the Revolutionary and Napoleonic Wars. Relations with Muscat, which had close trading links with British India, continued but with no reference to international strategy. A treaty signed with Afghanistan in 1809 was nullified immediately after by the fall of the Afghan government which signed it. Arrangements with Sind and the Panjab also sought in connection with the French threat quickly lost any link with that event and relations with those countries were governed by matters of local concern.

At first sight there seems little substance to the British reaction to French activities in the Near East between 1798 and 1815. A mixture of fanciful strategy and opportunism had sent British agents, troops or ships throughout the Near East, from Egypt and the Dardanelles to Afghanistan and beyond, but the only enduring result was the lame alliance with Iran. The importance of that first extensive British political involvement in the Near East lay in the future. The information acquired, the ideas formulated and the contacts made during that period were to be of considerable significance during the period from 1830 onwards when the strategies employed against France were to be refurbished for use against Russia, and Britain was to begin an involvement in the region which eventually, by 1919, was to make her mistress of the whole Near East.

Effects of the European struggle on the Near East.

The more intimate political involvement of European powers in the Near East was one consequence of the Napoleonic struggle. A second was the economic impact. The presence in the region of troops and ships with the consequent demand for supplies provided a stimulus to the economy of many parts of the region, notably Egypt which supplied grain and other stores to British forces in the region. British subsidies to Iran and other states gave a boost to the local economy. On the other hand the Russian occupation of the Principalities cut off Istanbul from a main source of food supplies, leading to severe problems in 1807 and a search for new supplies. The French occupation of Egypt in 1798 had had a similar disturbing effect. War affected patterns of trade in other ways. French trade with the Levant was destroyed and Britain became the chief supplier of goods to the area and achieved a dominance which she did not lose before 1914. But Britain lacked the ships to carry the trade and the war also provided a major opportunity for Greek shipowners, who had profited greatly by the opening of the Black Sea after 1774, to develop their activities. By 1813 there were 615 Greek ships amounting to 155,500 tonnes and 38,000 seamen involved in the trade of the region, a circumstance of crucial significance in the Greek War of the 1820s. In a smaller way Muscat also expanded its trade in the Arabian Sea.

A third effect of the Napoleonic struggle was the blow which was given to older institutions. The Russian involvement in Transcaucasia and the Russian occupation of the Principalities from 1806 to 1812 changed the course of events in those areas. So did the French and British occupation of the Ionian Islands. Most dramatic was the effect of French and British activities in Egypt. The French defeat of the Mamluks and the British failure to restore either Mamluk or Ottoman authority paved the way for a new political power to emerge in Egypt under Muḥammad ʿAlī.

Fourthly, the European struggle accelerated the penetration of the Near East by new ideas. These ideas had different effects according to whether they were adopted by Muslim rulers or by their subjects. To Muslim rulers the great lesson of the Napoleonic period was the power of disciplined military force as deployed by France. In the Ottoman empire, Iran and elsewhere rulers wanted European advisers and equipment, usually French, to enable them to build up their own military forces. The Napoleonic struggle gave a strong impetus to modernization in the Near East. To their subjects different ideas appealed. While the Ottoman élite was indifferent to the ideas of liberty, equality, fraternity or nationalism which were popularized by the French revolutionaries, and their Muslim subjects rejected them as infidel heresy, the matter was otherwise with their Christian subjects. Even in the cafés of distant Baghdad, it was reported, Armenians were eagerly discussing these ideas. To many Balkan Christians, especially the Greeks in the Ionian Islands and those on the Dalmatian coast this was their first real contact with the disturbing thoughts of the Enlightenment. Newspapers, Masonic lodges, merchants, students and soldiers were modes of transmission of these ideas. Those who served in the French Chasseurs d'Orient or the British Duke of York's Greek Light Infantry, like Theodore Kolokotrones, a former klepht, inevitably saw a different world. Todor Vladimirescu, who was to lead the Romanian peasants against the Ottomans in 1821 first fought against the latter in the Russian forces in 1806.

The character of the Eastern Question had changed since the eighteenth century: more European powers were involved and in different ways and their impact upon the Near East had become more profound. Yet in one respect there was no change from the eighteenth century. For all the European powers their interests in the East were subsidiary to their interests in Europe. The policies of each state towards the Ottomans and Iran was determined primarily by their relations with each other and by what was happening in central Europe. This situation was to continue throughout the nineteenth century. For two states, however, their Near Eastern interests, although not rivalling their European concerns, were assuming greater importance than in the past. Russia's interests via the Straits had already been plain before the war, but the growth of the economy of the southern regions of the Russian state and the exposure of the strategic significance of naval movements through the Straits had made control of the Straits of still more importance to Russia. And the question of the Balkan Christians and the future of Transcaucasia had assumed enhanced significance in Russian policy. During the war Britain's Indian interests had also emerged for the first time as a distinct and separate influence on British policy-making, to be accommodated with her European interests in a new foreign policy in the Near East.

THE EASTERN QUESTION IN THE NINETEENTH CENTURY

The essence of the Eastern Question during the nineteenth century was the conflict between Ottoman rulers and their Christian subjects, primarily in south-eastern Europe, the demand by those subjects for autonomy or independence, the Ottoman resistance to those demands, and the efforts of the major European powers to find a solution to the conflict which would accommodate the desires of both Ottomans and Christians and which would not upset the balance of power in Europe. The problem boiled down to that of preventing the matter being solved in such a manner as to make Russia the predominant power in the whole region. In the following pages the various independence movements will be described and the major diplomatic crisis briefly examined. First, it will be appropriate to make some general remarks about what is called Balkan nationalism.

Balkan nationalism contained economic, intellectual and political factors. There were three main elements in the economic factor. The first was the increasing prosperity of a Balkan Christian commercial class as a result of the growth of trade, especially with Europe. Mention has already been made of the activities of Greek sailors. Greeks were also active, together with Serbs, Bulgarians and Vlachs in the growing land trade with Europe. The European demand for Balkan food and raw materials was the basis of this increased trade and the availability of cheap European manufactured goods was its counterpart. The second element was linked with the first; increased demand sparked off a shift from subsistence to capitalist farming and efforts by notables, Muslim and Christian, to change the tenurial structure of agriculture to facilitate this change. This endeavour contributed to peasant dissatisfaction evidenced by the growth in the number of peasant bandits, klephts, haiduks, etc. The third element arose from the competition between notables, whose wealth was increasing, for government employment and their willingness to use their private armies against each other in this struggle.

The intellectual factor has already been mentioned. Each of the Balkan nationalities had a historical memory of a Golden Age, or, at least, the materials lay at hand from which such a memory could be constructed by intellectuals. So the Greeks could look to Byzantium, the Romanians to the Roman period, the Bulgarians to the tenth-century Bulgarian state, the Serbs to the fourteenth century and the Albanians to the fifteenth. Contacts with European ideas had an influence on shaping Balkan aspirations. Also, within the Balkan communities the growth of literacy was creating intellectual pressures for language reform and the creation of literary languages; and these movements were also promoting a new sense of cultural and ultimately political identity. One point must be made about this cultural and political identity. When the Balkan intellectuals came to describe their national struggles, they did so commonly in terms of secular nationality. This was a mode of description adapted rather to the aspirations of the new states than to the reality of their contemporary self-image. At the time the predominant element in the movements was religion; Bulgarian peasants fought as Christians against Muslims, not as adherents of a secular Bulgarian culture, which was created only by the actions of the new states and their apologists. All the Christian Balkan nationalities drew on a rich folk tradition of saints and martyrs in the struggle against Islam.

The political element emerged in two ways. First through the resentments by certain Balkan nationalities of the privileged position of others. The dominant position of the Greek Church, Greek culture and certain Greek families in Ottoman employment meant that much early Balkan nationalism emerged as a reaction to Greek rather than to Ottoman domination, for example the resentment of Romanians against the political authority of Phanariot Greeks or the later opposition of Bulgarians to Greek claims. Second, Balkan nationalism shaped itself in dealings with the Ottoman authorities themselves. In some cases resentment was directed against the increased claims of government under the Tanẓīmāt. In other cases the reaction was not so much against the strength of Ottoman control as against its weakness which permitted local Ottoman notables, officials and soldiers to exploit Christians. So the first stirrings of Serbian discontent were directed against the unlawful activities of unruly Janissaries and were approved by the Ottoman government. So also Christians in Bosnia rebelled against Muslim landlords who were themselves defying their government. And, in another permutation, the Christian reaction was at second hand; as the Ottoman government increased its demands on its own supporters so in turn these applied pressure to Christians.

Montenegro

Montenegro, the Black Mountain, was the first Balkan country to repudiate Ottoman control. In fact the remote mountain tribesmen had always been virtually autonomous, and under the rule of their prince bishops the state was shaped by a struggle against the Ottoman government (the Porte) and against the tribes themselves in which the rulers drew on the essential help of Russian subsidies. From the mid-nineteenth century the state was secularized and the princely office made hereditary in the Petrović family. In themselves these developments were of small significance to the Ottomans; the disturbing factor was the ambitions of the new state directed towards Bosnia, Hercegovina and Albania and, in particular, the acquisition of a port on the Adriatic. These ambitions were a major factor in the Eastern Crisis of the 1870s, which resulted in the achievement of independence by Montenegro in 1878.

Serbia

Much more serious to the Ottomans was the Serbian revolt, or to be more precise, the revolt of the Serbs of the frontier pashalik of Belgrade. As mentioned above, the Serbs first appeared as loyal Ottoman subjects resisting the excesses of the local Janissaries and of ʿOs̱mān Pasvanoglu, the rebellious notable from Vidin. Between 1791 and 1796 Sultan Selīm III granted the Serbs some autonomy, including the right to collect their own taxes and form a national militia to resist the rebels. In 1798 Selīm was obliged to abandon this policy and make terms with the rebels, but he continued to encourage the Serbs and remained ready to concede autonomy to them. But Serbian aspirations developed under the leadership of Karadjordje Petrović from 1804. Karadjordje (*c.* 1768–1817) had served with the Austrian forces and gained some administrative experience during the Austrian occupation of Serbian lands between 1788 and 1791 to add to the experience of his trading connections with Austria. He began to look outside for help and found encouragement from Russia, who urged the Serbs to refuse a compromise and to fight on, diverting Ottoman resources from the conflict with Russia. But although Russia won some concessions for the Serbs at Bucharest she effectively abandoned them to the Ottomans who suppressed the Serbian revolt in 1813. Karadjordje fled but in 1815 a new revolt took place under the leadership of Milos Obrenović and the Ottomans conceded a degree of autonomy to the Serbs. In 1830 the Serbs gained full autonomy and in 1867 the Ottoman garrisons were removed. By then the only traces of Ottoman authority were the Ottoman flag and an annual tribute. In 1878 Serbia achieved full independence and further territory. During this period Serbian ambitions had developed. The 1815 territory had had a population of well under 1 million although it included some areas in which the Serbs were a minority. In 1833 further territories had been conceded by the Ottomans. At an early date the Serbs mapped out a plan of further expansion chiefly at Ottoman expense. According to the national programme of 1844 the Serbs would work to promote national feeling among the Balkan Christians, bring about a general uprising against Ottoman rule and create a Greater Serbia. Between 1866 and 1868 the Serbs almost succeeded in bringing into existence a Balkan league, but the murder of Michael Obrenović in 1868 ended this prospect and this end was not finally achieved until 1912. Like Montenegro, Serbia became a major factor of unrest within the Balkans. Balkan nationalism was like a snowball; although for substantial periods it seemed as though a *modus vivendi* could be found between the Balkan states and the Ottomans the appearance was illusory; grants of autonomy fed the desire for independence and expansion.

Rumania

Of all the Ottoman Balkan possessions the Principalities of Moldavia and Wallachia were the most open to outside influence. For long they had been semi-autonomous under Greek Christian governors and their geographical position exposed them to Russian interference. Eight times between 1711 and 1853 Russian troops occupied the Principalities and in 1774 the Russian right of protection was admitted. But to the Ottomans they were most valuable possessions, for they constituted a rich agricultural region producing a surplus of foodstuffs for export which was vital to Istanbul, especially after the loss of the Crimea. Large estates had developed in the Principalities and hostility existed between peasants and landowners, although in Moldavia and Wallachia, unlike other areas, both of these groups were Orthodox Christians. In 1821 the Greek revolt began in the Principalities with the invasion of Alexander Ypsilantis, and although this invasion was unsuccessful in its main aims it did have the result of bringing to an end the system of rule by Greeks from Istanbul and led to the appointment of native governors. By the Treaty of Adrianople in 1829 the governors were appointed for life, the Ottoman fortresses on the left bank of the Danube were evacuated, Ottoman subjects were withdrawn from the area and the Principalities were left to pay a fixed tribute only. From 1829 Ottoman control over Romania was only nominal and Russian influence paramount; Russia chose the governors until the Crimean War, following which the Russian protectorate was abolished and the Principalities placed under the protection of the Great Powers. Between 1859 and 1861 Moldavia and Wallachia united and Romania finally achieved its independence in 1878. More than any other Balkan state Romania owed its existence to Russia and it is ironic that it was against

Russia and Austria in Transylvania, Bukovina and Bessarabia that Romanian ambitions were directed rather than against the Ottomans.

Greece

Greece, on the other hand, owed her independence especially to the interference of the Western European powers. The growth of Greek national self-consciousness through contacts with Europe and through commercial prosperity has already been mentioned. It was particularly among the colonies of Greek *émigrés* and merchants that national ambitions were kindled, notably in Odessa which saw the birth in 1814 of the Greek political society, Philike Etairia, which dreamed of a great Greek empire in the Balkans. It was from Odessa that Ypsilantis launched his invasion of the Principalities in 1821 with disappointed hopes of Russian assistance. It is a significant comment on the nature of the Greek self-image at that period that the Greek revolt began in Romania. In the same month of March the Greeks rose in the Peloponnesus or Morea and there the revolt assumed a more local and religious character. The revolt spread to the Greek islands and to the Greek mainland and the Ottomans found themselves unable to suppress the rising without assistance. Muḥammad ʿAlī's navy and disciplined troops were brought in, first to subdue Crete and, in 1825, to begin the pacification of the Morea. The divided Greeks could offer little resistance and it seemed that the uprising would be extinguished. Russia, however, was at odds with the Ottomans over several issues and refused to allow the extinction of all Greek hopes. Alexander I pressed for a European intervention. The European powers agreed to demand the grant of autonomy to Greece. After the destruction of the Ottoman and Egyptian fleets at Navarino on 20 October 1827 (see p. 70) the Ottomans had no means of breaking Greek resistance. In revenge the Ottomans denounced their 1826 agreement with the Russians at Akkerman and went to war in April 1828. The Ottomans were defeated. By the Treaty of Adrianople (14 September 1829) Russia made a number of gains: small territorial gains at the mouth of the Danube and large gains in eastern Asia Minor; a new regime for the Straits; a protectorate over the Principalities; and autonomy for Greece which was quickly transformed into independence and the Greek kingdom was founded in 1830. It was a small and discontented kingdom, with a population well under 1 million, and vast ambitions. As the prime minister, Ioannis Kolettis, said in 1844, "The Kingdom of Greece is not Greece: it is only the smallest and poorest part of Greece. Greece includes [every place] where Greek history or the Greek race was present."[4] Greeks dreamed of a revival of the Byzantine empire, a new Greek empire with its capital at Constantinople: more modestly, but no less disruptively, others aimed at the extension of Greece to include all the Greek islands, Epirus and parts of Macedonia. Independent Greece was another disturbing element in south-east Europe, threatening a further partition of the Ottoman empire.

Crete

Greek ambitions focused particularly on the recovery of Crete which remained under Egyptian control until 1840 when it was restored to Ottoman authority. Thereafter a series of uprisings took place in Crete. These disturbances took the form of protests by Greek Christian peasants against the dominance of the half of the population which had converted to Islam and which held the best lands including many large estates. After each revolt reforms were promised but never implemented; the Ottoman government was unwilling to coerce loyal Greek Muslims. In 1896 the greatest uprising took place: in February 1897 the Cretan rebels declared their unity with Greece: and in April Greece went to war with the Ottomans. The Greeks were heavily defeated but were saved from the consequences of their actions by European intervention which ensured that they lost very little and secured autonomy for Crete. The Cretans continued to strive for unity with Greece, however, despite constant refusals of support by the Great Powers, until, in 1913, they accomplished their aim.

Bosnia

Like Crete, Bosnia was an area in which there had been mass conversion to Islam and a similar situation had arisen. Muslim (and some Christian) notables opposed government pressure to reform and revolted against Ottoman authority on several occasions. Until 1850, when Ottoman troops enforced government authority, Bosnia remained virtually autonomous. There continued to be much Christian peasant discontent in Bosnia and in 1875 Bosnian peasants rose, following a similar revolt in neighbouring Hercegovina. The Ottomans lacked the resources to suppress the rising and the temptation was too great for Montenegro and Serbia, which went to war in July 1876 in the hope of acquiring Hercegovina and Bosnia respectively. The Montenegrins had some success but the Serbs were heavily defeated and were saved from the consequences of their rash ambition only by Russian intervention. In

1878 Bosnia and Hercegovina passed under Austro-Hungarian protection and in 1908 were annexed to that state.

Bulgaria

The Bulgars also began their journey towards independence in 1878. Bulgarian nationalism was slow to develop for three reasons: the region was heavily settled with Muslims; the notables (known as *chorbajis*), like notables elsewhere in Christian areas, were generally content with the Ottoman system which left them alone; and Greek cultural and administrative domination, through the Greek Church, was widespread. During the course of the nineteenth century the position of the notables declined as large estates were sold up and land passed into peasant hands. Greek influence was reduced after 1821 from which date the Ottomans were less inclined to rely on Greeks in administration, secular Bulgarian education developed, a Bulgarian literary language was created and in 1870 the Ottomans established a Bulgarian Church independent of the Greek. There was no real challenge to Ottoman authority in Bulgaria until after the Crimean War; peasant uprisings were suppressed and *émigré* efforts to organize resistance controlled. It was the spreading influence of Bulgarian intellectuals exposed to radical Russian ideas which led to the formulation of a Bulgarian national programme.

In the latter half of the nineteenth century several groups emerged amongst *émigré* groups ranging from the moderate conception of Liuben Karavelov, who favoured Ottoman–Bulgarian compromise on the Austro-Hungarian model, to independence through a mass peasant revolt advocated by Vasil Levski. In 1870 the Bulgarian Revolutionary Committee was formed to combine the various groups and it was this committee which organized the unsuccessful uprising of 1875 suppressed by the Ottomans. A new uprising was planned for 1876 but the Bulgarian disturbances which took place in that year had an economic rather than a political origin, although they were exploited by Bulgarian nationalists particularly for the propaganda value of their brutal suppression by Ottoman irregular forces. Essentially, it was the Russian intervention and war with the Ottomans in 1877–8 which brought about the creation of Bulgaria. The Russian plan called for the creation of a large Bulgarian state but at the Congress of Berlin this was divided into three, the southern part being returned to Ottoman rule, the northern part being made autonomous but under Russian control, and the remaining portion, known as Eastern Rumelia, being given a degree of autonomy under a constitution drawn up by an international commission in which different powers compiled various sections. The situation of Eastern Rumelia illustrates the way in which facts created nationalist ideas in the Ottoman Balkans. During the struggles of 1877–8 most Muslim landholders had fled and their lands had fallen into the hands of Christians who were anxious to prevent the return of the Muslims. It was this circumstance, as much as anything else, which made the Rumelians Bulgarian nationalists and caused them to seek speedy unity with independent Bulgaria. In September 1885 the Rumelian leaders staged a coup in favour of union with Bulgaria, a demand which was accepted by the powers in 1886. From 1886 the hopes of united Bulgaria turned towards the acquisition of the third area of big Bulgaria, namely Macedonia, but there Bulgarian ambitions came into direct conflict with those of Serbia and Greece. Rivalry between the Balkan states, already apparent in 1877–8, was soon to become a dominant theme in the area, but it was too late to save the Ottoman empire in Europe from almost complete destruction in 1912–13.

Macedonia

After 1878 the last major area of Europe which remained under full Ottoman control was Macedonia, a poor area with an ethnically very diverse population of rather less than 2 million made up of Turks, Bulgars, Greeks, Serbs, Albanians, Vlachs, Jews, Gypsies, Macedonians and many who did not know to what national group they belonged because the question had not occurred to them. The region was claimed by Greeks on the basis of the Greek Church and the predominant Greek urban Christian culture; by the Bulgarians on the basis of the Bulgarian Church and language; and by the Serbs on the grounds that they were entitled to some compensation for their disappointment in Bosnia. There was also a Romanian claim on the basis of the Vlach population and a claim for an independent Macedonia on the grounds that the language spoken was distinct from Bulgarian. This last group of claimants was represented by the Internal Macedonian Revolutionary Organization founded in 1893. The substantial Muslim population looked to a continuation of Ottoman rule. Each group sought to advance its claims through its own organizations, churches, schools and national societies and through violence against other groups. The Macedonian Supreme Committee, which represented the hopes of those who looked to annexation by Bulgaria, employed a policy of attacking Muslims in the hope of provoking reprisals and producing a revolt. Macedonia was the *reductio ad absurdum* of Balkan nationalism; no solution could be based upon national feeling. The Ottomans struggled to preserve order while the powers sought a solution through partition or reform. In 1903 a new reform programme involving the employment of a foreign-officered gendarmerie to keep the peace in Macedonia was adopted and in 1905 a system of international financial supervision was set up. But Ottoman rule was finally brought to an end by the action of the Balkan states themselves.

In 1912 Bulgaria, Greece, Serbia and Montenegro came to a rough agreement on the spoils, spurned the efforts of Austria and Russia to control them and attacked the Ottomans, winning a notable victory. They were not, however, allowed to decide the terms of the settlement; on the grounds that it constituted a revision of the 1878 Berlin settlement, peacemaking was reserved to the Great Powers who imposed the Treaty of London (1 June 1913) which involved the creation of a new and unexpected state of Albania.

Albania

Albania was the only European territory of the Ottoman empire where a majority (about 70%) of the inhabitants had adopted Islam, the remainder consisting of 20 per cent Orthodox Christians and 10 per cent Catholics. Albania resembled Montenegro in that it was a poor mountainous area dominated by tribal loyalties and enjoying throughout history substantial autonomy. In 1830 the Ottomans recovered some control after murdering 500 Albanian Muslim notables and introduced some elements of the Tanẓīmāt reforms. An Albanian national movement emerged only in 1878 and was directed not against Ottoman rule but against Bulgarian and Montenegrin claims. In fact Albania was left untouched in the 1878 settlement, the movement withered away and its remnants were suppressed by the Ottoman authorities in 1881. In the last years of the nineteenth century, however, there were signs of a cultural awakening in Albania with the familiar cycle of language reform (and the controversial adoption of the Latin alphabet in 1908), the development of a national literature and the writing of national histories. After 1908 the Ottoman authorities attempted to check these exhibitions of national sentiment with more vigour, the Albanian nationalists reacted, armed clashes took place and in 1911 the Ottoman government made some concessions relating to the Latin alphabet and schools. But the split between government and Albanians was not healed and by 1912 there was widespread disorder in Albania. In August 1912 the Ottoman government made further concessions, amounting to virtual autonomy for the four Albanian provinces. Even so the Albanian leaders remained very divided between those (mainly

Catholics) who looked to Austria-Hungary for support, those who favoured autonomy and those who wanted direct Ottoman rule. It was the result of the 1912–13 First Balkan War which decided Albanians for there was no longer the option of a continuation of Ottoman rule or even of autonomy within the empire. The choice was between division among the Balkan states or independence. To the Muslim leaders independence offered the only chance of preserving something of the traditional life and on 28 November 1912 the national assembly at Valona (Vlorë) proclaimed the independence of the Republic of Albania with Ismāʿīl Kemāl as president. The national claims were supported by Austria, who had no wish to see Serbia further enlarged, and a compromise was arranged by which the Albanians surrendered some territory to the Balkan states and an international control commission was set up to direct the administration of Albania. A constitution was drafted for the new country and a German prince was given the throne. Albania, with a population of less than 1 million, was launched shakily into the world.

The principal losers from the creation of Albania were: Montenegro, which coveted the port of Scutari (Shköder); Serbia, which had hoped for an outlet to the sea at Durazzo; and Greece, which had looked to southern Albania, known to the Greeks as northern Epirus. The problem was further complicated by the intervention of Romania, which had remained neutral during the war but now demanded compensation from Serbia for Serbia's gains in Macedonia. Accordingly, Serbia and Greece demanded a new share-out at the expense of Bulgaria. Bulgaria resisted and was defeated. By the Treaty of Bucharest (10 August 1913), which brought to an end the Second Balkan War, Bulgaria lost most of her gains which were taken by Greece and Serbia. It was a sign of the changed Near Eastern situation that the Bucharest treaty, unlike that of London, was the work of the Balkan states alone. The Ottomans took the opportunity of the dissension among their rivals to recover most o Eastern Thrace, including Edirne. By 1913 Eastern Thrace was all that remained of their European territories, which, as a result of the Balkan wars, had been reduced from 162,500 square kilometres and 6 million people to 27,500 square kilometres and 2 million people. Romania remained the largest of the Balkan states with 7.5 million people but Bulgaria, Greece and Serbia all had between 4 and 5 million populations.

The role of the Great Powers, notably Russia but also Austria and Britain, in these events was considerable. It is necessary now to examine the course of events again, this time from the viewpoint of the Great Powers in order to show the nature of their concerns.

This will be done most conveniently by concentration on a few key episodes.

The Greek Crisis

The first major Eastern Question crisis after 1815 arose over the Greek revolt of the 1820s. Among the Western European countries there was a dual reaction: at the popular level there was a surge of sympathy for the Greek rebels, based partly on their status as Christians but more on a romantic identification of the Greeks with their ancient forebears whose literature supplied one of the great formative elements of European thought. Philhellenism, although not as strong everywhere, and especially not in England, as is sometimes supposed, produced a flow of volunteers and some financial support for the Greeks. At the official level there was much more caution founded on a just apprehension that the Greek revolt raised the question of the partition of the Ottoman empire, the aggrandizement of Russia in particular, and threatened the balance of power in Europe. The Austrian chancellor, Metternich, went even further; to him the Greek rising was one more exhibition of the revolutionary excitement which had disturbed Europe since 1789 and the sooner it was suppressed the better. Although Britain did not share this view of revolution she had been content since 1815 to follow the lead of Austria in supporting the integrity of the Ottoman empire.

To Russia the case was different and popular sympathy and official policy ran hand in hand. Russia already had several causes of dispute with the Ottomans relating to frontiers, the Straits and the principalities. Nevertheless, Russia perceived the dangers of unilateral action and therefore pressed for a joint European intervention to obtain a settlement favourable to the Greeks although falling short of full independence. No more than Metternich did Alexander I wish to encourage revolution.

For long no joint action by the European powers proved possible to arrange because of the suspicion with which the other European states regarded Russia; joint intervention seemed likely to help Russia to obtain what she wanted from the Ottomans and leave her in an even stronger position as protector of the Balkan Christians. By 1825 Russia was losing patience and, concerned by the success of Egyptian troops against the rebels, threatened to go her own way. It was this threat which finally prompted Britain, whose naval power in the Mediterranean was a major factor in the situation, to agree to co-operate with Russia in persuading the Ottomans to grant autonomy to the Greeks. Shortly afterwards, on 7 October 1826, by the Convention of Akkerman, the Ottomans gave way to Russia on the other points at issue between the two states. It now remained to persuade the Ottomans to accept the Greek autonomy proposal. In the end persuasion took the form of the destruction of the Turco-Egyptian fleets at Navarino by a combined British and French squadron (20 October 1827). The Western European powers were shocked by this result, Russia rejoiced and Sultan Maḥmūd II called for war with Russia, a contest which began in April 1828.

Despite early setbacks the result of the war was a convincing victory for Russia; by September 1829 she had captured Edirne and her troops were within 65 kilometres of Istanbul. It was at this point that a momentous decision was made by Russia; she decided against taking Istanbul and the Straits on the grounds that this would precipitate a general partition of the Ottoman empire and a European war which would be likely to end to the disadvantage of Russia. Instead, Russia decided that her best interests would be served by maintaining the Ottoman empire; only if the empire's collapse was inevitable should Russia seize the Straits. Considerable as her gains were at the Treaty of Adrianople (14 September 1829), they were designed to preserve the empire, not to destroy it.

The other European states took a different view of the Treaty of Adrianople which seemed to indicate a Russian purpose to establish control over the Balkans and over the Ottoman empire itself. In particular, in Britain the treaty was one of a number of events at the time which accomplished a revolution in British thinking about Russia; from regarding her as a natural ally and a state with which Britain had no major point of disagreement, Britons came to see Russia as the principal threat to British interests. These other events included the suppression of Polish liberties in 1830, the conduct of Russia in the Muḥammad ʿAlī affair in 1833 and the behaviour of Russia in Iran and Afghanistan in 1838–9.

The Muḥammad ʿAlī Crisis

Muḥammad ʿAlī of Egypt was determined to have Syria, which he had been promised for his assistance in suppressing the Greek uprising. In November 1831 he invaded the region; the Ottomans resisted and on 27 December 1832 were roundly beaten at Konya. There appeared to be nothing to prevent the Egyptian forces from advancing to Istanbul. The Ottomans appealed to other states for assistance, and received it from Russia, which sent troops to the Bosporus and signed a defensive alliance with the Ottomans (Unkiar Skelessi, i.e. Hünkâr Iskelesi, 8

July 1833). Russian policy was in line with her 1829 decision to preserve the Ottoman empire, but to the other European powers, which had dithered in response to the Ottoman request for help, it seemed as though Russia had acquired a *de facto* protectorate over the Ottoman empire. In Britain it seemed to confirm the impression derived from Adrianople and it became the object of British policy to undo the effects of Unkiar Skelessi and to support the independence and integrity of the Ottoman empire against all threats. Britain had hitherto demonstrated no interest in Egypt and had spurned Muḥammad ʿAlī's repeated overtures for an alliance. Now she became committed to removing him from Syria, not because she cared about the Near East but because of Europe. As was stated in the instructions sent to the British representative in Egypt. "H.M.'s Government attach great importance to the maintenance of the integrity of the Ottoman Empire, considering that state to be a material element in the general balance of power in Europe."[5]

The British opportunity to undo the 1833 arrangement occurred in 1839–40. In April 1839 the Ottomans attacked Muḥammad ʿAlī, hoping to expel him from Syria by force. Instead, the Egyptians defeated the Ottoman army at Nazib on 24 June and shortly afterwards the Ottoman fleet deserted to Egypt. The new sultan, ʿAbd ül-Mejīd, appeared helpless and his empire likely to collapse. To prevent that event the European states decided on joint mediation between the sultan and Muḥammad ʿAlī. They found themselves unable to agree on the terms they should offer and the manner of enforcement. The problem was presented not by Russia but by France, which was toying with the alternative policy of seeking a pillar of French support in the eastern Mediterranean and did not wish to alienate Muḥammad ʿAlī by driving him from Syria by force. The British foreign secretary, Lord Palmerston, however, was determined not to lose this opportunity of binding Russia to act in concert with the other European powers and thereby depriving her of the special position she appeared to have gained in the Ottoman empire by Unkiar Skelessi. France was, therefore, left out on a limb while the other European powers took action to force Muḥammad ʿAlī out of Syria and leave him with only the hereditary possession of Egypt still within the bonds of the Ottoman empire. The system of international co-operation was completed on 13 June 1841 by the adoption of an international convention to regulate the use of the Straits and to replace the arrangements previously established by Russia in direct negotiations with the Ottomans. The convention, which forbade the use of the Straits by foreign warships when the Ottoman empire was at peace, was in accordance with the Russian desire to exclude the warships of other European states from the Black Sea, but Russia had admitted the principle that outside powers had a right to a say in the use of the Straits.

Iran and Afghanistan

The second Eastern crisis of the 1830s involved Iran and Afghanistan. During the late 1820s and early 1830s there was some discussion in Britain and India concerning a Russian threat to India. One view, which was not taken seriously in informed discussion, was that Russia might invade India through Turkestan. The other view, which was taken seriously, was that Russia might gain a preponderant influence in Iran, use that country as a means of attacking Afghanistan, gain a strong position near the borders of British India and, when she chose, stir up unrest in India so obliging Britain to increase her military garrison in the subcontinent to such an extent as to make it unprofitable to hold India. It was further pointed out that the ability of Russia to cause disturbances in India could be used as a means of compelling Britain to defer to Russian wishes in Europe and other areas. Accordingly, a search began for a way to prevent Russia from acquiring a position of preponderance on the borders of India, either by rebuilding British influence in Iran, where it had declined in consequence of the failure of Britain to support Iran in her war with Russia in 1826–8 and the subsequent removal from the Irano-British treaty of alliance of the clauses which bound Britain to assist Iran, or by creating an alternative position of strength in Afghanistan. During the 1830s some effort was made to regain influence in Iran, but this effort collapsed when Muḥammad Shāh rejected British pleadings and proceeded to attack the western Afghan principality of Herat in 1837. It was believed that he was acting under Russian instigation and evidence was discovered which seemed to indicate a Russian intention to establish her influence in Afghanistan. Accordingly, Britain decided to establish her own influence in Afghanistan by replacing the existing ruler with a ruler who would be under British control. This end was accomplished in 1839, although the burden of sustaining a British puppet in Afghanistan proved to be beyond the price the British Indian government was willing to pay and the Afghan position was abandoned in 1842. However, Russia also failed in an effort to establish her control over the Turkestan state of Khiva in 1839 and the period ended with Britain and Russia more willing to try co-operation in Iran and central Asia. The practice of co-operation between Britain and Russia in the East broke down in 1854 when the Crimean War began.

British interests

During the 1830s Britain strengthened her position in other areas of the Near East, notably in the Persian Gulf, Iraq and Arabia. Her activity has been taken to indicate a concern to protect the routes to India, although it must also be seen as related to her policy towards Muḥammad ʿAlī and therefore connected ultimately with the maintenance of the balance of power in Europe. If Britain had wanted merely to protect the routes to India there was much to be said for a deal with Muḥammad ʿAlī who was the strongest power in the region, but Palmerston always rejected this view in favour of support for the Ottoman empire.

In the Persian Gulf the possibility of Britain acquiring an island base was raised during the 1830s when the island of Kharg was occupied in 1838 in an attempt to dissuade Muḥammad Shāh from persisting in his attack on Herat. Since 1808 the Indian government had shown intermittent interest in acquiring possession of an island in the Gulf which could be used as a base for operations against pirates, as a centre for trade and possibly for wider purposes including the coercion of states bordering the Gulf and the prevention of any threat to India developing from that direction. This Gulf strategy was seen as an alternative to the need to cultivate good relations with the states of the region. The Indian government wished to retain Kharg but the London government ordered the island to be returned to Iran as part of the settlement. The Indian government reverted to the gentler strategy of acquiring influence in the Gulf by persuasion directed towards the petty shaykhdoms of the Arab shore. Only in 1856 was the Gulf strategy briefly revived at the instigation of the government in Britain which, in the course of a fresh dispute with Iran, ordered military operations against southern Iran from the side of the Gulf. The Indian government reluctantly complied and Iran was invaded before the war was concluded by the Treaty of Paris (1856).

A second area of British interest during the 1830s was Iraq. Britain rejected requests for aid from Dā'ūd, the last Mamluk ruler of Baghdad, until shortly before his overthrow when it was decided to take advantage of the opportunity presented by his requests to obtain an influence in Iraq. However, Dā'ūd was overthrown before anything could come of this change of mind. Instead, Britain began a new initiative in Iraq associated with the development of steam navigation and the possibility of developing shorter routes to India. It was observed that a steam service between Bombay and the Gulf, linked to an overland route from Basra to the Syrian coast and a steamer service in the Mediterranean, could provide very rapid communications between Britain and

India and this route could be made still more convenient if steamers could be employed on the Euphrates. It was decided that, although the principal British effort should be directed towards the development of the route through Egypt and the Red Sea, the Euphrates route might also be developed. During the 1830s a steamboat experiment was attempted on the Euphrates and on the Tigris and it was argued that a further merit of this scheme was the additional political influence which Britain might thereby acquire in Iraq, notably among the Arab tribes. In fact the experiment was very largely unsuccessful and the route was abandoned, although Britain continued to operate a steamship service up the Tigris from Basra to Baghdad.

The third area of interest was south-west Arabia. Early steamboats found it difficult to ply directly from Bombay to Suez and a coaling station midway between them was highly desirable. During the 1830s a search was made for such a station and attention focused on Aden. However, it was not simply in order to establish a coaling station at Aden that the port was occupied by Britain on 19 January 1839, because a coaling station could have been obtained by other means than force. Rather it was in order to administer a rebuff to Muḥammad ʿAlī, partly to discourage him from pursuing his aims in Arabia but more especially to dissuade him from declaring his independence of the Ottoman empire. In British hands Aden eventually became both an important station on the Red Sea route to India, a commercial entrepôt, and a base for the extension of British influence in south-west Arabia and the Red Sea area. It was not until the 1860s, however, that these advantages began to be reaped.

The Crimea

The period of modest co-operation between Britain and Russia in the East broke down in 1854 with the outbreak of the Crimean War. Although it was fought ostensibly over the problems of the Near East the Crimean War was essentially a European war in which the main issue was prestige. Its principal effects were to break up the conservative coalition of Russia, Austria and Prussia which had dominated European affairs since 1815, isolate Austria and convert Russia into a dissatisfied, revisionist power. The Near Eastern causes of the war included a dispute between France and Russia over their respective patronage of Catholics and Orthodox in the Holy Places in Palestine, and the effort of Russia to extract from the Ottomans further concessions on Russian claims to protect the Orthodox Christian subjects of the Porte. Backed by Britain and France the Ottomans resisted this derogation from their sovereignty and independence, whereupon Russia occupied the Principalities of Moldavia and Wallachia and the war commenced. It was fought, however, not in the Principalities but in the Crimea, which was one of the few areas in which Britain and France could apply their strength. The war ended with the formation of a European coalition against Russia and Russian acceptance of the conditions of peace offered to her. At the Peace of Paris (30 March 1856) the independence and territorial integrity of the Ottoman empire were guaranteed by the powers and in return the Sultan promised reforms and better treatment for Ottoman Christians. The Black Sea was neutralized, Russia was forbidden to have naval bases on its shores and the sea was closed to all warships, including those of Russia. The Principalities were left under Ottoman suzerainty but removed from Russian protection and allowed to maintain their own independent, national administrations and armies. These arrangements provided the basis for the future unification and independence of the Principalities. The autonomy of Serbia was also guaranteed by the powers and a European commission established to superintend the navigation of the Danube, a matter of concern to several states. Effectively the treaty demolished the special position in relation to Balkan Christians which Russia had established at Bucharest in 1812, if not even earlier, and substituted for it the action of the powers in concert. Whether this new situation could be maintained despite the geographical position and power of Russia depended on two main factors: whether the victorious coalition would hold together and whether the West European powers could make the Black Sea clauses effective. By 1870 the answer to both questions had proved to be no.

Russian expansion

In the period after the Crimean War Russia switched her attention to regions east of the Ottoman empire, completing her conquest of the Caucasus and extending her empire into Turkestan. Since the late 1820s the Russians had had to contend with major uprisings against their rule in the mountainous Caucasus region, in Circassia, Daghestan and Chechenia. In the latter two regions the uprisings had taken on the aspect of a religious war under the leadership of a Ṣūfī named Shāmil of the Naqshbandī order, although the movement was known to the world as Muridism. These uprisings were extremely difficult to suppress and dangerous to Russia because of the possibility that the rebels might sever communications between European Russia and the Transcaucasian provinces, which might be lost to Russia. It is a matter of interest and surprise that Britain and France did not attempt to exploit this opportunity during the Crimean War and may be indicative of the fact that it was not their intention to push back Russia in the East. At all events, after the close of the Crimean War Russia resolved to end the uprising and inaugurated a massive siege operation involving as many as 250,000 troops. These operations were crowned with success by 1870, when the Caucasus was firmly in Russian hands and the frontiers of the independent Muslim Near East definitely pushed southwards. The conclusion of the campaign was succeeded by a major emigration of Muslims from the region to the Ottoman empire, a movement comparable to the similar emigration from the Crimea. The places of many of the *émigrés* were taken by Christian settlers.

The second area of Russian operations after the Crimea was in Turkestan. From the time of Peter the Great the southern frontier of Russia in this region had been drawn along the northern boundary of the steppelands inhabited by the Kazakhs, a nomadic, Turkic-language-speaking, Muslim people divided into tribes. Across the steppe the Russians had maintained commercial links by caravan with the settled peoples of the oases of Turkestan, including the Muslim states of Khiva, Bukhara and Kokand. From the late 1840s Russia had begun an advance aimed at encircling the turbulent Kazakh steppe and this programme was pressed forward with increased vigour after the Crimean War. It was explained in a circular issued by the Russian chancellor, Gorchakov, in 1864 that the advance of a civilized power against wild tribes such as the Kazakhs was inexorable and unavoidable, but he indicated that the advance would stop when the Russian frontier came up against those of settled states, i.e. Khiva, Bukhara and Kokand. In fact the advance did not stop but continued during the 1860s and 1870s during which period Kokand was annexed and Bukhara and Khiva stripped of many of their lands and reduced to the condition of Russian protectorates. During the 1880s the conquest was completed by the extension of Russian control over the Turkomans and the Russian frontier was made conterminous with those of Iran, Afghanistan and China. The whole enormous area of Turkestan had been made part of the Russian empire, Russian and other Slav peasant settlers came to areas of Kazakhstan and Kirgizia, Russian officials and workers moved into the cities, the Transcaspian railway and Turkestan railways were constructed to link the region with European Russia and the economy of the region was transformed as it became a major producer of raw cotton for the Russian market.

The advance of Russia in Central Asia, apparently in despite of the assurances of Gorchakov, caused concern in Britain and in India and attempts were made to come to some agreement with Russia about the limits of territorial expansion and the spheres of influence of the two powers in Central Asia. The understandings reached were, however, insufficient to stabilize the situation and, combined with the Russian denunciation of the 1856 Black Sea clauses in 1870, the Russian activities in Asia led to a profound suspicion of Russia on the part of some Britons and a belief that it was necessary to resist her further advance. It was in this atmosphere that the greatest of all the crises of the Eastern Question occurred, that of 1875–8.

The Eastern Crisis 1875–8

The Eastern Crisis of 1875 to 1878 followed the pattern of other nineteenth-century crises involving the Ottoman empire, that is to say disturbances within the Ottoman empire attracted the interest of outside powers, first that of other Balkan states and then of the great European powers. Ottoman efforts to suppress the disturbances produced a stronger outside reaction and led to demands for concessions to the rebels and European-sponsored plans for the reform of Ottoman governmental practices. Attempts to organize concerted action among the European powers failed because of divisions between them and Ottoman exploitation of these divisions; Russia took unilateral action; and the problem was eventually resolved through a general European conference. The difference between the 1875–8 crisis and other crises lies in the dimensions of the crisis, which brought Europe to the brink of war, and the far-reaching consequences of the final settlement.

The crisis began with a revolt of Christian peasants in, first, Hercegovina and then Bosnia against tax demands and against their Muslim Bosnian landlords. Serbian propaganda may have contributed to the outbreak; certainly the rebels were assisted by volunteers from Serbia and Montenegro, and popular sympathy in those countries with the rebels threatened to drive Serbia and Montenegro into conflict with the Ottoman empire. In Austria and Russia opinion was divided on how to deal with the crisis. Both states were officially committed to the maintenance of the integrity of the Ottoman empire ("Turkey", said the Austrian foreign minister, Andrassy, in 1875, "is almost of a providential utility to Austria")[6] and to the settlement of disputes by international agreement, but in both states powerful voices were raised to support different policies. Austria, it was suggested, should gain control of Bosnia and Hercegovina for herself: Russia, it was argued by the Panslavs, should set herself to free the Balkans from Ottoman rule. At first the conservatives prevailed in both countries; the Andrassy Note

(30 December 1875) represented an attempt by Russia and Austria to solve the problem through securing a promise by the Porte to carry out administrative reforms in the two rebellious provinces. Such reforms, of course, meant not better Ottoman government but less; how much less, whether the pattern of government should consist of local or municipal autonomy or whether it should amount to full provincial autonomy, was a key question which was left unclear. In fact almost no one believed it possible to bridge the gulf between the wish of Bosnian Muslims to remain part of the empire and the contention of the rebels on 26 February 1876 that "only true liberty can disarm us".[7] Although the Andrassy Note secured both the support of the other powers and acceptance by the Ottoman government, it failed to end the rebellion and the crisis worsened. On 13 May 1876 Austria and Russia tried again through the Berlin Memorandum which called for further reforms, again left unclear, and threatened the use of force if the Ottoman government failed to respond. Behind this initiative was an understanding about possible shares for Russia and Austria if some form of partition were to result. The Berlin Memorandum also failed to achieve its purpose, partly because it was not supported by Britain but principally because the Bosnian crisis was engulfed by still more dramatic events in Bulgaria.

In April 1876 a rising occurred in Bulgaria which was suppressed by the Ottoman authorities using irregular forces which committed appalling atrocities. The Bulgarian atrocities changed the whole climate of the crisis because they produced a powerful European revulsion against the Ottoman government. Having failed to organize a general Balkan alliance against the Ottomans, Serbia went to war on 30 June spurred on by domestic pressure and a conviction that Russia would come to her aid even at the expense of a European war. Serbia was joined by Montenegro. The outbreak of war made it still more urgent for Austria and Russia to reach agreement and they did so at Reichstadt on 8 July. Their agreement covered the possibilities both of an Ottoman victory over Serbia and of an Ottoman defeat. In the former event the Ottomans would not be permitted to gain any advantage; Serbian and Montenegrin territory would be safeguarded and the Ottomans still obliged to carry out reforms in Bosnia and Hercegovina. In the latter event the two powers proposed that there should be a partition of a portion of the Ottoman territories, involving the transfer of Bosnia and Hercegovina to Austria; if Serbia was to be protected from the consequences of defeat she was also to be deprived of the sweetest fruits of victory. A flood of Russian volunteers went to the aid of Serbia, but they were unable to save her from defeat at the hands of the Ottomans and Russia was compelled to ask, on behalf of Serbia, for an armistice to preserve the country from destruction. A powerful wave of Russian sympathy for the Balkan Slavs threatened to sweep away those who stood for co-operation with Austria and the maintenance of the Ottoman empire.

As the developing crisis threatened the tender bud of Austro-Russian co-operation the attitude of the other European powers became of greater consequence. France was of little account in the crisis; since her defeat by Germany in 1871 she had been preoccupied by more immediate problems and it was the views of Germany and Britain which counted. Britain was hostile to a partition of the Ottoman empire, Germany more ambivalent, but neither was prepared to support any solution which was uncongenial to Austria. British views were strongly divided both in the Cabinet and in the country at large where the news of the atrocities had provoked a mighty agitation against the Ottomans. Some ministers, for example Lord Salisbury, favoured co-operation with Russia; others, including the prime minister, Benjamin Disraeli, now (12 August 1876) Lord Beaconsfield, wished to continue the traditional British policy of co-operation with Austria. The foreign secretary, Lord Derby, who pursued no policy with any resolution, invited the major powers to a conference in Istanbul to discuss the reform of the Ottoman government while maintaining the principle of the integrity of the Ottoman empire. The other powers agreed with some reservations and the conference met in December 1876 and produced a plan which in several respects foreshadowed the settlement eventually reached at Berlin. The conference, however, broke up without agreement, the Ottomans having produced a constitution for the empire which they claimed made talk of reforms in particular provinces unnecessary. As she had threatened, Russia, after further unavailing attempts to induce the European states to undertake any concerted action, went her own way. Having first secured the neutrality of Austria by a promise of Bosnia and Hercegovina and of restraint in her own demands, Russia went to war with the Ottomans on 24 April 1877.

Expectations of a speedy Russian victory were confounded: Ottoman resistance in eastern Asia Minor and at Plevna in Bulgaria held up the Russian advance for six months and it was not until January 1878, with the Russian forces approaching Istanbul once more, that the Ottomans sought peace. The Russian terms were severe. The military had at this point taken effective control of Russian policy-making and they recognized few restraints when they dictated peace at San Stefano (3 March 1878). In eastern Asia Minor Russia was to gain substantial territories, including Kars, Ardahan, Bayazid and Batum; and in Europe she was to have Bessarabia (from Romania). Romania, Serbia and Montenegro were also to receive territory (although only Montenegro made substantial gains) and to become wholly independent, the government of Bosnia and Hercegovina was to be reformed as was that of other parts of the Ottoman empire, and a large autonomous Bulgaria was to be created, stretching from the Black Sea to the Aegean. A proposal for a new regime for the Straits, more favourable to Russia, was dropped from the treaty but not before it had caused great annoyance among the other European powers.

Of all the provisions in the Treaty of San Stefano those relating to the new Bulgaria were the most obnoxious to other European powers, including Austria, for they went far beyond the agreement reached between the Austrian and Russian governments. The British reaction was especially sharp; she ordered her fleet up to Istanbul and war between Britain and Russia seemed a real possibility. It was averted only by the ultimate caution of the powers and by the decision to re-examine the settlement at an international conference at Berlin. It was, indeed, acknowledged on all sides that a European conference was necessary to ratify the settlement since it involved a modification of the Treaty of Paris of 1856, but there was a dispute about the powers of the conference. Russia did not want it to recommend a new treaty but Britain insisted that this was what it should do. The dispute was solved by prior agreement about the nature of its main recommendations.

Under the new settlement arranged by the Congress of Berlin Russian territorial gains in eastern Asia Minor were reduced; Batum, Kars and Ardahan were retained but Bayazid returned to the Ottomans. Of the Balkan states Serbia was given more territory and Montenegro less. Romania remained the same and Greece still had nothing, although in 1881 she obtained an improved frontier in Thessaly and part of Epirus. Bulgaria was divided into three; the southern portion was returned to full Ottoman control; the central part became the semi-autonomous province of Eastern Rumelia and only the area north of the Balkan mountains remained as an autonomous Bulgaria. Bosnia and Hercegovina were now placed under Austrian occupation and by a separate agreement Britain was given control of Cyprus on the argument that a base in the eastern Mediterranean was necessary to enable her to protect the Ottoman empire's Asian territories from Russia, to superintend reforms in the Asian provinces and to give Britain a more direct stake in the fate of the Ottoman empire.

The Eastern Crisis of 1875–8 had several important consequences. In the first place the Balkan states had made major advances in the acquisition of territory and in status. Nevertheless Serbia, Romania and Greece were discontented with their gains and the Bulgarians looked to recovering the glorious prospect of being the largest and most powerful state in the Balkans which had been briefly dangled before them by the San Stefano treaty. Secondly, the spirit of disappointed nationalism had now invaded Asia. During the Russo-Turkish War Armenian volunteers had fought with Russian troops and hopes of an independent Armenian state in eastern Asia Minor had been raised and disappointed. Hitherto the Armenians had been seen as a loyal Ottoman community. Henceforth they were regarded with suspicion by the Ottoman authorities and with a mixture of fear and hope by others. From the point of view of the Great Powers the settlement had only postponed the inevitable and final collapse of the Ottoman empire. "In the course of my travels", wrote Salisbury in 1876, "I have not succeeded in finding a friend of the Turk. He does not exist. Most believe his hour is come. Some few that it may be postponed. No one has even suggested the idea that he can be upheld for any length of time."[8] Bismarck and Andrassy were clear that the empire was doomed and that the best policy was to arrange a balanced partition in which no power emerged as the clear winner; in effect to balance any gains by Russia by acquisitions by other powers. Although France and Italy had received nothing at Berlin they were encouraged to seek compensation in North Africa, in Tunis and Tripoli. The concept of a balanced partition was, however, easier to contemplate than to accomplish. Of all the consequences of the crisis none was more pregnant with future disaster than that which put Austria in control of Bosnia because it brought her into conflict with Serbia and ultimately with Russia.

For Britain the crisis was notable for two factors. First, the emergence of public opinion as a major constraint upon policy in the East. The Bulgarian atrocities raised feelings against the Ottomans so strong as to overcome even traditional Liberal repugnance towards working with autocratic Russia. The persistence of this antipathy to the Turk was to have considerable influence in the future, especially during and immediately after the First World War. Secondly, the Eastern Crisis of 1857–8 was the first occasion on which the problem of the security of the routes to India was clearly and prominently stated in connection with the fate of the Ottoman empire, notably in Lord Derby's Note of 6 May 1877, in which he summed up British interests in the question. Further, the fate of Armenia and Mesopotamia were now given great significance in relation to Russian advances in eastern Asia Minor and the routes to India. The connection with India was made closer by Disraeli's gesture in summoning Indian troops to Malta and the corresponding Russian action in despatching a mission to Kabul in Afghanistan. The stress on India during the crisis has been linked with the emergence of the question of the moral basis of British policy. To those who asserted that it was immoral to support Ottoman rule it was replied that the alternative might be to sacrifice the interests of Britain and the Indian people alike in the continuation of British rule in India. In the end, however, it is difficult to explain British policy in terms of either the protection of the routes to India or even the maintenance of the balance of power in Europe. In the last analysis the issue was the prestige of Britain as a Great Power; having stated an interest in the matter she could not permit a settlement to be made without her opinion being sought.

In retrospect one can see the decade from 1869 to 1878 as constituting a watershed between the old Eastern Question and the new. In the old the issue had been the maintenance of the Ottoman empire as a pillar of stability in the Near East. The opening of the Suez Canal seemed to make Istanbul less important in the Near East and turn the focus towards Egypt and the Levant. The Russian denunciation of the Black Sea clauses in 1870 marked the end of the Crimean system by which the European powers had been able to guarantee the continued life of the Ottoman empire. The French defeat by Germany in 1870–1 removed one of the two powers which had believed in and supported the movement of reform in the Ottoman empire and after 1871 that movement also took a different turn. Finally, the 1878 settlement had shattered the framework of Ottoman rule in Europe. The old system of autonomous and semi-autonomous states was replaced by wholly independent states over a considerable area and those who had gained some degree of autonomy saw this only as a short chrysalis stage. In the new Eastern Question the problem was to find some stable substitute for the Ottoman empire in south-east Europe and beyond that to contemplate whether and in what form the empire could endure in Asia.

The Eastern Crisis of 1875–8 had an important by-product further east, where it was a contributory cause of the Second Anglo-Afghan War. It has been remarked that Russia responded to Disraeli's summoning of the Indian troops to Malta with a mission to Kabul. At that time Russians employed the very strategy which Britons had feared; to seek influence on the borders of India and, by hostile troop movements, to threaten India so as to divert British resources thither. It was a perfect answer to Disraeli's gesture – to show that far from being a source of strength to Britain India was in fact a source of weakness, a hostage to fortune and vulnerable to Russia. It was inevitable that Britain would make some response to the challenge to her position in the East and it was for the Viceroy, Lord Lytton, to determine what that should be.

Lytton's response produced the Second Anglo-Afghan War. He was a rare Viceroy who believed that India could actually support British actions in Europe. From his arrival in India he had pursued an active policy on the Indian frontier in reply to the Russian advance in Turkestan, and in 1877 had occupied Quetta. He was also determined to strengthen British influence in Afghanistan, and the Russian mission to Kabul was both an excuse to present his demands to Afghanistan and a slight to British prestige which had to be conspicuously avenged. He so arranged matters as to place Britain and Afghanistan in such a position that war was inevitable and, after a short, sharp campaign, by the Treaty of Gandamak (26 May 1879) he created what appeared to be a satisfactory position in Afghanistan. Certain frontier regions were taken from Afghanistan, a British political resident was placed in Kabul with a more adaptable ruler and Britain assumed control of Afghanistan's foreign relations. Within a very short period Lytton's settlement fell to pieces as a result of an uprising in Afghanistan and he was faced with an expensive and laborious campaign to reconquer the country. Lytton then fell back on another plan for Afghanistan involving breaking the country up into three main parts; Kabul under an independent Afghan ruler, Qandahar under a British-controlled puppet Afghan prince and Herat which should be given to Iran. In fact this plan was abandoned in favour of a united Afghanistan under a ruler who would accept British control over his foreign affairs, although British control fell far short of that envisaged by Lytton at Gandamak and there was no British political resident in Afghanistan.

Anglo-Russian relations

In the years which followed two alterations took place in the character of Anglo-Russian rivalry in the eastern areas of the Near East. First, the assumption of British control over Afghan foreign affairs implied some British responsibility for the protection of Afghanistan and, in its turn, this involved Britain in the definition of Afghanistan's frontiers with those of the Russian empire in Asia. Between 1884 and 1895 a series of boundary commissions demarcated the Russo-Afghan frontiers, punctuated by crises, one of which, the Panjdah incident of 1885 when Russian and Afghan forces clashed, momentarily appeared to threaten war between Britain and Russia. The second development involved a change in the British Indian view of the nature of the threat from Russia. After the experience of 1878 the possibility of a direct Russian invasion of India seemed much more likely and partly displaced the older perception of the Russian threat as proceeding from the encouragement of disorder within India from a position on the Indian frontier. In the last years of the nineteenth century and during the early years of the twentieth century British Indian military dispositions were made increasingly with the likelihood of a Russian invasion in mind. Calculations of the troops required to repel such an invasion grew steadily until they involved not only the retention of a large British garrison in India but also massive reinforcements from Britain in the event of a Russian advance. It was these military demands, as much as any other factor, which determined Britain to seek a diplomatic agreement with Russia which would end the rivalry in Asia. This settlement was reached in 1907. According to the Anglo-Russian agreement of that year Iran was divided into spheres of influence, the north being Russian and a small stretch in the south-east covering the Indian frontier being British with the intervening area constituting a neutral zone. Russia accepted British control of the foreign relations of Afghanistan. One effect of the 1907 agreement was apparently to impair British control of the Persian Gulf, the Iranian coast of which was left in the neutral zone. The Indian government under Lord Curzon had pressed hard for the total exclusion of all foreign powers from the Gulf, but the British government in London would not go so far and by the Lansdowne Declaration of 5 May 1903 merely said that Britain would resist the establishment of any foreign base in the region, leaving the way open to commercial activities by outside powers. In fact the Indian government was not consulted about the desirability of the 1907 agreement, European interests taking precedence over the views of India.

Rise of the Balkan states

During the years between 1878 and 1914 the implications of the events of 1875–8 and the features of the Eastern Question which had then appeared, became steadily more apparent. These were the increasingly independent role of the Balkan states, the growing importance of the fate of the Asian and African territories of the Ottoman empire, and the changing views of the major European powers concerning the maintenance of the integrity of the Ottoman empire and the possibilities of a partition.

The most prominent development was the conduct of the Balkan states as independent actors on the international stage and as competitors with the Ottoman power. Something has already been said about this change but it will be useful to rehearse the main features of it. Between 1878 and 1914 the population of the Balkan states more than doubled, even allowing for territorial changes. At the same time they underwent major economic changes, involving a shift from production geared mainly to local consumption to production for the international market. Competition from North American and Russian grain producers, combined with the protectionist tariff adopted by Austria, presented considerable problems for Balkan farmers and stimulated the demand for more radical political measures.

The most determinedly independent of the Balkan states was Bulgaria. In 1885 Bulgaria and Eastern Rumelia united, overthrowing a central feature of the Berlin settlement which the European powers had been determined to maintain. In 1886 Bulgaria threw off the close Russian supervision of her affairs which had been exercised since 1878. Thereafter, Bulgaria devoted her attention to the acquisition of the southern Bulgarian lands in Macedonia, to securing an outlet on the Aegean and even to the annexation of Istanbul itself and the control of the Straits. Her efforts were geared towards providing for the day when she would put into the field against the Ottomans the maximum force so small a country could create.

During the period from 1878 to the early twentieth century Serbia was comparatively quiescent. Her close economic links with Austria were reinforced from 1882 by a political clientage to that state, distasteful as such a state of affairs was to that majority of Serbs who hoped to unite with the Slavs of Bosnia and of regions of Austria proper. Only in 1903 did Serbia renounce Austrian patronage, an act which was followed by a rapid deterioration of relations between the two countries, marked by the economic contest known as the Pig War, which began in 1906, and by the outburst of Serbian resentment which succeeded the Austrian annexation of Bosnia–Hercegovina in 1908. Thereafter, Serbia joined Bulgaria as a dissatisfied Balkan state aiming at a radical change of the status quo, first by an attack on the Ottomans, and ultimately by pressure on Austria. Her old ally, Montenegro, was, as always, ready to fight for gain, in her case towards the Adriatic, into the Sanjak of Novi Pazar which separated her from Serbia, and into Hercegovina if opportunity ever offered.

For many years after 1878 Greece looked especially towards Crete, with which she attempted to unite in 1897 only to experience an ignominious defeat at Ottoman hands and to suffer once more the humiliation of being saved by the European powers from the Ottomans. Her ambitions unquenched by defeat and humiliation, she continued to look towards the annexation of islands in the Aegean and towards gains in Macedonia when the opportunity arrived. Like the other states her chief hopes for gain were at the expense of the Ottomans. Only Romania, cut off from Ottoman territory by Bulgaria, looked primarily to the territory of Austria and Russia for gain.

A feature of the emerging independence of the Balkan states was their increasing disputes one with another. Serbia and Bulgaria took their differences to war in 1885–6, a contest which ended in surprising defeat for Serbia and rescue by Austria. The two states remained rivals for the Ottoman heritage in Macedonia. Greece was also a contender for Macedonia and nursed a particular fear of Bulgarian ambitions on the Aegean, both states coveting the port of Salonika. In the Danube Delta Romania and Bulgaria were rivals. The rivalries between the Balkan states, no less than their strengths and ambitions, were to become major factors in dictating the form of development of the Eastern Question in the last years before 1914.

Asian and African developments

The second feature of the development of the Eastern Question after 1878 is the increased European interests in the Asian and African territories of the Ottoman empire. In 1881 France established a protectorate over Tunisia and in 1882 Britain occupied Egypt. British influence was expanded in Arabia and during the last years before 1914 Britain gave much more attention to Iraq. French investment in Syria grew and increasingly she marked out this area as her share of a partition, although she also retained an interest in northern Anatolia. Perhaps the most noteworthy developments occurred in connection with the advent of two comparative newcomers to the Eastern Question: Italy and Germany. In September 1911 Italy, having first carefully obtained the consent of the other European powers, went to war with the Ottomans for the possession of Tripoli. By the Treaty of Ouchy (15 October 1912) she gained Tripoli and also temporary possession of the islands of the Dodecanese, much to the dismay of Greece. Italy also began to take an interest in the Adriatic coast and even in the possibilities of colonization in Asia Minor. German interest in the Eastern Question centred round opportunities for trade and investment, and during the early twentieth century her inherent industrial strength carried her quickly to the position of being second only to Britain as a trading partner of the Ottomans and second to France as an investor. The central feature of Germany's investment policy was the Baghdad railway. In 1888 a German company was given a concession for a line from Konya to Baghdad and the Gulf, and in 1903 for a line from Baghdad to the Gulf. The German-controlled Baghdad railway appeared to other European countries to spearhead German economic and political penetration of the Near East and to threaten French interests in Syria, Russian interests on the Black Sea and in northern Iran, and British interests in the Persian Gulf.

The increased significance of the Asian and African territories of the Ottoman empire was also indicated by what appeared to be the extension to those regions of the national feeling among subject nationalities which had been a feature of the European lands since 1800. The nature and character of these national movements is discussed in detail in Chapter 4, where it is concluded that Arab nationalism did not present the threat to Ottoman integrity which has been claimed by some historians. Nevertheless, Muslim Arab nationalism was a new phenomenon which complicated the Eastern Question, while Armenian nationalism, in itself a Christian movement of a familiar type, was nevertheless novel in that it had not appeared before 1878 and that it was a Christian movement in the Asian territories of the Ottoman empire, comparable in that respect to Maronite nationalism in the Lebanon, although distinguished from it by several features. Armenian nationalism was essentially a product of the work of Armenian radicals in the Russian empire and was imported into the Ottoman empire, notably during the 1877–8 Russo-Turkish War when bands of Armenians fought for Russia. Thereafter, Armenians were suspect in Ottoman eyes and as nationalist propaganda increased so the Ottomans responded with repression leading to the massacres of 1894–6 which shocked Europe and brought more pressure for reform in the Ottoman territories.

Changing Great Power interests

The attitudes of the major European states towards the Near East underwent changes after 1878. Although the occupation of Egypt by Britain was undertaken doubtfully and reluctantly and was neither planned nor even intended, and although the retention of Egypt was not at first envisaged by British governments, the occupation of Egypt, particularly as it developed the signs of being of indefinite duration, contributed to a shift in British policy. Down to 1878 Britain had taken the view that the key to the Near East was Istanbul and the Straits and her efforts had been directed towards maintaining the integrity of the Ottoman empire and preventing the occupation of the Straits by Russia. In the years after 1878 she continued her efforts to this end. The Mediterranean agreements of 1887, which involved Britain, Austria and Italy and were backed by Germany, had as their purpose the maintenance of Ottoman rights and the prevention of Russian control of the Straits. After the formation of the Franco-Russian entente, however, Britain's relative naval strength in the eastern Mediterranean was severely reduced and it began to be accepted that she would not be able to act against Russia at the Straits so long as Russia could obtain the help of the French fleet. In this situation the possession of Egypt and control of the Suez Canal began to appear more important.

Although this revaluation did not mean that Britain ceased to support the older policy of the maintenance of Ottoman integrity, it did indicate that Britain would not fight so hard for that principle now that she had identified an alternative position in Egypt and was beginning to discern another in Mesopotamia. Furthermore, the new international alignments of the early twentieth century and the ententes with France (1904) and Russia (1907) had the effect of weakening British links with her oldest and most consistent ally in the Near East, namely Austria, a member of the Triple Alliance. Also, humanitarianism, which had risen to prominence in 1876, remained a factor shaping British policy towards the Ottoman empire. Britain took up the cause of the Armenians and of reform in Macedonia where she was the leading European supporter of changes during the years down to 1908. For similar reasons of sentiment Britain welcomed the Young Turk revolution of 1908, although she quickly turned against the Young Turks, seeing them as a dangerous clique of adventurers composed of Christians, Jews and Freemasons. Finally, Britain always remained sensitive to the danger that the Ottomans might use against her in India and Egypt the mysterious force of Panislamism and this fear acted as a permanent constraint upon Britain's Near Eastern policy.

Russian aims in the Near East were also changing. Largely as a consequence of Russian efforts the Balkan states had gained their autonomy and independence, but Russia received few tokens of gratitude; having achieved their new status the Balkan states rejected Russian influence. Romania remained embittered by the loss of Bessarabia and from 1883 allied herself with Austria. So did Serbia until she brought her problems back to Russia's door after 1903, while Bulgaria completely rejected Russian influence and became a competitor of Russia for control of the Straits. Far from the Balkan states being the instruments of Russian influence in south-east Europe, which had once been anticipated, they became problems for her. Russian interests in the Straits were, however, greater than ever. Although Russia's economic interests in the Ottoman empire were insignificant, through the Straits passed more than one-third of Russian trade, one-half of her exports and four-fifths of her grain in the early twentieth century. One-third of her population and most of her economic resources lay around the

Black Sea. On several occasions Russia discussed plans either to improve the regime of the Straits in her own favour (by allowing the passage of Russian warships) or for the seizure of the Straits by a *coup de main*. In 1896 and again in 1913 plans to take control of the Bosporus were seriously discussed, but it was decided that Russia could not hope to succeed in such an enterprise except in the context of a general European war when the event would be decided by the clash of armies in Europe. Russia's Black Sea fleet was, in any case, inferior to that of the Ottomans. In Transcaucasia Russia stood wholly on the defensive. Bereft of local allies and unable to act independently Russia could accomplish almost nothing in these years. Her only successes were in northern Iran and for some years before her defeat by Japan in 1905 she turned her main attention to the Far East.

Russian attempts to win the consent of other major powers for Russian gains in the Near East ended in rebuffs or humiliations. Yet still the great emotional forces of Panslavism, Orthodox Christianity and Russian prestige made it impossible for Russia to renounce her leading role in the Near East. Only France was willing to go along with Russian wishes and that out of loyalty to the entente rather than because of any enthusiasm for Russian policy in the Near East. France still supported the old policy of Ottoman integrity, although almost as much for financial reasons arising from the circumstance that she held two-thirds of the Ottoman Public Debt, as for political reasons, for her interests were concentrated on the Rhine and the Near East was of much inferior interest. Her financial and cultural interests in Syria were real as were her ambitions to develop economic opportunities in northern Anatolia, but in no sense were they decisive in shaping French policy.

Throughout the period after 1878 Austria remained a consistent supporter of the integrity of the Ottoman empire. From 1878 until the early twentieth century she was the dominant power in the Balkans through her alliances with Serbia and Romania and her generally good relations with Bulgaria. Austria employed her influence to hold the Balkan powers in check and to oblige them to respect the status quo in the Ottoman lands. The exception relates to her own conduct in Bosnia and Hercegovina which she annexed in 1908. During the decade before 1914 Austrian predominance in the Near East slipped away. The loss of control over Serbia was a severe blow to her policy, she was unable to prevent the outbreak of the Balkan War in 1912 and the result of the war was a diplomatic defeat for Austria. Although she was able to reduce the extent of the defeat by sponsoring the creation of Albania, the existence of which deprived Serbia of access to the Adriatic, Albania was a poor substitute for the Ottoman power in Macedonia while the result of the Second Balkan War was the great expansion of the power of Serbia and the defeat of Bulgaria, which had constituted a potential check upon Serbian ambitions. After 1913 nothing stood in the way of a struggle for mastery in the Slav lands between Austria and Serbia but an unlikely restraint on both sides. For Austria the principal issue now at stake in the Near East was the vindication of her own prestige. "We do not want to be the only power to come away empty-handed", wrote Berchtold in November 1913.[9] In south-east Europe it was Austria and not the Ottomans which was now cast for the part of the victim in the drama of the Eastern Question.

In the affairs of the Near East Austria had been able to count upon one reliable ally, Germany. For most of the period since 1878 Germany had been content to follow the Austrian lead and to lend her weight to support Austrian policies aimed at the maintenance of the integrity of the Ottoman empire. This policy was also indicated by Germany's economic interests in the Near East, although the Ottoman lands were of little importance for the German economy as a whole, despite the imposing appearance of the German presence in the region. Germany's policy of giving military assistance to the Ottomans, pursued with some consistency from the military mission of Colmar von der Goltz in 1882 to the employment of Liman von Sanders in 1913, arose from simple military concerns and had no especial political undercurrent. In fact, despite the complaints of her rivals, the flourish of Wilhelm II's pro-Ottoman Damascus declaration in 1898 and the clamour of colonial pressure groups in Germany, German political interest in the Near East before 1914 was slight. By a series of agreements made between 1911 and 1914 Germany went a considerable way towards eliminating the causes of dissension in the Near East involving herself and Russia, France and Britain.

The most restless of the European powers in the Near East was also the least significant – Italy. Italy had economic interests through trade, shipping and vague hopes of relieving present overpopulation in southern Italy through a programme of colonization in North Africa and Asia Minor. But her interests were political rather than economic and were connected principally with her desire to be recognized as a full member of the club of Great Powers, a state to be consulted on every Near Eastern issue. Italy's youthful assertiveness made her the single European power which hoped for a total collapse and partition of the Ottoman empire.

Contemplating the attitudes of the major European powers towards the Near East in 1914 one must conclude that they had changed less than one might have supposed since the end of the eighteenth century.

For every power the Near East was subsidiary to Europe and their relations with the Near East subsidiary to their relations with one another in Europe. Their main concern was that changes in the distribution of power in the Near East should not affect the balance of power in Europe. For most of the nineteenth century it had been agreed that this result could best be achieved by the maintenance of the integrity of the Ottoman empire. This did not mean that the system of government of the Ottoman empire should remain unchanged; on the contrary, the legal integrity of the Ottoman empire could best be secured, it was thought, by a reform of its system of government which could accommodate the wishes of the Christian Balkan peoples. It was this accommodation which proved to be impossible. The first breach in the system was made when Greece secured its independence instead of the autonomy which had been envisaged, but the system was split wide open in 1878 when Serbia, Montenegro and Romania became independent. Bulgarian independence had followed in 1908, when Bosnia and Hercegovina were also formally lost to the Ottoman empire. Thereafter the integrity of the Ottoman empire was no longer a question; the Ottoman empire was merely a convenience for delaying a solution to the intractable problem of Macedonia, an almost indispensable device for preventing a major conflict over control of the Straits, and a still valuable element for the disposition of the territories of western Asia, an empire whose existence yet prevented a struggle for preponderance within those Asian territories which could threaten a European war.

Although the preoccupation of European powers with Europe remained the same their interests in the Near East had developed in the course of the nineteenth century. Around the southern coastline of the region, from the Red Sea to the Persian Gulf Britain had marked out an informal system of control, buttressed at either end by the solid bases of Egypt and India. Through the north of the region, from the eastern shores of the Black Sea to the Tien Shan mountains, Russia had created a land empire from which was projected her further influence. And within the Near East France, Germany and Italy had established important footholds of economic, political and cultural interest and influence. It must be emphasized once again, however, that these European penetrations of the Near East did not threaten conflict between the powers or the replacement of the familiar political structure of the Asian Middle East. The most notable feature of international rivalries in the region before 1914 is not that they existed but that they were adjusted by agreement and by the continued recognition of formal Ottoman control. The one region where rivalries seemed incapable of adjustment was in the region where Ottoman control had vanished; Austria and

Russia had found it possible to reconcile their prescriptions for the Sick Man of Europe but they could find no way of reaching agreement on how to treat the lusty infant, Serbia.

By 1914 the outstanding element in determining the attitudes of the Great Powers towards the Near East was prestige. Neither the protection of the routes of empire nor economic interest nor even the balance of power in Europe weighed, in the end, against prestige. In order that they might remain great, Great Powers demanded to be treated as great. Important developments should not take place without their consent even if that consent was given only as the result of military defeat. The integrity of the Ottoman empire was like a bank on which the Great Powers could draw to make up the balance of their prestige. When the bank was exhausted there was no longer an easy line of credit in the Near East; such was the fate of Austria and Russia in 1914.

In the preceding paragraph one reason for the failure of the Great Powers to succeed in the design of maintaining the Ottoman power has been suggested; the prestige of a Great Power could be most easily salvaged at the expense of the Ottoman empire. Russia, the one power with major objectives to be won from the Ottomans had to be given something in recompense for her efforts, at least most of the time. And if Russia got something others also had to have compensation. The compensation might be justified by reference to arguments of national interest but essentially its purpose was prestige. A second reason was that local factors predominated in the Near East. However hard they might try the Great Powers could not control the situation on the ground and the situation became more and more unruly until, in 1912, the Balkan states, ignoring the Great Powers, took matters into their own hands in their assault on the Ottomans. The Great Powers, which had been willing and able to intervene to restrain the Ottomans, found it more difficult to restrain the Christian powers of the Balkans.

A new view of the Eastern Question

Throughout this chapter the Ottomans have been treated in the familiar fashion of writings on the Eastern Question as more or less passive recipients of European commands, occasionally managing to manipulate differences between the European powers but fundamentally the incompetent decaying government of the traditional European history textbook. In the next two chapters an effort will be made to redress that balance and to show the Ottoman empire as an active, reforming state bringing about great changes in its institutions. But here it is useful to pose three questions. Why should the traditional picture of the Sick

Man of Europe exist? What is wrong with it? And in what ways should the picture be modified?

Why should the traditional picture exist? Four reasons may supply the answer. First, the story has been told from the viewpoint of the major European powers and based upon their archives. Little use has been made of the archives of the immediate actors, whether those of the Balkan states or of the Ottomans themselves; the Ottoman empire has been seen from the outside. Second, much of the history of the Eastern Question was written by historians who were committed to a belief that liberalism and nationalism constituted part of a natural political order and multinational, autocratic empires such as the Ottoman empire (or indeed the Austrian empire) were unnatural creations. Their collapse scarcely needed explanation; once the artificial circumstances which kept them in being were removed they would automatically fall. Third, there was a peculiar antipathy towards the Ottoman empire because it was a Muslim empire, and to most historians reared on European history Islam itself was some sort of great historical aberration, a crude version of the Judaeo-Christian tradition which was suitable for illiterate tribesmen at a certain stage of development but which should have been discarded long ago. Instead, Islam had become the ideology of a state which figured on the European scene. In the eyes of most Europeans, however, Islam remained the same static, unprogressive religion resting on superstition, fraud and violence, and the Ottoman empire was an anachronism, even an excrescence on the face of Europe. Some writers, for example, Adolphus Slade, might protest against this picture, but it infused the views of very many Europeans who could not believe that the Ottoman empire was, indeed, changing its character. Lastly, the picture survived because there was no one with an interest in rehabilitating the Ottoman empire. Those Europeans who finally destroyed the empire after the First World War needed to believe that it had been invincibly bad and those Turkish nationalists who succeeded to its heritage in Anatolia also had to persuade themselves that the empire was a worn-out historical structure which had contributed to its own destruction.

The second question posed above was, what is wrong with the picture of the Sick Man? First and foremost the picture attributes to the Great Powers far too much interest in the Near East and too much power to control events. It fails to give sufficient weight to local factors and, in particular, to the extent to which opposition to Ottoman rule was a response not to the decay of the Ottoman system of government but to its active reforming style in the nineteenth century. The role of the European powers was not to persuade the Ottomans to provide better government but to try to stop them from introducing better (or, more precisely, more efficient) government and to induce them to provide less government. The influence of the European powers was mainly negative and it was exercised through military force and the threat of its employment. It was not that the Ottoman military forces were peculiarly inefficient – rather the contrary – but given their resources in money and manpower and the calls upon them the Ottomans could never hope to be more than a minor military power in European terms and no match for the major European powers in a prolonged war. Until 1912–13 the Ottomans were more than a match for any Balkan power or any combination which could be brought against them, and even in 1912 they were unlucky that circumstances did not enable them to bring their full power to bear against the Balkan alliance. The Ottomans could hold even a major European power for some time as they did Russia in 1828 and again in 1877. In 1911 they withstood Italy, despite the logistic difficulties which they faced, and in 1915 and 1916 they were to acquit themselves with distinction against the Entente forces. But, on each occasion, in a long war they were defeated; they could not sustain the effort required. To offset their military weakness the Ottomans required all the resources of diplomacy but they were not the equals of Europeans in diplomacy, a game invented by Europeans and played according to their rules. The Ottomans had some men of outstanding ability in foreign affairs, such as Fu'ād Pasha, but these were very few in number and far too few to staff the embassies in European capitals with men of the calibre required. The Ottomans were compelled to rely heavily upon Greeks who neither possessed the full confidence of the Ottoman government nor carried great influence. Musurus Pasha, the Greek Ottoman ambassador in London for much of the nineteenth century, was an efficient postman but he had no political weight. The absence of efficient diplomats added to the difficulty which the Ottomans experienced of being accepted as diplomatic equals. Italy, a power of no greater strength, was treated quite differently.

How should the traditional picture be modified? A revision must begin with an understanding of why the Ottoman empire lasted so long. The empire endured for 600 years and no other empire in the world during the same period came anywhere near such a lifetime. If one rejects the notion that this longevity could have been the outcome of fraud and violence alone then one is left to explain what seems a remarkable Ottoman talent for government and to seek reasons why this talent should have failed in the nineteenth century. Second, the modification must encompass a just account of the nineteenth-century

Ottoman reform movement and a study of the relationship between governmental reform and the emergence of "national" opposition. Thirdly, a more penetrating account of the development of nationalism in the Balkans and elsewhere is required. Fourthly, we need an account of the Eastern Question from the point of view of Ottoman diplomacy which is based upon Ottoman archives and which includes a full account of the changing character of Ottoman decision-making and the domestic constraints upon it. And, lastly, a better understanding of the goals of the European powers themselves is required. It is necessary to move beyond the arguments used to an examination of the reasons why those arguments were deployed. Some recent writing on the Eastern Question has failed to proceed beyond the arguments used and has given undue prominence to such arguments as those relating to the protection of the routes to India as an explanation of British policy, although it is plain that these arguments were used often by those who had in mind some special interest for which they required more general support. Other writers have moved in the opposite direction, have disregarded altogether the reasons why people said they were acting as they did and asserted that they were controlled by economic imperatives deriving from the manner in which their economic systems were developing. The theory that European powers were mainly actuated by economic goals in the Eastern Question has little to recommend it. And, finally, it is necessary to shift the emphasis upon research from a focus upon the actions of Britain and France towards greater concern with those of the eastern European powers. Russian archival materials are still only partially available and a fuller picture of Russian activity is required. But most of all a deeper study of Austrian policy is required for it was Austria which led first Britain and then Germany in the maintenance of Ottoman integrity.

In recent years work has been done in many of these areas of indicated research and some of the products are discussed in the bibliographical essay appended to this volume. This work displays two divergent tendencies. The first tendency has been to endorse the view of a passive and decaying Ottoman empire doomed to destruction at the hands of emergent nationalism and European power and to extend that picture from the European territories of the Empire to which it was formerly applied to the Asian territories. According to this view Arab nationalism and European greed were the two forces which contended for the remains of the empire in the early twentieth century while Turkish nationalism sapped the ideological basis of the empire. The second tendency has been to play down the importance of national feeling, especially in the Asian areas, to emphasize the European preoccupations of the European powers and to downgrade the significance of their Near Eastern interests. The outcome of this latter tendency has been an emphasis on the accidental elements in the Eastern Question; the problem is seen not in terms of determination and impersonal forces of economics or nationalism but rather in the choices of men, made in the turmoil of events with imperfect information and with all the weight of prejudice to which men are subject. In this view, which is also the view of the author, there was nothing inevitable about the way in which the Eastern Question developed and no historical ordinance which decreed that the Ottoman empire should disappear. There is no simple answer to the Eastern Question.

NOTES

1. *Parliamentary history*, XXIX, col. 9.
2. *Parliamentary history*, col. 77.
3. Napoleon to Talleyrand 9 June 1806, quoted E. Saul, *Russia and the Mediterranean 1797–1807*, Chicago 1970, 213–41.
4. Quoted E. Driault and M. Lheritier, *Histoire diplomatique de la Grèce de 1821 à nos jours*, II, Paris 1925, 252–5.
5. Palmerston to Campbell 4 Feb. 1833, Public Record Office, FO 78/226.
6. Quoted M. D. Stojanovich, *The Great Powers and the Balkans*, Cambridge 1939, 30–1.
7. *The Times*, 11 March 1876.
8. Lady Gwendolen Cecil, *Life of Salisbury*, II, London 1921, 107.
9. Quoted F. R. Bridge, "The Habsburg monarchy and the Ottoman Empire 1900–18", in M. Kent (ed.), *The Great Powers and the end of the Ottoman Empire*, London 1984, 44–5.

CHAPTER THREE

Reform in the Near East 1792–1880

THE CENTRAL GOVERNMENT OF THE OTTOMAN EMPIRE

The reign of Sultan Selīm III (1789–1807) marks the beginning of a period of major changes in the Ottoman empire. These changes primarily affected government but they extended also to social institutions. The concepts behind the changes were not wholly new, nor were the new policies pursued continuously from the time of Selīm III, but their direction becomes clear from his reign onwards and historians have come to regard his attempted innovations as marking a watershed in Ottoman development. Before examining the changes, however, it is necessary to establish a perspective from which to view the work of Selīm III and his advisers.

A generation or so ago teaching Ottoman history was a simple task. One described the formation of the state at the beginning of the fourteenth century; the gradual evolution of its institutions until they reached perfection in the age of Süleymān the Magnificent during the early sixteenth century, when the organization of the Ottoman empire could be represented by a clear and harmonious model based upon the work of the American historian, William Lybyer; the progressive corruption of its institutions and the loosening of the bonds of the empire until, by the late eighteenth century, the empire was faced with dissolution; and lastly, the valiant, but ultimately unavailing attempts by Ottoman reformers from the time of Selīm III onwards to reconstruct the empire on new principles. Since that delightful age of pellucid exposition the work of historians has contrived to blur the picture at all points, to qualify every generalization and to introduce nothing but ambiguity. No new great synthesis appears to be in prospect and none can be presented here.

It is plain that the idea that there was something amiss with the empire goes back even to the time which was regarded as its most splendid period, namely the reign of Süleymān the Magnificent. The causes of the empire's troubles were then held to be a departure from earlier practices and remedies suggested were characteristically Muslim: get rid of innovations and return to the customs of an earlier, mythical Golden Age. Even so, and even at this early period remedies proposed also included the adoption of European military and naval practices, essentially innovations. By the eighteenth century the complaints of decline were louder and the borrowings from Europe which were mentioned were more wide ranging and more detailed. Nevertheless, the reformers of the so-called Tulip Era retained their conviction that Muslim civilization and the Ottoman state were fundamentally superior to the institutions of the Christian West. In the end, it was claimed, Islam must prevail; all that was required was to adapt to Ottoman needs some of the military techniques which had enabled the West to obtain an unfortunate advantage. But ambiguity attended the contemporary debate: some of the reformers plainly held the undeclared view that reform could not stop with the army but must extend to other institutions of government; indeed military institutions were so entwined with those of government and society that no change could be made in one sphere without affecting the others.

By the eighteenth century the debate was sufficiently extensive to enable the main supporters and opponents of the projected reforms to be identified. The reformers came from the bureaucracy, especially the scribal bureaucracy, and they were assisted by recent converts to Islam and by some foreign diplomats. The opponents were strong among the ulema and the Janissaries, although these institutions were no more united in their opposition to change than were the bureaucrats in support of it. One of the chief supporters of Selīm III's reforms was ʿAbdallāh Efendi, chief judge of the council and a representative of the religious hierarchy and one of the leading opponents was Aḥmed ʿĀṭif Efendi, who had charge of foreign affairs. Ulema opposition was based partly on Muslim principle, manifesting itself in objections to any innovation, and particularly to the adoption of infidel practices, including the newly established military colleges; and partly on material interest. The lower ulema, with their close links with the artisan population of the great cities and with the Janissaries, perceived the proposed changes as a threat to their own status and interest.

The Janissary Corps itself, the last metamorphosis of the former élite Ottoman infantry, was the principal coercive factor at the disposal of the enemies of reform. By the eighteenth century the Janissaries consisted of the skeletons of regiments fleshed out at muster by large numbers of artisans. The sale of pay certificates was a lucrative business for Janissary officers and others. Any reform of the army represented a direct threat to the Janissaries' privileged existence and to the interests of the artisans who drew a small income as paper soldiers. In combination, the ulema and Janissaries could foment a riot which no Ottoman government could contain. To placate the mob the sultan was obliged to sacrifice reforming ministers; on the body of one luckless grand vizier the rioters placed a placard which read "The enemy of the *Sharīʿa* and the State."

Selīm III was the first sultan to place himself unequivocally on the side of the reformers. In part he was impressed by the evidence that provincial disregard of the sultan's government had progressed to the point when the desire for local autonomy by notables and non-Muslim groups was threatening to assume a separatist character.

By 1792 Ottoman control had long since broken down in North Africa: in Algeria and Tunisia power had passed to dynasties which had emerged from the Janissary garrisons; in Libya ruled the hereditary governors of the Qaramānlī family; and Egypt was disputed by Mamluk factions. Ottoman authority in Arabia had dwindled to a nominal suzerainty over the Sharifian rulers of the Hijaz. In the Fertile Crescent Baghdad and Basra were controlled by the Georgian Mamluks and in Syria local notables vied for power. Much of Anatolia and Romania was also under the control of local families or adventurers. More particularly, Selīm was shocked by the disastrous results of wars with Russia which, in 1783, had led to the loss of Muslim territory in the Crimea. The loss of territory populated by Christians could be regarded as the luck of the game, but the surrender of Muslims to Christian rule constituted a major reproach to any Ottoman ruler and challenged his claim to legitimate authority. If a Muslim ruler could not defend the land of Islam and provide the conditions in which Muslims could live as good Muslims should, according to the *Sharīʿa*, what title had he to rule at all? The failure of the Ottoman effort to recover the Crimea, signalized by the Treaty of Jassy (1792) was a clear indication that the old Ottoman system had comprehensively failed. Change was required and must begin with financial and military reforms.

Selīm's proposed reforms may be divided into three categories: the collection of information, financial and administrative reforms, and military reorganization. For information he looked first to the advisers who surrounded him, a small group of about twenty leading bureaucrats, slaves and friends; and beyond that group to a larger body of notables sympathetic to reform. In 1791 he asked a group of twenty-two notables for recommendations for reform. Second, Selīm sought information in Europe. More than previous rulers Selīm showed himself willing to employ European advisers, mainly French. Before 1789 he had himself corresponded with Louis XVI. Previously, Ottoman embassies had been sent to European capitals only for special purposes: now Selīm established permanent embassies in London (1793), Vienna (1794), Berlin (1795) and Paris (1796). It was within these embassies that many of the next generation of Ottoman reformers received part of their early training.

In central government Selīm's administrative reforms focused on the reorganization of his council, which was to consist of twelve ministers, and the redistribution of responsibilities among them. The redistribution involved an apparent reduction of the power of the grand vizier (Ṣadr-ı̊ Aʿẓem) but this was not an attack upon the keystone of the bureaucratic system; rather it was an early recognition of the increasing complexities of the tasks of government. Traditionally, the grand vizier was the deputy of the sultan in all matters, military and civil; only he advised the sultan formally and he could shed no part of his responsibilities. The grand vizier was assisted by clerks and soldiers who executed his orders. Plainly, the burdens were too great for any man and as governmental functions expanded a bottleneck was created. In the Ottoman empire, as in other Middle Eastern states, a distinctive element of reform in the nineteenth and twentieth centuries was the removal of this bottleneck by the shifting of some of the grand vizier's functions on to the shoulders of the clerks who eventually evolved into ministers responsible for departments of government. But the process was a slow one and often responsibility remained with the grand vizier long after functions had effectively passed beyond his control. Selīm also attempted provincial reforms through new regulations to reduce the period of service in any locality by governors (so as to diminish the chance of their becoming too independent of central government) and to change the system of taxation, particularly by reducing the prevalence of tax farming.

The third and most important group of reforms concerned the army. The Ottoman forces at the time of Selīm III may be divided into five groups: frontier garrisons usually located in fortresses, local forces raised by provincial governors, troops hired for campaigns and discharged at the termination of the campaign, the "feudal" army, and the professional army. Some effort was made to repair fortresses but little was done with the first three groups and Selīm concentrated his efforts on the reform of the feudal and professional corps. Selīm attempted to rejuvenate the "feudal" army by ensuring that a timariot lived on his *timar* and was ready to perform military service, that *sipahis* did not abandon campaigns to return to their holdings to collect their revenues and that military *timars* did not fall into the hands of non-military men. Where these conditions were not met Selīm sought to resume government possession of the grant of revenues. The attempted reform was a genuine attempt to make the "feudal" army an efficient military force once more. However, Selīm's efforts failed and government was still obliged to hire *sipahis* to perform the ordinary cavalry duties which they were supposed to provide anyway. Selīm's failure was followed by a precipitate decline of the *timar* system as grants were rapidly resumed by government in the succeeding years and converted into tax farms or *chiftliks*. By the early nineteenth century only 2,500 *timars* remained of the 50,000 which had existed in the early sixteenth century.

Selīm's principal military reforms were concentrated on the professional army, that is, the specialized regular army units, including engineers, the artillery, the regular cavalry, the various service corps and, most important of all, the Janissaries. With several of these corps Selīm had some success. The quality of the guns and powder supplied to the artillery was improved with the aid of European engineers and the standard of artillery and engineer officers raised through the use of European instructors in the new military and engineering schools which had been established. The main problem was the Janissary Corps. Selīm attempted to reform the Janissaries by relieving the officers of administrative duties, by organizing regular musters and inspections and by reducing the numbers from 50,000 to 25,000 in the Istanbul region. (The paper total for the whole empire was 150,000.) Selīm intended to bring the streamlined corps into barracks again, discipline it, pay and equip it adequately and turn it into an effective fighting force. The involvement of the Ottoman empire in the Revolutionary War frustrated his hopes, however, and far from being streamlined the Janissary Corps actually doubled in size during his reign.

In addition to the reform of the various units of the regular army Selīm established a wholly new corps, known as the *Niẓām-i Jedīd*, which was to be paid for by revenues from resumed grants and new taxes on tobacco, spirits and coffee. The formation of the new unit was first announced in 1791 but it made little progress for some years. In 1793 a call was made for 12,000 volunteers but few came forward. Only one regiment was established; a second was added in 1799. Only in 1802, when his other military reforms were plainly failing to produce the desired results did Selīm introduce conscription to fill the ranks of the new corps. In 1805 he ordered a general levy of men for the new regiments and by 1806 the strength of the *Niẓām* had reached 24,000, concentrated mainly in Anatolia and Istanbul.

Selīm had overreached himself. In 1805 the Janissaries revolted against the general levy (which would have resulted in Janissaries being drafted into the *Niẓām-i Jedīd*) and defeated the new troops. Selīm was obliged to dismiss his reforming ministers. In 1807 a further mutiny took place among auxiliary troops, mainly Albanian and Circassians, who were stationed near Istanbul and who protested against being required to wear new European-style uniforms. Their mutiny was supported by the Janissaries and the ulema; many of the sultan's close advisers were killed: and Selīm himself was deposed in favour of his cousin, Muṣṭafā IV (29 May 1807).

The principal reason for the failure of the reform movement under Selīm III was simply that the opponents of reform were more numerous and more powerful than its supporters. There were subsidiary reasons: Selīm was tactically inept and his close association with France allowed his enemies to depict his reforms as infidel innovations. And the circumstances of the Russian War, which broke out in 1806, did not help him for at the time of the May 1807 uprising the leading councillors were away on campaign with the grand vizier and their deputies in Istanbul sided with the opposition.

In 1808 the hopes of the reformers briefly revived. At the time of Selīm's fall some of his supporters had escaped and taken refuge at Ruschuk in Bulgaria with Bayrakdar Muṣṭafā Pasha and in July 1808 they attempted to restore Selīm to power. Their efforts, however, encompassed his death at the hands of Muṣṭafā IV who was himself deposed by Muṣṭafā Pasha in favour of Maḥmūd II (1808–39), the younger brother of Muṣṭafā IV and, except for his brother, the last surviving Ottoman prince. Muṣṭafā Pasha, who had helped to defeat Selīm's reforms in 1805, now put himself at the head of the reforming faction and summoned a meeting of notables to discuss a programme of reform, particularly military reform. But when he endeavoured to implement the programme he was confronted with the same hostile coalition of ulema and Janissaries. These revolted in November 1808 and demanded the restoration of Muṣṭafā IV. To protect himself Maḥmūd II ordered the execution of his brother so leaving no legitimate alternative to himself and made peace with the opposition, abandoning the reformers.

The problems which the reformers had tried to solve remained. The lack of control by the central government over the provinces persisted and local independence began to assume a more dangerous aspect from 1804 when a revolt commenced in Serbia which soon took on a separatist character. The continuing weakness of the Ottoman military forces was fully displayed in the war with Russia and the Ottomans were saved from more severe losses only by Napoleon's invasion of Russia, which obliged Russia to seek peace at Bucharest in 1813 before her objectives were accomplished. Nevertheless, the Ottomans lost Bessarabia and their authority in the Principalities was much impaired. And the Ottoman government in Istanbul remained at the mercy of popular disturbances led by the Janissaries, whose discipline deteriorated even more rapidly after 1808. The Janissaries became increasingly reluctant to go on campaign and when called out either mutinied or simply deserted. On 23 May 1811 13,000 Janissaries mustered in Istanbul to go on campaign but before they had travelled more than a few kilometres on the road to Edirne only 1,600 were left. The Janissaries fought no significant military action after 1812. Their character as a body of town bullies whose brawlings menaced the security of other citizens was now firmly established. Among the duties of the Janissaries of Istanbul was to serve as the city fire brigade. It was commonly asserted that they started fires and demanded payment to put them out.

Maḥmūd II was slow to confront the core problem of the Janissaries. Partly, his delay was due to his preoccupation with other matters; first the Russian War and then the task of trying to recover authority in provincial areas. Partly, it is attributed to the influence of his favourite, Ḥālet Efendi, who dominated Ottoman politics from 1812 until 1822 and who was reported to be a supporter of the Janissaries. But principally, Maḥmūd's procrastination seems to have been tactical; he was waiting for the right opportunity and in the meanwhile allowing time and the disorderly conduct of the Janissaries to work for him. The outbreak of the Greek revolt in 1821 and the utter incompetence of the Janissaries which was then revealed were the key and from 1822 Maḥmūd II worked steadily towards the assertion of control over the Janissaries and a fundamental reform of the empire's military structure. Maḥmūd placed his own supporters in key posts in the religious hierarchy including those of Shaykh al-Islām, Qāḍī-ʿasker and Qāḍī of Istanbul; he established his followers in senior posts in the Janissary Corps itself; and he selected as commander of the Bosphorus forts, Ḥüseyn Agha, a veteran Janissary who had risen from the ranks and committed himself entirely to the sultan.

In May 1826 Maḥmūd began his military reform campaign with an ordinance which declared the Janissary Corps to have become "nothing more than a great disorganized body into which spies have penetrated to foster disorder and to incite sedition", and called for the establishment of a new army "as trained as it is brave, and whose strokes, directed by science, will . . . destroy the arsenal of military inventions of infidel Europe".[1] The new force was to be formed by withdrawing 150 men from each of the 51 Janissary companies in Istanbul and subjecting them to discipline and training. Maḥmūd carefully avoided any reference to Selīm's *Niẓami* Corps and went out of his way to forestall accusations of infidel innovation. The instructors were to be Muslims, members of the ulema were to be attached to each company to conduct daily prayers and to act as religious commissars, and the ordinance was accompanied by a *fetvā*, or religious judgement, to the effect that the reform was in accordance with the *Sharīʿa*. Concessions were offered to the Janissaries. Although the sale of pay certificates was prohibited in the new corps it was stated that all existing Janissary pay certificates would be honoured during the lifetime of the holder.

The Janissaries revolted against the reforms. The first drill was held on 12 June and the Janissaries mutinied three days later. In reply the government assembled the loyal troops drawn from the artillery, bombardiers and service corps, together with the troops from the Bosphorus forts under the command of Ḥüseyn Agha and attacked the Janissaries in the Meat Square. Many were killed, others were hunted down, tried at summary courts and executed. Possibly 1,000 Janissaries died in Istanbul, 6,000 in the empire as a whole and the power of the corps was ended. On 17 June the abolition of the Janissary Corps was announced together with its replacement by a trained body of troops to be known as "The Triumphant Soldiers of Muḥammad" and commanded by Ḥüseyn Agha with the new title of commander-in-chief (Ser-ʿasker Pasha).

The destruction of the Janissaries in Istanbul was followed by the rapid subjection of the Janissary garrisons throughout the empire; only in Bosnia did they hold out for some time. Also, other disorderly and inefficient units were dissolved or reorganized. The destruction of the old Ottoman army was completed in 1831 when the *timar* system was abolished and all remaining *timars* resumed. The way was clear for the establishment of a new, European-style Ottoman army with all the momentous consequences of that innovation.

Ottoman historians referred to the destruction of the Janissaries as "the Auspicious Event" and it is evident that it was both a symbolic event and a real turning-point, a true revolution from above, the counterpart of such episodes as the storming of the Bastille or the Winter Palace. Yet, like those events, what strikes the historian is the smallness of the happening. Government forces numbered about 13,000; the Janissaries and their supporters were considerably fewer. The number of deaths was relatively small. That it was on such trivialities that a revolution turned may emphasize the point made previously about minimal government; so weak was the Ottoman government that it had for years lived in bonds to a puny foe. What had made the Janissaries formidable to a government which lacked a loyal and efficient coercive force had been their links with the artisan population of Istanbul and the lower ulema. It was especially the weakening of those links which marks the difference between 1807 and 1826. In 1807 the mass of the population had supported the Janissaries, but in 1826 only the porters' and boatmen's guilds stood by them and the assistance from the Kurds of Istanbul which the Janissaries received may have been more of a disadvantage than otherwise. In 1807 the Janissaries could plausibly represent themselves as the representatives of the popular will and of Muslim orthodoxy; in 1826 they were perceived as a self-interested, privileged rabble.

The claim of the Janissaries to be the guardians of Muslim orthodoxy was suspect as many of them were members of the heterodox Bektāshī dervish order, which was anathema to the orthodox ulema, as well as to members of rival brotherhoods. Representatives of all these latter Muslim groups were present at a council meeting called in July 1826 to condemn the Bektāshīs. The following month the order was proscribed throughout the empire.

The ulema were themselves not to escape the reforming impulse of the sultan. Although they had been brought to approve the measures taken against their former allies they remained an obstacle to the plans of Maḥmūd. He took a number of measures including restricting by administrative means the power of the Shaykh al-Islām, reducing the number of religious commissars in the army and establishing some measures of financial control by instituting the Directorate of *Waqfs* to superintend the administration of a major source of ulema income.

Another group which suffered a reduction in its power was the provincial notables. Maḥmūd had begun his operations against the notables early in his reign. In much of Anatolia he was able to restore government authority without the use of force. Heirs of local dynasties were offered attractive but distant posts and their places filled by loyal officials. Thus he asserted control over the hereditary pashaliks of Erzerum, Trabzon and Van and broke the power of the Karamanian dynasty. Diplomacy brought him success also in Izmir, Chios, Cyprus and Vidin. Elsewhere, a show of force was required as in Salonika, Jannina and Iraq. In 1834–6 Kurdistan and Mosul were reduced by Reshīd Meḥmed who built a road and marched south-east from Sivas to Mosul suppressing the power of all the valley lords (*derebeys*) on his way (see p. 126). Egyptian arms in Ottoman service restored government authority in Crete and, for a time, in the Morea. Against the successes must be set the loss of control over certain regions. In North Africa the loss of Algeria to France was little more than a bookkeeping transaction, so nominal had Ottoman authority become in the province. In 1835, however, the Ottomans recovered control over Libya, after the failure of the government of Yūsuf Pasha Karamanli. In the Balkans Ottoman authority was conspicuously reduced in consequence of the intervention of major European powers. Ottoman control over the Principalities was weakened in 1813; Serbia won autonomy and Greece her independence in 1830. The greatest reverse suffered by Maḥmūd, however, was that inflicted by Muḥammad ʿAlī of Egypt whose quest for autonomy and, eventually, independence had wrested from the sultan's direct control Egypt, Syria and much of Arabia by the time of Maḥmūd's death in 1839. Indeed, both the example and the competition of Muḥammad ʿAlī may be seen as significant factors in Maḥmūd's determined pursuit of reform during the latter part of his reign.

In place of the institutions which he had destroyed or remodelled Maḥmūd created the instruments of state power; a new army and a reformed administration. Following the destruction of the Janissaries Maḥmūd abandoned the caution which tactical imperatives had forced upon him and set about establishing new, European-style forces, trained and assisted by European officers, and supplied with an officer corps educated in the new military schools. Already in existence were the naval and military engineering schools which had been established in the late eighteenth century. Maḥmūd added a medical school for army doctors, a music school for bandsmen (a not insignificant component of a disciplined army) and a school of military sciences, intended as the Ottoman equivalent of the recently established officer training schools of Sandhurst, St Cyr and West Point. The language of instruction in these schools was French and French instructors were also employed.

The Ottoman empire did not acquire a new, efficient army overnight. Cobbled together from soldiers drafted from existing units mixed with unwilling conscripts, clothed in a strange mixture of military dress from several European armies, armed with indifferent weapons whose use the soldiers barely understood, the new army was the object of the amused contempt of European observers and its performance against Russia in 1828 and against Muḥammad ʿAlī's troops in the 1830s was dismal. It took a long time to develop the force which acquitted itself with such distinction at Plevna and Gallipoli. But the new army had one great quality which its predecessor lacked: it was politically reliable and so could become an effective instrument of internal security. The old army was an expression of social reality; the new army an instrument of state.

The second arm of the Ottoman state was the bureaucracy. Maḥmūd II continued the process of allocating responsibilities to clerks who now became ministers with European titles; the former Kâhya Bey became minister of civil affairs and then, in 1837, minister of the interior, the Reʾīs Efendi became minister of foreign affairs and the Defterdār finance minister. Around them were established ministries and, within the ministries, councils, which became instruments of control and planning. The status of bureaucrats was raised; they were given greater security of tenure, more regular pay and they were now exempt from their previous liability to have their property confiscated by the state at death. A significant change took place within the Ministry of Foreign Affairs partly in consequence of doubts about the loyalty of the Greeks who had formerly dominated the department (and who continued to be prominent within it). For the first time Ottoman Muslims were encouraged to learn European languages so that they might assume a more prominent role in the conduct of foreign affairs. Taken in conjunction with the similar requirement of a knowledge of European languages for military officers the situation led to a number of initiatives, notably the despatch of student missions abroad from 1827 and the opening of the Translation Bureau in 1833, which served both to provide translations of books and documents and as a training centre for civil servants. The reopening of overseas embassies in 1834 (these had been closed after the fall of Selīm III in 1807) also provided opportunities for junior bureaucrats to become familiar with European languages and European practices. The changes in the Ottoman bureaucracy have a double significance. In the first place they helped to create a more efficient instrument of state power. Secondly, they point to the nature of the revolution accomplished by Maḥmūd II. It was not a revolution of the type familiar to Europeans, in which some new group acquires economic power and translates that power, by violence or peaceful means, into political power; it was a revolution from the top in which holders of political power ousted their rivals and then enhanced their power by extending the scope of political power itself at the expense of other social institutions. It is unsurprising that the chief supporters of the revolution, the scribal bureaucracy, should have been the chief beneficiaries; their consolidation of their power under Maḥmūd II was to dictate the nature of the nineteenth-century reform movement.

It has been said of Maḥmūd II that his great achievement was to establish the respectability of change, symbolized by his order to replace the turban with the fez. Even that change is ambiguous, however;

a brimless hat which does not obstruct the act of prayer may be regarded as a characteristic Muslim compromise. Maḥmūd's successes may be attributed to his containment of change and his concealment of the extent of the changes which he wrought. Maḥmūd limited significant change to the army and bureaucracy; apart from that he built some roads, established the first official newspaper and set up a postal system. And he concealed the extent of his changes by presenting his reforms as the abolition of harmful innovations and the restoration of the essence of Ottoman institutions of the time of Sülaymān the Magnificent. Always he stressed that his reforms were intended to protect Islam.

What Maḥmūd and his tiny group of supporters had created was an instrument for change without any motive force for change; a motor car without an engine. No social or economic impulse prompted change; only the wish to preserve the empire from internal and external enemies combined with the ambition of officers and bureaucrats to improve their position. The mass of the population was indifferent or hostile to change. For the nineteenth-century reformers it would be a problem to discover some sustaining impulse to advance and guide their steps, particularly when they found themselves confronted by a sultan who was uninterested in change.

The Tanẓīmāt

The death of Maḥmūd II and the accession of ʿAbd ül-Mejīd in 1839 ushered in the second stage of the Ottoman reform movement, a stage commonly known as the Tanẓīmāt (literally, orders or regulations). The year 1839 also marks the beginning of a major ambiguity in the Ottoman reform movement which may be expressed in terms of a dispute both about the goals of the movement and about its success. According to one view the goals were set out in two great reforming edicts, the Khaṭṭ-i̊ Sherīf of Gülkhāne (1839) and the Khaṭṭ-i̊ Hümāyūn (1856), and in the Ottoman constitution of 1876 and in terms of these goals the Ottoman reformers miserably failed. According to another view the goal of the Tanẓīmāt reformers, like that of their predecessors, was the preservation of the Ottoman empire through the centralization of authority in the central government and judged by that end the reformers achieved some success. An examination of the problem may properly begin with an account of what the reformers actually did.

Measured simply by financial criteria the first priority of the reformers was the army. Between a half and two-thirds of Ottoman government expenditure went on a variety of coercive forces. Two major reorganizations of the army were carried out. In 1842–3, under Riżā Pasha, a conscript army of 400,000 was planned, although the burden proved too great and the target was reduced to about 250,000 which, with about 50,000 irregulars, yielded an Ottoman army of about 300,000, although by no means all were available at any time. At this size the Ottoman army was roughly comparable with European armies of the time, but the situation was altered in consequence of the arrival of the new-style European armies based on the 1860 Prussian model, which aimed to produce a small peacetime and large wartime force. The second major Ottoman military reorganization in 1869 carried out under Ḥüseyn ʿAvnī Pasha was intended to match this development and produce a wartime force of 700,000. The task was, however, beyond Ottoman resources and from that time onwards the Ottomans were always losing the battle to stay on equal terms with the Europeans.

One major difficulty for the Ottomans was that the Ottoman forces had to carry out much more varied functions than European armies. In addition to preparation for international warfare the Ottomans required a force suitable for colonial warfare in the Yemen and for substantial internal security duties. Although irregular, and later gendarmerie forces assisted the regular army the latter force was continuously employed to support the constabulary forces. In consequence the Ottomans required a large standing force as well as a large wartime force. The financial and manpower burdens were more than the empire could sustain although the effort to meet them never flagged until 1913.

The efforts required to sustain the momentum of army modernization dictated the shape of the entire reform programme. Money to pay for the army had to be raised by taxes and loans. In turn a larger and more efficient administration was required to mobilize the empire's resources. Educational reform was needed to produce the necessary officers and bureaucrats. When resources were taken from other institutions the state had to undertake the functions those institutions could no longer discharge. Thus the needs of the army supplied the impulse for the reform not only of the institutions of government but those of the society as well. The reform of the Ottoman empire was a classic example of military-led modernization. There was little money available for other reforms and many of the contemplated changes in Ottoman organization remained on paper.

Administrative reform was the necessary partner of army reform. Maḥmūd II had made substantial changes in central government and these were elaborated under the Tanẓīmāt, but the principal achievement of the Tanẓīmāt reformers was the remodelling of the system of provincial government, notably by the new *vilāyet* law of 1864. Unreformed Ottoman provincial government presented a variegated aspect; different areas were governed in different ways arising from their history. The basis unit was the *sanjak*, the origins of which were, not surprisingly, military. The duty of the *sanjak bey* was to assemble the timariots of his district and to bring them to the provincial muster. *Sanjaks* were grouped loosely to form provinces of fluctuating size. Extra governmental functions had been grafted on to the *sanjak bey* and, of course, his original function had entirely disappeared with the abolition of the *timar* system. What was now required was to evolve a system of provincial government designed to carry on the expanding duties of civil government. Under the 1864 law the older provincial groupings were remodelled, renamed *vilāyets*, and placed under a governor (*vālī*). The *vilāyets* were subdivided into districts (*sanjaks* or *livās*) under a *mutaṣarrif*, the districts into *qaḍās*, (under a *qāʾim maqām*) and the *qaḍās* into urban and rural districts (*kāriyas* and *nāḥiyes*). *Vālīs*, *mutaṣarrifs* and *qāʾim maqāms* were all appointed from Istanbul as were also senior provincial officials in charge of finance, public works, agriculture and other major functions. In addition, each official in the larger units was advised by a council composed of appointed and elected members who represented local interest groups. The system was designed to give scope for the initiative of the provincial governor tempered by central control exercised from Istanbul and the representations of local opinion through the councils. Under an efficient governor the system could produce impressive results as the often quoted performances of Midḥat Pasha as governor of Tuna in Bulgaria and, later, of Baghdad showed. Historians have tended to argue that the role of the councils was very limited, that they were dominated by conservative Muslims and they obstructed changes. More recent research into the working of the councils shows that this view needs much modification; it is clear, for example, that the councils in Palestine functioned as effective executive bodies giving due weight to local opinion which was by no means always opposed to change.

Reform of provincial government must be seen not merely as an attempt to establish a more uniform and efficient system of local government, to mobilize resources and to execute reforms, but also as a partial answer to the perennial problems of the Ottoman reformers, namely the establishment of a system of government which would meet the requirements of the various religious communities in the empire. For the *millets*, to which had been consigned many of the duties of administration, were changing. Hitherto the *millets* (by 1914 there were seventeen recognized by the Ottoman government and all under foreign protection) had been dominated by the higher clergy in each religious community. In the course of the 1860s a challenge to the authority of the higher clergy developed among the lower clergy and lay members of the *millets*. The Ottoman government abetted this challenge and allowed the remodelling of *millet* organization between 1862 and 1865. Partly, the Ottoman authorities were bowing to Western pressure exercised on behalf of their protégés, but also the Ottoman action proceeded from a view that the new *millet* movement tended towards secularization and hence was compatible with the elaboration of a universal, secular, state governmental system for the empire. In the long run, it was hoped, the remaining functions of the *millets* would be taken over by the new provincial authorities, the *millets* would wither away and there would be a single form of government for all Ottoman citizens. In fact this did not happen and the secularization of the *millets* operated to foster nationalist and separatist tendencies among many of the religious communities rather than to diminish separatism.

The Tanẓīmāt reformers placed much emphasis upon the development of a modern system of education. In 1838 the Board of Useful Affairs reported that "the acquisition of science and skill comes above all other aims and aspirations of the state".[2] Religion, it argued, was valuable for the next world, but it was science which facilitated the perfection of a man in this world. In 1846 a commission recommended the establishment of a comprehensive system of state education from primary to university level and in 1869 an even more ambitious plan called for free and compulsory primary education for boys and girls, leading to free lower secondary education and to selective higher education. The commitment of the Tanẓīmāt reformers was plain; they accepted the need to provide a modern education for Muslims to enable them to keep up with the advances in Christian education which were taking place in reorganized *millet* schools and in foreign missionary schools, and they recognized the desirability of a common system of secular education to further the aim of Ottomanization. The establishment of a Ministry of Education in 1847 removed education from the control of the ulema and the 1869 plan proclaimed that there would be no discrimination in state schools either through language or religion.

The Tanẓīmāt achievement in education was limited. At the primary level little was done but the provision of a few buildings and textbooks and primary education remained in the hands of the religious communities. In secondary education progress was slow but convincing and secondary schools were eventually established in all provincial capitals and other large towns. In higher education major developments took place. The Ottoman State University did not get under way until the beginning of the twentieth century, the first attempt to establish the institution in 1870 having ended in failure after only one year. But a number of high schools were established in the Tanẓīmāt period which offered an education comparable to that obtainable at the American Robert College and the Syrian Protestant College. In particular Galatasaray, a French-style *lycée*, and the Civil Service College (Mülkiye) trained many of the leading bureaucrats of the next generation.

The second area of social reform was law. Two problems confronted the Tanẓīmāt reformers: to establish a system of law which would provide more adequately for the complex transactions of a modernizing society; and to devise a system which would be acceptable to the Europeans and to their non-Muslim subjects who enjoyed virtual exemption from Ottoman law through the capitulations and the *millet* system. Only when all Ottoman citizens were subject to a single legal system could there be any hope of realizing the aim of Ottomanism, that is, the establishment of common institutions and a common focus of loyalty for all Ottoman citizens. Legal reform involved the drafting of new substantive law in the form of codes, new codes of legal procedure and the creation of a system of courts with trained judges who could apply the law.

A major difficulty was presented by the existence of the *Sharīʿa*, in theory a complete code of behaviour covering every aspect of man's conduct. To suggest that the rules God had provided were either mistaken or insufficient was plain blasphemy as Reshīd Pasha discovered to his cost when he introduced his proposed Commercial Code in 1841 and was dismissed for claiming that it had nothing to do with the *Sharīʿa*. The Commercial Code was not put into force until 1850. The code was administered by mixed tribunals of Ottoman and European judges, following European legal procedure. The device of mixed tribunals had come into unofficial existence at the beginning of the nineteenth century but received formal recognition under the Tanẓīmāt. Once established the system could be adapted for other purposes, including criminal cases, in which, for the first time, Christian testimony against Muslims was admitted. To reform criminal law itself was a more difficult matter for, unlike such matters as bills of exchange, the *Sharīʿa* had a good deal to say about punishments for criminal offences. Early efforts went no further than the codification of *Sharīʿa* law. In 1858, however, a radical change was accomplished by the new Penal Code which was basically an adaptation of the corresponding French code. It was applied in the state courts established under the Ministry of Justice.

The most difficult area of law was civil law and especially the law governing marriage, divorce and inheritance. This was the traditional area in which the *Sharīʿa* courts operated. In 1868, however, the establishment of the Council for Judicial Ordinances provided the possibility of a system of secular courts to try civil suits. All that was required was a civil code which they could utilize. Some reformers pressed for a completely secular code, but the matter was put into the hands of a commission chaired by one of the most distinguished Tanẓīmāt statesmen, Jevdet Pasha, who advocated a gradual approach. The result was the famous Mejelle, issued between 1870 and 1876 which was a most successful compromise between *Sharīʿa* and secular law and which endured until the end of the empire and persisted thereafter in many of the successor states. The Mejelle covered all areas of civil law except personal law which remained in the hands of the religious courts.

As with education, legal reform under the Tanẓīmāt had limited success. Much progress was made in establishing a comprehensive system of substantive law and courts to implement it. Most law was taken from the hands of the religious classes and placed under the state. There was a marked shift towards secularization. However, the legal reformers failed to persuade the Europeans to surrender the protection of the capitulations or to prevent their non-Muslim subjects from seeking the protection of the European consuls and exemption from Ottoman state law. In the longer term, however, the legal reforms of the Tanẓīmāt made possible the transition to a purely secular system and the ending of the capitulations under the Turkish republic.

In army, administration, education and law there were real changes under the Tanẓīmāt which can be seen as contributing to the building of a modern, centralized, secular state and to the realization of Ottomanism, the equality of all Ottoman citizens, the professed ideology of the Tanẓīmāt reformers. The limitations on success proceeded partly from the lack of trained personnel, partly from finance, partly from the interposition of the influence of the European powers, partly from conservative resistance, and partly from the hostility of the empire's non-Muslim subjects. It is in the context of those limitations that the edicts may be examined.

The Tanẓīmāt edicts of 1839 and 1856 should be seen primarily as statements of principles which should govern reforms rather than as decisions to be implemented forthwith. The main principles were equality and security for all citizens, the removal of administrative abuses and, in 1856, the notion of administrative and economic development. Each of these principles had an essential ambiguity in the Ottoman context. For example, equality could mean either the establishment of a common code for all Ottoman citizens, Muslim and non-Muslim, which was the interpretation inherent in the Tanẓīmāt reforms; or it could mean the removal of the special disabilities suffered by non-Muslims, which was the interpretation preferred by the *dhimmīs*. The implication of the non-Muslim interpretation was that Christians, etc., should preserve their identity, enshrined in the *millets*, and resist submergence in a common citizenship. Although the retention of that identity could in theory be consistent with continual membership of the empire, in practice it pointed towards the development of autonomy and, where the territorial situation permitted, eventual independence. Europeans wavered between support for either interpretation with the result that the edicts promised both equality for all citizens and a special status for the *millets*. The European complaint that the promise of equality was not implemented was therefore unreasonable for it was impossible to carry out in both senses. In fact the Ottomans could not afford to implement the promise completely in either sense. Equality in the Tanẓīmāt sense encountered the hostility of the Muslims; and in the non-Muslim sense would probably lead to the dissolution of the empire as the Christians sought independence. The dilemma of the Tanẓīmāt reformers was that, whatever their hopes that in the very long run their reforms might produce consent for their rule, in the short term they were sure that many of their non-Muslim subjects could only be held within the empire by force. To use force against Christians required the assent of at least some of the major European powers. The expression, "the removal of administrative abuses", however, was virtually a euphemism for refraining from the use of force against non-Muslims. The great crises of the Eastern Question arose mainly from the European efforts to prevent the Ottomans from enforcing their authority. One face of the Tanẓīmāt was therefore concerned with creating the instruments through which the state could enforce its will and the other with restricting the use of those instruments.

In the Tanẓīmāt, as in other institutions, one may make a distinction between the efficient and the decorative. The real, the efficient Tanẓīmāt was the drive for a modernized, centralized state; the unreal, the decorative Tanẓīmāt was the professions of unrealizable ideals made necessary by the need for some measure of European consent. The timing of the professions lends conviction to this view; the Gülkhane edict followed the Ottoman need for European support against Muḥammad ʿAlī; the Hümāyūn edict followed the Crimean War and preceded the admission of the empire to the status of a European power; and the 1876 constitution was issued just in time to avert the threat of a concerted European intervention in the affairs of the empire.

The Ottoman constitution of 1876 and the Young Ottomans

The Ottoman constitution of 1876 was not merely an exercise in deception; it was an attempted answer to problems inherent in the Tanẓīmāt. The Tanẓīmāt was a programme for the salvation of the empire which was directed by a small body of ministers drawn from the bureaucracy and the army. It had no roots in popular affections and was dependent upon the consent of the sultan. After 1870, Sultan ʿAbd ül-ʿAzīz, who had succeeded ʿAbd ül-Mejīd in 1861, opposed some features of the Tanẓīmāt programme and appointed ministers uncongenial to the reformers. In their turn ministers began to look for some device which would render them and their programme less dependent upon the will of the sultan and in this context began to study the possibilities of a constitution.

Although the leading reformers of the Tanẓīmāt period had approved the idea of representative councils at the local level they had resisted the extension of the representative principle to the centre, believing that non-Muslims would use a parliament to block the Tanẓīmāt programme. A parliament was advocated, however, by critics of the Tanẓīmāt, known as the Young Ottomans, who came to prominence in 1867.

The Young Ottomans were a small group of young men, mainly from the bureaucracy and possessing some knowledge of European languages who were united principally by common enmity towards the leading Tanẓīmāt statesmen, ʿAlī and Fu'ād Pashas. All wished to preserve the Ottoman empire but they differed widely in their suggestions of how this should be done. Among them, however, there was some support for a constitution and a parliament. The most articulate among them, Nāmiq Kemāl, grounded his arguments in Ottoman and Muslim history. The traditional Ottoman constitution, he claimed, had featured a system of checks and balances in which the ulema and the Janissaries had operated to balance the power of the state. The destruction of these checks had led to the unrestrained abuse of power by ministers which had placed the Ottoman empire in a dangerous situation wherein it was subject to control by the European powers. A new system of checks was required which could be best supplied by the establishment of a representative assembly to which ministers would be responsible. This institution, he argued, was further recommended by Muslim history. The Prophet had enjoined his followers to consult among themselves and the early Muslim community had taken its decisions after deliberation among all the members. It was now impossible for the community to forgather in this way, but the Prophet's injunction could be fulfilled through the device of a representative assembly. The particular model of parliament which Nāmiq Kemāl recommended bore a close resemblance to that of Britain, and it seems likely that it was with observation of the British institution rather than of Ottoman and Muslim history that he began, although his presentation reversed this order of events.

Mention of the ideas of Nāmiq Kemāl prompts a brief digression to comment on the line of argument which he represents and which is known as Islamic modernism. As remarked in Chapter 1, there were, among the Muslim peoples of the Near East, different attitudes towards modernization. One, which was represented by the Tanẓīmāt reformers and which has been that which has prevailed in almost all governments in the region, has been to adopt the goals of modernization, to assume that these implied the secularization of public life, and to push on towards the realization of these goals despite the opposition of the majority of the populations which they ruled. A second reaction was rejection, whether violent or passive; an assertion that, if salvation on this earth was only to be obtained by the sacrifice of what was enjoined by the *Sharīʿa* then it was not worth having, for it would mean the abandonment of the hope of eternal salvation. In a sense the point at issue between these groups is essential to the understanding of the internal debate concerning the Ottoman reform movement. The reformers claimed that their programme was essential to preserve the Ottoman empire. But that was to conceive of the empire as a territorial entity and to those who saw the empire as a Muslim empire the reformers appeared to be destroying the essence in order to preserve the shell. There was, however, a middle way which was represented by the Islamic modernists. If, by the use of arguments congenial to Muslims and based on the same mode of reasoning as that employed by orthodox Muslim jurists, the reforms could be shown to be in accordance with the *Sharīʿa* then they might be received readily by Muslims and take root in the society instead of merely being a veneer pinned on the outside of the social fabric. The mode of reasoning employed by Nāmiq Kemāl was to be adopted by many other reformers in the Near East and was brought to a high level of sophistication by the followers of the Egyptian social reformer, Muḥammad ʿAbduh. In their hands Islamic modernism was to become a vital tool for legal reform, making acceptable major changes in personal law.

The ideas of the Young Ottomans won a small following among the Europeanized intellectuals of Istanbul and, combined with the more limited notions of those ministers who sought a check upon the power of the sultan, were to form a significant factor in the making of the constitution. But it is unlikely that these ideas would have had any immediate result but for the peculiar events of 1876.

The 1870s were a decade of political crisis in the Ottoman empire. From 1840 until 1870 there had been much continuity of policy. Ministries had been dominated by three great reforming bureaucrats, Muṣṭafā Reshīd Pasha, Fuʾād Pasha and ʿAlī Pasha, who had between them held the office of grand vizier for nearly eighteen of these years. All were men of administrative ability and experience of the West and had a commitment to reform. After the death of ʿAlī Pasha in 1871 the empire entered a period of political instability. Between 1871 and 1880 there were twenty different ministries and fifteen grand viziers. The initial cause of this instability was the desire of Sultan ʿAbd ül-ʿAzīz to recover control over policy from the bureaucrats and his practice of constantly changing his ministers to prevent any of them from becoming too powerful or too independent. ʿAbd ül-ʿAzīz's policy led to a conflict between the sultan and the Porte which was not settled until Sultan ʿAbd ül-Ḥamīd took firm control.

The crisis was made worse by serious economic difficulties. Drought and floods had a disastrous effect upon an agricultural economy and as production fell so the pressure of taxation increased leading to a serious governmental financial crisis. The economic and financial difficulties contributed to the great international crisis of 1875–8 and the war with Russia which imposed great burdens on the state through the demands for money and soldiers and eventually set the empire the problem of absorbing a large number of Muslim refugees from the European provinces which passed under Christian rule in 1878.

Lastly, the period saw a new questioning of the direction of Ottoman policy. The secularist aims of the Tanẓīmāt statesmen came under increasing criticism from several directions and the concessions made to Christians since 1856 provoked resentment which found some expression in the revival of Islam which was noticeable throughout the empire. In his halting of some Tanẓīmāt policies ʿAbd ül-ʿAzīz could be said to be responding to the movement of public opinion, and ʿAbd ül-Ḥamīd's cultivation of Islam in the years after 1880 can be seen as a necessary compromise in an empire which was becoming, in population, much more Muslim than it had been when the Tanẓīmāt statesmen launched their reforms.

In 1875 the Ottoman empire went bankrupt, that is to say it could not pay the interest on its public debt. Finance had always been a major problem for the reformers. The early Tanẓīmāt reforms had been paid for largely by inflation achieved through debasing the coinage or printing money; from the time of the Crimean War the Ottomans had begun to borrow abroad, accepting as the corollary the need to stabilize their currency and formalize their financial system. In 1856 the Ottoman Bank was established and in 1863 the first budget was produced. Inflation was brought under control but the foreign debt mounted until by 1875 the Ottomans owed £200 million. Ottoman bankruptcy was the consequence of a fall in receipts due to bad harvests, and increased expenditure made worse by the need to suppress a revolt in Bosnia (see p. 77). In other times the Ottomans might have been able to borrow enough to tide them over their difficulties, but they were unlucky that their problems coincided with a general European financial crisis when high-risk borrowers went to the bottom of the queue. Bankruptcy and Christian uprisings provided the basis for European intervention to force the Ottomans to adopt a plan of reform under European superintendence.

A group of military and civilian leaders decided that drastic action was needed to avoid European intervention and they adopted the traditional mode of removing first the grand vizier, Meḥmed Nedīm, and then on 30 May 1876 the sultan himself, replacing the latter with Murād V who had a reputation as a liberal. About what should be done next ministers were divided. For many, nothing more required to be done; a bad sultan had been removed and a new sultan installed. For some, notably Midḥat Pasha, a more permanent remedy was required and these advocated the introduction of a constitution. There was some discussion but for the time being the majority of anti-constitutionalists prevailed. Two factors changed the balance of ministerial opinion. One was the plain threat of European intervention which became irresistible as news leaked out of the brutal suppression by the Ottomans of the rising in Bulgaria. The other was the evident mental incapacity of the new sultan. Murād would have to be deposed and be replaced by ʿAbd ül-Ḥamīd II, whose reputation was doubtful. With such uncertainty about the sultanate the arguments for some machinery which would give security to ministers became more persuasive. The necessity for his ministers to secure the approval of a representative assembly would limit the capacity of any sultan to pursue arbitrary policies. Having secured ʿAbd ül-Ḥamīd's prior agreement to a constitution, Midḥat and his colleagues deposed Murād and set up the third sultan of 1876 at the end of August.

A constitution was quickly drafted, by a committee which included a majority of constitutionalists using as a basis the Belgian constitution of 1831, itself approximating to a written version of the unwritten British constitution. The draft, however, was unacceptable either to

ʿAbd ül-Ḥamīd or to the majority of ministers. Midhat was obliged to accept amendments which strengthened the powers of the sultan, although it should be said that the original draft already left the sultan very considerable powers and the changes did not add substantially to them. All parties were anxious for agreement, however, because it was important that the constitution should be promulgated before the European statesmen met in conference in Istanbul. In fact the constitution was proclaimed on the day the conference opened and the Ottomans were able to say, in effect: you want a constitution for Bosnia – we have made one for the whole of the empire. The conference closed without agreement on a European policy so the constitution had achieved one end at least.

The constitution did not function for long. Its principal architect, Midḥat, was dismissed on 5 February 1877 and the assembly met only for one year, from March 1877 to February 1878 before being prorogued indefinitely by ʿAbd ül-Ḥamīd. The constitution was not abolished but it was not operated, and for the next thirty years ʿAbd ül-Ḥamīd ruled the empire autocratically.

To those who regard the Ottoman constitution as the end-product of a liberal movement in the empire its suspension in 1878 appears to mark the failure of that movement. In this chapter it has been argued that this view is inappropriate; there was a liberal movement but it was a puny affair which had only a modest impact upon a constitution which was essentially the product of the desire of a group of bureaucrats to protect their position and, in the difficult situation of 1876, to preserve the empire with whatever device was most suitable. There was little popular enthusiasm for a constitution and for the majority of ministers it was a leap in the dark which they happily declined when it became apparent that in ʿAbd ül-Ḥamīd they had the type of strong-willed and determined sultan which their experience indicated the empire required. The Tanẓīmāt was not a liberal, but a bureaucratic movement. There were ministers with liberal impulses such as Meḥmed Kābulī Pasha of whom the British ambassador, Sir Henry Layard, remarked that he "gave proof of his liberal opinions and of his desire to introduce social as well as political reforms amongst his Mussulman fellow-countrymen by having his wife taught French and the piano",[3] just as there were stern conservatives who criticized the reforms as going too far and too fast. But their ideological views were always subordinated to their responsibilities as state servants and their own interests as office-holders, Bureaucrats were at once the inspiration of the Tanẓīmāt and its chief beneficiaries. "A Pasha can scarcely remain poor", an informant explained to Nassau Senior, "unless he is absolutely indifferent to money."[4] Most of the Tanẓīmāt leaders died wealthy men.

ANATOLIA

One of the many surprising features of the writing of Ottoman history is that the history of Anatolia, which is sometimes described as the heartland of the empire and which composes most of the present Turkish republic, has hardly been written. Unlike other portions of the Ottoman empire, which have their separate histories, the history of Anatolia has been lost within the history of the empire as a whole. One reason for this circumstance is that Anatolia lacks geographical unity, although a similar deficiency has not prevented the writing of the history of other areas: a second reason is that modern Turkish historians have seen their historical past in the history of the entire empire, whereas other nationalities have concentrated their attention upon those areas which formed their inheritance or the centre of their aspirations. To write a history of Anatolia in the nineteenth and early twentieth centuries is, therefore, a difficult enterprise, but to present a Near East in which Anatolia is given much less attention than regions of far slighter significance would be to distort history.

Anatolia may be divided into innumerable regions but it will be convenient here to describe it in terms of five regions and subsequently to write about it as only two – western and eastern Anatolia. The largest part of Anatolia is the central plateau in the middle of which is situated Ankara. The plateau is a high (about 900 metres), dry region subject to extremes of temperature. Rainfall agriculture is possible almost everywhere, but amounts of rain are barely sufficient and urban centres and regions of cultivation have concentrated in districts which enjoyed a water bonus either because they lay in a depression or because they were adjacent to high ground. In 1800 most of the central plateau was the home of pastoral tribes, mainly Turkoman but including Arabs in the south and Kurds in the east. The principal products of the region were derived from animals, and included the famous Angora wool. The precariousness of life on the plateau was well illustrated by the Ankara famine of 1873–4 which is estimated to have killed 25 per cent of the people (up to a quarter of a million according to one estimate) and 60 per cent of the livestock. The drought of 1873 had pushed the region into danger, and heavy snow, followed by floods in the spring of 1874, prevented supplies from reaching the starving people.

On the north the plateau is bordered by mountains which slope down sharply to the Black Sea coast. The narrow strip of land so formed is one of the most fertile areas of Anatolia, heavily wooded (especially in the east) and producing a wide range of crops including fruit, nuts and tobacco. The Black Sea coast of Anatolia lacks major harbours but it was through the ports of this coast, principally Samsun, that the plateau was supplied. To the south of the plateau is the Taurus range which cuts off Anatolia from the Mediterranean and Syria. The southern slopes of the Taurus and the coastal plains form a fertile region often known as Cilicia. The large plain of Adana became a centre of sugar and cotton cultivation in the later nineteenth century. Further east, away from the Mediterranean, between Aleppo and Diyarbakr the region is drier and included some semi-desert. Nevertheless, there were substantial areas of cultivation. To the west of the plateau are the Aegean coastlands including the long valleys of the greater and lesser Menderes rivers and the Gediz. This region was a major cereal-producing area.

The fifth region of Anatolia is the tangled mass of mountains and valleys lying to the east of the central plateau forming the region commonly described as Turkish Armenia by Europeans, although this phrase had obvious political implications. In this book all the area lying east of a line drawn from Samsun on the Black Sea to Diyarbakr will be termed eastern Anatolia and the other four regions will be considered as western Anatolia. Eastern Anatolia included considerable cultivated plains and valleys, for example around Mush, Van and Erzerum, but much of the land was used as pasture by tribal peoples, mainly Kurds.

Estimates of the population of Anatolia in 1800 vary greatly but modern writers put it around 6 million people. By 1912 the population of Ottoman Anatolia (a somewhat smaller region) was around 17.5 million. A considerable part of this increase was the consequence of immigration. Throughout the whole period down to 1870 there was an influx of Tatar Muslims from the regions north of the Black Sea, the Kuban, the Crimea, the Caucasus and Transcaucasia. More moved in after the loss of the north-eastern lands of Anatolia to Russia in 1878 and other Muslims entered Anatolia from the European provinces of the empire. Many members of this last group preferred to settle in Rumelia but the Ottoman government encouraged them to move to Anatolia by offering them, under the 1857 refugee code, land and exemptions from taxes and conscription for twelve years compared with only six if they settled in Rumelia. Istanbul itself was a major staging post for immigrants moving on to Anatolia and held a large floating population throughout the nineteenth century. It is very difficult to estimate the number of immigrants; statistics for the earlier period are lacking, there are difficulties arising from the internal movements of immigrants and later figures are open to distortion through propaganda, but it is likely that immigrants to Anatolia may have been as many as 2 million which ranks the migration among the major human movements of the nineteenth century.

The immigration had several effects. First, it led to an extension of cultivation in Anatolia, notably in Cilicia where the development of cotton cultivation in the later nineteenth century was based on immigrant labour. Second, it contributed to continuing social unrest. Immigrants were given land but lack of capital or skills led many to abandon their land and become paid labourers for big landowners. Some, especially the Circassians and Nogay Tatars, took to pillaging travellers as well as their neighbours; relations between the immigrants and the existing communities were commonly bad and many of the immigrants harboured vengeful feelings against Christians following the treatment which some had received in Russia or the Balkan lands. Circassian relations with Kurds were no better, however. A third effect was to change the population balance of Anatolia. Taken in connection with the emigration of many Greeks and Armenians to the New World and elsewhere, the immigration made Anatolia more Muslim than it was in 1800. In 1912 the non-Muslim population of Anatolia was about 17 per cent; it is difficult to believe that it was not higher in 1800 although we have no statistical evidence.

The population of Anatolia also increased substantially by natural increase. Most writers consider that this increase took place principally from 1878 onwards but there is no certainty about the timing. That an increase did take place, however, is not to be doubted, despite the universal view of contemporary European observers which was that the population of Anatolia was declining and that the Muslim population was declining more rapidly than the non-Muslim groups. The Europeans were decidedly wrong on both counts, and their fundamental misapprehension not only affected their perceptions of Anatolian developments but it has continued to influence the views of subsequent writers who have busied themselves explaining a non-existent decline of Anatolia.

The population of Anatolia was also more divided linguistically than that of the Arab provinces. A majority spoke Turkish, although in a number of dialects which bore only a distant relationship to the Arabicized official Ottoman Turkish. Other languages spoken included Greek, Armenian, Kurdish, Persian, Arabic, Georgian and other Caucasian languages. Many of the speakers of these languages also spoke Turkish, but the total proportion of the population which did not speak Turkish as a first language may have been as high as one-third.

A final feature of Anatolia was that it was the least urbanized region of the empire, and remained so throughout the nineteenth century as the growth of the coastal towns, principally Izmir, was matched by the decline in the population of towns in the interior. Partly the lack of urbanization is to be explained by the existence of Istanbul across the Straits which acted as a magnet and a provider of services in place of other towns, for example Konya and Bursa, which might have fulfilled this role; but principally it was due to the very poor communications in Anatolia which meant that towns tended to serve only small regions. Long-distance trade outside the ports was conducted through periodic fairs well into the nineteenth century.

Western Anatolia

In 1800 the Ottoman government had little direct control over western Anatolia. Ottoman administration was confined to the provinces of Karaman and Anadolu: the remainder was the preserve of the valley lords (*derebeys*) who ruled over autonomous hereditary principalities. The *derebeys* were tax farmers, who controlled local officials and served with their own troops with the Ottoman army on campaign. The *derebeys* had proliferated in the last quarter of the eighteenth century. The best known were the Kara ʿOs̱mān-oghlu, who, from their base at Aydi̊n, dominated the valley of the greater Menderes; the Chapan-oghlu, of Turkoman tribal origin, who controlled a large part of the central plateau in the triangle formed by Amasya, Ankara and Kayseri; and further east, in the coastal region behind Trabzon (Trebizond), were the bitter rivals of the Chapan-oghlu, the Jānīkli family. Along the Mediterranean coastlands were several *derebeys* including the Küchük ʿAlī-oghlu around Adana and the Yilanli-oghlu who controlled the Koja valley from Isparta to Antalya.

Many distinctions have been drawn between the *derebeys* and the *aʿyān*, but it is easiest to think of the former as rural notables who had converted their local influence into political power. They were tolerated by the Ottoman government which found them indispensable as recruiters during the late-eighteenth-century wars with Russia. And they were not ruthless exploiters of the local populations; subsequently they were the objects of an exaggerated nostalgic admiration which contrasted favourably their government with that of the Ottoman bureaucrats who succeeded them. Some, like the Chapan-oghlu, who founded the town of Yeuzgat, populating it with Greek and Armenian settlers, fostered economic development within their territories. Nor were all of them opposed to reform; both the Kara ʿOs̲mān-oghlu and the Chapan-oghlu supported reform under Selīm III and Muṣṭafā Bayrakdar Pasha. Nevertheless, their defiance of the Porte, their diversion of revenues, the danger that they would make their own agreements with foreign powers, and their rivalries one with another which kept areas of Anatolia in a disturbed state were not to be tolerated by Maḥmūd II who devoted much of his reign to bringing them under control by political and military means. The notables of the Black Sea coast, including the Jānīklis, were eliminated in 1812–13; the Chapan-oghlu lands were taken under direct Ottoman control after the death of Süleymān Beg in 1814; and the Aydi̊n region was brought under Ottoman government after the death of Kara ʿOs̲mān-oghlu Hüseyn Agha in 1816 although full authority was not established until 1833. By the end of 1817 most of western Anatolia was under Ottoman authority, although the struggle continued in isolated areas and was not completed until 1866 when an expedition was sent from Istanbul to subjugate the last valley lords and tribal chiefs of Cilicia. The reassertion of Ottoman control over Cilicia was delayed by the Egyptian occupation of 1833–40, an important period in the history of the region because of the unprecedented power of Egyptian government under Ibrāhīm Pasha, the assault on local and tribal autonomy, the imposition of conscription and the promotion of economic development.

The defeat of the new Ottoman army in Anatolia by Ibrāhīm Pasha in 1833 and 1839 was one of the factors which led to the extensive military reorganization of 1841. In those new arrangements Anatolia was given a prominent place. It was, in effect, divided into two areas: in the west the old Imperial Guard, renamed the Imperial Army, was moved across the Bosporus to Scutari and took responsibility for the security of western Anatolia. Eastern Anatolia was given to the Ottoman Fourth Army based on Sivas. Anatolia also included two of the four imperial military reserve districts (at Izmir and Sivas), indicating the importance of Anatolia for recruitment. It was a sign of the progress of pacification in western Anatolia that in the 1869 military reorganization the Imperial Army was returned to Istanbul to become the Ottoman First Army and the Fourth Army was moved east from Sivas to Erzerum, indicating that the duties of external defence had become more important than those of internal security which were left to the police and gendarmerie.

The reimposition of Ottoman authority was followed by administrative reorganization. In the early years Anatolia was under military governors because of the eminence of internal security problems and the lack of trained administrators. As pacification proceeded and the new colleges produced their quota of trained bureaucrats civilian governors took over and by the second half of the century such men were the norm. At the same time the large old provinces were broken up into more manageable units until the whole provincial structure was remodelled under the 1864 law. By 1867 there were thirteen *vilāyets*, and eventually Anatolia came to be divided into seventeen provinces (including Aleppo which embraced parts of Anatolia as well as Syria).

As remarked above many European observers painted a picture of misrule and decay in nineteenth-century Anatolia, complained of the incompetence and corruption of Ottoman officials and saw hope for the region only in the activities of the Greek and Armenian minorities. Indeed, Greek and Armenian informants, many of whom hoped for European intervention in their causes, were a principal source of European information. Much of that information also came from European consuls in the seaports and their statements about insecurity in the interior were quite inaccurate. The European picture is altogether overdrawn and a true account of Anatolia in the nineteenth century must take account of great variations over time and place. There were good and bad Ottoman officials but their general quality improved over the period. And although insecurity existed, western Anatolia gradually became more tranquil until, by 1878, the region was on the verge of a period of unparalleled prosperity which endured until 1914.

Eastern Anatolia

In eastern Anatolia in 1800 the Ottomans had even less control than they had in the western region. In the east were three main groups of peoples: Turkish peasants, mainly in the north, Kurdish tribesmen and cultivators, principally in the south, and Armenian peasants, especially in the east. The geographical indications relate to emphasis only; in fact the three groups were intermingled almost throughout the area. It was among the predominantly Turkish population of the northern region that Ottoman authority was re-established early in the nineteenth century; in the southern and eastern areas progress was much slower, principally owing to the defiance of Ottoman authority by the Kurds.

The Kurds were a tribal people who inhabited the region from Diyarbakr eastwards to the Iranian frontier and beyond, and from Lake Van south to Sulaimaniyya. Until the end of the eighteenth century they were grouped in a number of loose confederations or amirates ruled by men selected from ancient noble lineages who were assisted by councils composed of the chiefs of the subordinate Kurdish tribes, by tiny bureaucracies and by small standing armies. In time of war the amirs could assemble the main tribal force. The authority of the amirs was not great and they ruled principally by balancing one tribe or clan against another. Several Kurdish tribes were outside the confederations altogether, although they commonly made tactical alliances with one confederation or another. The amirates were often at war with each other and fluctuated in number, size and influence. At the end of the eighteenth century there were five: Bitlis, the Jazira, Amadiyya, Julamerik and Sulaimaniyya. During the early nineteenth century another, Rawandaz, made a rapid rise to become the leading Kurdish amirate, taking over Amadiyya. Muḥammad the Blind, who, despite his name, could see perfectly well through one eye, ruled his Kurdish tribesmen with great severity and won recognition as a pasha from the Ottomans. Like the Bābāns of Sulaimaniyya the rulers of Rawandaz were able to use their position on the Iranian frontier to maintain some degree of independence by balancing between Ottoman and Iranian frontier governors.

During the first half of the nineteenth century the Ottomans broke the authority of the amirs in Kurdistan. The decisive period was during the 1830s when a three-pronged assault on Kurdistan was launched by Reshīd Pasha, former grand vizier and *Vālī* of Sivas, from Diyarbakr, by Muḥammad Pasha, the so-called Inje Bayrakdar from Mosul and by the *Vālī* of Baghdad. Sharīf Bey of Bitlis and Muḥammad the Blind were defeated by Reshīd and sent to Istanbul and the Jazira and Amadiyya were annexed to Ottoman authority in 1838. Later, Badr Khan of Botan was crushed in 1847 and the long-lived Bābāns of Sulaimaniyya finally succumbed in 1850.

The end of the Kurdish amirates was not succeeded by Ottoman authority except in a few areas such as Bitlis. In most of the Kurdish region the breakdown of the amirates was followed by anarchy as tribal chiefs struggled for power, which passed especially to the leaders of Ṣūfī orders. Among the heterodox Kurds Sufism had always been strong but in the new nineteenth-century situation they rallied to charismatic, religiously inspired military leaders, notably those from the Naqshbandī order, which had developed a new militant style. Developments in Kurdistan were similar to those in other remote areas of the Muslim world during the nineteenth and early twentieth centuries; comparable movements may be observed in Afghanistan, on the North-West Frontier of India, in Turkestan, the Caucasus, Libya, the Sudan and West Africa. It was with tribal chiefs and Ṣūfī shaykhs that the Ottomans had to deal and they never found a complete solution to the Kurdish problem before the end of the empire, although they experimented with several policies.

One possible answer to the Kurdish problem was settlement. Until the nineteenth century the great majority of Kurds were nomadic or semi-nomadic. Part of what they regarded as their lands, namely their winter pastures, they permitted to be cultivated by Armenian and Nestorian peasants, taking in return a share of the crop and demanding to be quartered free of charge in the Armenian villages during the winter. When the Ottomans endeavoured to stop this practice the Kurds justified their raids on Armenian villages by reference to their ancient rights to provision.

Under the Tanẓīmāt reforms the non-Muslim cultivators were less willing to tolerate their humble position and sought Ottoman government and European assistance to throw off Kurdish control and reduce the demands made upon them. It was Nestorian complaints which led to the expedition against Badr Khan, and Armenian peasant complaints against the exactions of the Dersim Kurds north of Diyarbakr were a persistent feature of eastern Anatolian history in the nineteenth century.

The Armenians also looked to Russian support and many committed themselves to Russia during the invasion of 1828–9 so that when the Russian Armies retired some Armenian peasants from the Erzerum region accompanied them. Many Kurds and Circassian immigrants settled on the vacant lands as well as on wastelands and former pasture lands and took up cultivation. Some of those who settled in this way, for example those in the region of Lake Van, abandoned their Kurdish identity, learned Turkish and called themselves ʿOsmānlis: others, such as those in the Tekman region near Erzerum, continued to maintain their Kurdish identity.

International warfare was another disturbing factor in eastern Anatolia. The interminable series of Ottoman–Iranian Wars on the frontier came to an end during the first half of the nineteenth century but only after they had long kept the region in a chaotic state. The 1823 Treaty of Erzerum, which ended the war of 1821–3, was no more than a truce but the Treaty of Erzerum of 1847 did mark the beginning of a long period of frontier delimitation which made it more difficult for the Kurds to exploit the differences between the two great states. The new nineteenth-century factor was the Russo-Ottoman Wars which caused great devastation in the area, not merely through the movement of troops but through the religious and social animosities which they fostered in the region. The war of 1828–9 led to temporary Russian occupation of Erzerum, in 1855–6 there was a second Russian invasion and in 1878 the Ottomans were heavily defeated and lost Kars, Ardahan and Batum. The Russian successes, as indicated in Chapter 2, had a powerful effect in rousing Armenian expectations and in promoting

Muslim hatred towards Christians in the region. The forces released were a significant factor in establishing the base for the greater unrest which overtook the region after 1878. By that time the scene was set for a major confrontation between Kurds and Armenians, a clash similar in kind but far greater in scope than the conflict in Lebanon between Druze and Maronite.

SYRIA

During the nineteenth and early twentieth centuries Europeans and others often referred to the area which now contains the modern states of Syria, Lebanon, Israel and Jordan as "Syria" and it is with that meaning that the term is used here. "Syria", in this sense, is a terminological convenience; the legend of "historic Syria" is only a legend and in 1800 the people of the area had none but local feelings of loyalty to the land they inhabited. For Ottoman government purposes the area was divided into four provinces: Aleppo, Damascus, Tripoli and Sidon. During the course of the nineteenth century the administrative divisions fluctuated but at no time was the region treated as a unity. The term "Surīyya" was coined during the nineteenth century and from 1864 was incorporated in the title of the province of Damascus, namely "Vilayet Surīyya", but in no way did the region subjected to Damascus correspond to Syria in the wider definition. The suggestion that the Ottomans divided the region for political rather than administrative reasons, that is, they hoped thereby to neutralize Syrian national feeling, is quite anachronistic.

Geographically, the divisions all run north–south. Syria consists of four geographical features which run parallel to the coast: the coastal strip and two chains of mountains which are separated by a great valley, most conspicuous at the Dead Sea, the same rift-valley which includes the Red Sea and runs through East Africa. In consequence east–west communications were difficult and limited to a few passes through the mountains. It is in those passes that one finds the recurrent names of the historic battles of the region. By contrast north–south communications were easy; the coastal strip afforded easy passage between Anatolia and Egypt as well as being the site of ports which had been centres of Mediterranean trade from the time of the Phoenicians at least. The mountains, a barrier to movement, were also a refuge. Rainfall was sufficient to maintain pasture and settled agriculture and minority groups found the hills provided shelter from governments and other enemies. Syria was, therefore, at once a great meeting-place of people moving, trading and fighting between the great population centres of Anatolia, Mesopotamia and the Nile valley, and a shelter from the forces based on those regions, a paradox summed up in the spectacle of modern Beirut, a great cosmopolitan city fought over and partitioned between particularist communities.

The communities which inhabited Syria were distinguished neither by racial nor by linguistic differences. Arabic was the daily language of the whole region and older languages survived mainly in liturgies. Separate identities were maintained partly through religious loyalties; Syria contained many religious communities – Muslim, Christian and Jewish, orthodox and heterodox. To a limited extent these religious communities possessed regional or economic characteristics; thus the towns were especially the homes of the orthodox, whether Sunnī Muslim (70 per cent of the population) or Greek Orthodox and the heterodox groups sought isolated mountain areas, for example the Maronites, the Ismāʿīlīs, the Druzes and the ʿAlawīs. But this distinction cannot be pressed too far; a Maronite community existed in Beirut and Aleppo and fiercely independent Sunnī communities lived in isolated hill areas of Palestine. The greatest number in all communities was peasants.

In its main features the economy of Syria resembled that of other regions but three aspects call for note. These are first the presence of a great open desert frontier on the east which made relations with the bedouin a major preoccupation for all Syrian governments and peoples: second, the circumstance that rainfall agriculture was much more widespread in Syria than in other parts of the Arab Near East; and third, the presence of several substantial towns rather than of any very large town with the consequence that there were several economic foci leading to the development of distinct economic regions involving the exchange of agricultural produce from the countryside for the manufactures of the towns. Some larger towns were also engaged in production, especially of silk manufactures, for a wider market within the Ottoman empire and Europe.

Syria had come under Ottoman rule in 1516. By 1800 Ottoman authority had greatly declined. The Janissary garrisons had undergone the same evolution into urban factions observed elsewhere: the *timar* system had withered away to be replaced by usually hereditary tax farmers: and without the means to support their authority the pashas were unable to enforce their will. In particular, the encroaching bedouin flouted their commands and the Wahhābīs of Arabia interrupted the passage of the annual pilgrim caravans from Damascus, responsibility for which was one of the principal concerns of the pashas of Damascus. Syria paid little to Istanbul, probably no more than a quarter of the taxes raised, and in total little more than £100,000 a year or about 20p per head of the population.

The principal arbiters of the destinies of the various parts of Syria were the local notables, whose consent was necessary to carry on government. In Aleppo in the north no dominant figure emerged; the anarchic character of Aleppine politics was determined by the contention of many factions. In Damascus, during the eighteenth century, the ʿAẓm family of local notables established the basis of a considerable power and forced the government in Istanbul to recognize their influence by making them governors of Damascus. In north Palestine a tribal leader, Shaykh Ẓāhir al-ʿUmar, became the dominant power for a time and he was succeeded in the same area by Aḥmad al-Jazzār Pasha, a Bosnian by origin whose authority eventually extended to Damascus. On Mount Lebanon the Shihāb family attained unprecedented power.

Certain features distinguished the notables of the eighteenth and early nineteenth centuries from most of their predecessors. They broke away from the old traditions of power building by alliances with other local notables and sought an independent source of power in the form of an army recruited from outsiders – bedouin, heterodox groups, Bosnians, Albanians and men from North Africa. These were mercenary soldiers who had to be paid in cash. Cash payments meant heavier taxation and the exploitation of new techniques for raising money through monopolies and trade with Europe. The demands for money set up pressures which reached down the scale. Thus the tax demands of Jazzār Pasha forced Amir Bashīr II Shihāb to squeeze the landholders of Lebanon harder and contributed to the breaking of the old alliance system on Mount Lebanon. Also, the growth of mercenary armies made the inefficient traditional forces superfluous and the diversion of revenues to support them unnecessary.

None of the new-style ruling notables sought to break away from the empire. At one time Ẓāhir threatened to do so in alliance with ʿAlī Bey of Egypt and the Russians but Ẓāhir was murdered in 1775. Neither the ʿAzms nor Jazzār sought more than the maximum of autonomy they could extract from Istanbul. Nevertheless, they posed a challenge to the Ottomans both by the possibility that they might seek independence with the support of a foreign enemy and because their activities diverted resources now urgently required for the remodelling of Ottoman imperial institutions. The new order was applied to Syria soon after the destruction of the Janissaries; in particular, in 1831 a new personal tax was levied on Muslims which led to a revolt in Damascus and the murder of the Ottoman governor and several Ottoman officials. Before authority could be restored Ottoman efforts at reform were interrupted by the Egyptian occupation of 1831–40 which itself was an important factor in bringing about change in the region.

The Egyptian government in Syria was the most efficient and comprehensive the country had seen for many years. Public security was established by relieving bedouin pressure and repressing local sources of disorder, including the enforcement of disarmament over large areas, the reform of justice and the execution of rebels. Egyptian government was also more extensive; the bureaucracy was increased by between 30,000 and 90,000 people and a substantial army was maintained, consisting of Egyptian troops and forces raised locally by conscription. A programme of public works was mounted including the building of roads, bridges and fortresses. To pay the expenses of government and carry out its policies the Egyptians increased taxation, substituting direct taxation for tax farming, and employed forced labour. The new government also fostered economic development; trade expanded and there was a considerable import of manufactured goods. To raise revenue the production of cash crops (silk, cotton and olives) under a monopoly system was encouraged. The period was characterized by a general increase of prices and a rise in urban land values. Finally, the Egyptian government brought about changes in the relations between the communities in Syria. The majority, Sunnī Muslim community, was politically unreliable in that most of its leaders remained attached to the Ottoman connection. For the expanded administration the Egyptians particularly recruited Christians and Jews; Ḥannā Baḥrī, a Greek Catholic, was head of the financial department. There was nothing new in the employment of the minorities; what was new was the scale of their employment and the other privileges given to these groups through the removal of discriminatory practices. The Egyptians relied on Christians in other ways; Amir Bashīr II Shihāb was the principal support of Egyptian rule and was employed to quell a Druze uprising.

One should not exaggerate the Egyptian patronage of the minorities. The Egyptians remained a Muslim government and used Muslim allies when they could find them; for example the rise of the ʿAbd al-Hādī family in central Palestine owed something to Egyptian support. And Christians were already improving their position through educational advance which made them more qualified to fill positions demanding especial skills. But there seems little doubt that the period of Egyptian rule did contribute to the development of communal tensions in Syria; during the occupation there was a diminution in the power and influence of the traditional Muslim notables and a rise in the status of the minorities and there was in consequence much resentment on the part of the Muslim population, illustrated by uprisings against Egyptian rule, and this resentment became very apparent in the years which followed the end of Egyptian control.

Another factor which contributed towards change in Syria was the influence of Europe which manifested itself in three ways: through religion, trade and political pressure. Religion was the oldest source of European interest in the region and derived from the existence of the Holy Places in Palestine, which had never ceased to attract a flow of pilgrims, and from the presence of various communities of Eastern Christians to which different European powers gave protection. So the Russians claimed to speak for the Greek Orthodox and the French for the Catholics, especially the Maronites of Lebanon. Further, Europeans engaged in missionary activities in the area. Catholic missions confined their attention to the welfare of Christian communities linked to Rome and the Russian effort (after the Crimean War) was directed towards the Orthodox community but missionaries from the Protestant powers, Britain, the United States and Germany, possessing no obvious community among which to work, appealed to all. For them the ultimate target was the Muslim community, but missionary work among Muslims was forbidden so they confined their efforts to the conversion of Christians to Protestantism in the disappointed hope that eventually these would be the agents of the conversion of Islam. In practice, however, their activities were more practical and focused on the provision of schools and hospitals for local Christians.

The trading connection of the European states with the Levant was an old one and at different times various groups had predominated. During the Napoleonic period, however, British traders became dominant and the trade itself underwent a change; purchases of local manufactures were reduced, there was an increase in the purchases of food and raw materials and exports of European manufactures, especially textiles, greatly increased. The extent of this change and the effect of it upon the various sectors of the Syrian economy are matters of dispute, as indicated in Chapter 1, but there is no doubt that the trade with Europe provided a new dynamic for change in Syria and one which was maintained throughout the nineteenth century as new areas of the country were brought within the orbit of the European market in consequence of improvements in communications. So, for example, the grain-producing region of the Ḥawrān which had traditionally supplied the Damascus market became orientated towards the European market after the development of road and rail links with the ports of Beirut and Haifa.

The third source of European interest was strategic and political. From the late eighteenth century the European powers manifested a greater interest in the Levant. In the war of 1768–74 Russia linked with dissidents in Egypt and Syria: France began to re-examine her traditional policy and looked to the establishment of influence in Syria to facilitate the acquisition of that region in the event of an Ottoman partition: and, with the enlargement of her Indian empire, Britain became concerned about the safety of communications through the Levant. The change in the character of British consuls in Syria during the 1830s is noticeable. The old Levant Company agents had been almost wholly concerned with trade but the new breed of consuls sought to justify their position by political activity. All European consuls endeavoured to interfere in the government of the region in the hope of advancing the interests of their own governments, or in some cases of furthering their personal ambitions or enthusiasms.

The last, and perhaps the most important factor for change in Syria, was the activities of the restored Ottoman government after 1840 and the application to Syria of the Ottoman reforms. The new Ottoman policies were not applied at once. In the early years after the restoration the Ottoman governors reversed Egyptian policies, abandoning conscription, disarmament and direct taxation, restoring the power of the ulema in education and law and giving them back control of *waqf* administration. Muslim notables were conciliated. But from the mid-1840s onwards, and especially from 1860, new policies, which closely resembled those of the Egyptians, were introduced.

The major contribution of the restored Ottoman government was the establishment of public security and the repression of local groups which opposed Ottoman power and threatened public order. As the Ottoman commander-in-chief, Nāmiq Pasha, expressed the matter: "Formerly the Turkish Government was weak in Syria and we could not expect you always to obey us, but now we are strong and if you are insubordinate I will throw you into the sea."[5] The main agency of order was the reformed Ottoman army which came to be recruited by conscription in Syria. Syria resisted the application of conscription; attempts to enforce it led to uprisings in 1843–6, 1848 and 1850–2, but after the suppression of the Damascus riots of 1860 conscription was accepted by all but the wildest areas such as those of the bedouin, Druzes and ʿAlawīs and the latter groups were also subjected to conscription by the early twentieth century. The Syrian Fifth Army had an active strength of about 20,000–30,000 with a much larger number of reservists available who were summoned when required. The rank and file was composed of Syrians, mainly Arabic speakers, and the officers were drawn from all parts of the empire. The army was supported by a gendarmerie force which was gradually recruited to replace the old irregular forces and by various police organizations. The army became the agency for the subjection of unruly groups, for the pushing back of the bedouin by the re-establishment of a fortified eastern defence line and for the socialization of large parts of the population, especially through service in other parts of the empire. It is often suggested that Ottoman government was negative but this view neglects the positive contribution which greater security made to economic development and social life. Against this, however, it must be observed that military demands also imposed great burdens on the population; in particular the Russian war of 1877 led to a massive drain of manpower from the region, to a heavy cost in taxation and forced loans, and contributed to a revival of banditry, bedouin raids and other episodes of disorder.

A second contribution of Ottoman government lay in the improvement of communications, telegraph, postal service, roads, railways and port works, many constructed with European capital. All the principal towns of Syria were linked by telegraph by the late 1860s; the carriage road from Beirut to Damascus, opened in 1863, reduced the journey time from three days to twelve hours and by 1891 all of the main towns of Syria were linked by roads suitable for wheeled traffic; and from 1888 a programme of rail construction was launched. The second half of the century also saw major developments in education, in law courts and in the administration, notably after the application of the 1864 *vilāyet* law to Syria and the creation of local councils to assist officials. The tax-farming system, however, was continued.

The new Ottoman system inevitably had its effect upon the traditional politics of the area. The consequences will be considered in greater depth in Chapter 4, but here it may be noted that the main effect of reformed Ottoman government was not so much to diminish the power of the notables as to channel that power into government. Whereas formerly factional politics in the Syrian cities had sought to hold government at arm's length and to set goals outside government, now the objects of notables were to seek government posts and use those positions to increase their wealth, status and influence. So, whereas before 1860 it is true to say that the most esteemed of the Damascus notables were those who held one of the prized religious offices, after 1860 the notable families who prospered most were those who secured posts or achieved influence with government. Such posts or influence were, of course, used for the acquisition of wealth which, in turn, could be used to maintain family and followers, although there was an increasing tendency to use it to sustain a more conspicuous style of life. Looking at the course of politics in Syria in the period after 1840 it is plain that it did not pay to oppose government except for short periods; in one town after another local factions were brought under control either by being played off against one another, as in Aleppo, or by force, as in Damascus in 1860. Even among the Druzes of the Jebel Druze those who fared best, like the Aṭrash family, were those who sought a compromise within the Ottoman government system.

In one area the reformed Ottoman government failed to restore and consolidate Ottoman authority. This was Mount Lebanon and it is instructive to look at Lebanon in some detail to see how the various factors contributed to change the development of that area. Under the traditional system the basic building blocks of the Lebanese polity were the *muqāṭaʿajīs*, who held land on effectively military tenures, could put fighters into the field and wielded local power. Through alliances and patronage they coalesced in groups under certain notables to whom they paid tribute and rendered military service. The notables, as *ḥākims* or *amīrs*, dealt with the Ottoman governors. During the seventeenth and eighteenth centuries political struggles in Lebanon centred round factional rivalries for control of these offices and the patronage they brought with them. In these struggles confessional alignments played a part but not a dominant one. Most political alliances bestrode confessional groups.

During the course of the eighteenth century the situation in Lebanon changed owing to three factors. The first was the rise of the Maronite Church as a more significant political factor with improved organization, a more powerful position for the higher clergy, better financial resources and greater independence of the *muqāṭaʿajīs*. Inevitably, the influence of the Church tended to give a more confessional character to Lebanese politics. The second was the expansion of the Maronite community itself from its original base in north Lebanon southwards into Druze areas where Maronite peasants rented land from Druze landlords but looked for guidance to the Maronite Church. The third factor was the rise of the Shihāb family (originally Sunnī Muslim), many members of which embraced Christianity in the late eighteenth century and formed a close alliance with the Church. In their rise to power the Shihābs defeated *muqāṭaʿajīs*, seized their holdings, giving some to their own followers but retaining others to give themselves a greater degree of independence. Until 1825 the confessional factor was obscured by the dependence of the Shihābs on their alliance with the great Druze family of the Janbalāṭs (Jumblatts) but after the defeat of the Janbalāṭs the Shihābs had no rival and the power of Bashīr II was enhanced by Egyptian support.

Even so, before 1840 communal rivalries were not the main force in Lebanese politics. The old factions, with their antique labels of Qaysī and Yamanī, Yazbakī and Janbalāṭī persisted: Maronite *muqāṭaʿajīs* opposing the demands of the Shihābs and the Church sought alliances with their Druze counterparts; and when Bashīr II fell it was as a result of a Maronite uprising against an Egyptian order to disarm the community and fears of conscription. In the end the Maronite Church itself turned against him.

The effect of the change in the balance and organization of the communities became evident after 1840 when the problem was exacerbated by the efforts of European consuls to intervene on behalf of the communities they favoured and the attempts of the Ottoman officials to re-establish Ottoman control by playing off one group against another. The Ottomans hoped to break the power of the Lebanese notables and replace them with Ottoman officials and direct rule from Sidon. Communal clashes took place in 1841 and 1845 and changes were introduced which were designed to achieve a *de facto* separation between the Maronite north and the Druze south but the Maronite expansion had made this solution difficult. Another device was the introduction of representative councils. These efforts were nullified by the great disturbances of 1858. Beginning as a struggle of Maronite peasants against Maronite *muqāṭaʿajīs* in the north, the uprising spread into Druze areas where it assumed a communal form; Maronite peasants supported by their priests against Druze landlords. The Druzes retaliated violently and effectively. In June 1860 the Maronites were heavily defeated, thousands were killed or died of starvation and up to 100,000 became refugees. In July the communal disturbances spread to Damascus where between 5,000 and 10,000 Christians were massacred. Although efforts have been made to explain the Damascus massacre in terms of factional rivalries and economic changes there was also a substantial element of Muslim popular hostility to the new pretensions of Christians shown by their reluctance to accept former disabilities. Similar, albeit smaller, anti-Christian riots had taken place in Aleppo in 1850 and Nāblus in 1856. In each case these riots were directed against Christians and not Jews, who maintained a much less conspicuous demeanour.

The Damascus uprising turned the scale in favour of European intervention in the form of a French army; Napoleon III was obliged to appease outraged French Catholic opinion. Although order was restored before the arrival of the French troops and severe punishments were given to those held responsible for the disturbances, whether by sins of commission or ommission, France insisted on major governmental reforms in Lebanon. Under the new system, introduced in 1861 and revised in 1864, Mount Lebanon (not including Beirut, the Biqāʿ, Tripoli or Sidon) was to be autonomous under international guarantee with a Christian governor assisted by an elected council on which all communities were represented (4 Maronites, 3 Druzes, 2 Greek Orthodox, and 1 each from the Greek Catholic, Sunnī and Shīʿī communities). The system of *muqāṭaʿajīs* was abolished and taxation was severely limited.

In retrospect it is clear that the 1861 settlement began the process by which Lebanon became an independent state, and to some extent the 1861 solution indicated the type of polity that would emerge within that state, namely power sharing on a communal basis and its corollary of a very limited role for government. From the beginning the Maronites sought to preserve and enhance their independence, even refusing to participate in elections to the Ottoman Parliament in 1876 and 1908 lest this action should jeopardize their autonomy. The system was also protected by Britain and France who endeavoured to look after the Druzes and Maronites respectively. From the Ottoman point of view the 1861 settlement was only a temporary reverse, however, and they hoped for the increase of Ottoman influence and the eventual restoration, under favourable circumstances, of full Ottoman control, an event which took place in 1914. And the Ottomans were correct in their view that Mount Lebanon, although possible as an autonomous entity, was not viable as an independent state without access to the sea and greater resources. From the beginning the resistance of the council to any increase of taxation made the province dependent upon an Ottoman subsidy and the reluctance to consent to a sufficient military force obliged the governors to call upon Ottoman Muslim forces from outside to suppress disorders. The instability of the Lebanese settlement was a powerful factor in causing men to look for new, more radical political solutions in the late nineteenth and early twentieth centuries.

IRAQ

It is even more anachronistic to write of the history of Iraq in the nineteenth century than to write of that of Syria. Although the term "Iraq" was an old one it did not correspond to the area of the modern state and was not used to designate any of the Ottoman administrative divisions of the area. The Ottomans divided the area into provinces or subordinate units based upon Baghdad, Basra, Mosul, Kirkuk and, occasionally, Sulaimaniyya. Part of northern Iraq fell under the governor of Diyarbakr. Although the governor of Baghdad was often accorded some pre-eminence, comparable to that of the governor of Damascus in Syria, this was a military and administrative convenience rather than any recognition of the unity of the area; to group Basra with Baghdad made some sense economically and some unified control of border relations with Iran was also desirable. Nor did Europeans perceive any unity in the area. The old term "Mesopotamia" referred only to the area between the Tigris and Euphrates and excluded the north and south of the country; the favourite British designation was Turkish Arabia, indicating an inability to see any clear dividing line between Arabia and Iraq, a view which was evidently shared by those who inhabited the area.

Geographically, Iraq consisted of two distinct parts: the mountainous areas of the north and east, which provided suitable conditions for pasture and rainfall cultivation; and the plains of the centre and south where, as with the Egyptian Nile, the Tigris and Euphrates rivers carved a belt of land cultivable by irrigation from the desert. On the east the Zagros mountains formed the frontier with Iran, although in the seventeenth and eighteenth centuries this frontier had several times been called into question in wars between Iran and the Ottomans and as recently as 1775–9 the Iranians had occupied Basra. Not until the 1847 Treaty of Erzerum was the frontier defined, although it was not delineated with precision. On the west Iraq merged into the Syrian and Arabian deserts: the inroads of nomadic Arab tribes from the desert had been one of the most conspicuous features of the political history of the region; and regulating the activities of the tribes one of the greatest preoccupations of its rulers.

The population distribution reflected the geography of Iraq; in the mountainous areas lived non-Arab peoples, predominantly Kurds; and in the plains the population was overwhelmingly Arabic speaking. Only in the towns, notably Baghdad and Kirkuk, was there a substantial Turkish-speaking population. The countryside was the home of the tribes. Both the Kurdish and Arab populations were largely tribal in social structure. The great, loose tribal confederations of the ʿAnaza, the Muntafiq and the Shammar dominated Lower Iraq. A substantial portion – between one-third and one-half – of the population was nomadic or partly nomadic, but many of the Arabs who had settled and taken up cultivation retained their tribal structure and allegiances. Settled agriculture in 1800 was confined to only a few areas, of which the most significant were the areas north of Baghdad, lying between the rivers, and that in the south around Basra. The urban population was small, no more than 150,000. An important division was religious: Iraq was the only major area of the Ottoman empire where a majority of the population was not Sunnī but Shīʿī. South of Baghdad the overwhelming majority of the Arab population was Shīʿī and the area contained the two most cherished Shīʿī towns of Najaf and Karbala. In Baghdad itself there had already appeared in 1800 the distinction between the predominantly Sunnī right bank and the Shīʿī left bank of the Tigris, although the great Shīʿī shrine at Kāẓimiyya was itself on the right bank. North of Baghdad on the Euphrates the Arab population was predominantly Sunnī as were the northern mountains; Shīʿī Kurds were few in number. Unlike Syria, however, non-Muslim groups were small in number and politically unimportant, although the old-established Jewish community played a substantial role in commerce and in financial administration, and Assyrian Christians were prominent in the affairs of Mosul.

In Iraq, as elsewhere, the institutions of Ottoman rule had greatly changed by 1800. The *timar* system had never been fully applied to Iraq; there were no *timars* in the south, only a few in the Baghdad region and most were concentrated in the north, around Mosul and Kirkuk. By 1800, however, few were left. The Janissary garrisons had gone through the familiar evolution as members of the eighteen regiments had acquired local interests; in earlier centuries they had been a dominant political factor but in the latter part of the eighteenth century their power to control events in Baghdad was waning. Iraq paid little revenue to Istanbul and Ottoman profits were derived from the payments made by officials for appointments in Iraq and such tribute as they sent to Istanbul after appointment. The system encouraged a rapid turnover of officials, but during the eighteenth century good evidence of declining Ottoman control is to be seen in the appointment of pashas for long periods and the infrequent payments of tribute. More and more the Ottoman government was ready to settle for a strong ruler who would pay tribute regularly and look after the frontier with Iran; for the rest he could be left to his own devices.

Power in Iraq resided in a variety of groups of local notables. One group was the shaykhs of powerful tribes. It is wrong to think that the tribes were independent of the state. It is true that the state had no control over the internal affairs of tribes but it did have a say in the leadership of tribes. It is an oft-repeated truism that competition is a prominent feature of intra-tribal relations and competitors for tribal leadership perceived recognition by the state to be a significant factor in enhancing their claims and one for which they were willing to pay either in services or money. Tribes paid more taxes and tribute than is often realized; for example, in July 1813 the shaykh of the Khazaʿil paid 100,000 piastres plus a quantity of rice in return for confirmation of his position by government. It followed that the shaykhs were required to maintain agents at the appropriate seat of government and to attempt to influence the direction of political events in a manner favourable to their interests. In its turn government sought to influence tribal affairs by alliances, a policy of divide and rule and sporadic coercion of vulnerable groups.

Other groups of notables had an urban base, notably those whose influence was based upon Janissary support, or bureaucratic influence, or trade (merchants being in a position to finance government activities) or religion. The ulema were as important in Iraq as elsewhere, both for their role in legal and educational affairs and especially because of their position as the custodians of the great shrines, including the Shīʿī shrines mentioned above and Sunnī shrines. In Baghdad was the centre of the Qādiriyya order maintained by members of the Gaylānī family, the Naqībs of Baghdad, and powerful voices in the legitimization of any activity of government.

From these various sources and one other emerged a number of families which controlled the various parts of Iraq in 1800. In Sulaimaniyya was the influential Bābān family: in Mosul the very large Jalīlī family controlled the district from 1726 until 1834 and in Baghdad were the Georgian Mamluks of the household of Sulaymān the Great. The rise of the Georgian Mamluks was the leading feature of the political history of Iraq during the late eighteenth century. They were men from the Caucasus, mainly Christian slaves converted to Islam, who entered the service of the pashas of Baghdad as bureaucrats, who possessed no local loyalties and therefore were deemed to be more reliable than locals. They subsequently formed a military corps of some 2,000 and in 1747 took control of the government of the pashalik. Ottoman attempts to remove the Georgian Mamluks failed and the Porte was compelled to acquiesce in their rule which reached its apogee under Sulaymān the Great, 1780–1802. The Mamluks broke the independent power of the Janissaries; the last major intervention of the Janissary Agha in politics was in the struggle for the succession to Sulaymān in 1802. They created their own military force composed of the detribalized ʿUqayl Arabs, Lurs, Kurds and tribal levies. For some elements of their forces they purchased modern weapons and employed European instructors to train them in disciplined tactics. They endeavoured to foster trade and the improvement of communications and they sought links with European powers, particularly with Britain. These developments especially characterized the reign of Dā'ūd Pasha (1816–31), the last of the Georgian Mamluk rulers of Baghdad, whose policies in many ways resemble those of Muḥammad ʿAlī of Egypt, albeit in a slight and superficial fashion, and it was only Dā'ūd among the Mamluks who seems to have contemplated breaking away from Ottoman domination and endeavouring to create an independent state in Baghdad and Basra – he had no control over the Kurdish areas.

The Mamluk regime was brought to an end in 1831 when Ottoman authority was restored. One major factor in the fall of Dā'ūd was the increased Ottoman determination and ability to restore authority over the provinces of the empire. A second factor was the opposition to Mamluk rule within Iraq from several groups of notables and particularly from the Turkish bureaucratic families whose employment had been restricted by Mamluk policies. Several writers have also pointed to the divisions among the Mamluks themselves and it is true that the absence of any stable system of succession led to factional disputes which were a feature of the period 1802–16, when the average length of rule by the pashas was three and a half years and opportunities were provided for Ottoman interventions to influence the succession in 1810 and 1816. But under Dā'ūd factional disputes were repressed and it does not seem that this was an important cause of the Mamluk collapse. The major cause of the fall of Dā'ūd appears to have been natural; the floods and plague which wasted Baghdad in 1831. In 1830 Dā'ūd had treated an Ottoman attempt to dismiss him with disdain, murdering the envoy who was sent: in 1831 he had no resources with which to oppose the new Ottoman Pasha, ʿAlī Riżā.

In the following years Ottoman rule was slowly confirmed in Iraq. Direct rule over Mosul was restored in 1834; plague and a loss of their traditional skill in the management of local groups having brought about the failure of Jalīlī rule. In the same decade an Ottoman force marched through Kurdistan, from Diyarbakr to Rawandaz, pacifying the tribes and reducing the power of the chiefly state of Rawandaz itself. The Bābāns of Sulaimaniyya submitted in 1850 and the independent power of the Shīʿī *mujtahids* of Karbala and Najaf was abridged by force in 1843 and 1852–4 respectively. There was no quick solution to the problem of the Arab tribes; the Ottomans were obliged to rely upon the traditional means of tribal management and only in the long term could they hope that the gradual improvement of their powers of coercion combined with the effects of reforms in government and economic development would ease the tribal problem. Both the Arab tribes and the Kurds remained a problem for the provincial governments, although settlement, education and military employment, in the army, gendarmerie and in the irregular Ḥamīdiyya battalions founded in 1885, alleviated the Kurdish problem.

The new institutions of Ottoman rule were the army and the reconstructed bureaucracy. The *Niẓām-i Jedīd* reforms had been applied to Iraq nominally in 1826 when the Janissary regiments were converted into eighteen *Niẓāmī* battalions. These forces, with the new Ottoman troops which were introduced, formed the nucleus of what was to become the Ottoman Sixth Army. As time went on and conscription was extended to various parts of Iraq the Sixth Army became more distinctively local in rank and file and Ottoman in its officers. The process was a slow one, however; conscription was applied to Mosul in 1835 and to Lower Iraq in 1870, although there was little attempt to apply it to the tribes. The formal adoption of a territorial system did not take place until 1885. The pattern of recruitment ensured that the Sixth Army was much slower to be Arabicized than the Fifth Army in Syria: by contrast, Iraqis, including Arabs, were much more ready than Syrians to choose a military career as officers and Iraqis formed by far the largest portion of the Arab officers of the Ottoman army. The Sixth Army, poorly paid and equipped, remained something of a Cinderella force, however. As in Syria the army was supplemented by a gendarmerie which was used increasingly in tribal operations as well as for the security of roads.

The bureaucracy also provides some slight contrast with that of Syria. Only the highest appointments were filled by appointment from Istanbul; most posts below that of *vālī* were filled from local applicants, especially Turkish speakers from Kirkuk. A number of Caucasian recruits also entered the bureaucracy, preserving the Mamluk tradition, and some notable families began to specialize in administration at an early date, including the Jalīlīs of Mosul and the Bābāns of Sulaimāniyya. In the north the Ottomans were compelled to rely upon Kurds, in particular those who had been educated in Ottoman Turkish. Despite the preponderance of local officials the introduction of men from outside did bring some new ideas, particularly Western ideas, into Iraq.

Down to the late 1860s Iraq remained a sleepy backwater of the Ottoman empire, reasonably quiet by comparison with its turbulent past, and paying revenue with commendable regularity. From that time onwards, however, Iraq seemed to change gear, both in terms of economic and governmental activity.

The governmental change of gear is associated with the introduction of the new *vilāyet* system and the governorship of Midḥat Pasha (1869–72). Midḥat fostered an active policy in several spheres, including education, land reform, communications, economic development, conscription, municipal improvement – Baghdad was transformed during his rule – and the extension of Ottoman power into Arabia. The economic shift is seen in an expansion of agricultural production and a switch towards production for the international market. Iraq became a cereal exporter; and the value of her grain exports increased twenty times during the forty years before 1914. Also Basra became the date capital of the world with exports worth £500,000 a year by 1914. Over the same period Iraq increased her imports from outside; textiles, coal, coffee, tea and sugar.

The development of communications is an important indicator of change. In 1835 steam navigation had been commenced on the Tigris and Euphrates and a regular service was eventually established. The telegraph system was extended through Iraq in the 1860s and a postal system in 1885. Roads were built and just before 1914 railways at last made their appearance in Iraq with the beginnings of construction of the Baghdad railway. The port of Basra was developed. By comparison with Egypt, however, there was no major development of irrigation; not until 1910 was a comprehensive plan for the control of the waters of the Tigris and Euphrates drawn up and implementation begun; and only in 1913 was the first major element in the system, the Hindiyya barrage on the lower Euphrates, opened. The slowness of the Ottomans to realize the agricultural potential of Iraq affords a useful example of the contrast between military-led modernization and the economic inspiration characteristic of Egypt after 1841.

Land reform also assisted in changing the structure of Iraq. Midḥat introduced the 1858 Ottoman land law into Iraq. The 1858 law established a category of *tapu* land, that is, state land on a perpetual, transferable registered lease. In introducing it into Iraq Midḥat hoped to create a class of industrious peasant proprietors who, most importantly, would also be taxpayers. But, although the *tapu* system worked quite well in areas where there were already peasant proprietors, it did not work well in Iraq where the notion of peasant proprietorship conflicted with established tribal custom and concepts of communal landholding. Land was registered not in the name of tribesmen or peasants, who feared registration was merely a cover for additional taxation, or, even worse, conscription, but in the name of tribal shaykhs, former tax farmers or merchants. This unintended result had the effect of enhancing and altering the power of the tribal shaykhs by turning them into landlords. When the government realized what had happened it endeavoured to reverse the process with some success; by 1914 80 per cent of land in Iraq was on the old *mīrī* tenure and only a small part was *tapu*. Nevertheless, the reform did have an important effect in further weakening the bonds between shaykh and tribesman, which had already been loosened by the assumption of the role of tax farmer by some shaykhs, and by helping to incorporate the tribal leaders into the Ottoman system; they lived more in towns, sent their sons to Ottoman schools and engaged themselves in the new administrative councils. One would not wish to exaggerate the change in tribal structure; as noted above the Ottomans attempted to reverse the policy when they observed its effects and in some tribes relations were unaltered. But in the Muntafiq tribe, the most important confederation in the Basra region, a major change was accomplished and the Saʿdūn family moved measurably into the Ottoman system.

Other factors also affected the tribal structure, including communications, urbanization and irrigation; the Hindiyya barrage had the incidental effect of removing much of the isolation and inaccessibility of the Khazaʿil Arabs. Over the period there was a substantial decline in nomadism; in 1867 35 per cent of the population were nomadic, by 1905 only 17 per cent and by 1930 this had sunk to 7 per cent. Settled cultivators increased from 41 per cent in 1867 to 59 per cent in 1905 and 68 per cent in 1930.

The most dynamic area was the urban sector, the seat of government and the home of educational development. As in Syria and Egypt there were two spheres of educational development apart from the traditional religious education. The government system consisted of free primary schools in each subdistrict capital, secondary schools in certain larger towns and a number of military schools. Beyond the secondary level education required a move to Istanbul or some other centre. The private system was operated chiefly by foreign missionary organizations, Catholic, Protestant and Jewish; possibly the best school in Baghdad was that founded in 1865 by the Alliance Israélite Universelle and its facilities undoubtedly assisted the continued advance of the Iraqi Jewish community. Educational advance was, therefore, chiefly at the secondary levels and was especially designed to produce government servants, but within these limits it was successful and achieved a measurable growth in urban literacy from an estimated 0.5 per cent in 1850 to between 5 and 10 per cent in 1900.

The changes in Iraq had affected the position of the notable families of the region. Some groups had risen in esteem and influence notably the minorities and, in particular, the Jews who had specialized in international trade and finance. The Sāsūn family, whose fortunes were founded by the chief banker to Dāʾūd, the last Mamluk ruler, developed international connections stretching from Bombay to London. Muslim merchants had also increased their standing, although they were active primarily in local trade. The successful career of Muḥammad Chalabī Sabunjī in Mosul (1895–1911) illustrates what a merchant could achieve. The other groups who had risen were those who had secured places in the Ottoman bureaucracy and administrative councils; especially the Turkish speakers of Kirkuk but also other families. And those who had declined in influence and prestige were the group which had been most eminent in the early nineteenth century, that is those men whose status depended upon the possession of religious office or influence and who were descended from families of Arabian, Persian or Syrian origin settled in Iraq for three centuries and more. In 1894 there were officially twenty-one Sunnī *ashrāf* from five families: the Alūsīs, Gaylānīs, Ḥaydarīs, Jamīls and Sināwīs. It was an evolution reminiscent of that which had taken place in Syria during the same period and the movement had a similar significance which will be considered in Chapter 4. At the end of the nineteenth century, however, Ottoman rule in Iraq was more firmly based than it had ever been.

EGYPT

At the end of the eighteenth century Egypt was in a state of political anarchy. Ottoman authority had dwindled to little more than a symbolic presence and Mamluk factions fought for influence and the spoils. No faction, however, could prevail; for a time it seemed that the ruthless ʿAlī Bey, who recruited a mercenary force financed by confiscations, monopolies and trade, might succeed in establishing a strong government once more in Egypt but after his death (1773) and that of his killer, Abu'l Dhahab (1775) no Mamluk achieved similar stature. The weakness of government permitted inroads of bedouin from the desert who roamed unmolested through the fertile Delta.

The French invasion of 1798 greatly weakened the defeated Mamluks but it did not establish a strong government throughout Egypt; French power was limited to Cairo and the Delta, and Upper Egypt remained in the hands of the Mamluks. Within Cairo French rule was detested and popular hostility was shown in major uprisings.

The removal of the French in 1802, followed by the British withdrawal in 1803, opened the way for a fresh contest of power in which the participants were the Ottomans, represented by the pashas Khusraw and Khūrshīd, the Mamluks, still divided into factions of which the most prominent were those of al-Bardīsī, al-Alfī and Ibrāhīm Bey, and an Albanian soldier named Muḥammad ʿAlī. Muḥammad ʿAlī (*c.* 1770–1849) had arrived in Egypt in 1801 as second-in-command of the Kavalla contingent of the 6,000 Albanian troops in the 10,000-strong Ottoman force sent to collaborate with the British forces against the French. In 1803 he became leader of the Albanian contingent, which was the most powerful military force in Egypt, and chief rival of the Ottoman pasha, whom he deposed in 1805 with the support of the ulema and people of Cairo. In 1807 Muḥammad ʿAlī gained recognition as governor of Egypt from the Porte and also defeated a British invasion. Muḥammad ʿAlī was then free to attend to his last rivals for power, the Mamluks. As it happened the two most dangerous of the Mamluk leaders, ʿUthmān al-Bardīsī and Muḥammad al-Alfī had died in 1806–7 and the Mamluk numbers had been considerably reduced through death and the inability to replenish their numbers in their former fashion by recruiting from the Crimea and Caucasus and other Ottoman territories. They had come to rely increasingly on the unreliable support of bedouin irregulars. Between 1809 and 1812 Muḥammad ʿAlī destroyed Mamluk power, the most dramatic event being his massacre of a considerable number of Mamluks in the citadel of Cairo on 1 March 1811. By 1812 Muḥammad ʿAlī was supreme throughout Egypt and able to embark upon a comprehensive programme of modernization.

As in the Ottoman empire the first steps in modernization involved the rebuilding of the army and the administration. Muḥammad ʿAlī's early experiences had convinced him of the value of European-style disciplined forces. His problem was to find the men to fill the ranks. The older source of military manpower in Egypt, namely the Caucasus, was closed to him by the Russian occupation and recruitment within the Ottoman empire was difficult. His Albanians refused to accept discipline and were politically unreliable; from time to time they even shot at the pasha. The bedouin were unsuitable except as irregular cavalry. Muḥammad ʿAlī looked at a fresh source of recruits, slaves from the Sudan. Between 1820 and 1824 he brought 20,000 to Egypt for training but no less than 17,000 died and Muḥammad ʿAlī abandoned the idea. Instead he took the unprecedented step of conscripting resentful Arabic-speaking Egyptian Muslim peasants and these, with officers drawn from groups which originated in the Turkish areas of the empire and in the Caucasus and who are usually termed Turko-Circassian, became the main strength of his army. Recruitment began in 1822 and with the help of European (mainly French) instructors six disciplined regiments were ready by 1824. The new *Niẓām-i Jedīd* regiments proved their value in the Morea campaign and he rapidly increased their numbers to a peak of 38 regiments (115,000 men) in 1840. By then Muḥammad ʿAlī also had a well-trained European artillery corps, an engineer corps, 10,000 regular cavalry and a large number of irregulars, and the largest navy in the eastern Mediterranean (having more than replaced the vessels sunk at Navarino). All in all Muḥammad ʿAlī had by far the strongest military force in the Near East. It was also a very burdensome force to support for it meant something approaching 4 per cent of the population of Egypt were under arms, or 12 per cent of the population of working age, a proportion far in excess of that common in European countries at the time. The costs of this force in money and manpower go a very long way to explaining the policies of Muḥammad ʿAlī.

After Muḥammad ʿAlī's defeat at the hands of the European powers in 1840–1 there was a dramatic change in the position of the army, for it was reduced by treaty to 18,000. Although Muḥammad ʿAlī was able to evade the restrictions to some extent and in 1848 his son Ibrāhīm reintroduced conscription and increased the army to 70,000, the demands of defence never again imposed a similar burden during the nineteenth century. Under his successor, ʿAbbās Ḥilmī I, the army was again reduced in size and when it was raised to 80,000 under Ismāʿīl Egypt's resources were much greater and able to support the burden more easily, although it still proved to be a very considerable weight on Egyptian finance. But, by comparison with the Ottoman empire, Egypt was not subject to the same pressures of military-led modernization after 1841 and a different, economic impulse took the place of defence.

To mobilize the resources to support his army and to replace the loose Mamluk system Muḥammad ʿAlī was obliged to create a new administrative system. At the centre he established a system of executive departments corresponding to ministries; by 1837 there were six such departments dealing with the Navy, War, Finance, Industry, Education and Foreign Affairs. Others were added by his successors: Interior (1857), Public Works (1864), Justice (1872) and Agriculture (1875). In each department the minister was advised by a council and Muḥammad ʿAlī also formed a council of officials and notables to advise himself. There is, however, no suggestion of anything corresponding to a Cabinet under Muḥammad ʿAlī; the pasha kept firm control of major decisions and his ministers were essentially executives. Only in the 1870s can one see some degree of ministerial independence emerging. More significant than his changes in the central administration were his innovations in provincial administration because Muḥammad ʿAlī laid the foundations of the system which prevailed in Egypt thereafter. From 1824 onwards he divided Egypt into provinces, districts and subordinate divisions down to the villages and urban quarters. All were placed under a central office of inspectorate and the whole provided a highly centralized scheme of administration. Under Muḥammad ʿAlī the central administration and the provinces were placed exclusively under Turko-Circassians; Arabic speakers served only in the lower divisions. Only in the 1850s were a small number of Arabic-speaking Egyptians appointed to head provinces and more rarely ministries. Between 1849 and 1879 there were only eight Egyptian ministers and more important posts were held by Armenians and Europeans. The whole military and civilian bureaucracy was dominated by Turko-Circassians right down to the British occupation and the Muḥammad ʿAlī family held a controlling position.

One of the striking features of the new provincial administrative system which differentiates it from previous systems is the extensive duties of the provincial officials. They were responsible for conscription, taxation, local security, public works and a range of economic functions including the organization of labour corps, supervision of cultivation, distribution of seeds and the direction of industrial development. The very considerable stress upon economic management distinguishes the Egyptian system from that which obtained at the same period in the Ottoman empire and underlines the different impulse towards modernization.

To supply trained officers and administrators Muḥammad ʿAlī was obliged to undertake educational reforms. In the longer term he looked to the establishment of modern educational institutions in Egypt but his needs were more urgent and he turned to Europe. The first student mission to Europe was sent in 1813 and substantial missions were sent to France from 1826 onwards. The students stayed for five or six years, the majority were Turks and went for military training but an increasing number were sent to acquire skills which they could teach on their return to Egypt. The Turko-Circassians taught in the military schools and Egyptians taught elsewhere. Within Egypt Muḥammad ʿAlī concentrated on the establishment of a small number of institutions which would offer a modern curriculum to the élite who were needed for the army and administration; virtually nothing was done for primary education despite the recommendation of an 1834 commission that fifty primary schools should be established and this sector was left to the ulema. No attempt was made to link the modern and traditional sectors. There were specialized schools for military officers from 1816, for accountants (1826), for civilian administrators (1829 and 1834), for medicine and related topics (1827–34) and for languages (1835). The language school also produced translations, especially from French. It is indicative of the origins of Muḥammad ʿAlī's educational reforms that until 1837, when the Department of Education was created, education was administered by the War Department. After 1841, when the army was reduced, there was also retrenchment in education. The pattern of educational development established by Muḥammad ʿAlī was continued under his successors. Despite an ambitious plan in 1867 to reform the traditional schools and integrate them with the modern sector, little was done for primary education and the emphasis continued to be on secondary and higher education in Europe and in foreign schools established in Egypt, of which there were 146 by 1878. In government schools the object was still to train officers and bureaucrats. Between 1865 and 1875 63 per cent of graduates of the so-called civilian schools went into the army and 19 per cent into the civil bureaucracy. The Azhar, the home of traditional Islamic higher education, remained unreformed but a modern teacher training college was opened in 1873.

Muḥammad ʿAlī's modernization of the army, administration and educational system had to be paid for and this required both gaining control of a larger share of Egypt's resources for the state and also increasing the total of those resources. The main source of wealth was agriculture and in this area Muḥammad ʿAlī made major changes which may be considered in relation to tenure and products.

At the beginning of the nineteenth century most land in Egypt was held under the *iltizām* system as tax farms, often hereditary. From Muḥammad ʿAlī's viewpoint there were two things wrong with the *iltizām* system. First, it alienated most of Egypt's revenues to his enemies, the Mamluks; and second, it was rapidly collapsing. Insecurity, the French administration and the flight of peasants had weakened the system to the point where *multazims* could not raise enough money from their lands to pay the taxes due and were returning their tax farms to the Treasury. In 1814 Muḥammad ʿAlī abolished the *iltizām* system and recovered direct control for the state. A substantial amount of land had been converted into *waqf* land to avoid taxation; Muḥammad ʿAlī left genuine charitable *waqfs* alone but resumed control of the bogus *waqfs*. For some time Muḥammad ʿAlī administered land directly but he found this to be unworkable and began to regrant land to his family and followers as *chiftlik*, especially from the 1830s. At first the grant related only to the government share of the produce, but as time went on the new landholdings tended to be transformed into a form of ownership, so establishing a system approaching private property in Egypt, dominated by large landowners, in particular the Muḥammad ʿAlī family which, by 1845, held nearly one-fifth of the land of Egypt. Military and civil officials, rural notables and tribal chiefs also became substantial beneficiaries from the new arrangements.

Muḥammad ʿAlī made considerable efforts to extend the area of cultivation by special inducements, for example tax-free tenancies for peasants, to cultivate waste land. In addition he encouraged the repair of old canals and dikes and the construction of new works. By these means and through the growth of population the area under cultivation increased by about one-third under Muḥammad ʿAlī's rule. Muḥammad ʿAlī also encouraged more intensive cultivation by the construction of irrigation works in the Delta (involving the employment of very large gangs of labourers) in order to make water available for an increased production of summer crops – rice, sugar, indigo and, above all, cotton. Muḥammad ʿAlī encouraged improvements in these crops, notably the introduction of long-staple cotton suitable for the European market and they became a major source of revenue. In particular, cotton came to dominate Egypt's export trade and indirectly the whole economy of Egypt. By 1849 cotton already accounted for some 31 per cent of total exports.

The profits from these cash crops formed a substantial part of the revenues of Muḥammad ʿAlī. Until 1841 the pasha took his profit through a system of monopolies according to which producers were obliged to sell their produce to government at a fixed price, well below market price. Muḥammad ʿAlī then resold the produce and pocketed the difference. The system was applied especially to cash crops for export but monopolies on crops grown for local consumption were also established. The system was resented by producers and Muḥammad ʿAlī was often obliged to use coercion to compel cultivators to grow crops which were relatively unprofitable to them. After 1841 monopolies were made illegal when the Anglo-Ottoman commercial treaty was applied to Egypt and Muḥammad ʿAlī was compelled to find other means of extracting the surplus for the state. This he accomplished by switching to taxation: government revenue increased from just under £E3.0 million in 1842 to £E4.2 million in 1846.

Muḥammad ʿAlī's industrial policy was ambitious but much less successful. The pasha established industrial monopolies, acting like an entrepreneur in the domestic system, supplying raw material and buying the finished product at a fixed price. More importantly, Muḥammad ʿAlī established new factory industries especially those concerned with military needs, and food and other primary product processing and including wool, cotton- and silk-mills, sugar refineries, iron foundries, arms, glass, paper, leather and shipbuilding. Excluding domestic handicrafts it has been calculated that up to 200,000 workers were employed in industry, although this figure exaggerates the strength of the industrial sector as 40,000 were in building and 80,000 were weavers who worked in a traditional fashion but in large workshops. These industries were never profitable and Muḥammad ʿAlī spent an estimated £12 million with no permanent return.

The reasons for the failure of the Egyptian industrial experiment under Muḥammad ʿAlī include the climate, which created problems for machinery, the lack of skilled management and a skilled labour force, want of capital and, above all, the absence of any suitable native power source; Muḥammad ʿAlī's factories used animal power. Egyptian historians have disputed this view and contended that the industries were profitable or on the verge of profitability and that the main cause of their failure was British and other European competition in textiles and other manufactures to which they were exposed after 1841; a continuation of protection for a longer period, they argue, might have enabled Egyptian industry to achieve a breakthrough which would have changed the entire course of Egyptian and possibly Middle Eastern economic history. Their arguments, however, are not convincing. The appearance of profitability in some industries seems to be the result of inadequate accounting techniques and there is good evidence that the industrial decline began in the late 1830s before any exposure to European competition.

During the reign of Muḥammad ʿAlī there was a very considerable increase in Egyptian trade; exports rose from £200,000 in 1800 to £2 million in 1840 and imports increased in the same proportion. There was also a change in the direction of trade; at the end of the eighteenth century more than half of Egypt's trade had been conducted with the Ottoman empire and only 14 per cent with Europe; by 1823 the Ottoman proportion was down to one-seventh and Europe dominated the trade of Egypt. And there was a major change in the control of trade; Egyptian trade was now in the hands of government. In 1836 it was calculated that 95 per cent of exports and 40 per cent of imports were on government account. This characteristic was the consequence of Muḥammad ʿAlī's monopoly system; like ʿAlī Bey before him he had always looked to foreign trade to provide him with a large cash income. During the Napoleonic Wars he had made a fortune selling grain to British forces in the Mediterranean and he continued the system through the sale of cash crops after 1815. The application of the Anglo-Ottoman treaty of 1838 to Egypt after 1841 did not change the direction of Egyptian development. The new duties on imports and exports were, in fact, higher than those charged previously. It is claimed that the end of the monopoly system opened Egypt to foreign traders but it seems likely that it merely facilitated a development which was well under way before 1841.

There were significant developments in communications in Egypt, notably in the use of steamboats on the Nile and on canals. The opening of the Maḥmūdiyya Canal in 1819 linking Cairo and Alexandria, greatly assisted the growth of the latter city. From a population of 15,000 in 1805 Alexandria rose to 150,000 in 1847, including a large foreign element. There was no railway construction under Muḥammad ʿAlī; that initiative was reserved for the second half of the nineteenth century.

Under Muḥammad ʿAlī Egypt underwent a major change. Politically it was transformed from a condition of anarchy into a strong centralized state which possessed unprecedented power over the lives of its citizens. It has been estimated that at one time in rent and taxes Muḥammad ʿAlī secured over 80 per cent of the agricultural production of Egypt and that one-third of the entire Egyptian labour force was employed, mainly unwillingly, on public works or in the army. Travellers wrote of villages denuded of able-bodied men. Economically, Egypt entered a period of rapid growth based upon the production of cash crops for sale abroad. Socially, Egypt changed much less but some elements of a modern educational system were created, important changes took place in the legal system, especially with the development of Mixed Courts (that is, courts with European and Egyptian judges which evolved their own system of law), and there were alterations in the positions of some groups within society; in particular foundations were laid for the greater participation of the native Arabic-speaking Muslims in the activities of government. It seems likely that many of these changes would not have taken place without Muḥammad ʿAlī and the question must be asked: what was his purpose?

To try to answer that question it is necessary to look at his policy outside Egypt. From 1811 until 1841 the pasha was engaged in a series of foreign adventures. His first series of campaigns in Arabia was apparently undertaken at the instigation of the Porte which had been pressing him since 1807 to attack the Wahhābīs who had extended their control from Najd to the Hijaz, raided Iraq and Syria and stopped the pilgrim caravans. Their activities constituted a threat to the sultan's position as a Muslim ruler. For some time Muḥammad ʿAlī resisted the pressure from Istanbul, but in 1811–13 undertook a successful campaign to subjugate the Hijaz and in 1818 carried on to destroy the Wahhābī base in Najd. Later, a Wahhābī recovery drove him from Najd, but in 1838–9 he mounted a new campaign which pushed Egyptian control as far as the shores of the Gulf through the occupation of al-Ḥasā and Qaṭīf and also drove southwards into Yemen.

Muḥammad ʿAlī's second series of campaigns were directed up the Nile into the Sudan, which was brought under Egyptian control in 1820–6. His objects appear to have been to secure supplies of gold and slaves and to control the whole trade of the Nile and the Red Sea. Until 1838 tribute from the Sudan was paid in slaves. The Sudan did not prove to be a profitable conquest, however, any more than did Arabia. Muḥammad ʿAlī was unable to develop any new types of cultivation and the area remained a backwater of the Egyptian empire.

Muḥammad ʿAlī's intervention in Greece during the 1820s was also at the request of the sultan, who sought help to quell the Greek rising which had begun in 1821. In 1822 Muḥammad ʿAlī agreed to reconquer Crete and subsequently Cyprus. In 1825 his forces were employed in the Morea and in 1826 in mainland Greece. The Egyptian involvement in Greece threatened to bring Muḥammad ʿAlī into conflict with the European powers who were pressing for a settlement which would save the Greeks from destruction (see p. 69). Muḥammad ʿAlī had no direct interest in the contest – there is no good evidence to support the theory that he planned to dominate the trade of the eastern Mediterranean by control of Greece – and the pasha offered to withdraw in return for British recognition of his independence. This was the first suggestion of what was to become a recurrent theme of Muḥammad ʿAlī's policy during the next decade and more. In fact Egypt was compelled to withdraw from the Morea in 1828 after the naval defeat at Navarino in 1827.

The Greek campaign led on to Muḥammad ʿAlī's greatest conquest. In return for his support for his sultan in Greece he had been promised the governorship of Syria and when Maḥmūd II refused to honour his agreement Muḥammad ʿAlī invaded Syria in November 1831, fulfilling an ambition cherished since at least 1811 (see p. 70). Syria offered manpower, revenues, timber and control of the two great Muslim cities of Damascus and Jerusalem and the prestige which went with them. Control of Syria has been an object for almost all rulers of Egypt. The question remains whether Syria was the limit of Muḥammad ʿAlī's ambitions because his troops under his son Ibrāhīm did not stop in Syria but marched on into Anatolia as far as Kütahya. It seems possible that Muḥammad ʿAlī might have considered continuing his advance as far as Istanbul and imposing himself as a mayor of the palace and master of the Ottoman empire. However, the threat of Russian intervention caused him to halt and the opportunity was gone. In 1833 he negotiated an agreement which left him in control of Syria, Adana and Crete but still no more than an Ottoman official; he rejected the advice of Ibrāhīm to make independence a condition of a settlement.

For the following decade Muḥammad ʿAlī sought confirmation of his possession of Syria and some form of international recognition which would protect him from the evident intention of Maḥmūd II to recover Syria. In 1839 Maḥmūd tried to expel Muḥammad ʿAlī by force and failed disastrously losing his army and his fleet before his own death. Muḥammad ʿAlī was deprived of the fruits of his victory by a European coalition which, combined with a popular rising against the detested Egyptian rule, drove him from Syria in 1840. The pasha was compelled to settle for the hereditary governorship of Egypt.

Four theories have been advanced to explain Muḥammad ʿAlī's external policy. The first, taking into account his activities in Arabia, Syria and an apparent threat to Iraq, contends that he had in mind an Arab state. This theory, which was popular with contemporary British commentators, has nothing to recommend it. Muḥammad ʿAlī spoke Turkish and regarded himself as a Muslim; there is no evidence that he thought in Arab terms and much to support the view that he regarded Egyptian Arabic speakers with contempt. There is, on the other hand, some evidence to suggest that his son, Ibrāhīm, may have been more sympathetic towards Arabic speakers, although nothing to argue that he translated this into political terms. The second view is that the pasha regarded himself as an Egyptian ruler and adopted traditional Egyptian national goals, including the unity of the Nile valley and control of Syria. It is certainly true that Muḥammad ʿAlī regarded Egypt as his base and as the core of his power but no evidence that he had any notion of Egyptian nationalism. The third view sees Muḥammad ʿAlī as acting in a Muslim and Ottoman context, and seeking advancement within the Ottoman system. This view has much to recommend it for the period down to the occupation of Syria, but from that time onwards Muḥammad ʿAlī's hopes within the Ottoman context were increasingly difficult to realize and he was obliged to consider more and more the possibility of independence. From 1828 onwards he often sounded British and French representatives on the possibility of support for his independence but whether it was his main goal or an alternative to Ottoman hopes is unclear. The fourth view sees Muḥammad ʿAlī as a military adventurer with no ideological views beyond personal power. In this view Egypt was simply a base for the conquest of more territory, the end being merely the acquisition of wealth and power. According to this interpretation the modernization of Egypt was merely a by-product of his personal ambitions and Muḥammad ʿAlī an able man making use of whatever opportunities came his way.

During the short reign of ʿAbbās I (1849–54) there was a reaction against modernization. The army was reduced, secular schools closed, foreign advisers dismissed and there was a substantial retreat in government power, evidenced by the halving of tax yields. The policies of Muḥammad ʿAlī were resumed under the next two rulers, Saʿīd (1854–63) and Ismāʿīl (1863–79), both of whom were European educated and French speaking, wore European dress and were committed to the modernization of Egypt on a European model and in association with Europe.

Economic development, based on the expansion of the cotton economy, remained the driving force of development. This is true even when allowance is made for the unreliability of Egyptian trade statistics which omit important items, overstate the export surplus and overestimate the importance of cotton: the figure of 75 per cent commonly given as the share of cotton in Egyptian exports during the 1860s and 1870s is too high. The growth of the cotton economy was most marked during the 1860s when the cessation of supplies of US cotton in consequence of the American Civil War led to a quadrupling of the price of cotton and a very considerable increase in Egyptian production. Between 1863 and 1865 Egyptian exports (mainly cotton) rose from £4 million to £14 million. Although cotton exports fell back temporarily after the restoration of US supplies, exports remained well above their former level; by 1872 they had recovered almost to the 1865 peak and by 1880 were 50 per cent above the peak. Production and export of other crops was also stimulated, notably sugar exports which increased by 600 per cent, although sugar yet failed to produce all the results for which Ismāʿīl had hoped. Wheat exports could not compete with cheap North American wheat.

The foreign exchange earned from cotton exports was available to finance investment in Egypt, notably by permitting borrowing from abroad. Much of the money so raised went into communications. The most spectacular achievement was the Suez Canal (opened in 1869) but Egypt also acquired a railway system. The first railway from Cairo to Alexandria had been planned under ʿAbbās and was opened in 1856, the first railway in Africa, and it was shortly followed by a link from Cairo to Suez. Under Ismāʿīl a network of railways was built in the Delta which facilitated the movement of the cotton crop and a further line was built into Upper Egypt. Much expenditure also went into roads, bridges, the telegraph and harbour works at Alexandria. A second major area of investment was in irrigation; 13,500 kilometres of canals were opened. There was investment also in factories; sixty-four sugar factories were built. In all Egypt invested about £50 million of which railways, irrigation and the Suez Canal took the greatest part.

Although it was the major item of government expenditure economic development was not the only element in increased spending under Ismāʿīl; considerable sums were spent on education, on what might be called conspicuous consumption, for example the lavish entertainments ordered for the opening of the Suez Canal, and on foreign policy. Ismāʿīl endeavoured to buy greater freedom from the Ottoman government, including the title of khedive. A series of agreements between 1867 and 1873 cost Ismāʿīl a substantial sum in bribes and in increase of tribute. The khedive also had ambitious plans for expansion up the Nile and down the Red Sea and intended to found a great empire in northeast Africa. These plans necessitated an expansion of his army which rose to 80,000. Lastly, Ismāʿīl spent money on what may be termed civilization, whether from conviction or from a desire to impress Europe. The suppression of slavery and the abolition of forced labour were expensive pursuits.

Egypt paid for these developments by mobilizing internal resources and by borrowing abroad. Government revenue rose from just over £2 million in 1861 to £10.5 million in 1875. This last figure was inflated by mortgaged revenue; the law of the *Muqābala* of 1871 allowed holders of state land to halve their tax bill in return for paying six years' extra tax in advance. The full wealth of Egypt was not tapped by government, however; *ʿushūrī* land (held mainly by notables) paid tax at only one-third of the rate levied on state lands; the foreign communities in Egypt paid almost no tax; and no tax was levied on the lands of the Muḥammad ʿAlī family although this property amounted to one-fifth of the cultivated land of Egypt. The main burden fell on the peasant. While cotton leaped in value the peasant could afford the higher tax bill, but as the pressure grew heavy after 1875 he ran into debt, his creditor sought judgement against him in the Mixed Courts, his land was sold under him and he found himself a tenant or labourer on the land of others. Such was the fate of many peasants.

Foreign borrowing was a major source of funds for investment. Neither Muḥammad ʿAlī nor ʿAbbās had borrowed abroad and Egypt was handicapped in raising loans by the 1841 firman which required Ottoman government consent for public loans. Accordingly, Saʿīd and Ismāʿīl preferred to raise money by short-term devices rather than by long-term loans. For this privilege they paid dearly; Egypt paid rather more than twice as much as India for capital. How much Saʿīd contributed to Egypt's indebtedness is a matter of dispute; estimates range from just over £3 million to £16 million. Ismāʿīl was, without doubt, the principal borrower. In 1863 he declared that "the basis of all good administration is order and economy in finance",[6] and he bore a reputation before his accession as the most prudent and successful farmer in Egypt. He was to become one of the most controversial figures in Egyptian history with opinion divided between those who saw him as an extravagant incompetent and those who regarded him as a far-sighted but unlucky modernizer. Certainly, Ismāʿīl was unlucky to run into the European credit crisis of the early 1870s, but it is difficult to argue that Egypt acquired fixed assets worth the £98.4 million at which his debt was assessed in 1880. Long before that date the Egyptian government was bankrupt. In 1875 Ismāʿīl could not pay the interest on his debt and was obliged to seek a composition with his creditors. Between 1875 and 1880 came a series of efforts to ascertain the amount of the debt and to devise a system of payments acceptable to the bondholders and affordable to Egypt. These efforts included the Cave Mission (1875), the establishment of the Caisse de la Dette (1876) to represent the bondholders, the Goschen–Joubert Mission (1876), the appointment of two European financial controllers and the imposition of a government which included several Europeans (1878). Efforts were concentrated on reducing public expenditure and increasing tax yield. All efforts failed because they overestimated Egypt's ability to pay (an ability seriously weakened by drought and floods in the late 1870s) and because of Ismāʿīl's constant efforts to prevent the European controllers from gaining full control of Egypt's resources. Only after 30 June 1879, when Ismāʿīl was replaced by his son Tawfīq, did the European prescription have a chance of success. In 1881–2, however, this chance was frustrated by the ʿUrābī revolution.

THE SUDAN AND THE MAGHREB

The metamorphosis of political authority in Egypt was imitated in a pallid fashion in other parts of North Africa. North Africa also witnessed other elements of modernization, although the agency was different. The similarities and the differences are of sufficient interest to make it worth including in this section a short sketch of developments in the Sudan, Libya, Tunisia and Algeria, although no attempt will be made to offer an account comparable to that given for other parts of the Near East.

In the Sudan the Funj sultanate, which since the early sixteenth century had exercised overlordship from the Ethiopian marches to the

Third Cataract of the Nile, lost power during the second half of the eighteenth century to a clan of regents and to local tribal leaders. At the same time, further west in Darfur, another Sudanese sultanate attained the peak of its power. Throughout the territories of both sultanates a rigorous folk-Islam with strong Ṣūfī characteristics flourished. In the early nineteenth century this latter feature was reinforced by the development of two new orders, the Sammāniyya, which originated in Medina as a branch of the Khalwatiyya, and the Khatmiyya, a purely Sudanese order, whose founder, Muḥammad ʿUthmān al-Mīrghanī, was, like Muḥammad ibn ʿAlī al-Sanūsī of Libya (see below), a disciple of Aḥmad ibn Idrīs in Arabia. These Sudanese religious movements remained active during the Egyptian conquest of the Sudan.

The Egyptian conquest, the most important event in Sudanese history during the first eighty years of the nineteenth century, was launched in 1820 by Muḥammad ʿAlī, who was interested in gold, slaves and closing a possible refuge to his Mamluk rivals. From 1820 until 1825 there was almost continual fighting in the Sudan, but by the latter date resistance was quelled and the Egyptian governors had established a relationship of collaboration with Sudanese notables. Between 1825 and 1853 the Sudan was a quiet backwater. The accession of Saʿīd Pasha was accompanied by two new developments. First, there was an influx of private traders into the southern regions of the Sudan beyond the pale of Egyptian administration and, second, there was much stronger European pressure to suppress the slave-trade. A solution to these two problems was left to the Khedive Ismāʿīl who launched a campaign against the slave-trade which involved the extension of Egyptian authority over the equatorial regions of the Upper Nile and Baḥr al-Ghazāl. Ismāʿīl also extended his control over Darfur and eastwards to the Red Sea, acquiring the ports of Suakin and Massawa from the Ottomans in 1865. The suppression of the slave-trade was, indeed, only one aspect of a dynamic policy of change launched by Ismāʿīl in the Sudan, which included plans, only partly realized, for a railway, steam vessels, the telegraph and the development of cotton cultivation.

By the time of Ismāʿīl's deposition in 1879 the Sudan had experienced sixty years of a steadily expanding, modernizing government which had brought about major social, economic and political changes in the Sudan. These changes – a revolution imposed from above and from without – contributed to a Sudanese reaction which took the form of the uprising of the Mahdiyya in 1881.

In the Maghreb a new pattern of authority emerged during the eighteenth century when the Ottomans recognized the establishment of relatively stable local political systems. The countries of the Maghreb apart from Morocco were not independent of Ottoman authority: they continued to acknowledge Ottoman suzerainty and the Ottomans were able to exercise a degree of influence through control over supplies of military equipment and recruitment of Turks to serve as soldiers in the Maghreb, through the ability to employ religious sanctions and through the denial of access to Ottoman harbours to recalcitrant Maghrebi rulers. A principal cause of dispute between the Ottoman and local governments was the activities of the Barbary corsairs operating out of Maghrebi ports, especially Algiers. Although the great age of the corsairs was over and during the eighteenth century the activities of the pirates in the Mediterranean were declining as they became more and more restricted in the areas in which they operated, there were still continual complaints directed to the Ottomans by the European powers and attempts by the Ottomans to limit still further corsair activities. The justification for the attacks on Christian vessels by the corsairs continued to be the prosecution of the Holy War, and the Maghreb was regarded by the Ottomans as a frontier region which had the theoretical duty to expand the frontiers of Islam either against the Christians or against the pagans to the south. The Ottomans were in something of a dilemma: to stop the corsair campaigns was to deny a basic attribute of the Ottoman state but the Ottomans were well aware that they could not afford the resources to prosecute the struggle. On tactical grounds they sought, therefore, within their means, to restrict the Maghrebi states in their relations with the European powers. One effect of the limitation of corsair activity was to reduce the incomes of the Maghrebi states and to bring about a financial crisis, especially in Algiers.

In Libya the Ottomans recognized the hereditary rule of the pashas of the Qaramānlī family in Tripolitania from 1711 to 1832 with only a brief interruption in 1793–5. The penultimate ruler from this family, Yūsuf Pasha (1795–1832) tried without success to modernize his state and in 1835 his successor, ʿAlī, was deposed by the Ottomans who suppressed local opposition and installed direct rule in Tripolitania, which endured until 1912. Cyrenaica remained independent of direct control and for this reason was chosen as the headquarters of the conservative and puritanical Ṣūfī order of the Sanūsiyya, an offshoot of the Idrīsiyya founded in Mecca by Muḥammad ibn ʿAlī al-Sanūsī (1791–1859). The Sanūsiyya was established in Cyrenaica in 1843. Under Sayyid Muḥammad al-Mahdī (1845–1902) the order spread among the bedouin of Cyrenaica and the western desert of Egypt. By means of the establishment of branch lodges in each tribal area the order was able to attach itself to the existing tribal structure. The Sanūsīs themselves, who came mainly from the western Maghreb, appeared as outsiders and therefore as acceptable arbiters within the tribal system. Their lodges became centres of Islamic teaching, elementary education and retreat and the basis of the political power of the Sanūsiyya.

In Tunisia the Ḥusaynid dynasty, which ruled until 1957, became established as beys in 1710, reduced the power of the Janissaries and built up a local following. During the early nineteenth century Aḥmad Bey al-Ḥusaynī (1837–55) launched himself on a career of modernization which in several features resembled that of Muḥammad ʿAlī in Egypt. In particular Aḥmad tried to create a strong centralized government based on a new European-style army raised by conscription of the peasants and on a powerful administration supported by monopolies and a host of taxes levied on the rural areas. To raise money he sought to substitute olives for grain as the chief export. Other reforms were aimed at the abolition of slavery and the improvement of the position of the non-Muslim minorities. Finally, Aḥmad endeavoured to free himself from Ottoman control. His modernizing policy failed: Tunisia lacked the resources to pay for his programme; he aroused the hostility of the peasants and notables; and he came under increasing pressure from the European powers. Under Aḥmad's successors Maḥmūd Bey (1855–9) and Muḥammad al-Ṣādiq (1859–82) Tunis slid deeper into trouble, suffered a rebellion in 1864 and in 1869 went bankrupt and was obliged to accept British, French and Italian representatives to superintend the finances of the state. It was under European pressure also that Tunis began the first hesitant steps towards a constitutional system. In 1857, in imitation of the Ottoman Khaṭṭ-i̊ Hümāyūn, Muḥammad Bey announced the principles of the Fundamental Pact and in 1861, with French approval, his successor promulgated the first constitution in the Near East, which established a grand council to assist the bey in government.

Since the seventeenth century Algeria had been governed by a dey nominated by the officers of the Janissaries. The system was formally countenanced by the Ottoman government in 1711. The power of the deys was in practice shared with three beys who ruled three of the four provinces into which Algiers came to be divided and within each beylicate tribal chiefs possessed substantial autonomy within their tribal zones. During the late eighteenth and early nineteenth centuries Algeria experienced a ferment of religious revival through the establishment of new Ṣūfī orders similar to that witnessed in Arabia and the Sudan. During the early nineteenth century the deys made an attempt to break away from their dependence upon the increasingly unruly Janissaries, but the experiment was brought to a sudden end in 1830 by the French invasion of Algeria, following the celebrated incident in 1827 when the dey had struck the French consul with a fly-whisk. French prestige had to be vindicated even more than French trade had to be protected and the expedition of 1830 was the result. Honour avenged, France decided to establish a *de facto* protectorate over the coastal regions but there was resistance and France was drawn into a full-scale war of conquest in 1840. There were several centres of Algerian resistance but the best known was that of ʿAbd al-Qādir (1808–83) which continued until 1847. Even after his capture resistance continued, the Berber confederacies of the Kabylie were not subdued until 1857, there was a major uprising in 1871 and peace was not completely established until 1884. In 1848 Algeria was annexed to France and a programme of colonization implemented. Colonization proceeded much faster after 1871 and by 1881 there were 336,000 Europeans in Algeria, mainly in the towns but also including 140,000 in the countryside. With Turkestan, the Crimea and the Ukraine, Algeria was one of the few countries in the region which underwent extensive European colonization involving settlement on the land. Many local cultivators and landowners were dispossessed, individual landholding imposed, the tribal structure was profoundly altered and the Algerian population fell by, it has been estimated, nearly 1 million between 1830 and 1872. Algerians were regarded as uncivilized. Muslim criminal law was abolished, *qāḍīs* dismissed and *waqfs* confiscated.

It has been argued that Algerian society was affected more profoundly than any other Near Eastern society during the nineteenth century. It should be noted, however, that other countries underwent extensive programmes of modernization and equally destructive wars and in many there was also a strong outside element influencing events. Further, the continuation of Muslim personal law for the Muslim population ensured that Muslims retained their identity and a Muslim élite of judges continued in existence. Finally, to link with the Muslim population the French required a group of Muslim collaborators and this they found through the maintenance of an important Muslim landholding group, in effect notables who operated in the familiar Near Eastern fashion. Muslim society was not broken by modernization in Algeria: indeed, it seems likely that the weakening of tribal bonds contributed to the enhancement of Muslim identity.

IRAN

One difficulty in describing Iran in 1800 is to know where it began and ended. The western frontier with Iraq was fairly well determined and the southern frontier was effectively on the Gulf, for, although Iran claimed Baḥrayn, she had no means of asserting her claim. The northern and eastern frontiers were, however, much less certain. Beyond the Aras Iran claimed suzerainty over Transcaucasia and parts of Georgia, and on the east her claims penetrated deep into Turkestan and Afghanistan. As a result of wars with Russia and by the Treaties of Gulistan (1813) and Turkmanchay (1828) her northern frontier was fixed on the Aras. Following the Russian conquest of Turkestan between 1864 and 1885 Iran's claims in that area lapsed; and by agreement with Britain her frontiers with Afghanistan and British India were defined in the second half of the nineteenth century. From 1828, therefore, effective Iranian rule was limited to an area roughly corresponding to the present boundaries of the state and it will be simpler to concentrate on that area.

Geographically, Iran presents a curious spectacle, rather like a bowl of which the rim represents the chains of mountains which almost encircle Iran and the bowl proper the central plateau. It is, however, an empty bowl for the central plateau of Iran consists principally of two large deserts and it is the rim which contains most of what is worth having in Iran. The mountains receive enough rainfall to permit the pasturing of flocks and the cultivation of various crops; elsewhere agriculture is only possible through the beneficence of rivers (neither numerous nor large) or the ingenuity of man, who, through the device of underground tunnels (*qanāts*) has conducted water for many kilometres to supply areas of the central plateau. Even so, only about 20 per cent of Iran was arable and most of this cultivation was concentrated in the northern part of the country. The implications for Iranian communications and, therefore, political and economic characteristics, of the distribution of the major centres of population around a mountain rim are easy to appreciate.

Estimates of the population of Iran in 1800 are little more than guesses; these put it in the region of 6 million. Of this population about one-third was composed of nomad or semi-nomad tribal peoples; not more than 10 per cent lived in towns of over 20,000 inhabitants; and the remainder were settled cultivators, proportions similar to those of Iraq. In 1900 the total population was estimated at 10 million, representing a rate of growth considerably below that of Egypt and also below that of the provinces of the Ottoman empire. The urban population grew only slowly. The population of the large cities showed no net increase before

1870, the growth of Tabriz and Tehran being offset by the decline of Isfahan and Shiraz. After 1870 there was an increase in urban population, particularly in Tehran, which reached 250,000 in 1900. The proportion of nomads is estimated to have fallen to one-quarter indicating some degree of settlement although it would be unwise to build much upon these estimates.

The population was almost entirely Muslim; numerically, non-Muslims were insignificant, although the small Armenian community did play a role of some importance in commercial and financial matters. A large majority of the Muslim population were Shīʿīs; within the Shīʿī community there were some important divisions between different groups among the orthodox and between orthodox and Ṣūfī of which more will be said below. There were also substantial Sunnī groups among the Arabs of the Gulf, the Balūchīs of the south-east and the Kurds of western Iran, although none of these had any great political significance. Linguistically, there were very sizeable groups of non-Persian speakers, depending on how one classifies Iranian dialects; possibly, in 1800, these constituted a majority. Among them were the Balūch, the Kurds, Arabic speakers of the south and south-west and the substantial groups of Turkish speakers, notably the Turks of Azerbaijan. There is no evidence, however, that linguistic differences had any political significance; Persian was the language of administration as it was also the principal literary language.

Politically, Iran was ruled by the Qājārs, a dynasty of Turkish tribal origin, newly come to power at the end of the eighteenth century when the founder of the Qājār dynasty crushed the Zand dynasty of southern Iran and established his own capital at Tehran. In 1800 the dynasty was represented by Fatḥ ʿAlī Shāh (1797–1834) and his family held most of the provincial governorships. The Qājārs were assisted by a bureaucracy which had a very old tradition and style of work and was staffed by men of varied origins but often of considerable ability.

Although a number of changes did take place in Iran during the nineteenth century these changes were very far from being of the order of those which took place in the Ottoman lands or in Egypt, a factor which was of considerable importance for the future development of the region. A central question which may form the basis for a consideration of Iranian history during this period is why did Iran fail to modernize in the fashion of either the Ottoman empire or Egypt? Consideration of the development of those states has revealed two quite different patterns of modernization, namely military-led modernization, which characterized the Ottoman empire throughout the period and Egypt until 1841; and economic-led modernization, which characterized the development of Egypt after 1841 and particularly from the 1860s. It will be useful to look first at the achievement of Iran in these two areas of activity.

Just as the Ottoman empire, in the face of a threat from Russia, determined to modernize her military forces on a European model, so did Iran under similar circumstances during the early nineteenth century. The initiative was taken by ʿAbbās Mīrzā, governor of Azerbaijan and heir to the Qājār throne, who was chiefly responsible for the conduct of the war with Russia. With the aid of first French and subsequently British instructors he began to create a force of disciplined infantry and artillery, and built up a respectable army, which, although it suffered defeat at the hands of Russia in 1812 at Aslandaz, yet survived into the peace which followed. This initiative was, however, dissipated and, despite frequent attempts by Iranian rulers and statesmen to revive it, Iran never possessed any force remotely resembling the Ottoman army. ʿAbbās Mīrzā died in 1833 without succeeding to the throne. The military initiative was revived by his son Muḥammad Shāh with British assistance in the 1830s but his force disintegrated after the repulse at Herat in 1838. In subsequent years French and Austrian military missions came and went and new schemes were introduced and dropped after a year or two. By the end of the period the Iranian army existed on paper only; all that could be put into the field was a few thousand ill-disciplined, ill-paid, ill-equipped, ragged soldiers. "The untidiness, the carelessness, the technical ignorance, the general fecklessness of the Persian soldier exist in as great a degree as any imagination, military or civil, can conceive", wrote one British traveller who visited Iran in 1881.[7] Provincial governors raised their own forces for particular operations and by the end of the century the only reasonably efficient force in Iran was the small, 2,000-strong, Russian-officered Cossack Brigade which had been instituted in the 1870s. The major dynamic provided by the problem of raising, training, equipping and paying a modern army was wholly lacking in Iran.

Iran also failed to achieve any substantial progress in economic modernization. The principal factor in this failure was the absence of any considerable development of communications. It is true that Iran experienced some benefit from steam navigation, which became established on the Gulf and the Caspian Sea from the 1830s onwards and on the Karun river from 1888. Also Iran acquired a telegraph link by the 1860s. But there was little port, road or, above all, railway construction during the nineteenth century. Consequently, there was no means of moving bulk goods into and out of most areas of Iran; production remained geared to local markets or to subsistence except in a few areas which had access to the communications systems of other countries. In the latter part of the nineteenth century there was some new development of cash crops in such areas including rice production and a revival of silk production in Gīlān, where access to the Caspian made transport easier, of cotton in the eastern province of Khurāsān, where use of the Transcaspian railway made it possible to reach Russian markets, and of opium in the south whence it could be exported via the Gulf. Otherwise Iran was obliged to rely upon exports the price/weight ratio of which was high enough to cover the heavy transport costs which were the inevitable consequence of dependence upon animal transport. It is notable that the only significant industrial development was of a traditional industry where the product had a high value, namely the handwoven carpet.

In percentage terms there was a considerable increase in Iran's foreign trade during the nineteenth century; one writer estimates the increase at twelve times in real terms between 1800 and 1914. Between 1875 and 1914 the increase was especially marked; the Gulf trade (mainly with British India) increased from £1.7 million to £4.5 million and the Russian trade from about £1 million to £9.4 million. There was evidently some dynamism in the international trade sector and this factor is reflected in the rise of a substantial merchant class which was to become one of the principal elements in the demand for change at the end of the nineteenth century. A good example of the new-style Iranian merchant is Ḥājjī Muḥammad Ḥassān Amīn al-Żarb, whose interests extended from trade into investment in banking, industry, mining and even the construction of a small railway to help him develop his iron-ore mines. He profited greatly from the Gīlān silk revival of the 1800s and was reputed (improbably) to have acquired a fortune of 25 million tomans (£7 million).

Although there were wealthy Iranians and some of them were willing to invest in economic development, Iran lacked the institutions which would have permitted the mobilization of internal resources on any scale. There was no bank until 1888 and the credit system remained elementary until 1914 and was geared towards the financing of international trade, not domestic investment. The alternative to the use of private capital was government investment or borrowing from outside. Government investment was not a serious possibility; revenues, always low in proportion to national income, showed a decline in real terms through the nineteenth century. Borrowing from outside could be accomplished either by government agency or by private means. Iran did not resort to government borrowing until the end of the nineteenth century, the sums involved were small (in 1914 the total foreign debt was under £7 million as compared with about £200 million each for the Ottoman empire or Egypt), and the money was used primarily to finance the overseas visits of the shah or to pay compensation for cancelled concessions. Iran failed to attract private foreign capital in any large amount. An effort was made in 1872 through the Reuter Concession to initiate a large-scale economic development involving railways, mining and banking but the concession was cancelled the following year and, in any case, it represented a poor bargain for Iran; substantial concessions were given to a lightweight capitalist enterprise with no obvious ability to promote economic development on the scale required by the concession. Arguments about the concession impeded new development for some years and further concessions were much smaller in scope.

With the minor exception of the foreign trade sector there was no economic impulse to modernization comparable with that supplied by cotton in Egypt or in Turkestan. Iran remained a traditional economy, involving mainly subsistence farming or production for local markets, pastoral production and, in the towns, the familiar handicrafts.

Nor did Iran see any substantial changes in social organization. Educational development was much slower than in regions further west. Although Iran sent her first student mission to England as early as 1811 there was no consistent policy in subsequent years comparable to that pursued under Muḥammad ʿAlī and most Iranians who acquired a foreign education did so through private means. There was no major change in the educational system within Iran. In 1851 the Dār al-Funūn was founded with a modern French-style organization and curriculum and some foreign teachers. Military subjects were taught and the institution was essentially an élite school for training higher bureaucrats and officers. Further specialized institutions were added subsequently; in 1873 a school of languages, military colleges in 1883 and 1886, an agricultural college in 1900 and, in 1901, a school for foreign service officials. These developments were in the area of specialized high school training and therefore comparable to similar developments which had taken place in the Ottoman empire and Egypt some fifty years earlier. There was no considerable educational development at lower levels and such efforts as were made were largely the work of groups of enlightened ulema who founded private modern schools from the 1890s onwards. There was some missionary work among Christians by American Presbyterians in the north and Anglicans in the south. Nor was there any legal reform comparable to that which took place elsewhere; Iran was left with an unresolved conflict of *Sharīʿa* and state law and a judicial system in the hands of the ulema. Although a printing press was opened in 1812 and the first newspaper established in 1837 the press and publication in Iran remained much less developed than in neighbouring states.

It remains to try and explain why Iran should not have developed on the models of the Ottoman empire and Egypt during the nineteenth century. Some factors have already been mentioned, in particular the geography of the country which made the development of adequate communications so difficult and expensive and which limited the degree of control exercised by government. The substantial tribal population also represented an obstacle. Whereas experience proved that traditional nomad forces were no match for disciplined troops armed with modern weapons it was equally true that against ill-disciplined and poorly equipped forces they were a formidable enemy indeed, with their organization, rapidity of movement and willingness to endure hardship. Another factor already mentioned was the absence of significant minority populations which could take the lead in economic and commercial development as did the Greeks and Armenians in the Ottoman empire, or the foreign minorities established in Egypt, or the Jewish community in Iraq. A further feature of the presence of minorities in the Ottoman empire was, of course, the interest which they attracted from European powers. Although this interest proved a considerable embarrassment to the Ottomans it also provided the basis of considerable pressure for change in Ottoman government and institutions to which the Ottomans responded; no such interest existed in Iran.

One difference between Iran and other countries is that Iran is Shīʿī and the others are Sunnī and some writers have found in this difference an explanation for Iran's failure to modernize. Two points have been stressed. One is a psychological argument, according to which Shīʿīs are more "other worldly" than Sunnīs, less orderly and more inspirational and therefore have a lower propensity to organize for material development. The second is more specific and is concerned with the role of religious leaders in Shīʿī Islam in general and in Iran in particular. The Iranian ulema, it is contended, were more powerful than those in Sunnī areas and used their influence to oppose modernization in general and to resist government efforts to promote change in particular. The hostility of the ulema to government, it is argued, derived from two factors: ideological and material. Ideologically, it is pointed out that according to majority opinion among the *mujtahids* all government was illegitimate since authority was properly invested in the "Hidden Imam", that is the twelfth Imam, Muḥammad al-Mahdī, who had disappeared from human sight in AD 873, but who continued to rule the world unseen. Certain powers remained with the Imam and could not be devolved, but it was a question who should exercise the day-to-day powers of regulation of human affairs. The answer to the majority of the ulema was clear; it was the *mujtahids* themselves, who, by their learning and knowledge of God's rules as contained in the *Sharīʿa*, were best fitted for this duty. The claims of secular rulers to undertake these duties were unsound and should be resisted. The material interests of the ulema also led them into opposition to government. Their incomes were derived from fees, contributions from the faithful, their personal activities including trade, and *waqf* incomes, notably the great revenues from the shrine of the Imam Rižā at Mashhad. Any attempt by government to undertake a more active role in modernization must have had the effect of reducing their influence (in law and education) and their incomes. The ulema, it is argued, perceived modernization to be both a threat to their interests and authority and a threat to Iran and Shīʿī Islam because it meant the adoption of infidel modes of organization and the admission of infidel advisers. Finally, it is argued that the influence of the ulema was enhanced by two other factors: they had the support of the masses of the people, particularly in the towns; and the government was disabled from combating their influence by the circumstance that the principal Shīʿī shrines and the leading *mujtahids* were outside their reach, being in Iraq.

These arguments are persuasive in theory but much less so in practice. In the first place not all of the ulema accepted the theoretical arguments about the exercise of authority in the absence of the Hidden Imam; some agreed that government had a role to play. Second, whatever their theoretical opinions most Shīʿī *mujtahids* took the view that in this evil world one must accept imperfections and they espoused the doctrine of the lesser evil. If a Muslim ruler conducted affairs in such a manner that good Muslims were not prevented from living as good Muslims should, then he was entitled to the obedience of Muslims for the alternative was anarchy and that was much worse; better a little injustice than chaos. Shīʿī views in this matter could be similar to those of Sunnī jurists. Third, not all the material interests of the ulema pointed against co-operation with the state. Several prominent members of the religious classes were dependent upon government patronage, for example the Imām Jumʿa of Tehran. Much depended upon the source of income of each member of the ulema in deciding whether his interest was aligned with that of the state or opposed to it.

If one examines the record one finds that the ulema were by no means universally hostile to modernization or to government. No objection was made by the ulema to ʿAbbās Mīrzā's *Niẓām-i Jedīd* which he presented carefully as a revival of old practices and not as innovation. It was members of the ulema who took the lead in the modernization of education in the 1890s, and government and ulema co-operated in the suppression of the Bābī movement.

The Bābī movement grew out of a theological argument within the Shīʿī community concerning the mode by which the knowledge of the Hidden Imam was made accessible to the community. One group, the Shaykhīs, stressed the idea of the Perfect Shīʿī, a being without sin who could act as the vehicle or "gate" of the Hidden Imam. In 1844 Mīrzā ʿAlī Muḥammad, a young man from a merchant family in Shiraz, proclaimed or allowed it to be believed that he was the gate or *bāb*. The claim was anathema to the orthodox, who determined to suppress it. In this they co-operated with the state which became alarmed at the element of social and political protest which entered the Bābī movement. The Bāb was executed in 1850 and his followers repressed with great savagery.

Discussion of the role of the ulema in Qājār Iran has been greatly influenced by theoretical arguments and by the evidence of the leadership of the anti-government movement of 1890–1906 by members of the ulema. It is clear, however, that the part which the ulema played is much more ambiguous than the simple view that they were the principal opponents of modernization would lead one to suppose; sometimes members of the ulema co-operated with reform efforts and sometimes they opposed them. It is doubtful whether Shīʿīsm and the role of the ulema constitute a sufficient explanation for the failure of modernization in Iran.

Another factor which must be considered is the role of the Qājār family. During the whole of the period there were only three monarchs: Fatḥ ʿAlī Shāh (1797–1834), Muḥammad Shāh (1834–48) and Nāṣir al-Dīn Shāh (1848–96). There was no generally accepted system for succession and Britain and Russia intervened to procure the succession of Muḥammad in 1834 and Nāṣir al-Dīn in 1848. In the circumstances contenders for the throne looked for outside support and this fact undoubtedly contributed to some weakness by the government. In 1834 there was a short civil war. However, it is difficult to believe that the succession question was a major factor in the weakness of government – Egypt and the Ottoman empire also had some problems – and there is some compensation in the lengthy reigns of the rulers concerned. The Qājār rulers were men of ability and intelligence but they were heavily criticized for weakness and a frivolous attitude to government. Certainly, they adhered to that ancient tradition which asserted, in contradiction of Shakespeare's Henry IV, that being a king was fun, or ought to be. The early Qājārs spent a great deal of their time in hunting – Tehran was only the winter capital and during the summer Fatḥ ʿAlī lived like a nomad. The later Qājārs developed a passion for trips abroad; the last Qājār, Aḥmad Shāh, could not bear to be away from Europe. And yet they were certainly men who were receptive to new ideas and aware of the problems which Iran faced. All were willing to sponsor schemes of modernization: their weakness lay in failing to carry them through and it can be argued that it was scarcely in their power to do so given the structure of Iranian government.

The Qājār family was very numerous and its members were supported by being given offices at court or in the provinces. Whereas in the Ottoman empire and in Egypt provincial governorships were held by bureaucrats, in Iran they were all held by Qājār nobles who maintained their own mini-courts in each province, where they conducted their own policies. Even foreign policy was consigned to their care. Dealings with the Ottomans were assigned to the governor of Kirmānshāh, those with the Russians to the governor of Azerbaijan, the most important and wealthiest province which was always given to the heir apparent, those with Afghanistan to the governor of Khurāsān and those with the British to the governor of Fārs, the enormous province which included most of southern Iran. These provincial governors were great potentates who could not readily be given orders: the Ẓill al-Sulṭān, governor of Isfahan for nearly forty years, was easily the most powerful man in Iran during the 1880s, maintaining a military force much larger than that of the shah. Each of the great provincial governors maintained his agents at court and resisted any effort to strengthen the central government at the expense of the provinces. The factions at court, dependent as they were upon the receipt of pensions and salaries for their sinecures, were also inclined to oppose reforms which might result in the diminution of their incomes and influence. Given the geography of Iran it is not easy to see how a centralized system of government could have been conducted without prior investment in communications but the decentralized system operated against modernizaion. The provincial governors opposed the increase of central power and the central government prevented any provincial ruler from making himself too great a rival to the shah.

A key factor in the modernization of the Ottoman empire was the commitment of the civil and military bureaucracy to reform. There was no such commitment in Iran in the nineteenth century. The Iranian bureaucratic tradition was an ancient one and the system was surprisingly open to recruits of ability who came from very diverse backgrounds; great notables and the sons of kitchen servants each held high office. And a succession of reformers emerged from the bureaucracy: Mīrzā Abu'l Qāsim Khān, the Qā'im maqām (in effect the chief minister) of 'Abbās Mīrzā was committed to reform as was Mīrzā Taqī Khān, the Amīr Kabīr, first minister of Nāṣir al-Dīn (1848–51) who proposed many reforms in the army, administration, education and economic development. Both of these ministers encountered opposition from worried court factions, were abandoned by their masters and murdered. Under Ḥājjī Mīrzā Ḥusayn, Sipah Sālār (1827–81), who was chief minister from 1871 to 1873, a far-reaching programme was launched, including reform of the army, administration, taxation, law and economic development. It was the Sipah Sālār who was responsible for the Reuter Concession. Like the Amīr Kabīr, who had visited Russia and the Ottoman empire, the Sipah Sālār had some experience of life outside Iran having served in the foreign service in India, Russia and the Ottoman empire. The Sipah Sālār was especially impressed by the Tanẓīmāt reforms on which he modelled his own schemes. But like other reformers he fell victim to forces which opposed either reform or the reformer; a coalition of ulema, court factions and Russia procured his dismissal.

The history of the bureaucratic reformers of Iran prompts three observations. First, they were far less numerous than those of the Ottoman empire; individual bureaucrats were interested in reform but there was no group commitment to reform. As one minister, himself sympathetic to the cause of change, wrote: "We servants, possessing every privilege and extravagant incomes, are carefree and at ease, and it is time to graze and laze about."[8] Mīrzā Āqā Khān Nūrī, chief minister of Nāṣir al-Dīn after the Amīr Kabīr, advised his master not to concern himself with military reform: "Why do you want to bother with watching the army practising?" he inquired. "Take a few women and have a good time."[9] Many refused to admit that there was anything radically wrong in Iran. As the Sipah Sālār complained, "We believe that we have reached the highest degree of progress, and there is nothing we have to do or worry about."[10] And, second, even the reformers lacked consistent purpose. Sipah Sālār remained minister of war for seven years after he ceased to be prime minister but failed to achieve anything apart from the foundation of the Cossack Brigade which remained in a state of inefficiency until his departure. He did, however, acquire an unrivalled reputation for corruption. Another subsequent reformer, Mīrzā 'Alī Khān, Amīn al-Dawla (1844–1904) was Nāṣir al-Dīn's private secretary for twenty-three years and abounded in schemes of reform; at the same time he made a fortune out of the post office and the mint. And, thirdly, the reformers were not strong enough to prevail against the forces opposed to them, in particular the Qājār court factions. Mīrzā ʿAlī Asghar Khān, Amīn al-Sulṭān, the corrupt and much hated minister who became the leading figure of the 1890s, was also a man with realistic schemes of improvement, but many of his efforts were stultified by the opposition of his rival, Kāmrān Mīrzā, son of Nāṣir al-Dīn. Their separate control over different spheres of administration virtually paralysed Iranian government.

The last factor alleged to have contributed to the lack of Iranian development is foreign influence. It is claimed that it suited the interests of Russia and Britain to preserve Iran as a weak buffer between them and that by their constant interference they handicapped Iranian development, aligning themselves with conservative groups and contributing to the downfall of reformers. There is some truth in this argument. Russia certainly did not want to see Iran grow in power. Politically, a powerful Iran could threaten the Russian hold over her Muslim subjects in the Caucasus and Turkestan: economically, as long as Iran remained undeveloped Russia would encounter no serious rival in the markets of northern Iran for geographical reasons. British views were more mixed. It was a fairly consistent British view that her interests would be best served by a strong Iran which would form a better buffer against the advance southwards towards India or Russia and which would also offer a better field for British economic enterprise. On the other hand, experience showed that a stronger Iran was as likely to assert herself in the direction of Afghanistan or the Gulf as against Russia and so act against British interests. More importantly, Britain would not aid Iran to become strong if Russia was thereby alienated. Accordingly, although at times Britain pursued policies aimed at the modernization of Iran, at others she opposed changes which might lead to a clash with Russia in which Britain would be at a disadvantage. There were offsetting advantages for Iran from the presence of Britain and Russia, notably in the development of international trade, in the control of internal disorder (as in the matter of the succession), and in regional security through the containment of disputes with the Ottoman empire and Iran. The peaceful definition of Iran's frontiers was a valuable gain. Nevertheless, it seems clear that the net effect of the action of the two powers in Iran was to impede change and this is nowhere more clear than in the matter of railway development. It was Russian jealousy more than any other factor which prevented any serious railway development in Iran even to the extent that Russia acquired in 1890 a veto over any railway construction in Iran. Attempts by Iran to enlist the help of another power in an effort to break out of this control failed.

ARABIA

No estimate of the population of Arabia in 1800 can be other than a complete guess: 1 million is as likely to be correct as any other figure. Most of the peninsula was desert; cultivation depended upon rainfall or underground water resources, such as those which supported the oases of eastern Arabia, for example al-Ḥasā. Two mountainous areas embraced much of the settled agriculture: Oman and Yemen, and probably the largest part of the population lived in these areas. The principal crops were grain, fruit and dates. Specialist crops included Yemeni coffee (an industry declining in the eighteenth century) and *qāt* a narcotic shrub. A large part of the population was pastoral, dependent upon flocks of sheep, goats and horses; the last formed an important item of export. Industry consisted principally of handicrafts for local use together with fishing around the coasts. The only major industries were pearling in the Gulf, which attracted thousands of pearlers during the annual season, and the pilgrimage, which also attracted thousands of would-be *ḥājjīs* at the appropriate time. Pearling, fishing and trade (including the trade in slaves from East Africa) created a demand for ships, and shipbuilding was an activity in several small ports. Most of the principal towns were on the coast: on the Gulf coast were several small ports from Kuwayt to Muscat; near ṭhe mouth of the Red Sea was Aden, much reduced in size, and the main port of Yemen was Ḥudayda. Jiddah, which served Mecca, was principally noted for the pilgrim traffic. Mecca and Medina owed their eminence to their religious prestige although they still retained some local significance as market towns for the surrounding tribes and as centres of government. Elsewhere were small oases which were the sites of settlements, for example Ḥā'il and Darʿiyya. Rastaq, the ancient capital of Oman, was the centre of a more considerable population but probably the largest town in Arabia was Ṣanʿāʾ, the capital of the Yemen. The towns contained government servants, artisans and religious experts.

Socially, the structure was tribal. Whether men were nomadic or settled their status was determined by their membership of a tribe which was the principal focus of their loyalties. Those who stood outside the tribal structure – artisans, some merchants, slaves, certain religious figures, especially those claiming descent from the Prophet – were dependent upon tribal protection or tolerance. The *sayyids* played an important role in Arabia as the mediators of tribal disputes, their knowledge, prestige and tribal neutrality making them valued for this purpose. Members of the ʿAydarūs family, who were custodians of the main shrine at Aden, were the most respected and authoritative figures in the locality and a point of reference for local tribal leaders. But although the *Sharīʿa* might prevail in the towns, elsewhere tribal custom was the code of rules by which men lived.

The population was overwhelmingly Muslim. Only a very few non-Muslims lived in Arabia, including a Jewish community in Yemen and Aden, and some Hindu merchants on the Gulf coast. The Muslim population was divided into Sunnīs, who prevailed throughout the north and west, Imāmī Shīʿīs who lived in certain areas of the Gulf coast, notably Baḥrayn and al-Ḥasā, Ibāḍīs in Oman and Zaydī Shīʿīs who formed the highland population of Yemen, the lowland areas being principally inhabited by Sunnīs of the Shāfiʿī rite. One would not wish to over-emphasize the significance of these religious differences. Doctrinally, the differences were small. The Zaydīs were the most Sunnī-like of the Shīʿī groups and the Ibāḍīs regarded themselves merely as good Muslims. Only in the context of religious revival did the differences become significant.

Politically, Arabia in 1800 was virtually independent of outside influence. Ottoman power had declined to almost nothing. The Ottomans had been expelled from Yemen in the 1630s and their place had been taken by the imams of Ṣanʿāʾ, whose power had also diminished during the eighteenth century, and various groups had established local independence in the south-west. The Ottomans had lost Aden and Hadramaut in the early eighteenth century. ʿAsīr, where Aḥmad b. Idrīs finally settled, was virtually independent, power being divided between the tribes of the Tihāma lowlands and those of the highlands. In the Hijaz the sharīf of Mecca had complete autonomy, although he continued to acknowledge Ottoman suzerainty. In eastern Arabia the Ottomans had had no power since the sixteenth century. The main political development in Arabia during the nineteenth century was the assertion of outside power over much of the peninsula: in the north and west the Ottomans; in the south and east the British.

In 1800 the major political power in Arabia was that of the Wahhābīs. Wahhābīsm was a puritanical Muslim movement which represented a development of the teachings of the strict Ḥanbalī school of Sunnī Muslim interpretation by Muḥammad ibn ʿAbd al-Wahhāb (1734–1792). It was given new force when it was adopted as the ideology of a political movement based upon the tribes of eastern and central Arabia led by Muḥammad ibn Suʿūd (d. 1765) of Najd. At the end of the eighteenth and during the early years of the nineteenth century under the leadership of ʿAbd al-ʿAzīz I ibn Suʿūd (1721–1803) and Suʿūd II ibn Suʿūd (1748–1814) the Wahhābī/Saʿūdī alliance expanded its power to the shores of the Persian Gulf and to the Hijaz and mounted raids into the Ottoman provinces of Iraq and Syria. The Wahhābīs also interrupted the pilgrim caravan from Damascus.

By their criticism of the laxities of Muslim observance the Wahhābīs constituted a challenge to orthodox Islam, and by their disregard of his claims they presented a challenge to the political legitimacy of the Ottoman sultan. Like the Bābīs in Iran the Wahhābīs opposed the social order and it became the object of the sultan to crush them, a goal which was eventually achieved through the agency of Muḥammad ʿAlī of Egypt between 1811 and 1818. The Egyptians evacuated Najd in 1824, returned in 1837 and finally withdrew in 1840, leaving central Arabia to the Saʿūdis.

Muḥammad ʿAlī had no better success to his repeated efforts to subjugate ʿAsīr and Yemen. Eleven expeditions were launched against ʿAsīr between 1814 and 1840 but the region remained independent. In the Yemen the Egyptians could only acquire a foothold on the coast. The Egyptian defeat in Syria in 1840 allowed the Ottomans to return to Arabia but the recovery of Ottoman power in Arabia was slow. The Hashemite rulers of the Hijaz remained virtually autonomous; the Ottoman *vālī* was generally disregarded by them. Only from 1880 did ʿAbd ül-Ḥamīd attempt to recover some control, mainly by playing off one faction in the Hijaz against another, but he had little success and more or less abandoned the attempt after 1886. The situation was only changed by the construction of the Hijaz railway and the advent of the Young Turks which events were the prelude to a more active Ottoman policy in the Hijaz.

The Ottomans reoccupied Ḥudayda in 1849 but made no serious effort to occupy the interior of Yemen until 1872. The Hijaz provided a base for Ottoman efforts to extend their power down the Red Sea coast and the opening of the Suez Canal in 1869 was an important factor in enabling the Ottomans to bring ships, troops and supplies to the region. In 1869 they mounted a campaign to recover control of ʿAsīr and in 1872 they extended the campaign into the Yemeni interior. There followed a prolonged colonial war waged by the Ottomans with the object of subjugating the Yemen, a war which was expensive in manpower with heavy losses through disease and which was unpopular within the empire. In 1911 the Ottomans called a halt and by agreement with the Imam Yaḥyā conceded autonomy to the Yemen. During the last part of the nineteenth century the Ottomans also made a major effort to recover power in central and eastern Arabia through an expedition launched from Iraq in 1871 which successfully re-established Ottoman control over al-Ḥasā and gave them a base for the extension of their influence over eastern Arabia where the Saʿūdī power had revived since

1840. By an alliance with the Rashīdī family of Ḥā'il the Ottomans were able to control the area successfully, at least until the resurgence of the Saʿūdīs after 1902.

British power rested primarily on control of the sea and therefore rooted itself on the coasts of eastern and southern Arabia. On the shores of the Persian Gulf and the Arabian Sea in 1800 were a number of small states. The largest was Oman where the Āl Bū Saʿīd dynasty had come to power in 1749 and created a large trading empire in the Indian Ocean based on the coastal strip of Muscat, a number of ports in the two gulfs and the island of Zanzibar in the west. Interior Oman, where the Ibāḍī community lived in traditional fashion with a mainly subsistence economy, had little involvement in these dynastic adventures. The Persian Gulf coast of Oman, which later became known as Trucial Oman and now forms the United Arab Emirates, was dominated in its northern section by the Qawāsim Arabs and in its southern reaches by the Banū Ya's Arabs and was divided politically into a number of small shaykhdoms. The Qawāsim lived by fishing, trading, pearling and occasionally piracy. Further up the Arab shore of the Gulf, Kuwayt and the island of Baḥrayn had passed during the eighteenth century under the control of the ʿUtūb Arabs, who had considerably expanded their trading activities. Like all Gulf Arabs they were involved in the pearl fishing on the banks off Baḥrayn.

British interest in the Gulf arose from her involvement in India and was related to trade, the defence of India and the routes to it, and humanitarian impulses. The combination of these factors led to an effort to control the waters of the Gulf, partly by combating piracy and regulating maritime warfare conducted by the Arabs of the region. British efforts to suppress Arab attacks on trading vessels included armed expeditions in 1809 and 1820, but a solution to the problem was eventually found through British-sponsored voluntary action by the shaykhs, which took the form of annual and eventually permanent truces. Britain was the sponsor and policeman of this system and her role provided the basis for the gradual extension of her influence, the regulation of the slave-trade and the arms traffic, and the negotiation of agreements which excluded foreign influence. During the last twenty years of the nineteenth century agreements were reached with Baḥrayn, the Trucial states, Oman and Kuwayt which amounted to veiled British protectorates. Although the Gulf did not become an exclusively British preserve because of the presence of the Ottomans and Iran, Britain was the predominant power in the region.

The establishment of British influence along the coasts of southern Arabia derived from her possession of Aden which was taken in 1839.

The annexation of Aden was the consequence of two factors: the search for a suitable coaling base for the technically primitive steamers newly introduced on the Bombay–Suez route; and the threat to British interests in the Ottoman empire in general and in Arabia in particular posed by the activities of Muḥammad ʿAlī in Egypt. For many years after the capture of Aden Britain was content to sit tight behind her fortifications and to eschew further expansion in south-west Arabia, but after the opening of the Suez Canal in 1869 Aden's importance and prosperity rapidly increased and Britain, concerned by the advance of Ottoman forces in Yemen, began to extend her own sphere of influence. In 1873 Britain made an agreement with the tribal shaykhs of West Aden (or south Yemen) which excluded foreign influence and in 1882 concluded a similar agreement with the Qu'aytī ruler of Hadramaut. British control was also extended to the Somali coast.

By 1900 Arabia presented a very different picture from that of 1800. Wahhābī power was eclipsed and the Ottoman empire and Britain had seemingly asserted themselves in the region. In fact there was much less change than this formulation suggests. Both Ottoman and British power was confined almost exclusively to the coasts. The Ottomans abandoned the effort to control the interior of Hijaz, Yemen and eastern Arabia directly and contented themselves with incorporating autonomous rulers within their system. British control was based upon cheap sea power and hardly extended more than a gunshot from the coast. Further inland Britain attempted to do no more than exclude foreign influence, leaving the inhabitants to run their own affairs. Accordingly, although British and Ottoman efforts to influence events had some effect on the power structure of the interior this effect was very limited and the social and economic life of Arabia was almost unaffected. The promotion of trade and the improvement of navigation, the control of the slave-trade and quarantine measures had some distant consequences but for tribesman and cultivator life was little changed.

NOTES

1. Quoted H. A. Reed, "The destruction of the Janissaries by Mahmud II in June 1826", unpublished Ph.D. thesis, Princeton 1951, 131.
2. Quoted N. Berkes, *The development of secularism in Turkey*, Montreal 1964, 105.
3. Sir Henry Layard, *Autobiography and letters*, II, London 1903, 94.

4. Nassau Senior, *Journal kept in Turkey and Greece in the autumn of 1857 and the beginning of 1858*, London 1859, 107.
5. Quoted M. Ma'oz, *Ottoman reform in Syria and Palestine, 1840–61*, Oxford 1968, 78.
6. Quoted G. Douin, *Histoire du règne du Khédive Ismaīl*, I, Rome 1933–8, 1.
7. E. Stack, *Six months in Persia*, II, New York 1882, 165.
8. Muḥammad Ḥasan Khān I'timād al-Salṭana, *Rūznāma-yi khāṭirāt*, Tehran 1966–7, 1025. Quoted S. Bakhash, *Iran: monarchy, bureaucracy and reform under the Qajars 1855–1896*, London 1978, 268.
9. Khān Malik Sāsānī, *Sīyāsatgarān-i dawra-yi Qājār*, I, Tehran 1958–66, 17. Quoted G. Nashat, *The origins of modern reform in Iran*, 1870–80, Urbana, Ill., 1982, 21.
10. Quoted Nashat, *Origins of modern reform in Iran*, 36.

CHAPTER FOUR

Nationalism and Revolution in the Near East 1880–1914

THE CENTRAL GOVERNMENT OF THE OTTOMAN EMPIRE

It was once the convention of European writers to contrast the liberalism of the Tanẓīmāt with the despotism of ʿAbd ül-Ḥamīd II and to represent the dismissal of Midḥat Pasha in 1877 as a watershed in the Ottoman reform movement. A closer study of events shows that this view was mistaken; in all essential lines of policy the Hamidian era was a continuation of the Tanẓīmāt; the differences are those of emphasis, presentation and style.

The army continued to be the principal object of attention; organization was improved, conscription was extended and new weapons were introduced, including the Mauser rifle for the infantry and artillery from Krupps. Particular care was given to the education and training of army officers with the aid of a German military mission. In addition, to relieve the regular army of some of the burdens of constabulary duties, the gendarmerie was expanded and new irregular cavalry formations, known as Ḥamīdiyya, were created. In the interests of economy, naval development was held back. The administrative system was also elaborated through the development of municipal government, and was further centralized under the control of the Ministry of the Interior. Education and training were of especial concern; the Civil Service College, the Mülkiye, was reorganized and new schools for legal and financial specialists were opened.

Education and law were major preoccupations of the Hamidian regime. In education most attention was given as before to secondary and higher education with the intention of supplying suitable recruits to the army, navy and bureaucracy. In 1900 the reorganized Ottoman University was opened. Legal reform focused on providing judges with a modern legal training to operate the expanded system of state courts, the introduction of new codes of procedure, and the extension of state control exercised by the Ministry of Justice which was reorganized and given control over all state courts other than the *Sharīʿa* courts. The consular and Mixed Courts continued their independent existence.

Much attention was given to the development of communications by the extension of the telegraph network, road building and the construction of railways, mainly through the device of concessions but also by direct government action as in the case of the Hijaz railway. Through investment in communications, as through the establishment of greater public security, the state made some contribution to economic development; during the Hamidian period, far more than was the case under the Tanẓīmāt, there is evidence of state efforts to promote the growth of certain industries and, more especially, the improved cultivation of crops. It would be wrong to suppose, however, that there was any change in the older, *laissez-faire* attitude to economic development during the Hamidian period; state interventions were primarily related to revenue enhancement and military ends; the industries which received most attention were those which were linked to war. There was no movement towards tariff protection or economic investment by the state; foreign capital, placed primarily in railways, public utilities and banking, was the principal element in investment.

Under ʿAbd ül-Ḥamīd government was even more centralized than previously. Within the Porte there was greater stability than during the years prior to the establishment of the sultan's authority. Five prime ministers – Meḥmed Saʿīd, Meḥmed Kāmil, Aḥmed Jevād, Khalīl Rifʿat and Meḥmed Ferīd – held sway for nearly twenty-eight of the last thirty years of ʿAbd ül-Ḥamīd's reign and individual ministers ruled their departments for long periods, giving much continuity to the execution of policy. Although ministers did not possess such independent power as the indifference of ʿAbd ül-Mejīd had permitted the ministers of the early Tanẓīmāt or the acquiescence of ʿAbd ül-ʿAzīz had given to ʿAlī and Fuʿād, it would be wrong to suppose that ʿAbd ül-Ḥamīd's ministers were merely clerks who executed his will. Saʾīd and Kāmil, in particular, were men of considerable ability who designed and carried through policies which they believed to be important. Nevertheless, ʿAbd ül-Ḥamīd did intervene much more in the affairs of government than his predecessors had done and sought advice from various sources outside the bureaucracy.

During the reign of ʿAbd ül-Ḥamīd much greater influence was exercised by the sultan's personal staff in the palace (Yi̊ldi̊z), led by the military hero Ghāzī ʿOs̱mān Pasha and including a number of powerful secretaries who also served in the official bureaucracy. The sultan also developed his own secret police and an elaborate spy network to provide information directly to him.

One source of advice was unorthodox religious figures, principally Arabs from Syria, including Abu'l Hudā al-Sayyādī, the head of the important Rifāʿī Ṣūfī order in Aleppo (who rose under the sultan's patronage to become Qāḍīʿasker of Rumelia in 1885), Abu'l Hudā's protégé, Aḥmed ʿIzzat Pasha, and Muḥammad Ẓāfir from Tripoli in North Africa. These men were popularly credited with considerable powers to shape Ottoman policies under ʿAbd ül-Ḥamīd, but the evidence suggests that with the exception of ʿIzzat Pasha who also served as a palace secretary, their influence was overrated. Primarily they functioned as the sultan's propaganda agents, emphasizing his role as caliph and offsetting arguments intended to stress differences between Arab interests and those of the Ottoman empire. In return they were able to promote the interests of their own families, friends and orders. During the reign of ʿAbd ül-Ḥamīd there was a growth of Ṣūfī Islam by comparison with orthodox Islam.

The new salience of Islam in the Ottoman empire is one feature which distinguishes the reign of ʿAbd ül-Ḥamīd from those of his nineteenth-century predecessors. Although in no way hostile to Islam the Tanẓīmāt statesmen had steadily restricted its public functions and had often perceived organized Islam as an opponent to particular reforms and to their general programme of Ottomanism, a secular political ideology. Under ʿAbd ül-Ḥamīd this policy was not changed in its essentials; the public role of Islam in law and education was further limited and Ottomanism remained the ostensible basis of the state. But Islam was now embraced as an ally in this programme, a device which could fasten the bonds of the empire more tightly and which could also attract support to the empire in the outside world.

Panislamism, as it was called by Europeans, had two aspects. Within the empire it served to rally Muslims to the defence of the polity, encouraging them to see the embattled empire as their defence against the sea of infidelity. In this context the pious appearance of the sultan's court, the money made available for mosque construction and the volume of religious publication all contrived to give the Hamidian regime a far greater popularity than the Tanẓīmāt regimes had enjoyed. Islam served to socialize the Tanẓīmāt reforms without changing their nature. Outside the empire Islam served a different purpose. In earlier times the office of caliph had combined both religious and temporal authority. From the late eighteenth century, in response to external developments beginning with the separation of the Crimea from the empire in 1774, a novel doctrine had been asserted, namely that the caliph possessed a religious authority over all Muslims, distinct from political authority. To this doctrine was added another new assertion, that the Ottoman sultan was the true and rightful caliph having inherited his office from the last ʿAbbasid caliph following the conquest of Egypt in 1517. In combination these two doctrines were used, from the 1860s, to justify Ottoman interest in the fate of the Muslim khanates of Turkestan, then falling under Russian control. Under ʿAbd ül-Ḥamīd the new theory of the caliphate became a powerful diplomatic weapon against all European powers which ruled over substantial numbers of Muslims, in particular Russia, France and Britain.

It is difficult to judge the extent to which these doctrines were accepted by Muslims; some found it convenient to embrace them; others repudiated them as novel and unfounded arguments. It is clear, however, that the assertions reinforced an existing sentiment among Muslims who looked to the Ottoman sultan as the most powerful independent Muslim ruler, a pillar of support in a world which was becoming increasingly hostile to the claims of Islam and one in which the great majority of Muslims lived under alien rule. The necessity for Muslims to reform their ways and to unite to oppose infidel encroachment was one which was expounded by several writers, most notably Jamāl al-Dīn al-Afghānī (1838/9–97) who in his last years enjoyed the protection and patronage of the sultan. The appeal of ʿAbd ül-Ḥamīd to Muslims was a real one; the contributions of Muslims throughout the world to the costs of the Hijaz railway, ostensibly designed to facilitate the pilgrimage, show the strength of the sentiment. To Europeans Panislamism was a serious threat. They found it easy to accept the notion of religious authority divorced from temporal power for it was one embedded in the political organization and theory of Europe since the Middle Ages. They also found only too persuasive the idea that Muslims were essentially fanatical and prone to resort to violence in response to a religious appeal. Accordingly, they accepted that there was a danger, if the sultan was pressed too hard, that Europeans might be confronted with agitation, even rebellion in their colonial dependencies. Equally, a satisfied ʿAbd ül-Ḥamīd could make life easier for Europeans in all their contacts with Muslims.

If ʿAbd ül-Ḥamīd was perceived by Europeans as the protector of Muslims he was also seen as the murderer of Christians, as Abdul the Damned, or the Red Sultan, the epithet referring to the colour of blood and not, of course, to his politics. ʿAbd ül-Ḥamīd acquired this soubriquet in consequence of the massacres of Armenians during the 1890s. Thereafter, Armenian *émigrés* in Europe were numbered among his most powerful enemies and their attacks upon his regime became the major factor in forming the extremely unfavourable view of the Hamidian system which has since prevailed among writers on the subject.

ʿAbd ül-Ḥamīd was an intelligent man, an able politician, a ruthless modernizer, a patriotic ruler strongly sensible of his duties and, by most standards, mad. In ʿAbd ül-Ḥamīd suspicion of those about him was carried to absurd and dangerous lengths. He refused to delegate real power, maintained a spy system which struck fear into his subordinates without being especially effective, and operated a strict and grotesque censorship. Lest his subjects should find inspiration in the murder of foreign rulers no Ottoman newspaper ever permitted any foreign potentates to depart this life by other than natural causes. His pervasive mania handicapped the working of the Ottoman government. It was ʿAbd ül-Ḥamīd's suspicions which led him to reject an opportunity provided by Britain to regain control over Egypt, and the Armenian massacres were a brutal display of his fears which cost his regime dear. The comparison with Joseph Stalin is irresistible.

The Young Turk revolution

The Hamidian regime was overthrown by revolution in July 1908 and, nine months later, in April 1909, the sultan himself was deposed. The revolution, known as the Young Turk revolution, was unlike previous movements of opposition within the empire both in its success and in the composition of the revolutionary group. Previous movements of opposition were of three types: in the provinces revolts by discontented Christian minorities which aimed at autonomy or separation from the empire; movements of tribal groups or notables whose power was abridged by the Tanẓīmāt reforms; and disputes within the civil-military élite of the empire, particularly the episode of 1876. The Young Turk movement, however, was composed mainly of junior army officers and minor bureaucrats and had two aims: the salvation of the empire and the restoration of the constitution of 1876 or, more precisely, of those parts of the constitution which had been suspended since 1878, principally the Ottoman Parliament. Although minorities gave some support to the movement it was essentially directed by Ottoman Muslims, in particular those who had been brought up within the new reformed institutions.

This view of the Young Turks was not held by British observers at the time. Under the guidance of the oriental counsellor at the British Embassy, G. H. Fitzmaurice, British officialdom regarded the Young Turks as Freemasons and Jews engaged in a conspiracy to impose upon the empire an alien system of ideas. How Fitzmaurice came to this quite false view is a mystery, but it was an interpretation which Britons found very convenient during the First World War when it was their object to try to discredit the Young Turks among their Muslim subjects, and it was one which was not uncongenial to the Nationalists who succeeded the Young Turks and also wished to make them a scapegoat for the ills of the empire. The Young Turks, and especially the leading party among them, the Committee of Union and Progress, have been the subject of consistent misrepresentation.

There were two strands in the Young Turk movement: first, the activities of a number of *émigrés*, mainly civilians who left the empire because they were discontented or involved in a conspiracy and who published their complaints and prescriptions in Europe; and, second, the operations of secret societies within the empire, particularly those involving military officers. The links between these two strands are tenuous and consist of the alleged transmission of ideas from the first group to the second through literature smuggled into the empire, and organizational links forged in 1907 which appear to have had no influence on the conduct of the secret groups within the empire. Indeed, from the point of view of understanding the 1908 revolution it would be possible to disregard the *émigrés* altogether, but some account of them is justified by the interest of their ideas and the demonstration of the variety of their prescriptions. It will be convenient to examine the *émigrés* through the personalities of three of the most notable among them.

One line of thought among the critics derived from the Islamic modernist ideas of Nāmi̊q Kemāl and was particularly linked with a former associate of the Young Ottomans, Murād Bey (1853–1912), who left the empire in 1895 and went first to Cairo where he published a paper, *Mīzān* (the Balance). Murād believed that a constitution was necessary to protect the empire from the vagaries of the sultan but it must be a constitution which was compatible with the *Sharīʿa*. Under the constitution and through education the empire would be saved. In exile Murād found himself linked to some unwanted companions, in particular the Armenian critics of ʿAbd ül-Ḥamīd, and the European opponents of the Ottoman regime. The reconciliation of Islam and constitutionalism began to appear more difficult and the sultan seemed a lesser evil to Muslims than the dangers of Christian intervention. In 1897 Murād made his peace with the sultan and returned to Istanbul where he was rewarded with high office. Murād was criticized for having sold out to ʿAbd ül-Ḥamīd but this simple version of events fails to do justice to what was a real dilemma for all Muslim Ottomans. Murād had solved the problem as Muslim jurists had done in the past –

by concluding that it was better to tolerate some injustice if the alternative was chaos or the rule of infidelity.

A second element in the Young Turk critique was represented by Aḥmed Riżā (1859–1930), a former Director of Education who had gone to Paris in 1889 and in 1895 began to publish *Meshveret* (Consultation). Aḥmed Riżā supported the restoration of the 1876 constitution but in other respects his ideas were not dissimilar to those which were the stock in trade of the Tanẓīmāt reformers, namely Ottomanism, centralization and long-term salvation through education. His emphasis upon education, if not an occupational reaction, is perhaps the principal evidence of the influence upon him of Positivist ideas which also provided the slogan of his newspaper – "Order and Progress". Otherwise, in his emphasis upon a powerful role for the state outside the field of education his ideas are not in keeping with those of the Positivists and his selectivity may again endorse the view that the Ottoman reformers took from Europe the ideas which suited them and were not the slavish adherents of inappropriate models. What Aḥmed Riżā lacked, however, was any prescription for winning power since he rejected, until shortly before 1908, any violent revolution and he would not co-operate with those groups, including the Armenians, who sought to bring about reform in the Ottoman empire through European pressure on the sultan.

The third and most revolutionary prescription for reform was that of Prince Ṣabāḥ ül-Dīn (1877–1948), the son of an Ottoman prince who fled to Europe in 1899. Whereas the universal answer to the empire's problems provided by all previous reformers had been a more powerful state, Ṣabāḥ ül-Dīn argued that centralization merely exacerbated the problems of the empire and that salvation lay in decentralization. At first sight this recommendation seems very similar to those of the minorities and Europeans who had called for the devolution of authority to more or less autonomous provinces and the creation of a confederal imperial structure, and it is true that Ṣabāḥ ül-Dīn's views provided a bridge through which he could hope for an accommodation with the minorities and particularly with the Armenians and also meant that he need not rule out reform through the agency of European pressure. But in fact Ṣabāḥ ül-Dīn's views went deeper than this. What he was really concerned with was not the devolution of political power to other governmental bodies – in fact he never proposed the reduction of control from Istanbul – but the limitation of the sphere of political action and the greater responsibility of the individual for decision-making. In particular, unlike other Ottoman reformers, Ṣabāḥ ül-Dīn saw salvation not in politics but in economics. Economic individualism would both remove conflict from the political arena and usher in a great advance in material prosperity. Contented subjects would ensure the preservation of the empire. The origin of these ideas is easy to perceive; they were essentially those of the Anglo-Saxon *laissez-faire* philosophers led by Herbert Spencer and they came to Ṣabāḥ ül-Dīn through the writings of Edmond Demolins. They were chosen by Ṣabāḥ ül-Dīn because they offered an apparent answer to the particular problems of the empire. After 1908 the same ideas were to influence the Liberal Party just as the ideas of Aḥmed Riżā were prominent in the Committee of Union and Progress.

Unlike the *émigrés* who conducted their arguments through newspapers in Cairo, Paris and Geneva and aired their differences at well-reported congresses, the conspirators within the empire carried on their affairs in a secrecy which not only defeated, for the most part, the attentions of ʿAbd ül-Ḥamīd's secret police but have also commonly vanquished the historian who is obliged to rely upon the memoirs of interested parties written in very different circumstances years after the events concerned. The sad truth is that we know very little about the origins of the July 1908 revolution or how it was planned and directed.

At the heart of any inquiries must be the question of why the army, the principal beneficiary of the Ottoman reform movement, should have turned against the regime it served, in particular why the college-trained officers should have led the opposition in 1908. One attempted explanation alleges that the composition of the officer corps changed during the Hamidian period. Cadets now came forward, it is claimed, from provincial families with no military tradition and these men found themselves the objects of discrimination resulting in unattractive postings and slow promotion as compared with officers from more acceptable backgrounds. Disgruntled and disappointed they were ready material for conspiracies and their concentration in the Third Army in Macedonia made that army the main centre of the 1908 revolution. It is an attractive theory, particularly to those acquainted with the evolution of revolutionary sentiment in the Egyptian and Syrian armies after the Second World War when something very like this process did take place. Unfortunately, apart from the career records of a few individual officers it has no evidence to support it; no one has discovered, or examined the records of officer cadets in the Ḥarbiye which would permit a judgement on the merits of the theory.

The cadets involved in the first conspiracy of which we have knowledge do fit the pattern above. In 1889 a group of students in the Istanbul Medical College formed a party known as the Ottoman Union (later Union and Progress), built around the ideas of Nāmiq Kemāl. This group and others extended their influence (we are led to believe) and a coup was planned for 1896 which was discovered by the sultan and the conspirators were obliged to flee or conceal themselves. In fact some doubt attends the projected coup, whether it was so extensive as was claimed or whether it had the goals alleged. It has been suggested that the plot was magnified by those in authority as a device for taking measures against their rivals. What we do know, however, is that from early in the twentieth century there are records of several groups within the Ottoman field armies engaged in discussing reform and revolution. The best known of these was the Ottoman Freedom Society which was founded in Salonika in September 1906 and which included both military officers and civilian officials among whom the most prominent was Ṭal ʿat Pasha, a post office official. It was this group which, in September 1907, established links with Aḥmed Riżā's group in Geneva and adopted the name of the Committee of Union and Progress (CUP). Branches of the Ottoman Freedom Society were founded elsewhere, notably in Monastir, where the members were probably more numerous and more active than those in Salonika. Many men who were to become leaders of the CUP in the following years joined the society in this period.

The confusion and contradictions of the various accounts of these societies, of their membership and activities and importance and, above all, of their connections with one another may indicate that they were insubstantial groups, often mere meetings of discontented men to exchange ideas rather than organizations engaged in a conspiracy to seize power and carry through a far-reaching transformation of the empire. Another theory, however, asserts that such obscurity was inevitable in an organization to which secrecy was all-important; the conspirators could not know each other because that would open them to the danger of penetration by the sultan's spies. In fact, it is claimed, they had an elaborate network of communication exploiting other secret societies, including Freemason lodges and Ṣūfī orders. The question remains, however: whatever the secrecy should not more evidence have survived of so general a conspiracy if it existed?

The course of events in the summer of 1908 has the appearance of a series of unplanned responses to a developing situation. Apparently suspecting the existence of disaffected groups within the Third Army the Ottoman government ordered an investigation followed by a second. Neither investigation uncovered any elaborate organization, possibly because none existed, but some dissidents, alarmed at the possibility of discovery, took evasive action. Among them was an officer named Niyāzī who left Monastir and took to the hills accompanied by some 200 men, including soldiers and civilians. In the name of his 200 men Niyāzī issued an appeal for the restoration of the constitution of 1876. Niyāzī's appeal was the first clear statement of an objective for the opposition and one which found wide support during the following weeks for it possessed the two essentials of a revolutionary slogan: it was simple and it was meaningless. In 1878 the constitution had proved to be no restriction on the sultan's power and no answer to the problems of the empire. Around so inoffensive and innocuous an appeal almost all groups could rally. Some of those who declared for the constitution did so because they believed it was what the sultan wanted. No other, more specific goals were ever stated.

There followed a number of mutinies and demonstrations throughout Macedonia accompanied by demands for the 1876 constitution. That they were part of a calculated plan seems doubtful although they were exploited by the CUP. An example is the Firzovik incident when a group of Albanians destroyed a picnic site prepared for an Austro-German society, allegedly because the Albanians thought the picnic was to be the occasion of an orgy. A CUP member persuaded the Albanians that what they truly wanted was not the simple, hooligan pleasure of destruction but a constitution and a demand was duly sent to the sultan. The response of the Ottoman government to these events was confused and tended to accelerate their development. The Porte ordered investigations, arrests and sent in troops from outside. All failed: investigating officers were assassinated, suspects took to the hills and the fresh troops refused to fire on their fellow soldiers. On 23 July ʿAbd ül-Ḥamīd gave way and proclaimed the restoration of the constitution.

The Young Turk revolution of July 1908 appears to have been an unco-ordinated but widespread reaction of frightened men to the threat of a Hamidian purge. It took place within a very general context of disaffection towards the regime, especially marked in Macedonia, and in a situation in which outside events had set an example of radical and liberal opposition. The Japanese victory over Russia was an event frequently discussed and was perceived as an example of what could be achieved against European power by a determined, modern and liberal Asian state. The Russian Revolution of 1905 also appeared as a victory of liberalism as well as a weakening of the empire's principal antagonist. The revolution in Iran in 1906 and the demonstrations in Egypt in 1907 were still nearer examples of activity in favour of a more liberal system. In revolution, as in other affairs, fashion is a significant factor. To the Third Army in Macedonia these examples must have seemed especially relevant for it was in Macedonia that the problems of the Ottoman empire seemed most acute. The province had become the focus of inchoate national aspirations, of the ambitions of its Balkan neighbours and of widespread political and social violence. It was also the object of the particular attention of the European powers who had already obliged the Ottomans to accept a packet of reform measures involving the establishment of an international gendarmerie, with which the Third Army compared its own condition unfavourably for the gendarmes were much better paid for doing the same work. It was feared that the next step might be a European-imposed partition of Macedonia among the Balkan states, and it was believed that the May 1908 meeting of Edward VII and Tsar Nicholas II at Reval had been concerned with planning such a partition. How much all these events contributed to the revolution is unclear; all one can say is that the rapid spread of opposition to the regime in July 1908 indicates either careful planning, for which no good evidence exists, or considerable receptivity to the idea of radical, violent action.

The Young Turks in power 1908–18

The events of July 1908 did not constitute a revolution but they made a revolution possible. The key development was the establishment of a Parliament with the requirement of elections and the need for party organization to win elections and to be effective in the new Parliament which opened in December 1908. In this new political arena the CUP had a head start over its rivals for, rightly or wrongly, it was widely credited with having master-minded the July events. Its leaders were thrust into prominence and many men hastened to obtain the endorsement of the CUP during the elections. Equally, the CUP aroused strong animosities among those who regretted the passing of the former system and those who belonged to different factions among the Young Turks, notably the liberals. From 1908 until 1913 the CUP was engaged in a struggle with these and other elements for mastery.

In the struggle for political domination in the Ottoman empire the first major confrontation took place in April 1909. According to one view, what happened in April 1909 was that the forces of reaction, led by the sultan, attacked the CUP with the intention of overthrowing the constitution but were ultimately confounded when the CUP assembled a force in Macedonia, marched on Istanbul and defeated the reactionaries. It is now clear that this view is wrong. There was an element of Muslim opposition to the CUP, which was represented by an organization known as the Muhammadan Union which attacked the CUP on grounds of infidelity and called for a return to the *Sharīʿa*. But the principal element in the uprising was military and sprang from the old antagonism within the army between the college-trained officers and those promoted from the ranks. It was the first group which had been the particular beneficiaries of 1908 and had promptly engaged themselves in politics in the hope of rapid promotion and other benefits. They had left the former rankers (who numbered 80% of the officer corps) to carry out the ordinary regimental duties. Resentment first manifested itself among the Arab and Albanian soldiers of the sultan's Palace Guard and spread to soldiers of the First Army. Supported by religious students and others the mutinous troops took control of Istanbul, attacked known CUP supporters and demanded the dismissal of certain ministers. The liberal chief minister, Hüseyn Ḥilmī Pasha, resigned and was replaced by Aḥmed Tevfīq who quickly restored order. There is no evidence that the sultan or his ministers were involved and the orthodox ulema subsequently denounced the Muhammadan Union for creating anarchy. The whole affair was at an end a week before the so-called Action Army, assembled from the Second and Third Armies and accompanied by volunteers, arrived in Istanbul.

The April 1909 uprising was a turning-point in the Young Turk revolution. The principal beneficiaries of July 1908 had been the bureaucracy for they had Parliament to provide them with bargaining power against the sultan, just as the ministers of 1876 had foreseen. The old bureaucrats had remained firmly in charge of government and the new men of 1908 had been left on the sidelines. As a result of the April events the constitution was amended, the powers of the sultan virtually eliminated, those of the bureaucrats reduced and the powers of Parliament enhanced. The long domination of the Ottoman reform movement by the civil bureaucracy, which had endured since 1826, was coming to an end. Power was shifting towards men who had a quite different political base but the immediate beneficiary of 1909 was the army.

In the Young Turk revolution as in other episodes of Ottoman and Turkish history it is crucial to keep in mind the distinction between the activities of politically minded junior officers and the operations of the army as an institution. It was the army as an institution which was the clear winner in April 1909. The commander of the Action Army, Maḥmūd Shevket Pasha, a senior career staff officer, emerged as the principal influence on Ottoman political development during the next three years. Shevket exercised his influence in a negative fashion. He did not claim to interfere directly in government; government was a matter for bureaucrats and politicians and in his view the army was above politics; it represented the state. But the demands of the army must have priority over all other policies; its needs for money and manpower must take precedence over everything else and so great were these demands that there was no room left for the political groups to accomplish any revolutionary changes in Ottoman policies. At Shevket's behest ministers were obliged to seek loans abroad and Parliament to swallow the painful necessity of the conscription of Christians into the army.

The army's demands were given additional force by the perilous international situation of the empire during these years. Naïve hopes that the international community might give the Ottoman empire another chance under a constitution were quickly disappointed. Bulgaria took advantage of the July revolution to announce its independence, Austria annexed Bosnia and Crete united with Greece. In 1911 the empire was forced into war with Italy when that state took Tripoli. In October 1912 the empire was attacked by a league of Balkan states and lost nearly all its European territories, although in the Second Balkan War, fought in the summer of 1913, it recovered Eastern Thrace including Edirne (see p. 68). These desperate events left little opportunity for the execution of new policies and helped to shape the political events of the period: in particular it was the threatened loss of Edirne which was the occasion of the coup of 23 January 1913 when the CUP finally seized power.

Between 1908 and 1909 the CUP made unsteady progress against its rivals. In 1908 it had been little more than a label covering a multitude of disparate factions but it steadily improved its central organization and hammered out policies at its party congresses. Almost nothing is known about its provincial organization. Its first members entered the government in November 1908 and the party took a major step forward in the summer of 1909 when two of its members, Ṭalʿat and Javīd, became ministers of the interior and finance respectively. At elections the CUP regularly emerged as the largest party and in 1912 its control of government was sufficient to enable it to secure a landslide victory over its main rival, the Liberal group, a coalition which favoured policies nearer to those espoused by Ṣabāḥ ül-Dīn than the centralist policies of the CUP. But in July 1912 the tenuous hold of the CUP was exposed by a movement of disgruntled army officers, who called themselves the Saviour Officers, condemned the CUP's handling of the Italian war as well as its heavy-handed domestic policy and with the support of Shevket Pasha acted to replace the CUP government by a coalition under the military hero, Ghāzī Mukhtār Pasha. Parliament was dissolved, new elections held and the old bureaucrat, Kāmil Pasha, emerged at the head of an anti-CUP government. The new government, in its turn, was discredited by defeat at the hands of the Bulgarians and, as mentioned above, the CUP seized power, ostensibly in protest against the decision to surrender Edirne. In appearance the January 1913 seizure was a true military coup. Within the CUP was a military nucleus of some forty or fifty officers including a number known as the Faithful willing to perform any act including the sacrifice of their own lives for the sake of the party. Some of these men, led by Enver Pasha, the most adventurous of all Young Turk leaders, broke into the Cabinet room and shot the minister of war, forcing the resignation of the government of Kāmil. Shevket became chief minister, but after his murder in May 1913 the CUP assumed complete control over the army as well as the other institutions of state. The 1913 coup ushered in something like a true revolution for the CUP was now able to begin to implement the programme of change which it had worked out since 1908. It was, however, to be a brief and incomplete revolution because of the involvement of the Ottoman empire in the First World War in the autumn of 1914.

In essence there was no change in the main direction of the Ottoman reform movement under the Young Turks. The liberal alternative of decentralization was rejected and the programme of the CUP was basically the old formula of Ottomanism, centralization, a strong, modern army and administration and a modernized, secularized educational and legal system. Their only novel addition was a greater emphasis upon economic development and the most striking feature of their policies was the extent to which they were willing to pursue them. The Young Turks were much more impatient, much less willing to compromise than were their predecessors.

It is unnecessary to describe in detail the efforts to streamline the central and provincial administrations, reduce the power of the *millets* and to reform the system of taxation. The modernization of the army and navy was conducted with the aid of German and British missions and with much success; the achievements of the Ottoman army in 1914–16, coming after the defeats of 1911–13, are striking. A complete reform of the gendarmerie considerably increased the power at the disposal of provincial governors. In education the most interesting developments were, first, the beginnings of advanced education for women, who were admitted to high schools; the first *lycée* for women was opened in 1911; second, the campaign for adult education conducted by the Turkish Hearth society; and, third, the much greater interest in primary education, hitherto left mainly to the religious sector. The new Primary Education law of 1913 prescribed six years of free and compulsory education for all children and defined the curriculum. The emphasis on primary education raised a problem which had hitherto been obscured. So long as the state confined itself mainly to secondary and higher education the medium of education was not a major question and as the principal object of the schools was to produce government servants it made sense to educate children in the state language, namely Ottoman Turkish. But Ottoman Turkish was an unsuitable medium for primary education and was almost incomprehensible to Anatolian children. Accordingly, a movement began to introduce a form of the language much closer to that spoken by Turkish children, that is, with a large part of the Arabic element eliminated. But in its turn this movement raised the question of what should be the language of primary education in the non-Turkish provinces and this latter question became connected with problems of cultural and political identity. The state interest in primary education also brought it into conflict with the ulema, the end of which was the assumption of control over all religious schools by the Ministry of Education and the secularization of their curricula.

From 1911 onwards the previous policy of *laissez-faire* gave way to the idea of state-led economic development with the objects of developing Ottoman industry to replace imported foreign goods and encouraging Muslims to replace non-Muslims in certain occupations; thus vocational training was provided to permit Muslims to take over jobs performed by Greeks on the railway. It was, of course, after 1914 under both the pressures and the freedom of war that state economic development made most progress. In 1917 a national credit bank was established. The pressure of war also obliged the Ottoman government to assume unprecedented powers to control production, prices and distribution, especially in Istanbul.

It has been claimed that during the Young Turk period there was a major change in the ideology of the Ottoman empire and that Ottomanism was abandoned in favour of Turkish nationalism. This claim requires closer examination. A convenient starting-point is a work entitled *Three kinds of policy* written in 1904 by Yūsuf Akchura. Akchura was born in Russia, was educated at the Ḥarbiye in Istanbul and later returned to Russia to work as a teacher in Kazan where he wrote his best-known work. In 1908 he returned to Istanbul where he became a prominent historian and writer linked to Turkish nationalist causes. He was a founder member of the Turkish Society (1908) and its successor the Turkish Hearth (1912) and edited the principal Turkish journal, *Turkish Homeland*.

Akchura distinguished three lines of policy for the Ottoman empire: Ottomanism, Panislamism and Pan-Turkism. Ottomanism, he claimed, had failed and was rejected both by minorities and Muslims. Panislamism would encounter the opposition of the Great Powers. The most suitable policy for the future was likely to be Pan-Turkism because it was in keeping with the nationalist spirit of the age and because it was less likely to encounter the hostility of the powers, with the exception of Russia. Akchura did not, however, commit himself completely as between Panislamism and Pan-Turkism.

There was no support for Akchura's ideas in 1904. Turkism as a cultural movement was accepted and was represented by an interest in the history of the Turkish peoples, a concern with the Turkish language and the cultivation of Turkish literature. All those had been features of Ottoman life since the second half of the nineteenth century. But to Ottomans Turkism as a political programme held no appeal. However, it has been argued that during the years after 1908 views changed, particularly after the loss of almost all the Ottoman possessions in Europe and the evidence of discontent among Albanians and Arabs, and that the Young Turks came to share Akchura's view that Ottomanism and Islam were unsuitable bonds to hold the empire together and that the state should rest primarily upon the supremacy of Turks; other nationalities should be held in subjection and ultimately Turkified. The most prominent ideologue of Turkish nationalism was Żiyā Gökalp (1876–1924), a collaborator of Akchura in the Turkish Hearth. Gökalp rejected Ottomanism, selected from Islam those elements which could be harmonized with Turkism and made the Turkish nation the basis of his programme.

There is no good evidence that the intellectual speculations of men like Akchura and Gökalp ever became the basis of Young Turk policy. They had some influence on educational policy and some members of the CUP, notably Enver Pasha, found them attractive. But the CUP programme remained that of its predecessors: Ottomanism, centralization, modernization. All that was required as the writer, ʿAbdallāh Jevdet (1869–1932), put it, was to go further and faster in the direction of the adoption of European civilization. This could only be achieved through the driving force of an élite in control of the centre; the people would not do it themselves. Exhibitions of ethnic nationalism were sternly repressed by the Young Turks; only when they had no alternative did they compromise and they abandoned the compromise as soon as it was convenient to do so. The appeal of Pan-Turkism was more particularly to men like Akchura, whose connections were with the Turks of Russia, or to marginal men like Gökalp whose background in a mixed Turkish–Kurdish area obliged him to consider problems of political identity which to others ranked a poor second to the practical problems of governing the empire. Only when the non-Turkish areas had gone would the way be open to develop a theory of Turkish nationalism to fit the new political reality. So long as the Ottoman empire existed it required an imperial ideology.

ANATOLIA

During the period 1880–1914 western Anatolia enjoyed unprecedented prosperity. The population of Anatolia increased by approximately 50 per cent and by 1914 had reached a figure of 17.5 million. The greater part of this increase occurred in the northern coastal belt and in the west. There was considerable agricultural development. According to one estimate cereal production between 1876 and 1908 rose by 500 per cent. Although this figure seems far too high, there was certainly a substantial expansion of production. It was during this period that Anatolia displaced Russia and the Balkans as the principal supplier of grain to the huge Istanbul market, providing 75 per cent of its soft wheat by 1914. Other crops also showed large increases, especially raisins, tobacco and cotton. There was greater use of agricultural machinery, including ploughs, threshing machines and food-processing equipment. Perhaps because the revenues of Anatolia were not assigned to the payment of the interest on the Ottoman Public Debt the Ottoman government gave its attention to the improvement of Anatolian agriculture with agricultural schools, model farms and the agricultural banks which loaned 600 million piastres to nearly 800,000 cultivators in Anatolia during the reign of ʿAbd ül-Ḥamīd II. There was a predominance of smallholdings in the region; large landed estates existed chiefly in Adana which was the scene of settlement by Circassian immigrants who often gave up their lands to work as labourers on the large cotton estates which became a feature of the province. Unlike Egypt, however, there was little investment in large-scale irrigation schemes; several were planned at the end of the period but the only project which was completed was the Konya irrigation scheme in 1913, once again with the object of settling new immigrant workers. There can be little doubt that the constant influx of cheap labour supplied an important impetus to western Anatolian economic development. The major factor in the economic expansion, however, was certainly the development of railways from the 1860s onwards and the concentration of these in the western and north-western areas explains the location of the growth. It is quite easy to relate economic development to the arrival of the railway in each region; thus the dominance of cotton in Adana follows the opening of the Adana–Mersin railway in 1886. The railway also facilitated the development of Anatolian minerals, including chrome, iron, lead, silver, copper, lignite and coal, although the location of deposits in some cases made it difficult to utilize the potential of the railways without large investment.

A disproportionate share of the economic benefits went to the Greek population of Anatolia which was concentrated especially in the western and northern regions as well as in Istanbul and in towns generally. By 1914 the Greek population of Anatolia amounted to about 1.25 million, or a little over 7 per cent. The Greeks were especially involved in economic activities related to international trade. Accounts of their relations with the Muslim population differ: some observers comment upon the absence of hostility between the two communities; others write of Greek ambitions to achieve a special political position or even to link their fortunes to Greece. But although this ambition had grown during the period there is no evidence to suggest that it was dominant among the Greek population and it is plain that there was no disharmony between Greeks and Muslims in Anatolia which equalled the animosities of Armenians and Kurds in eastern Anatolia.

There were, however, new developments among the Muslim population of Anatolia especially after 1908. In the new Parliament Anatolia was under-represented in relation to its population: Anatolian delegates each represented twice as many people as delegates from the European provinces. The holding of elections in the towns and the connection with national politics did help to arouse Anatolian political consciousness, and another factor was the attention given to Anatolia by those who espoused the cause of Turkish nationalism, notably the members of the Turkish Hearth society. For these theorists Anatolia began to acquire a new status within the empire as the heartland of the Turkish people; the Anatolian peasant was romantically cherished as the pillar of the empire instead of being despised as a primitive yokel as in the past. Further, his language was taken increasingly as a model by language reformers and western Anatolia became the scene of the major drive to expand elementary education. By 1914 western Anatolia was not only the economic success story of the empire; it was also acquiring a new political significance.

In eastern Anatolia the situation was very different. Outside the Black Sea coastal region there was little economic development; the region remained a network of small local economies isolated from each other by poor communications. There was no railway development east of Ankara. Politically, the region was dominated by the problems of defence against any further encroachment from the side of Russia and by the growing conflict of Armenian and Kurd.

The Armenian population was spread throughout Anatolia, as well as including a substantial part of the inhabitants of Istanbul. In every town there was an Armenian element and there were also areas where Armenians were settled in large numbers as cultivators. One such area was Cilicia in western Anatolia, but the largest single concentration was in the six eastern provinces of Erzerum, Van, Bitlis, Kharput, Diyarbakr and Sivas. Of the total Armenian population of Anatolia of about 1.5 million in 1914 rather more than 860,000, or about 58 per cent, lived in the east. In none of the six provinces, however, did Armenians constitute a majority.

During the nineteenth century there was a growth of Armenian political consciousness and an increasing unwillingness to accept their often inferior status. There were several factors in this change in Armenian attitudes, many of which recall the similar changes in Maronite attitudes during the same period. One factor was the reforms in the Armenian Church and the improvement of the education offered to Armenians. A second factor was the arrival of US Protestant missions. The first mission in the region was established at Erzerum in 1839 and by 1914 the American Board for Foreign Missions had 174 missions in the area which in 1923 came to form the Turkish republic, many of these in Anatolia. At that time there were 17 principal mission stations, and 426 schools with 25,000 pupils. The missionaries provided a source of education and of ideas and also attempted to enlist the interest of outside powers in the fate of the Armenians, although they had little success with their own government. The presence of the missions also had a disturbing effect upon Muslims; there is evidence of the hostility of Kurdish shaykhs to the establishment of the Bitlis mission in 1858.

Down to 1878 Armenian nationalism existed almost exclusively among *émigrés* who continued to be important in its subsequent evolution. The increasing tendency of Armenians to travel abroad, to western Europe, notably Italy and France, and to Russia, was a source of new ideas. One well-known incident in 1894, which led to Muslim retaliation on the local Armenian population, was found to be the work of an Armenian returned from Italy who appears to have adopted the Bulgarian technique of attempting to provoke reprisals which might lead to European intervention. The policy of Russia had, of course, led some Armenians to commit themselves to the Russian cause in 1828, 1855 and 1878 only to find that they and their co-religionists were left exposed to retaliation by the Russian withdrawal. The demand of the Armenian delegation to the Congress of Berlin in 1878 for an autonomous Armenian province in eastern Anatolia was an important factor in creating suspicion of Armenian designs. Russian Armenians, waging their own struggle against tsarist policy also appealed to their Ottoman fellows. The well-known Armenian political party, Dashnak, was founded in 1890 in opposition to Russification in Armenia, and launched an armed revolt in 1903 which the Russian authorities suppressed with the aid of Cossack forces, in an almost carbon copy of the Ottoman use of the Ḥamīdiyya against the Armenians. The 1905 revolution in Russia gave the Russian Armenians new hope and they looked again to the Ottoman territories. To the Dashnaks the Ottoman lands were of secondary interest to Russian Armenia. The other Armenian party, Hunchak, based among *émigrés* in western Europe, was more concerned with the Ottoman lands and operated there from its foundation in 1886.

Another unexplored factor in the Armenian awakening is the political consequence of a new phase of Armenian urbanization. In 1879–80 a British traveller noted that the Armenians of the town of Kayseri spoke Turkish, even at home, whereas those living in the countryside around about spoke Armenian. In general it is true that in the traditional Ottoman polity the urban Armenians, above all those of Istanbul, were the most integrated into the Ottoman system. It is quite possible that these urbanized Armenians underwent a change in their political identification and aspirations during the nineteenth century, following a similar evolution in the Greek community. (The same traveller also noted that Greeks in Kayseri who had formerly spoken Turkish at home now spoke Greek in response to the appeal of Hellenism.) It is also possible, however, that a situation familiar in other regions was duplicated in Armenia and that Armenian nationalism owed much to the demands of new immigrants to the towns who retained their traditional culture and language and embodied these attributes in their new political articulations. There is also evidence from Van which suggests that Armenian nationalism may have been a convenient ideology for a new Armenian counter-élite which wished to challenge the dominance of the old Armenian élite which was wedded to a policy of accommodation with the Ottomans.

Another factor in the development of Armenian nationalism was the extension of Ottoman government. Although the Armenians looked to the Ottoman authorities for protection against the Kurdish tribes it was noticeable that it was after the assertion of central government control in any area that Armenian nationalism became more obvious. As another traveller, Henry Lynch, observed: "No sooner had the centralising tendencies in the Ottoman Empire come near to establishing upon a permanent basis the unquestioned supremacy of Ottoman rule in these remote districts than the Armenian movement commenced to make itself felt."[1] Armenian nationalism was a more useful claim against a multinational empire than it was against tribal oppression or religious intolerance.

To some extent Armenian nationalism was simply reactive. Paul Cambon, the French foreign minister, once commented that "the Armenians were told for so long that they were plotting that they finally plotted; they were told for so long that Armenia didn't exist that they finally believed in its existence".[2] Apart from the suspicions of the Ottoman authorities the Armenians were subjected to attacks by Kurds. In the later nineteenth century the story of massacres unfolded; in 1877–8 massacres accompanied the Russian invasion; in 1890 there was the Erzerum affair; in 1894 that of Sasun in the south where Armenians worked as sharecroppers on Kurdish lands. In 1895–6 major massacres took place and following the attempt by Armenian revolutionaries on the Ottoman Bank in Istanbul on 26 August 1896 there were massacres of Armenians in Istanbul. In April 1909 there was a massacre of Armenians in Adana in obscure circumstances but in some way linked with the anti-CUP coup in Istanbul in the same month. The Adana massacre may have destroyed Armenian hopes temporarily elevated by the 1908 revolution.

The agency of several attacks upon the Armenians was the Ḥamīdiyya. The Ḥamīdiyya was formed in 1891 on the model of the Russian Cossack regiments, in the same way as the Persian Cossack Brigade, but it was much larger than the Iranian formation and served different purposes. It was planned initially with 30 regiments of 600 men each but was steadily increased until by 1899 it consisted of 60 regiments. The regiments were recruited primarily from Kurdish tribes although some were formed from Turkoman or Circassian tribes. Soldiers served under their own tribal chiefs with regular Ottoman officers and NCOs attached as inspectors and instructors. The regiments were paid only when they were called out for active service, but the troops were exempt from all taxes except the tithe and the land tax, no great concession because of the difficulties which government had in collecting taxes from the tribes. The tribesmen served only occasionally; the paper strength of the regiments was rarely realized. The Ḥamīdiyya was intended to serve three purposes: to defend the frontier with Russia in the light of the experience of 1878 which revealed a serious lack of irregular cavalry for reconnaissance duties; to provide for local security against disturbances; and to help to civilize the Kurds in much the same way that colonial powers elsewhere enlisted tribal groups in irregular formations as a means of controlling their propensity to raid their neighbours. The formation of the Ḥamīdiyya had two main consequences. First, it served to enhance the Kurdish sense of their own Kurdishness. The existence of the tribal regiments became a source of pride and identification. Whereas formerly Kurds had often sought to conceal their identity, Lynch remarks that in the area of Mush, Kurds, after the establishment of the Ḥamīdiyya, were willing to acknowledge their origin. Second, the Ḥamīdiyya contributed to the insecurity of the region. Around Erzerum Ḥamīdiyya officers led Kurdish bands on raids which the Ottoman authorities could not control.

Between Kurds and Armenians the Ottoman officials sought to hold a balance as they had tried, also without success, in the Lebanon before 1860 and as they tried in Macedonia. There is some evidence that they leaned increasingly towards the Kurds, partly out of fear of Kurdish attacks; it is claimed that they commonly referred to Kurdish raids as the work of brigands because it was impolitic to name the Kurds as offenders. In the first half of the nineteenth century the Kurds were acknowledged to be the principal disturbers of the peace and Ottoman officials boasted of their success in hunting them down; by the early twentieth century the Ottoman attitude was much more ambivalent and under the Young Turks after 1908 it became more so. The Ḥamīdiyya was allowed to fall into disuse and ethnic and religious identifications were alike held to be dangerous to the state. But the Armenians after 1908 appeared as the greater threat to the continuation of the empire.

For all the people of eastern Anatolia the fifty years which preceded the First World War were a time of upheaval in their lives and questions were posed concerning their loyalties which had not previously been asked. Their dilemmas may be illustrated by the histories of two men born about the same time in the same region. One has already been mentioned. Żiyā Gökalp was born in Diyarbakr and grew up speaking Turkish and Kurdish. But he did not choose a Kurdish identity; instead he became the prophet of Turkish nationalism emphasizing a Turkish identity based upon folk tradition and language. The other, Badr al-Aʿzam Saʿīd Nūrsī (1873–1960) was born in Bitlis of a mixed Turkish–Kurdish family, had a traditional madrasa education and acquired a reputation as a skilled tribal arbitrator. He became more widely known for familiar attacks on the corrupt state of Islam and as a spokesman for Muslims at the time of the 1895–6 massacres. Brought to the attention of ʿAbd ül-Ḥamīd he went to Istanbul and became one of the foremost spokesmen of Panislamism. Oddly enough, both men were able to obtain positions of prominence under the Young Turks.

SYRIA

During the latter part of the nineteenth century Syria prospered. Trade expanded, towns grew, cultivation was extended at the expense of the nomads and the desert, and the population reached approximately 4 million by 1914. Partly this was the consequence of the greater security offered by Ottoman government: partly it was the result of the increased opportunities afforded by better communications with the outside world. Some writers have associated this economic advance with social change and new political ambitions, namely the rise of a modern middle class and the emergence of Arab nationalism, but this theory must be approached with great caution for while it may have some merit in relation to the Christian population it has little in relation to the Muslims of the region.

One decided area of social change was education. Until well into the nineteenth century education in Syria had been the concern of the religious communities alone, and their objects had been similar: to provide basic literacy for the great majority and a specialized training for the few who sought a career in law, teaching or the religious affairs of the commmunity. Of all skills possibly the most highly prized was the ability to write a fair hand, for that facility could assure secretarial employment. The religious schools continued to provide this type of education throughout the period, with some minor attempts at modernization, principally in the Christian schools. The religious schools were supplemented by new schools described below.

For Muslims a more modern type of education came to be available in the Ottoman state schools, which were used primarily, although not exclusively, by Muslims or in certain reformed private schools, for example that founded in 1895 at Beirut by Shaykh Aḥmad ʿAbbās al-Aghasī. The principal beneficiaries of these schools were town-dwellers, mainly Sunnī Muslim; the heterodox Muslim groups tended to fall further behind.

For Christians quite new opportunities were provided in the missionary schools, which were first set up during the Egyptian occupation and subsequently developed into a large network. The French Catholic missions concentrated on providing education for the Catholic Christians, Greek and Maronite. By 1914 there were about 500 French mission schools in the whole region with between 50,000 and 60,000 pupils. From 1901 these schools were put under French government protection. Similar efforts were made by the Protestant missionaries, British, German and, especially, American. The Protestant missionaries concentrated on training teachers drawn from the Christian communities who might one day become the agents of the conversion of the Muslims. But the demand for education was such that they soon found themselves diverted from their original object and engaged in providing services, primarily educational, for pupils drawn from all the Christian communities and from some others. The Protestants established a network of schools including in 1866 the Syrian Protestant College (SPC), the precursor of the American University of Beirut. In turn the Catholics set up the University of St Joseph (1875). The Russian effort came later and was especially the result of fears of the appeal of the Protestant schools to the Greek Orthodox community. In the years after the Crimean War the Russian missionaries also established an extensive school system. Finally, in the years before the First World War, Italian and German schools were also introduced.

It has been asserted, particularly by the historian, George Antonius, that these schools were the principal means by which Western ideas penetrated Syria, an important agency for the development of the Arabic language, and, indirectly, the source of the seeds of Arab nationalism. Subsequent research has cast doubt on this view. In the first place the number of students on advanced courses was small; only five graduated from the SPC in 1879. Secondly, educational activities were always subsidiary to evangelization for Protestants and the controlling authorities in the United States frowned upon diversions from the main objective. The curriculum was limited to subjects which offered no obvious scope for introducing Western political ideas, although it is also plain that some teachers transcended these limitations such as the SPC teacher who devoted his French lessons to political thought. Nor was the contribution to the Arabic language so great. Contrary to common belief, teaching at the SPC was usually conducted in English before 1885 and the publications programme concentrated on the production of textbooks. The development of modern standard Arabic was much more the work of writers in Cairo, Istanbul and Beirut. The French schools always taught in French and set out to cultivate affection for France among the leading Catholic families. Above all, the missionary influence was almost wholly confined to the Christian communities, which, for social, economic and other reasons were much more open to penetration by Western ideas. Some Jews and Druzes attended the missionary schools but the great majority of Syrian Muslims would have nothing to do with them. It was said that a Muslim who sent his sons to a Christian school was equivalent to a man who commits adultery in public. It would be wrong to deny the missionary schools any influence; their contribution to the development of the Syrian Christian communities was considerable. But for the mainsprings of Arab nationalism it is necessary to look elsewhere.

One factor in the development of a sense of cultural Arabism was the Arabic literary revival, a phenomenon of the nineteenth century which was associated with the expansion of education, the spread of printing in Arabic and, above all, the development of journalism. During the later nineteenth century many Arabic journals and newspapers appeared in Syria, Egypt and elsewhere and it was in those publications that a form of Arabic universally intelligible to educated Arabs and capable of expressing modern scientific and political concepts was forged. It was through the journals that new European ideas were transmitted to Arab readers and they also became the forums in which problems and policies were discussed, commonly at a very high level of sophistication. In this golden age of Arab journalism which endured through the forty years or more which preceded the First World War Syrian writers played a leading part, both in Syria and in Egypt and Europe.

Among the more prominent of the writers were Nāṣīf al-Yāzijī (1800–71) a Greek Catholic and one of the earliest teachers of modern Arabic; Buṭrus al-Bustānī (1819–83), a Maronite convert to Protestantism who emphasized the ideas of Arab culture and Syrian patriotism; Fāris al-Shidyāq (1805–87) who founded the influential Arabic periodical, *Al-Jawāʾib*, in Istanbul; Salīm Taqlā (1849–92), a Greek Catholic who founded the best known Arabic newspaper, *Al-Ahrām*, in Egypt in 1875, and two Greek Orthodox writers, Yaʿqūb Ṣarrūf (1852–1927) and Fāris Nimr (1860–1952) who founded two of the leading Arabic periodicals, *Al-Muqtaṭaf* and *Al-Muqaṭṭam*, also in Egypt. The career of Jurjī Zaydān (1861–1914) may serve to illustrate the versatility of these writers and the diversity of their literary output. Zaydān studied medicine in Beirut where his ambition was kindled by that very influential Victorian injunction to virtuous self-improvement, Samuel Smiles's *Self-Help*. He also read Sir Walter Scott and Alexandre Dumas, and was led to write a series of historical novels in Arabic in which he described episodes in the history of the Arabs. As editor and principal writer of the journal *Al-Hilāl*, which he founded in Egypt in 1892, he was responsible for introducing to Arabic readers a great deal of contemporary European scientific and philosophical work. These and other writers also produced translations of European writings, new editions of classical Arabic texts, dictionaries and grammars and new important literary and scientific works in Arabic. The result of their work was not only to introduce a wide public to a new range of experience but to form a vocabulary which was capable of expressing a range of new concepts. The immediate significance of their work for the development of cultural Arabism is clear, but these Christian writers also laid the essential foundations for the future development of political Arabism.

The political ambitions of Syrian Christians were diverse and corresponded to the position of the different communities. Among the most prominent of these communities was the Maronite community of Lebanon which now lived under the system of local autonomy provided by the 1861 arrangements. Many Maronites were satisfied with the 1861 regime. The elected council provided an outlet for their ambitions which were directed towards preserving the system, endeavouring to influence the governor, particularly by enlisting the aid of European powers in bringing pressure to bear either within Lebanon or in Istanbul and, if possible, securing the appointment of a Lebanese governor, which was forbidden under the 1861 system. Many believed, quite rightly, that it was the intention of the Ottoman government to undo the 1861 settlement at the first opportunity and the justice of their fears was proved in 1914 when Lebanon's autonomy was removed.

Other Maronites believed that Lebanon, within its 1861 frontiers, was unviable and wished to include within it Beirut, Tripoli, Sidon and the Biqāʿ. Such a Greater Lebanon would offer more scope to their ambitions, particularly to those whose interests were commercial rather than landowning, and it would also possess the capability of a wholly independent political existence, with both a sufficient resource base and access to the sea. In such a state, however, the Maronites, although they would be the largest single religious community, would lose the majority which they possessed on Mount Lebanon. The ideological basis of such a state could not be purely Maronite but must include some wider appeal, whether linguistic, through Arabic, or economic, or historical, through an appeal to continuity from the time of Phoenicia.

The situation of other Christian communities in Syria was different. Whereas the Maronites of Lebanon could hope to create a political unit in which they predominated because of their territorial concentration, other communities were dispersed among the predominantly Muslim population. Unlike most of the Balkan Christians and the Armenians they were not differentiated by language for they spoke the same Arabic as their Muslim neighbours. Those Christians who hoped to improve their position by new political arrangements giving them increased control over their own affairs dared not make an appeal to loyalty to the religious community but had to find some way of formulating their ambitions which would also appeal to Muslim Syrians. It was in this context that they began to talk about Arabism as a cultural, linguistic identity separate from religion, and about Syria as a geographical and historical unit. The largest Syrian Christian community, the Greek Orthodox, was also the one which was most familiar with the notion of Syria as a political unit for the boundaries of Syria roughly corresponded to those of the patriarchate of Antioch, the *millet* unit in which they lived and which was a principal forum for their ambitions. It was during an internal conflict within the Greek Orthodox community of Antioch that Arabism began to assume a political significance because the higher clergy were Greek and the lower clergy and laity were Arabic-speaking. In the mid-nineteenth-century struggle for control of the affairs of the community it was inevitable that the Arabic speakers should stress that circumstance. The effects of *millet* secularization were, therefore, to give a more Arab emphasis to the Syrian Orthodox.

Expressions of national ideas among Syrian Christians are more confused than the above presentation would suggest. Political ambitions are commonly constrained by what is seen to be possible and there is always a danger of reading into the words of nineteenth-century writers unintended meanings. Thus when Buṭrus al-Bustānī wrote of his "Arab blood" and of love of his homeland he was not suggesting an Arab or Syrian state. Bustānī was writing in sentimental or cultural terms and was always content that Syria should remain within the Ottoman fold. Down to 1908 at least there were many Christians in Syria who thought that the liberal movement within the Ottoman empire offered much the best prospects for Christians through the gradual disappearance of religious discrimination, the end of despotic rule, the steady improvement of local government and access to better opportunities. For others, Arabism in politics was worse than Ottomanism for whereas the latter had a secular aspect, Arabism was inseparably connected with Islam: in an Arab state Christians would always be second-class citizens.

Nevertheless, it is also true that in the later nineteenth and early twentieth centuries the expression of distinctive political ambitions by Syrian Christians became more common. In the writings of Ṣarrūf and Nimr there are clear political demands for greater control over their own affairs by Syrians, and the increased use of Arabic in schools, courts and government offices. Small, short-lived secret societies, consisting of a few students, were formed and advanced more ambitious demands for autonomy or independence for Syria. In 1905 a book published in Paris, *The awakening of the Arab nation*, envisaged the establishment, by an armed rising if necessary, of an Arab state including Syria and Iraq with an Arab caliphate in the Hijaz. The author was a Syrian Catholic named Najīb ʿAzūrī (d. 1916) who claimed to speak on behalf of a League of the Arab Country, although there is no evidence that the league ever existed. Subsequently ʿAzūrī joined with Eugene Jung to produce *L'Indépendance arabe* in 1907–8. ʿAzūrī hardly represented any group, however, and his book was written mainly to further French interests in the Near East.

These various political ideas found little support from Syrian Muslims. This is not to say that there was not Syrian Muslim discontent with Ottoman rule. The application of Tanẓīmāt policies led to violent protest and concessions to Christians caused resentment. During the Russian war of 1877–8 the despatch of conscripts to fight in the European provinces led to demands from notables for the use of Syrian troops in Syria alone and greater autonomy for Syria. There was also expressed a view of Turks as degenerate Muslims, not to be compared with the Arabs who had received the original revelation, and, by implication, an opinion that it was the Arabs and not the Turks who should rule. This concept was to find some expression in the often reported notion that there should be an Arab caliphate. The idea of an Arab caliphate was set out in *The future of Islam* (1882) by Wilfrid Blunt in which the author reflects the views of Arab writers, notably Muḥammad ʿAbduh, the Egyptian reformer, and in the writings of ʿAbd al-Raḥmān al-Kawākibī (1849–1903), a notable from Aleppo who settled in Cairo whence he attacked the government of ʿAbd ül-Ḥamīd.

The great majority of Syrian Muslims had little or no interest in Arabist ideas. Their concerns were like those of other Ottoman Muslims: they were for or against the Hamidian regime, they were for or against the Islamic reform movement represented by al-Afghānī and ʿAbduh. When Arabism does come into their writings it is subordinated to their interests as Muslims as in the case of Muḥammad Rashīd Riḍā (1865–1935), the follower and biographer of Muḥammad ʿAbduh, who also settled in Cairo where he edited the famous periodical, *Al-Manār*. The centre of Rashīd Riḍā's interest was the reform of Islam and he is best known as the leading proponent of the Salafiyya, a movement to purify Islam. But, although there were critics of the despotic features of Ottoman government among them, Syrian Muslims regarded the Ottoman government as their government, a defence for Muslims against infidel pressure and infidel ideas. That they spoke Arabic and that some of them claimed Arab tribal descent they knew, but they did not think that this cultural identity had any political significance and even the cultural identity of "Arab" was questionable. The Arab was still a man who lived in a tent in the desert and one with whom an Ottoman gentleman of Damascus had little in common.

According to a widespread view the turning-point for Syrian Muslim Arabs came after the Young Turk revolution of 1908. After the failure of Ottomanism and Panislamism, the Young Turks, it is asserted, adopted Turkish nationalism and began a policy of Turkification, including making Turkish the official language, and its use compulsory in courts and schools and even in the naming of streets. The Ottoman administrative reorganization of 1909–10 is alleged to have led to a disproportionate number of dismissals of non-Turks, who returned to Syria complaining of discrimination against Arabs. New Ottoman officials in Syria knew no Arabic. And it is claimed that Arabs did not receive a just proportion of seats in the new Ottoman Parliament.

These claims have little evidence to support them. It has already been argued that the theory that the Young Turks adopted Turkish nationalism is erroneous; official policy remained Ottomanism. Ottoman Turkish had always been the official language for use in state courts, schools and administration; the difference was that under centralization there were more courts, schools and administrative offices. Residents of Syrian towns would have been surprised to learn that most streets had name-plates and puzzled to distinguish in Arabic script whether the names were in Turkish or Arabic. There is no evidence of deliberate discrimination against Arabs in bureaucratic appointments or that more or fewer Ottoman officials in Syria knew Arabic than in former times. And seats in the Ottoman Parliament appear to have been apportioned in rough correspondence to population distribution; only by the inclusion of the population of Egypt as Arab can one arrive at a disproportion and Anatolia appears to have fared worst.

Whatever the merit of the claims it is clear that there were complaints of discrimination in Syria and some anti-Turkish feeling did spread throughout the community. There were also political demands put forward by Syrian Muslims through various societies. These societies may be divided into two groups: public and secret.

The public societies include the Beirut Reform Society established in 1912, which comprised roughly equal numbers of Christians and Muslims in its leadership. Its programme was essentially a development of the programme of the liberal faction among the Young Turks and, indeed, the society was established in response to a request by the Liberal Union government. Its programme included making Arabic the official language in Syria and the corollary that all government officials in Syria should know Arabic, devoting local resources to local government, local military service and more power to local government. The society was closed by government action on 8 April 1913. A very similar programme was put forward in Cairo by the Ottoman Administrative Decentralization Party.

The secret societies present to the historian the usual problems of such organizations. It is difficult to know either their strength or whether those who claimed to speak on behalf of the society were entitled to do so. Much of the evidence concerning them appeared in an Ottoman official report in 1916, but the circumstances of the report do not suggest that overmuch confidence should be reposed in it. Other evidence appeared after 1918 when their alleged ideas were much more popular than they had been at the time and when many men were anxious to prove that they had jumped on the bandwagon at an early date. Among these societies were al-Qaḥṭāniyya, founded in 1909, and alleged to have advocated an Arab–Turkish condominium over the Ottoman empire on the lines of the Austrian Dual Monarchy. Al-Qaḥṭāniyya soon withered away for lack of support. Another society was al-Fatāt, or the Young Arab Society, founded in Paris in 1909 by Syrians living in France and subsequently moved first to Beirut and then, in 1914, to Damascus. Little was known of al-Fatāt before 1914; neither the Ottomans nor the French had any apparent record of its early years, suggesting that it could not have been extensive. Even less is known of al-ʿAhd, the Covenant, which was founded between 1912 and 1914 by ʿAzīz ʿAlī al-Miṣrī, an Ottoman army officer, and which recruited especially among Arab Ottoman officers, many of whom were from Iraq. It is claimed that of 490 Arab officers in 1914 no less than 315 were members of al-ʿAhd. What the secret societies stood for is quite uncertain as there was no official programme. Claims range from the Dual Monarchy solution to complete independence but little confidence can be placed in these claims.

The most public statement of Arab nationalist claims before 1914 appears in the programme adopted by the Arab Congress which met in Paris in June 1913 and included members of al-Fatāt and the Ottoman Decentralization Party. The delegates were nearly all from Syria and were fairly evenly divided between Muslims and Christians. Christians were prominent in the meeting which appears to have been preoccupied with their demands. The original organizer was Shukrī Ghānim, a Maronite who had long lived in France and who became the principal advocate of Greater Lebanon, but he lost control of the congress.

The president of the congress was a Muslim, ʿAbd al-Ḥamīd al-Zahrāwī, who subsequently accepted a seat in the Ottoman Senate and who complained that most of the delegates cared nothing for Arab nationalism or Syrian unity but were interested only in Beirut. The demands were essentially decentralist in character: in a general Ottoman reform there should be autonomy for the Arab provinces, with Arabic as an official language there and in the Ottoman Parliament, and local military service. There was, however, no wish to leave the Ottoman empire and there were specific requests for more jobs for Arabs in Istanbul and more Ottoman government financial assistance for the mutasarrifate of Lebanon. It is interesting that there was no mention of French help and French protection was rejected; to that extent the views of the Decentralization Committee prevailed over those formerly advanced by the Beirut Reform Society.

Following the congress there were negotiations with the Ottoman government on the basis of the programme and agreement on a package involving the use of Arabic in schools and administration, the reservation of ministerial and provincial governors' jobs for Arabs and the limitation of military service. The agreement was never ratified by the Ottomans on the grounds that the Arabs had published it prematurely. Arab resistance was dispelled by a mixture of arrests and government jobs. In the spring elections of 1914 many of the reformers were defeated by CUP candidates who were themselves Syrian notables, often from the same families.

It seems likely that there was no extensive Arab nationalist movement in Syria in 1914. Most of the Syrian élite remained pro-Ottoman. But there is no doubt that political ideas based on Arabism had advanced and their proponents embraced both Christians and Muslims. There was no clear programme because the interests of different groups led them to favour various political solutions, within and without the Ottoman empire. Only among Catholic Christians, who could envisage the possibility of independence under French support, was independence strongly favoured. To Muslims French control was less attractive than a continuation of Muslim Ottoman rule. The position on which nationalists could agree, therefore, was greater autonomy for the Arab provinces within the framework of the Ottoman empire. This autonomy featured the greater use of Arabic, more jobs for Arabic speakers and limitations on military service, the longest-standing complaint of Syrians.

Who were the Arab nationalists? The theory that they were the new Arab middle class which found nationalism a more convenient outlet for its economic interests does not stand up to examination. A study of the pre-1914 Muslim nationalist leaders shows that they were part of the traditional élite of Syrian notables, predominantly Sunnī Muslims from Damascus and almost indistinguishable in their attributes from other members of the same élite who were loyal Ottomanists in the same period. Only in one respect do they differ; the Ottomanists were much more likely to hold government jobs than the Arabists. Taken in conjunction with the stress placed upon the reservation of jobs for Arabic speakers the evidence points to the conclusion that Arab nationalism among Syrian Muslims in this period was primarily a dispute about jobs. If a knowledge of Arabic was made an essential condition for the holding of office native Arabic speakers would be at an advantage as compared with other Ottoman subjects. This view was sturdily denied by one of the leading reformers of the time, Shukrī Aslī Bey, who refused an appointment to Latakia. "It is not lucrative posts that we Arabs want", he remarked, "but serious reforms."[3] The weight of the evidence, however, is against him.

The rise of Arab nationalism in Syria reflects the changed outlook of the Sunnī élite. In earlier periods they had stood outside government and measured their status in competition for religious offices. The progress of centralization had made government employment much more important than in the past, both for income and for the possibilities of patronage through which they could support their families and retainers. The leading Damascus families were now those who were most successful in the pursuit of government jobs. The competition for jobs led to disputes among themselves and between them and the Ottoman authorities. In previous times these disputes might have been expressed in religious terms or even in the vocabulary of Arab tribal politics. Exposure to European ideas had presented the Damascus notables with a new range of ideas which, in a modernizing world, could serve as a more suitable vehicle of their ambitions. The adoption of the terminology of linguistic nationalism was not a light fashion copied frivolously from Europe but one which corresponded precisely to their needs. In its origins Arab nationalism was not dissimilar to other nationalisms and it served the same ends.

It was the misfortune of the Syrian nationalists that what had been mere dissent before 1914 became treason afterwards. During the war Syria was under constant threat of an Allied landing. Conscription, the despatch of troops from Syria to Gallipoli and elsewhere, requisitions and inflation caused widespread discontent and suffering, notably in Lebanon which was visited by famine. Relaxation of border controls led to bedouin inroads long before the bedouin were drawn into the Arab revolt. In this situation many of the pre-war reformers contemplated the end of Ottoman rule in Syria and the need to plan for what would follow, even to the extent of an understanding with the Allies. To the Ottoman authorities, led by Jemāl Pasha, such behaviour was intolerable. In 1916 there were arrests, executions and deportations to other parts of the empire. The Arab nationalist movement was dispersed and was re-created in very different circumstances in 1918.

IRAQ

Increased political activity among the various communities in Syria was not paralleled in Iraq where new political demands couched in a "modern" idiom appeared only just before 1914 and possessed little support or substance. The main reason for the lack of political development in Iraq as compared with Syria appears to have been the general slowness of modernization in the former region, but it is also possible to identify some more specific reasons.

One marked contrast between the two regions is presented by the position of the non-Muslim minorities. In Syria, the Christians, far more numerous and affected not only by changing circumstances within their own communities but also by close contact with Europe, began to express their new ambitions through a new vocabulary of politics: in Iraq the most prominent of the non-Muslim minorities was the Jewish community which eschewed political activity, concentrated on commerce and finance and lent its support to the Ottoman regime; the Christians were much less conspicuous except in the north and much less exposed to outside influences.

Two substantial groups among the notables held themselves aloof from government and confined their opposition to traditional forms of protest. These were the tribal shaykhs, who, with few exceptions, stayed out of politics – no tribal shaykh sat in the Ottoman Parliament; and the Shīʿī notables who also expressed in traditional terms their continued resentment of Sunnī dominion.

Of those notables who formed part of the Ottoman system the Turkish and Caucasian families continued to dominate public employment. As government employment became a more significant measure of status and wealth due to the increased role of the state, the position of the largest group of the traditional notables of Baghdad and Basra was adversely affected. These were those whose claim to position was based on religion, namely on their status as descendants of the Prophet or as holders of positions connected with the religious system. These *sayyids* had always been most prominent in Iraq, whether in support of government or in opposition to it, and it is therefore not surprising that it should have been among this group that the first stirrings of new forms of political protest were visible. It may, therefore, be unnecessary to look for reasons for their activity but the coincidence with the Syrian situation cannot escape notice; the increased role of the state and the relative decline of the importance of religious office-holding helps to account for the change.

It was the 1908 Young Turk revolution which marks the turning-point in Iraqi politics. The revolution was greeted with little enthusiasm in Iraq but the effects were as inescapable in Iraq as in Syria. The new factors were elections, the formation and organization of political parties to fight the elections and the development of a political press: in 1910 there were only six official papers in Iraq; by 1914 there were fifty newspapers expressing a range of opinions which included both Arabist and Islamic views. Contacts were formed with outside groups, with Syrian and other deputies through the Ottoman Parliament in Istanbul and with members of the Ottoman Decentralization Party in Cairo. A further source of outside influence was India which had close contacts with Basra. In the years immediately before the First World War Arabist political societies begin to appear in Iraq, including the Baghdad-based Arab Patriotic Society (1912) and a Basra group built around an able and ambitious member of the Naqīb family, Sayyid Ṭālib. These groups advanced demands similar to those of the Syrian nationalists, namely calls for greater autonomy, increased use of Arabic in schools, courts and government offices and more jobs for local men. Although Iraqis were virtually unrepresented at the 1913 Paris Congress the Iraqi provinces were included in the concessions promised by the Ottoman authorities and disappointment was felt at the result. Nevertheless, the claim that there was widespread discontent with the Ottoman government and connection in Iraq in 1914 seems unfounded; the evidence suggests only the first stirrings of discontent among small groups of notables; the great majority remained loyal Ottomans.

One final source of political activity in Iraq relates to the secret society al-ʿAhd. Iraqis had always formed the most numerous group among the Arab officers in the Ottoman army and it has generally been supposed that they comprised the bulk of the members of al-ʿAhd, which was reported to aim at the achievement of radical changes in the Ottoman empire including the independence of the Arab provinces. Something has already been said of the difficulties of determining the size or the aims of such secret societies; the claims subsequently made by individuals in very different circumstances afford no reliable guide to the situation in 1914. On balance one would incline to the view that before 1914 there were few Arab nationalist Iraqi officers and that it was the ill-fortune which attended Ottoman arms in the war and the prospective separation of Iraq from the empire which brought Iraqi officers in large numbers to the support of nationalist aims. But some already did harbour such ideas before 1914 and it is important to note that these men came from outside the old notable classes. Those Iraqis who went into the officer corps of the Ottoman army were mainly Sunnī Arabs from middling families; Nūrī al-Saʿīd was the son of a minor government auditor and Yāsīn al-Hāshimī, the founder of the Mosul branch of al-ʿAhd, was the son of the headman of a Baghdad quarter. After 1918 these men came to leading positions in the new Iraq which was created as a result of the war.

The war brought substantial changes to Iraq which was, from the beginning, the scene of armed contest, unlike Syria, which, although an Ottoman base, did not see the march of hostile armies until the end of 1917. The British occupation of Basra closed the main port and source of imports and the incomplete Baghdad railway was unable to supply the deficiency. Exports from Iraq were equally affected. The demands of the Ottoman armies – confiscations, restrictions and requisitions and the widening of the area of conscription also pressed heavily on the areas which remained under Ottoman control. The result of the war was economic disaster for central and northern Iraq. The operations of Russian armies on the eastern borders also added to the distress. These operations and the Russian appeal to the Christian groups, the Assyrians and Armenians also had the effect of worsening relations between Christian and Muslim communities in Iraq and between the Christians and the Kurds in particular. By contrast the south of Iraq under British occupation enjoyed much prosperity. Trade with India was still open and the presence of the British Indian forces created employment through the reconstruction of the port of Basra so as to be able to take in supplies, and through the building of railways to assist in the movement of troops and supplies northwards. From 1917 a new scheme of agricultural development under British guidance led to an expansion of food production. Notable beneficiaries of the British occupation were tribal shaykhs, whose control of movement and meat supplies made them useful allies to be cherished and subsidized. By 1918 the economic and political balance in Iraq had already changed as a result of the war.

EGYPT

Between 1882 and 1914 Egypt underwent a revolution and foreign occupation, and saw the beginnings of a national and constitutional movement. This section will consist primarily of an examination of the nature, causes and effects of these events, but it will be useful at the outset briefly to rehearse the leading changes of the preceding period which were described in detail in Chapter 3. These were, first, a political revolution in which Muḥammad ʿAlī destroyed the old political system and constructed the basic institutions of a modern state; second, an economic revolution marked by the growth of the cotton economy, the development of private landholding and the involvement of Egypt in the international economy; and, third, social changes which, although they left the vast majority of the population untouched, had a significant effect upon the emergent élite. These social changes were the expansion of education and the introduction of Western curricula in schools, the development of a press, the changes in the legal system and the adoption by sections of the élite of European fashions and aspirations. Some of these changes may be related directly to the events which are the subject of this chapter; others may be said to have contributed to them indirectly through creating new pressures, new possibilities and permitting new forms of articulation of protest. But to attribute the events of the years from 1882 to these causes alone would be mistaken because it will be apparent that the history of Egypt in these years can only be fully explained by reference to older forms of social organization and older political aspirations.

The scene was set for the ʿUrabist revolution of 1882 by the breakdown of Egyptian government finances with the consequent establishment of European financial control and its extension to political control with the imposition on Egypt of the government of Nubar Pasha in August 1878. This government introduced a programme of reform designed to limit the power of Ismāʿīl, separate his finances from those of the state and implement a policy of strict economy in public expenditure. The Nubar government also included European ministers. A financial commission produced a draft plan of financial reconstruction in April 1879 which involved the reduction of interest on the funded debt to 5 per cent, the cancellation of the *Muqābala* law which had alienated revenues in favour of landholders, and an increase of land tax on the category of lands known as *ʿushūrī* which were held mainly by the large landowners.

Ismāʿīl resented his loss of control over affairs and fought back. Nubar's government was both unlucky and unpopular; the Nile floods failed and the economies in military expenditure were resented by officers who were put on half-pay. In February 1879 a military demonstration against Nubar's government took place. The mutiny was quickly quelled by Ismāʿīl, but there was a strong suspicion that he had actually instigated it as a means of showing that only he could control Egypt and of getting rid of the Nubar government. In the last endeavour he succeeded and in March 1879 Nubar's government resigned and was replaced first by a ministry under Ismāʿīl's son Tawfīq and then, in April 1879, by a purely Egyptian, or, to be more precise, a purely Turko-Circassian ministry under Sharīf Pasha. Ismāʿīl also produced his own financial plan calling for a unilateral reduction of interest on the debt, an offer which on the face of it was more generous to creditors than that of the European-controlled financial commission. Ismāʿīl sought support from several quarters. He was supported by the notables because of their dislike of the financial commission's proposals concerning the *Muqābala* law and the *ʿushūrī* lands and he won over army officers with promises of promotion, the recall of dismissed officers and a plan for army expansion. He also turned to the Ottoman government for help. Ismāʿīl's projects were plainly beyond Egypt's ability to carry out and it was this circumstance which sealed the fate of Ismāʿīl for the Great Powers, led by Germany, brought pressure to bear at Istanbul to procure his dismissal and replacement by Tawfīq as khedive, on 30 June 1879.

The deposition of Ismāʿīl was quickly followed by the formation of a new government, first under Tawfīq and then under Riyāḍ Pasha in September 1879. Riyāḍ's government included two immovable European councillors (de Blignières and Baring) appointed by the French and British governments. They were allowed to make suggestions but they could neither vote nor take part in administration. Nevertheless, their influence was dominant in the policy of the new government which proceeded on the lines of the financial commission report: government expenditure was reduced, the *Muqābala* law abolished (January 1880) and the interest on the debt reduced. By the Law of Liquidation of 17 July 1880 the interest on the privileged debt was reduced to 5 per cent and that on the unified debt to 4 per cent. The new government also tightened control over the opposition; the press, which had considerably expanded since 1876 was brought under some control, the so-called "Young Egypt" Party, an indistinct group of reformers of mainly Syrian origin was repressed, and the Islamic reformer, Jamāl al-Dīn al-Afghānī, who had become the leader of a group of dissident intellectuals, was expelled from Egypt. Despite the continued discontent arising from the difficult economic situation and from government financial pressures, it seemed that under the Riyāḍ government Egypt was on the way to recovery.

The process of stabilization in Egypt was interrupted by the ʿUrabi revolt. The ʿUrabi revolt was primarily a mutiny of Arabic-speaking Egyptian army officers but it also included other ingredients which require consideration. These included a general spirit of intellectual awakening and criticism embracing elements of liberal and national feeling, a demand for a greater share in government by two distinct factions, one a group of Turko-Circassian notables led by Sharīf Pasha, and the other a group of rural notables, of whom the most prominent figure was Muḥammad Sulṭān Pasha; and a degree of generalized discontent of mainly economic origin within the urban and rural classes in Egypt. The situation was further complicated by the actions of the European powers and of the Ottoman government, which sought to exploit the course of events so as to recover its lost power in Egypt.

The first element in the intellectual awakening was the growth of a sense of Egyptian identity distinct from that of Islam. One of the starting-points for this development was the European discoveries concerning the early history of Egypt. These discoveries were taken up by Egyptian writers who developed a novel sense of Egyptian identity based on a continuity between pre-Islamic Egypt and the Muslim period. It is important to emphasize how novel was this sense; it is remarkable how Egyptians were formerly indifferent to the spectacle of the immense monuments of what is inaccurately called Pharaonic Egypt which surrounded them. The Pyramids and the Sphinx played some part in popular superstition but were not an item of serious intellectual interest; to Muslim Egyptians Egypt before Islam had been a land of uninteresting barbarians and there was nothing of value to be learned from their relics. Of course, one can find parallels to this attitude in Europe but there the visible remains of pre-Roman civilizations were puny compared with the legacy of Rome itself.

The best-known Egyptian writer who shaped this cultural change was Shaykh Rifāʿa Rāfiʿ al-Ṭahṭāwī (1801–73) who had studied first at al-Azhar and then in France, whither he had gone (as imam) on one of Muḥammad ʿAlī's student missions, one of the few Arabic speakers to be included. It was in France that he came into contact with the work of the great French orientalists. To Rifāʿa it was a great cultural shock and he recorded his experiences in a book, *Takhlīs al-ibrīz*. His book was not well received by orthodox Muslims. E. W. Lane heard it described (misleadingly) as an account of "his voyage from Alexandria to Marseilles; how he got drunk on board the ship and was tied to the mast and flogged; that he ate pork in the land of infidelity and obstinacy and that it is a most excellent meat; how he was delighted with the French girls, and how superior they were in charms to the women of Egypt; and having qualified himself, by every accomplishment for an eminent place in Hell, returned to his native country".[4]

On his return Rifāʿa taught in the School of Languages, was exiled to the Sudan under ʿAbbās and restored to favour under Saʿīd, when he became director of the Military School. In 1869 he published his most notable book, *Manāhij al-albāb al-Miṣriyya*, an account of the growth of Egyptian civilization in which he distinguished an Egyptian nation within the general cultural body of Islam and set out a programme for the reform of Islam through the adoption of Western ideas and for the modernization of the Arabic language. One whole volume was devoted to the history of pre-Islamic Egypt. The ideas popularized by Rifāʿa achieved general circulation within the modern Egyptian élite of the 1870s when a sense of a romantic Egyptian nationalism based upon history and geography was widespread although its content was cultural rather than political. The new ideas were promoted under Ismāʿīl by the establishment of a national library and museum and by the introduction of the teaching of pre-Islamic Egyptian history in high schools. For Ismāʿīl the promotion of an Egyptian nationalism was helpful in his struggles with the Porte. Ismāʿīl and many notables also patronized the Helwan Society where similar ideas were discussed.

A second element in the intellectual odyssey of Egypt in the nineteenth century was that of liberalism. To Rifāʿa liberalism was of no interest; an absolute ruler ruling justly was his favoured formula. But others took from Europe the ideas of liberal parliamentary democracy. The best-known exponent of such ideas, or rather the man who became identified with them in the minds of others because he himself was a politician rather than a writer, was Sharīf Pasha, a Turk who had come to Egypt in early life and acquired considerable wealth in landed property. Cromer later described him as "the incarnation of the policy of 'Egypt for the Turco-Egyptians' ",[5] which may indicate that his liberalism did not run deep. In fact Sharīf merely advocated the replacement of the arbitrary rule of the khedive with that of a relatively small oligarchy of wealthy landlords who wished to retain the advantages of light taxation and forced labour. One historian has said of him that "he adopted liberal principles in the same spirit as a Florentine gentleman during the renaissance might have patronized a new painter".[6] It seems inevitable that Egyptian liberalism should have been of this insubstantial character: there were no powerful interest groups independent of the court and bureaucracy or any independent Egyptian base for such views within the modern sector, no press support for constitutionalism before 1878, and no checks on the ruler which could provide the ground for debates similar to those which led to the formulation of doctrines of European liberalism. Egyptian liberalism was inevitably a pastiche. Nevertheless, there was a demand for constitutional liberties and parliamentary machinery which under suitable conditions could flourish. It was Turko-Circassian liberals who formed a self-styled Egyptian

National Party which issued a liberal manifesto on 4 November 1879 (in French) attacking the government of Riyāḍ.

A third new intellectual current was that which is called Islamic modernism and is especially associated with Jamāl al-Dīn al-Afghānī. Afghānī presents a puzzle to the historian who directs his attention to states, for Afghānī was, first and foremost, a Muslim thinker who thought, moved and acted in a Muslim context from the Ottoman empire to India. Born, despite his name, in Iran, he taught, wrote and advised in every Muslim country of western Asia and also lived for a time in France and Russia. His ideas were various and contradictory; at times he favoured reform carried through by an autocratic Muslim sovereign and at other times reform through a constitutional government. Some recent writers have seen him as a consistent enemy of British colonialism, but although this theme provides a prominent element in his writings it does not seem to have been pursued any more continuously than others. The one idea which persists through all his writing is the notion of the reform of Islam in the face of the challenge of the modern world, and it brought him into frequent conflict with the ulema and attracted to him a circle of admirers who subsequently developed his ideas. So rich and varied were those ideas, embracing as they did social, educational and political change, ideas of political and cultural identity based upon religion and language and the whole range of philosophy, that they still form a fertile source of inspiration for Muslim writers.

What is most significant about those ideas is that they were always related to traditional Muslim thinking in style and content even when they were plainly adopted from the West, and it is this feature which is the heart of Islamic modernism and the key to the embedding of these ideas in Muslim thought. Western ideas could be insulated from Muslim ideas and those who adopted them could be ignored. It may well be, as was alleged by his orthodox critics at the time and has been claimed by historians since, that Afghānī himself cared nothing for Islam or any religion and was an atheist and a free thinker. And it cannot be argued that this suspicion was of no consequence because it made his ideas repugnant to many ulema. But because of the way they were set out the ideas of the Islamic modernists could not be treated as of no account by Muslims. They struck directly into the centre of Muslim thinking and could not be insulated from it. To many Western readers Afghānī's ideas often seem superficial and naïve and he seems imprisoned within a pattern of thinking which forever limits the range of his thought. But to those young men who gathered round him in the cafés of the Near East and listened to him expounding his ideas while he smoked his incessant cigarettes it was as though he was opening to them not only a new world but one which was comprehensible. Afghānī may have done little by direct intervention in Egyptian politics before his exile in 1879. He appears to have been a protégé of Riyāḍ Pasha employed to attack Ismāʿīl and made an unfortunate decision to desert his patron in favour of Sharīf after Ismāʿīl's fall. Nevertheless, his influence on others, especially young students at al-Azhar, was profound. The modernists were uninterested in Egypt as a unit of loyalty; their loyalty was to an Islam purified and reformed by changes in education and law by the extirpation of the influence of those secularists who were corrupting Islam by introducing Western practices into society and infidel advisers into government. In an essay written in 1881 Shaykh Ḥusayn al-Marsafī attacked all the enemies of progress – the ulema, the bureaucrats and the landlords – condemned the spread of decadence through luxury and urged that Egypt should become more self-sufficient.

The major expression of the intellectual revival in Egypt was in the press. By 1879 there were sixteen well-established newspapers, ten of them in Arabic. It is dangerous to deduce too much about the currents of Egyptian thinking from the press. Writers and newspapers were dependent upon patrons and wrote to serve their interests; the opinions they expressed were not necessarily their own, still less those of substantial numbers of Egyptians of the time. Many were deeply influenced by French opinions: French schools and newspapers were strong in Egypt and several writers who began their careers in Egypt subsequently moved to Paris where anti-British views were popular.

Another feature of the writers is the number of non-Egyptians, or members of minority groups within Egypt, who were prominent among them. Among the many Syrian Christian immigrants was Adīb Isḥāq (1856–85) who arrived in 1875 and later edited *Miṣr*. Adīb Isḥāq was a follower of Afghānī but strongly opposed to the claims of religion and concerned to emphasize the secular bonds which united communities. James Sanūʿa was an Egyptian Jew who also stressed the notion of an Egyptian identity which transcended religious differences. In 1870 he founded a theatre and in 1877 began to publish *Abū Naḍḍāra*, a satirical journal attacking the Egyptian government.

Perhaps the best known of the journalists was an Egyptian, ʿAbdallāh al-Nadīm (1844–96), whose paper *Ṭarīq* took a strong populist line in supporting the grievances of Egyptian peasants and opposing European and other non-Egyptian influences. He too placed great emphasis on Egyptian patriotism. Later, he formed close links with ʿUrābī himself and made his paper a vehicle for ideas attributed to ʿUrābī and the radicals of 1881–2. Lastly, one must mention

Muḥammad ʿAbduh, the best-known follower of Afghānī, who edited the government newspaper, *Al-Waqāʾi ʿal-Miṣriyya*, which he made a vehicle for his own ideas on reform.

Another group which became influential during the ʿUrābī movement was the rural notables, that is, landowners of Arab as opposed to Turko-Circassian origin whose power and wealth were based in the provinces and not in Cairo. Unlike the Turko-Circassians their interests were not in maintaining government expenditure on the army and administration but they shared with other landowners a desire to retain the tax concessions on their *ʿushūrī* lands and the *Muqābala* law. The foundations of the wealth of this group had been laid under Muḥammad ʿAlī, but its members had prospered during the reigns of Saʿīd and Ismāʿīl and had profited from the growth of cotton cultivation. Their institutional outlet was the Assembly of Delegates, or Chamber of Notables as it is sometimes named, which had been created by Ismāʿīl in 1866. The assembly was not an impressive body; it was chosen by indirect election, had advisory powers only and met for a mere two months each year, when it did everything Ismāʿīl asked of it. The assembly was an emblem of civilization rather than an instrument of power but its membership was drawn especially from those with a power base in the villages. An example of the careers of these men may be seen in that of Muḥammad Sulṭān Pasha (1825–84) who came from a family of some education, moderate means and no influence in the province of Minyā. Sulṭān became a village shaykh and built up a local and provincial influence. Coming to the notice of Saʿīd Pasha, he was made a provincial governor in 1860 and in 1866 was appointed to the Central Inspectorate. Sulṭān's main power base remained in Minyā where he amassed large estates amounting by 1882 to 10,000 *faddāns* (42 sq. kilometres) in addition to another 3,000 *faddāns* (12.6 sq. kilometres) elsewhere in Upper Egypt. Sulṭān also strengthened his connections in Cairo where he built a palace. Sulṭān was a well-paid broker who represented the *fallāḥīn* to government and government to the *fallāḥīn*. In 1881 he threw in his lot with the constitutionalist group and played a significant role in formulating the demands of ʿUrābī.

The generalized economic discontent arose from natural disasters – floods and droughts – in the 1870s, the depression in the world economy (which is usually dated from 1873), the bankruptcy of the Egyptian government, which forced a policy of financial austerity, and the increased vulnerability of different sections of society. The spread of a cash economy in Lower Egypt led to the payment of debts and taxes by the *fallāḥīn* in cash rather than kind. Under the Land law of 1858 the *fallāḥ* on many categories of landholding could mortgage, sell or rent his land. In consequence the *fallāḥ* was able to borrow on the security of his land or sell his crops in advance. With the crop failures of the late 1870s the *fallāḥ* was often unable to repay his loans and the money-lender, usually a foreigner, Greek or Copt, obtained possession of the land through the new Mixed Courts which were in operation in 1876. What we do not know is how extensive such transfers were or whether they frequently resulted in eviction. But peasant grievances and the image of the foreign money-lender figured largely in the propaganda of 1881–2.

The factor which gave substance and a stage to all these vague elements was the action of the army in 1881–2, or rather of the Arabic-speaking officers. It has already been remarked that Egyptian *fallāḥīn* were recruited to the army from the time of Muḥammad ʿAlī. Later, they achieved commissioned rank, but none succeeded in advancing beyond regimental rank; ranks higher than that of colonel were the preserve of the Turko-Circassians. This circumstance was defended by reference to the particular military talents of the Turko-Circassian community, although this argument was discredited during the Abyssinian campaign when Turko-Circassian officers did not distinguish themselves. The exclusion of Arabic speakers from higher ranks caused some resentment, but the sense of injustice was much enhanced after 1876 when economy measures brought about a substantial reduction in the army. In 1878 the Nubar government ordered a reduction from a nominal 90,000 men, and an actual strength of 15,000, to a nominal 36,000 and an actual 7,000. At the same time the police force was to be reduced to 7,000 and the navy abolished. Out of 2,600 officers, 1,600 were to be put on half-pay. Inevitably, the principal economies were to be achieved at regimental level which signified that, even without any intention to discriminate against Arabic-speaking officers (although one certainly cannot exclude the possibility of such an intention), Arabic-speaking officers would suffer disproportionately. The economies played some part in the 1879 army demonstrations. At that time the army was brought under control and after the accession of Tawfiq its size was fixed at 12,000. On 15 January 1881 there was a new mutiny which appears to have been set off by fears among certain officers that they were about to be dismissed and resentment at the policy of the minister of war, a Turko-Circassian named ʿOsmān Rifqī Pasha, who was believed to favour his own community. The rebel officers demanded and obtained the dismissal of Rifqī, an increase of pay for unemployed officers and a promise of equal treatment for Egyptian and Circassian officers in promotion.

The spokesman for the Arab officers in 1881 was Aḥmad ʿUrābī

Pasha (1841–1911), the son of a village shaykh from the area of Zaqāzīq, who had received some education at al-Azhar, joined the army in 1854 and was promoted to lieutenant-colonel in 1860, in which rank he remained. ʿUrābī's promotion record does cast some doubt on the genuineness of the Arabic-speaking officers' grievances, for although he had held his rank for twenty-one years in 1881 he was still only forty years old, which in most peacetime armies would have been considered exceptionally young to command a regiment. His record may, however, also suggest that promotion in the Egyptian army was something of a lottery.

It has been claimed that the demand of the officers represented more generalized grievances, but although many of them were exposed to the general intellectual currents of the time, both Western and Islamic, and most had contacts with villages and were aware of the distress of the rural population, there is no evidence that there was any political content in their demands in January 1881. Their action and their demands appear to have been those of aggrieved officers and ʿUrābī took the lead not because of any nationalist sympathies he may have had but because he was regarded as an excellent speaker who could best present the demands of his colleagues. The officers' action, however, had political implications even if these were unintended because they threatened the success of the policies of the Riyāḍ government and its European backers. The officers could expect that the government would endeavour to reverse its defeat and to punish those who had set an example of successful mutiny. Fear, as well as the hope of further improvements in their conditions, drove the mutineers to further intervention.

The rebel officers made their second, more far-reaching intervention in September 1881. The immediate cause of this further mutiny was the dismissal on 13 August 1881 of Maḥmūd Sāmī Bey al-Bārūdī, ʿOsmān's successor as minister of war, a Turko-Circassian who was believed to be sympathetic to the aspirations of the rebels. Bārūdī (1839–1904) came from a family long established in Egypt and he had had a military and diplomatic career. In his writings there is evidence of a genuine sense of Egyptian patriotism, although this was historical rather than related to any consciousness of an Egyptian Arab identity. The strongest element in his political consciousness appears to have been Islam and his guiding principle was hostility to injustice. Bārūdī, like many of those concerned in the events of 1881–2, responded to traditional rather than modern political rhythms.

The officers made their first response on 20 August with a demand for better conditions of service. This was refused by Riyāḍ. Between the presentation of this demand and their demonstration in the Abdin square on 9 September, a political element entered the officers' thinking for the first time. This new element derived from contacts with rural notables including Sulṭān Pasha. In their September demands, in addition to the increase of the army to 18,000, these officers demanded the dismissal of the Riyāḍ government and the summoning of the Assembly of Delegates.

The rebels were again successful. Tawfīq replaced Riyāḍ by Sharīf and summoned the assembly, which met on 26 December after elections in November. In fact Sharīf's government was even more Turko-Circassian in composition than that of Riyāḍ and had a similar programme. Sharīf was unhappy about the conduct of the army and had no time for the rural notables of the assembly. "These peasants want guidance", he remarked later to Wilfrid Blunt.[7] He declined to accept dictation from either group and his coming to office ushered in a three-cornered conflict between the Turko-Circassians, the rural notables and the army. The Ottoman government and the European powers were very interested onlookers.

At first co-operation between the Turko-Circassians and the rural notables in the assembly seemed likely to succeed in producing an agreed plan for government. Sharīf produced a draft scheme of modest constitutional reform designed to strengthen the ministry against the khedive rather than the assembly against the government, a device similar to that evolved by the Ottoman bureaucratic reformers of 1876. It seemed probable that this scheme would be acceptable to the rural notables, but hopes were killed by the action of Britain and France who issued a joint note on 28 January 1882 in which they affirmed their support for the khedive and the status quo. The assembly was no longer willing to accept Sharīf's draft. The delegates demanded the right to vote on that part of the budget which was not assigned to the payment of the debt, but this the Great Powers would not permit. Sharīf resigned and was replaced by al-Bārūdī.

By many contemporary writers the new government, which included a number of non-Turko-Circassians and ʿUrābī as minister of war, was depicted as a species of radical military dictatorship. This picture is inaccurate. It is true that the reputation of ʿUrābī and the rebel officers had risen greatly after the Abdin square demonstration of September 1881. ʿUrābī had become a national hero, feted when he returned to his native province of Sharqiyya, and praised throughout the radical press as the protector of the people of Egypt against the Turko-Circassians and the Europeans. It was at this time that ʿAbdallāh al-Nadīm constituted himself a sort of publicity agent for ʿUrābī and, perhaps, grafted on to the officer ideas and aspirations of his own which were strange to ʿUrābī. ʿUrābī's own statements were replete with fine sentiments about law and justice, echoing Islamic traditional views, but he also apparently took over from its Coptic author the phrase, "Egypt for the Egyptians", a novel conception to Muslim ears, containing as it did the implication that Copts and Muslim Arabic-speaking Egyptians might have in common a bond not shared by Turko-Circassians, Syrians and Europeans. But it is not easy to penetrate the meanings men drew from such slogans. In private, to Europeans ʿUrābī readily acknowledged a debt to European ideas and appeared much more liberal and conciliatory.

Neither among the Arab army officers nor among their political associates in government or the assembly was there any conviction in favour of a radical programme of expropriation in the spring of 1882. Al-Bārūdī's government passed a law increasing the powers of the assembly but the rural notables were not radicals and had no wish to oust the Europeans from Egypt. The army officers, however, decided to redress the balance within the army in their favour: 754 officers, mostly Turko-Circassians, were retired and there were promotions for ʿUrābī's followers, 5 of whom became brigadier-generals. It was an extensive, but not a wholesale purge and it produced a strong reaction from the Turko-Circassian officers who entered a conspiracy against the Bārūdī government. When the plot was discovered forty of the conspirators were reduced to the ranks and exiled to the Sudan. It was this incident which lent colour to the reports of a military dictatorship bent on destroying its opponents. The Turko-Circassian plot also brought about a confrontation between Tawfīq and his government.

From May 1882 Egypt began to slip rapidly into disorder. On 20 May an Anglo-French fleet appeared off Alexandria and on 25 May, in a joint note, the two powers demanded the dismissal and exile of ʿUrābī. Al-Bārūdī's government resigned but ʿUrābī refused to accept his own removal and demanded the deposition of Tawfīq, who agreed to reinstate ʿUrābī on 28 May. Both sides looked to the Ottoman authorities for support and both received encouragement, but it is clear that ʿAbd ül-Ḥamīd was playing his own game and hoped to exploit the crisis so as to get rid of both ʿUrābī and Tawfīq and install his own favoured candidate, ʿAbd al-Ḥalīm, a son of Muḥammad ʿAlī, as khedive.

The crisis was brought to a head by riots in Alexandria on 11 June which resulted in more than fifty deaths, the looting of the European quarter and a panic among Christians. It was supposed that law and order in Egypt had completely broken down, that ʿUrābī or even Tawfīq had instigated the riots. In fact the riots were probably spontaneous and the ʿUrabists do not seem to have been involved, although some of the authorities, including the gendarmerie, appear to have been implicated. On 11 July the British fleet bombarded Alexandria and two days later Tawfiq put himself under the protection of the British troops. On 17 July ʿUrābī issued a proclamation stating that Tawfiq had gone over to the infidel and that he himself would defend Egypt. ʿUrābī summoned a council of notables (not to be confused with the Assembly of Delegates which had been ignored by everyone since May), to legitimize his position. The notables were divided and ʿUrābī then appealed to the people and called up yet another assembly. There was almost complete polarization in Egypt: the great majority of the Turko-Circassians and the wealthiest of the rural notables supported the khedive; while the bulk of the rural notables and the people of the streets supported ʿUrābī. The basis of ʿUrābī's appeal had now become entirely religious and the national element disappeared; ʿUrābī was the defender of Islam against the infidel and those who associated with the infidels.

ʿUrābī's resistance was ineffectual. British troops landed in Egypt in August and on 13 September routed the Egyptian army at Tel-el-Kebir. Cairo was occupied immediately afterwards, Tawfiq restored and ʿUrābī and his confederates arrested, tried and exiled to Ceylon. The British occupation of Egypt had begun.

The ʿUrābī revolution was a significant event in the modern history of the Near East. It was a revolution brought about by the consequences of modernization; it was focused within one of the principal institutions created by modernization; and it displayed several novel features. Ultimately, however, it was dominated by traditional modes of expression. The movement embraced two modern features: the desire to constrain the autocratic power of the ruler through the development of modest constitutional machinery; and the idea of nationality contained in the antipathy of Arabic-speaking Egyptians to Turko-Circassian domination, most prominently displayed within the army. The element of antipathy to foreigners extended to a desire to reduce the influence of, first, the Syrian and Greek immigrants who had been attracted to Egypt by the cotton boom and who were involved in commerce and banking; and, second, the Europeans, who increasingly dominated the policies of government and occupied more and more of the top positions in the bureaucracy; by the end of 1881 there were 1,325 Europeans in Egyptian government service holding jobs worth about £350,000 per annum. In the last stage of the revolution Egypt divided partly on class lines; those who had most to lose went with Tawfiq while popular support went to ʿUrābī. But in that last stage the demands of the ʿUrabists were enunciated not in national or in class terms but in basic religious terms. In the summer of 1882 everything was rolled up in the old notion of the fight for Islam against injustice and it was this notion which ʿUrābī personified.

The British occupation of Egypt in 1882 bears a misleading impression of inevitability and design. In fact, a study of the sequence of events shows that the British action was unplanned and undesired. To demonstrate the truth of this contention it will be useful to consider the event which is generally supposed to have made a British occupation inevitable, namely the construction of the Suez Canal.

The idea of a canal to link the Mediterranean with the Red Sea is an old one. Bonaparte's engineers considered the feasibility of the enterprise but their false belief that there was a difference of 10 metres in the levels of the two seas delayed the project for many years. The Suez Canal was eventually built on the basis of a concession granted to the French engineer, Ferdinand de Lesseps, in 1854 and was completed in 1869. Britain had long opposed the construction of a canal on the grounds that the existing arrangements for transport were satisfactory to Britain and that a canal would be of primary benefit to Mediterranean powers such as France. But once the canal was opened Britain had to live with it: she must use it to retain her mercantile superiority and she could not afford to have it closed against her. This view implied a greater concern with Egypt as well as an interest in the management of the canal. In this context it should be noted that the purchase of the canal shares by Disraeli in 1875 was of little significance for it gave Britain only a minority position among the shareholders in the Suez Canal Company and no more than three of the twenty-four directorships. The root of the problem was the rules for the use of the canal and, even more, control of Egypt. Nevertheless, the purchase was a public recognition of Britain's concern with the canal. As one of Disraeli's colleagues, Cairns (who like most of his fellow Cabinet ministers had been opposed to the purchase of the shares before the event), put the matter: "It is now *the Canal and India*; there is no such thing now to us as India alone. India is any number of cyphers; but the Canal is the unit that makes these cyphers valuable."[8] The orthodox British view, however, still held that it was through support for the integrity of the Ottoman empire that the canal was to be secured and not through direct action in Egypt.

Throughout the growing crisis in Egypt, from the time of Ismāʿīl's bankruptcy onwards, Britain followed the lead of France in the hope of averting unilateral French action. Unlike France, Britain declined to intervene in support of the British bondholders; their investments were their own affair, said government; only after the matter assumed a political aspect with the deposition of Ismāʿīl did Britain consent to nominate a financial controller. The deposition of Ismāʿīl was unwelcome to Britain; before that event she had been the leading European power in Egypt; thereafter, she was only equal with France. Britain was also reluctant to participate in the joint note of January 1882 which destroyed Sharīf's government; she co-operated only to prevent unilateral French action under the direction of Gambetta, who drafted the note whose implications the British foreign secretary, Lord Granville, apparently did not understand; the Cabinet believed it would weaken ʿUrābī but instead it strengthened him. When it became clear that intervention in Egypt to restore order might be necessary Britain preferred that it should be Ottoman intervention or a combined action by all the powers; no member of the Cabinet wanted unilateral British intervention and only a small minority wanted a joint Anglo-French intervention. But ʿAbd ül-Ḥamīd was busily looking after his own interests and Bismarck killed any hope of an international intervention by a declaration of his complete lack of interest in the matter. France also opposed an Ottoman intervention and Britain was obliged to go along with France during the spring of 1882. Eventually, France agreed to a British suggestion of a naval demonstration (intended only as a bluff) and to the use of Ottoman troops under Anglo-French control. But France withdrew from the Ottoman arrangement and swung round to favour a deal with ʿUrābī; so also did Austria and Germany. By June it seemed likely that no European power would join with Britain and prolonged efforts to obtain agreement with the Ottomans also failed to achieve any result. Should Britain go on alone?

In June and July 1882 the Cabinet finally reconciled itself to the notion of unilateral British intervention in Egypt, although to the end most members continued to hope that the rebels would capitulate to the threat of force. The question remained of the nature and purpose of any intervention. Some members were for action to protect the Suez Canal alone while others argued that there could be no security until ʿUrābī was overthrown and that object would entail an expedition to Cairo. But, while France would consider action to protect the canal she would not agree to an expedition against Cairo. On 20 July the Cabinet decided to send an expeditionary force and on 29 July the government of Freycinet in France fell over its request for funds to implement a scheme to defend the canal. The new French government refused to contemplate any intervention at all and Britain went on alone. With a Cabinet so divided and so much at the mercy of events it is difficult to say what motives finally predominated. Dislike of one who was seen as a military adventurer was one factor, the safety of the canal another, but perhaps the decisive factor was prestige. Once the naval demonstration had taken place the government had to be able to show some success for its efforts.

As soon as she was in Egypt Britain considered how she could get out. Any evacuation was dependent on securing a stable government in Egypt, with suitable provision for orderly financial arrangements, and a guarantee that no other European power would dominate Egypt and that British vessels would be guaranteed the free use of the canal. Britain hoped to achieve these ends through Ottoman intervention within a framework agreed among the powers and she did not finally abandon hope of agreement with the Ottomans until 1887. In the meantime she set about reconstructing the Egyptian government under Tawfiq on the basis of a report drawn up by Lord Dufferin which set out the principle of "enabling [the Egyptians] to govern themselves under the uncompromising aegis of our friendship".[9]

Under the Egyptian constitution of 1883 Egypt was to be governed by the khedive and his ministers assisted by a Legislative Council of 30 members (14 elected) and an 82-member General Assembly composed of members of the Legislative Council, ministers and 46 members elected on a restricted franchise. The General Assembly's role was primarily consultative but it was given a veto on new direct taxation. Small councils were also to be established in each province to assist the governor in dealing with local matters. The constitution amounted to a very limited experiment in participatory government; real power remained with the khedive and whoever could have the greatest influence over him. Who that latter power was to be was finally determined by events in the Sudan.

The event which made it impossible for Britain to leave Egypt was the Mahdist uprising in the Sudan (see p. 243). The rising began in 1881. The annihilation of an Egyptian force under Hicks Pasha in 1883 meant that there was no Egyptian force to defend Egypt and the Red Sea ports and Britain would have to accept the responsibility. Britain could not withdraw from Egypt.

Britain had assumed the management of Egyptian affairs under unsatisfactory conditions. By the various arrangements made to superintend the repayment of the Egyptian debt several international bodies had been established to manage Egyptian assets. Of these the most important was the Caisse de la Dette set up to collect revenues assigned to the debt. By 1885 the Caisse included representatives of Britain, France, Austria, Italy, Germany and Russia and the other powers were able to use their extensive influence over the financial affairs of Egypt to create difficulties for Britain. Had Britain made an early decision to stay in Egypt she might have insisted on different financial arrangements, but because of the way British occupation evolved she was left in a situation in which she could not employ Egyptian resources to the best effect. Not until the 1904 entente with France was this embarrassment relieved.

British control over Egypt was exercised in two ways: by military and political means. An army of occupation was introduced, at first 12,000, later reduced to 5,000 although it was easily supplemented when required as in the 1894 dispute with ʿAbbās II. Second, Britain controlled the Egyptian army. The old army had been destroyed at Tel-el-Kebir and was subsequently disbanded. From what was left was formed a basic corps of officers and non-commissioned officers to whom were added *fallāḥīn* conscripts and, subsequently, Black troops from the southern Sudan. The higher officers, including the commander-in-chief (the sirdar), were British. Originally, the Egyptian army was designed solely as a local police force but later it came to be posted mainly on the frontiers, especially that with the Sudan. The British Consul-General, Lord Cromer, wrote that it had to be efficient for use against Britain's enemies but also inefficient lest it be a danger to Britain. In fact the army remained firmly under British control throughout the period of occupation and was a useful instrument for the reconquest of the Sudan.

Political control was exercised through the Egyptian government. Theoretically, the Egyptian government was independent under the suzerainty of the Porte but in practice the dominant figure was the British consul-general. From 1883 to 1906 this post was held by Evelyn Baring, Lord Cromer, who had already gained experience of Egypt as one of the two European financial controllers. Tawfiq, it is said, used to turn pale whenever he heard the approach of Cromer's carriage and never offered any objection to his advice. His son and successor ʿAbbās II did try to resist Cromer after his accession but was sternly rebuffed. In retrospect it is clear that ʿAbbās held strong cards and if he had played them right he might have regained substantial independence. The Liberal government in England would have liked to have left matters as much as possible to the khedive in the hope of paving the way for a British withdrawal, and was unwilling to support Cromer in his desire to control Egyptian government more closely. Had ʿAbbās moved cautiously and confined his attention to civilian matters he might gradually have gained more control of affairs. "The Khedive", wrote Cromer in 1897, "if he knew it, is in reality much more the master of the situation than he imagines."[10] But in 1894 Cromer took advantage of

ʿAbbās's attempt to intervene in army affairs, a point on which the Cabinet was bound to support him, and so humiliated ʿAbbās that the khedive made no further, direct attack on Cromer's control. Cromer was able to continue to control the choice of Egyptian ministers. Chief ministers who attempted to resist British control, like Nubar and Riyāḍ, were dropped and Cromer eventually settled on the complaisant figure of Muṣṭafā Fahmī Pasha, who surrounded himself with a Council of Ministers, which Portal, the first secretary at the consulate, described as "this collection of supine nonentities and doddering old pantaloons".[11] It is noteworthy that the great majority of ministers continued to be drawn from the Turko-Circassian families; Cromer thought little of their capacity but greatly preferred them to Arabic-speaking Muslim Egyptians.

British control did not stop with the selection of Egyptian ministers but extended through the appointment of British advisers, to the management of policy within Egyptian ministries. The process began with the Ministry of Public Works in 1883 and continued through those of Justice (1891), Interior (1894) and Education (1906). Defence and Foreign Affairs were always effectively under British control but the most important area of control was Finance. The British financial adviser had a seat in the Council of Ministers and formed the chief link between the Egyptian government and the consul-general. Around them the British advisers accumulated British assistants. The number of these had increased to 286 by 1896 and 662 in 1906. In 1905, so the Milner Commission later reported, only 28 per cent of higher government posts were occupied by Egyptians (many of them Copts), 42 per cent by Britons and 30 per cent by Syrians and Armenians. British control also extended into the provinces through the appointment of European police inspectors.

Under British direction the major priorities of Egyptian government were financial stability and the development of public works, especially irrigation works. Financial stability was achieved. In 1882 Egypt's situation was gloomy; revenue was falling, nearly half being consumed in debt repayments, to say nothing of the compensation Egypt had to pay for the damage of 1882. In 1885 a new arrangement with the Caisse de la Dette provided a basis for steady financial improvement. As revenue rose the burden of debt repayment (fixed at about £5 million p.a.) became less and a surplus was available for tax reduction and the financing of investment. British financial strategy reversed that of Ismāʿīl, who had looked to rapid growth and a high level of government expenditure. British policy was to reduce the burden of tax, especially on land, in the hope that this would encourage private investment and expand agricultural production. Between 1881 and 1914 the proportion of revenue derived from land taxation fell from 58 to 33 per cent. An expansion of agricultural production was especially necessary in view of the steady fall in prices over the whole of the last quarter of the nineteenth century which meant that Egypt had to export far more cotton to meet her external payments. Cotton exports did, in fact, double over the period. After the end of the nineteenth century there was a substantial rise in cotton prices and so a very large increase in the value of Egypt's exports. Over the period 1880–1914 Egyptian exports increased from £13 million to £32 million (over 90% cotton) and imports from £7.4 million to £27.9 million. It is worth commenting that, despite the fall in cotton prices during the late nineteenth century, cotton remained by far the most profitable economic investment in Egypt.

The conservative financial policy of the British controllers (partly imposed by the Caisse) meant that comparatively little was borrowed for public investment; only £13.5 million between 1886 and 1904. Although this rate of borrowing was later increased it remained relatively low and the burden of public debt was substantially reduced. This was claimed as a major achievement by Britons but some doubts about these claims may be appropriate. The expected corollary of low public investment was high private investment and this did take place, especially after 1900, in public utilities, manufacturing and especially land, both purchase and mortgage. By 1907 foreigners owned 13.5 per cent of Egyptian land. By 1914 total foreign debt (public and private) was around £200 million and total overseas interest repayments about £9 million per annum, a figure well in excess of the balance on visible trade. On the face of it Egypt's financial position had actually deteriorated compared with the 1870s when interest payments had been covered by the favourable balance of trade. But this criticism should not be taken too far. Egypt had acquired some valuable assets, including large gold reserves, and during the fortuitous circumstances of the First World War when cotton prices reached an all-time high, she was able to earn so large a surplus that she could repatriate almost the entire overseas debt.

Public investment during the British period was concentrated on public works, notably irrigation. During the earlier development of the cotton economy in Egypt there had been no constraint arising from the total amount of water available; the problem had been essentially one of distribution. But further development of the cotton economy entailed making more water available in summer. The summer flow of the Nile is around 35 million tonnes of water a day; cotton requires about 25 tonnes of water per *faddān* per day. Simple arithmetic gives a theoretical maximum area under cotton of around 1.3 million *faddāns* (5,461 sq. kilometres) unless there is provision for summer storage (the limits on rice, which requires about 70 tonnes per *faddān* per day, are much more severe). The new problem was, therefore, that of increasing water storage through the construction of dams. Three major enterprises were carried out: the reconstruction of the Delta barrage, which was completed in 1890, a barrage at Asyut, completed in 1902 and the construction of the Aswan Dam (1898–1902). The Aswan Dam held about 1,000 million tonnes, that is, an extra 10 million tonnes a day for 100 days during the summer, or a maximum of 400,000 extra *faddāns* of cotton. In 1910–12 the height of the dam was raised and the storage capacity increased to 2,300 million tonnes. The results of this activity were dramatic in the life of Egypt. Down to 1900 cotton was grown almost entirely in the Delta but the Asyut barrage permitted the extension of cotton cultivation to Middle Egypt and the Aswan Dam to Upper Egypt. During the period 1882–1914 the cultivable area grew from 4.8 to 5.7 million *faddāns* and the crop area (i.e. allowing for the cultivation of two or more crops in a year) to 7.7 million *faddāns*. Agricultural development was further assisted by government investment in roads and light railways, by technical assistance, by the abolition of tolls and, above all, by the general security. Nor was cotton the only crop which was developed. The substitution for wheat of maize, which increased from about one-quarter of total agricultural production to nearly one-half by 1913, enabled Egypt to remain almost self-sufficient in food production, although she was a net importer of food after 1900.

Against this favourable picture of development which enabled Egypt to continue to support its population, which more than doubled during the British period, at an apparently rising standard of living it is necessary to set some counterbalancing elements. Some corollaries of development were unpleasant; waterlogging and salination in the Delta and disease among crops and people. These problems could be overcome but more expensive investment was required. After the great rise in the productivity of land which took place between 1880 and 1896, when it nearly doubled, productivity fell back until by 1909 it was not much above the 1880 level, although it increased again thereafter. But the great question is whether it was sensible to concentrate investment on raising agricultural production or whether it was time to diversify. Beyond reasonable doubt investment in agriculture paid better than any apparent alternative down to the early years of the twentieth century. After that time the indicators begin to suggest diminishing returns to further investment in agriculture and the desirability of greater investment in industry and related activities, including education.

There was very limited growth of industry in Egypt before 1914. Most developments were in cotton, sugar and food processing and in construction. Lack of indigenous sources of energy, of raw materials, want of a skilled labour force and low tariff protection (8%) all held back the growth of industry. Government did not invest in industry, regarding it as no part of its job to do so. Nor did it put much into education; expenditure amounted to only 1 per cent of budget and costs were shifted to parents and students. In 1881 70 per cent of students received some form of government subsidy; by 1892 only 27 per cent did so; educational development was left to private enterprise. By 1914 there were 68 government-supported primary and secondary schools, 328 private foreign schools and 739 private Egyptian schools. The Egyptian University was established in 1907 by subscription.

The British view was that choice of investment opportunities was best left to market forces, and that the focus on cotton was merely a reflection of the judgment that cotton offered the best long-tem investment opportunities. To some extent the experience of the First World War, when there was a boom in investment in manufacuring and the rise of a class of Egyptian entrepreneurs, justified this view. Between 1914 and 1918 the cessation of supplies from Europe and the demands of the Near Eastern theatre of war did provide the incentive for investment; when profits were to be made businessmen would respond. But in the particular situation of Egypt there is a question whether an opportunity was not missed during the early twentieth century to begin to diversify the Egyptian economy to prepare for the time when cotton could no longer carry the burden of meeting the increased expectations of a larger population.

Britain also had a view of desirable social development for Egypt. Partly for political and partly for romantic reasons British policy favoured the growth of a class of small peasant proprietors and sought to achieve this by various measures, including the sale of state land, lending through the Agricultural Bank (established 1902), and through legislation to prevent the seizure of the land of small proprietors for debt (the Five Feddan law of 1912). This policy was unsuccessful. The state lands went largely to large landholders and especially to foreign investors, the Agricultural Bank would lend only to those who already possessed land, and the Five Feddan law had the additional consequence of making it impossible for the peasant to borrow on his land and so to develop it. In fact the period of British control saw a steady decline in the position of small landholders, a substantial increase in the number of landless peasants and the continued domination of Egyptian agriculture by big landholders. The number of middling (5–50 *faddāns*) and large landholders (over 50 *faddāns*) and the amount of land in their possession changed little but the number of those with very small holdings or no land increased very greatly. By 1919 60 per cent of landholders held only 9 per cent of the land.

During the British period Egyptian agriculture was dominated by a new type of large estate. The abolition of forced labour had obliged landlords to develop a new mode of cultivating their estates by giving peasants small plots of land in return for labour services and by the employment, at harvest time, of gangs of itinerant labourers mainly from Upper Egypt. The growth of these estates and of an agricultural proletariat marked the end of the traditional Egyptian village, at least in the Delta. Beneath the British wrapping Egypt continued to be ruled by notables who owed their position to their landholding and especially to cotton cultivation. They were, however, not the same families who had dominated Egypt before 1882. Although the Muḥammad ʿAlī family still possessed very large holdings these were considerably reduced by the sale of domain lands during the British period. Also, the Turko-Circassian official class declined in significance as landholders, reflecting the decline in their political position. The new classes who rose to prominence were the foreigners, the Copts and the new urban rich. The foreign community reached its peak in size and influence in 1907 when there were about a quarter of a million foreigners in Egypt (not counting Ottomans and Sudanese) of whom about half were Europeans. The great majority of them lived in the five big cities of Cairo (where they formed 16% of the population), Alexandria (25%), Port Said (28%), Ismailia and Suez. Their influence on economic and social life was profound. For example, foreigners dominated the trade of Alexandria which handled over 90 per cent of Egyptian trade. Foreign influence began to decline after 1907, first slowly and then, from 1915, quite rapidly. Syrians played a major role in the press, administration and business. The rise of the Copts was associated with educational developments within their community, American missionary schools and British patronage.

During the British period Egypt maintained its contrast with Ottoman development. In the Ottoman empire it was political pressures which provided the largest impulse for change. Although political pressures and state demands on resources had a substantial effect in bringing about the ʿUrābī revolution, political pressure relaxed when British control was established and it was once more the pressure of economic changes, arising through the continued expansion of the cotton economy, which was the major factor in the evolution of Egypt. Those groups which were most influential in Egypt, whether Egyptian or foreign, derived their wealth and power from land and cotton. To some extent those groups did attempt to assert their power in the political arena and it is to that area that it is now necessary to turn.

The period of British control saw the development of new forms of political expression, distinct from those which had prevailed in earlier periods and emanating from different sources. These new forms may be loosely described as Egyptian nationalism but they include a number of components which make this simple description misleading. It will be most useful to describe their evolution in terms of three stages of growth: the period from 1882 until 1892, when there is very little political expression; the period from 1892 until 1906, when the new forms develop especially through the press; and the period from 1907 until 1914 when the political demands become embodied in institutions and operate in a changing political environment. After 1914 ordinary political activity came to a halt until 1918.

Between 1882 and 1892 there was almost no legitimate basis for political opposition. ʿUrabism was a crime, comparable to Jacobitism in Britain after 1745, and was represented only by the attacks on the British occupation maintained by *émigrés* abroad, notably by Afghānī and ʿAbduh who founded the newspaper *Al-ʿUrwa al-Wuthqā* in Paris in 1883 and advocated a Muslim uprising against British rule. Within Egypt the attitude of the Khedive Tawfīq towards the British, to whom he owed his throne, made it impossible for the palace to become the rallying point for opposition as it had been under Ismāʿīl between 1876 and 1879. The landed notables also saw Britain as guarantor of their position against the radical threats apparently embodied in the last stages of the ʿUrabist movement. Further, it was evident that Britain also constituted the chief protection of Egypt against the threat that Mahdism might spread from the Sudan. Finally, it was expected, not least by the British themselves, that they would soon leave Egypt, and there appeared no urgent need to press for a British withdrawal. Accordingly, such discontent as existed was confined to discussions in the salons of certain notables who, for one reason or another, were aggrieved by their treatment. Such were the salons of Princess Nazlī Fāżil, daughter of Muṣṭafā Fażil, the patron of the Young Ottomans; ʿAlī Pasha Mubārak, an Arabic-speaking former minister and writer; and Riyāḍ, who attracted discontented members of the ulema. Salon nationalism was important because it was in the salons that some of the young men who were to be prominent in the next stage of political development had their introduction to political debate and acquired the contacts and patronage which were to serve them well. Thus Saʿd Zaghlūl was taken up by Princess Nazlī, Muṣṭafā Kāmil by ʿAlī Mubārak and Shaykh ʿAlī Yūsuf by Riyāḍ.

The second period was ushered in by the accession of ʿAbbās II Ḥilmī, a young man who believed he should rule. The early and fatal rebuff administered to him by Cromer has been described. ʿAbbās might still have recovered part of his lost position by better tactics, but he failed to take advantage of the opportunities presented to him and drifted into a niggling opposition to British rule, during which he sought support in Istanbul, Europe and Egypt. It was ʿAbbās's evident dissatisfaction with his position and his wilingness to patronize critics of what was nominally his government which legitimized opposition to British control of Egypt. The khedive was the legal ruler of Egypt and those who professed loyalty to him could not be accused of treason as the ʿUrabists had been. ʿAbbās was willing to subsidize writers who would advance his cause through the newspapers.

The press in Egypt is the main source for our information about the development of nationalism in this period, but it is a treacherous source because without a full knowledge of who paid for articles it is difficult to know how to evaluate their contents. Al-Kawākibī's advocacy of an Arab caliphate takes on a new colour when we know that he was being paid by ʿAbbās II, to whom such an argument could be of assistance in his complicated dealings with the Ottoman sultan. One of the most popular of all Egyptian papers during this period was *al-Muʾayyad*, which was almost entirely written by Shaykh ʿAlī Yūsuf, who was a consistent supporter of ʿAbbās II to whom he was greatly indebted both for money and for saving him from the consequences of a scandal. At various times Muṣṭafā Kāmil and Aḥmad Luṭfī al-Sayyid were also dependent upon the patronage of the wealthy. The efflorescence of the Egyptian Arabic press and the coming into existence of a new, literate public with a keen interest in modern developments was a major element in the development of the new style of politics for it enabled modern political debate to take place in a language which was developing the necessary vocabulary and concepts.

Another factor was the acquisition by young Egyptians of a modern education, either in private schools within Egypt or abroad, and the opening up of careers outside government employment, notably in journalism, education and in law in the Mixed Courts. Public employment, however, remained the principal goal of most young Egyptians who had received a modern as opposed to a religious education and among them was increasing resentment at the growing domination of public employment at the highest levels by Europeans and other foreigners and the persistent hold of the Turko-Circassians at lower levels.

The third phase of the development of Egyptian nationalism was ushered in by a political crisis known as the Dinshawāy incident of 1907, when a British officer died following a scuffle with some villagers in a trivial dispute over pigeon shooting. Heavy punitive sentences were passed on the villagers concerned and these produced a major press agitation against the sentences which broadened into general popular condemnation of British rule. Partly this Egyptian reaction was the consequence of the campaign of the new nationalists, but there were other factors including the severe economic difficulties and financial crisis of 1906–7 and the example of Japan. Muṣṭafā Kāmil wrote a book entitled *The Rising Sun* drawing attention to the achievement of an Asian power successfully defying the might of Russia. The Egyptian reaction to the Dinshawāy incident called into doubt the claims made by Cromer to the effect that the great mass of Egyptians were favourably disposed towards British control and that opposition was confined to a tiny minority of malcontents. The new Liberal government which had come into power in Britain in 1906 decided to try a different line of policy to be implemented by the new consul-general, Eldon Gorst.

Gorst aimed to conciliate the moderate nationalists by concessions, while adopting more severe coercive measures against the extremists. He built his system primarily around winning over the Khedive ʿAbbās II, giving more power to Egyptian ministers, enlarging the powers of the three ineffective consultative bodies established by Dufferin in 1883, and trying to reduce the employment of European advisers, a circumstance which made him very unpopular with the British community in Egypt. Press censorship and deportation were the other side of the coin.

Gorst succeeded in dividing the nationalists but not in checking the growth of opposition to Britain which assumed more dangerous proportions with the assassination of the Coptic prime minister, Buṭrus Ghālī Pasha, in 1910, after he had put forward an unpopular proposal for the extension of the concession of the Suez Canal Company. The murder of Buṭrus had the additional result of inspiring the Copts with mistrust of the Muslim Egyptian nationalists. They were especially alarmed by the declaration of the chief *mufti* that the execution of Buṭrus's assassin was illegal as Buṭrus was a Christian. The Copts had presented themselves as Egyptians rather than as Copts and had joined with ʿUrabists in 1882 and with the nationalists in 1907. From 1910 there was a distinct tendency for the Copts to stress their Coptic identity and in 1911 they organized a Coptic Congress at Asyut at which they stressed the notion of an Egyptian nationality transcending religion, demanded equality in government employment, government financial help and a weighted electoral system which would have favoured the Copts. The Coptic Congress provoked the calling of a Muslim Congress at Heliopolis in 1911 at which the delegates opposed the Coptic demands, claimed equality for all citizens and demanded that Islam should be recognized as the state religion. In both cases underlying the public statement of equality was a recognition of religious rivalry.

After Gorst's early death in 1911, he was followed as consul-general by Lord Kitchener who modified Gorst's policy by abandoning the plan of cultivating ʿAbbās (whom he contemplated deposing) and the process of Egyptianization of the administration. He made a bid for support from the peasants through the Five Feddan law, and from the moderate nationalists through the creation of a new political forum by amalgamating the old Legislative and General Assemblies into a new Legislative Assembly with a large elected majority, although with severely limited powers. The new assembly quickly became the chief centre for nationalist opposition to government. Inevitably, it was dominated by large landowners (49 of the 65 members in 1913 were in this category) but it quickly came to include lawyers who developed political skills in the assembly and played a significant role in Egyptian politics during the 1920s.

From 1907 the suffocating effects of the Cromer system on Egyptian political life began to be dissipated. In the effort to divide and conciliate the opposition Britain created new opportunities for the politicians and the divisions among the nationalists led to the formation of new interests and their political representation. In particular political parties came into being, the three most prominent all being founded in the turbulent period of 1907. These were the Constitutional Reform Party which was really a one-man party in which ʿAlī Yūsuf supported the interests of the khedive and orthodox Islam and demanded British evacuation (through persuasion not force), universal free education in Arabic, a representative assembly and Egyptianization of the administration; the Nationalist Party of Muṣṭafā Kāmil; and the People's Party of Muḥammad ʿAbduh and Aḥmad Luṭfī al-Sayyid.

The Nationalist Party was the creation of one of the most interesting figures in Egyptian political life: Muṣṭafā Kāmil (1874–1908), editor of the newspaper, *Al-Liwāʾ* (*The Standard*), founded in 1900. A French-educated lawyer, Muṣṭafā Kāmil was an extremely talented writer and speaker. His ideas were usually extreme and always inconsistent; their most persistent feature was a desire to get the British out of Egypt as quickly as possible. At different times Muṣṭafā Kāmil supported the claims of the khedive, the Ottomans, of Islam and of secular nationalism. That he felt a genuine sense of Egyptian identity, built around the idea of the unity of the Nile valley, is evident, but what the precise constituents of his nationalism were is unclear. He died only two months after the foundation of his party which thereupon emphasized the Islamic content of Egyptian nationalism and links with the Ottomans under the guidance of Muḥammad Farīd and ʿAbd al-ʿAzīz Shāwīsh. The party had a powerful urban following and although it was in no sense a mass party it reached further down the social scale than any other Egyptian political grouping of the period. After 1908 the party became associated with violence and was the subject of attacks by government. By 1912 it had virtually collapsed in Egypt and its leaders took refuge in Istanbul, although the party revived under the renewed patronage of ʿAbbās II before 1914.

The Umma or People's Party represented what Britons thought of as moderate Egyptian nationalism. It was built around some of the ideas of Muḥammad ʿAbduh who had renounced his radical past after his return to Egypt in 1888 and devoted himself to social reform in law and education where his Islamic modernist ideas had brought him into a long conflict with orthodox Islam represented by al-Azhar, which he vainly endeavoured to reform. His efforts at legal reform had some success both in the improvement of the *Sharīʿa* courts and in their replacement by state courts in 1906 after the codification of *Sharīʿa* law gave the state courts a body of law which they could apply in cases involving personal law. Politically, ʿAbduh preached Egyptian patriotism, a loyalty owed to Egypt equally by Muslims and non-Muslims and he opposed the idea of a politics based upon religious loyalties as in Panislamic doctrines, but he never developed any sophisticated ideas about the mode of government appropriate for Egypt and continued to uphold the idea of the just ruler governing in consultation with his people. The evolution of constitutional ideas was left to his followers and especially to Aḥmad Luṭfī al-Sayyid (1872–1963), son of a village shaykh, editor of *Al-Jarīda* and the most distinguished intellectual proponent of early Egyptian nationalism. Luṭfī rejected religion as a base for political activity. "I emphatically reject the suggestion that religion is a suitable basis for political action in the twentieth century", he wrote. "Our nationalism must rest on our interests and not our beliefs."[12] Luṭfī's nationalism was a secular system, based upon geography, history and language; the system of government which he advocated was taken directly from nineteenth-century European liberal thought – constitutionalism, toleration and all. He stressed also that Egypt was not yet ready to adopt such a system and advocated a considerable investment in education. In the meantime there should be a gradual evolution towards a constitutional system. The People's Party, which attracted several wealthy landowners and some Copts, sought co-operation with the British but was unable to secure real concessions from either Cromer, who would share power with no one, or from Gorst, who preferred to deal with ʿAbbās, who was the enemy of the People's Party. Indeed, one could argue that the attitude of Egyptian nationalists towards British control was heavily conditioned by what they thought would follow it. All argued that Britain should go, but those who supported ʿAbbās (ʿAlī Yūsuf consistently and the Nationalist Party intermittently) demanded that Britain should go at once because evacuation could only be followed by the transfer of power back to the khedive (if it were not to go to the Ottomans). The People's Party, on the other hand, believed that Britain should first create a constitutional structure which would ensure that they would not be left to the mercies of ʿAbbās. Under Kitchener the People's Party became the dominant political grouping and was able to exploit the Legislative Assembly. In 1918 it formed the core of the Wafd.

It remains to disentangle the various strands in Egyptian nationalism as it developed during the period before 1914. Religion remained a prominent ingredient as it had been in the ʿUrabist movement. The doctrine of Panislamism put forward by Jamāl al-Dīn with its ideas of violent Muslim resistance won little favour, but Islam was a prominent element in the nationalism of ʿAlī Yūsuf and also of the Nationalist Party. It is clear that any effort to expand political mobilization outside the narrow European-educated élite required the injection of Muslim appeals. The persistence of Islamic political appeals in turn led to religiously based politics among the Copts, disguised as an appeal to Egyptian patriotism. There is a close relationship between the Islamic element and the anti-foreigner element which was also present in Egyptian nationalism in these years and was directed against Europeans, Greeks and Syrians, whom Muṣṭafā Kāmil called intruders. The Syrian Christians found it increasingly difficult to maintain their support for the British occupation and for gradual constitutional evolution; Fāris Nimr found it impossible to get his cotton picked unless he supported the nationalist demands. Also linked with Islam was Ottomanism. The continuing current of support for the Ottoman connection among all but the People's Party rested on two elements, emotional and tactical. To some extent it was a response to the view of the Ottoman empire as the Muslim state *par excellence* and of the Ottoman sultan as the protector of Muslims everywhere. This view was fostered by ʿAbd ül-Ḥamīd's Panislamic policy and found especial favour among the Turko-Circassians who had the closest ties to the Ottoman state. Tactically, the emphasis on the Ottoman links was related to the circumstance that Egypt was still legally part of the Ottoman empire and therefore the Ottoman cause represented a way of legitimizing opposition to Britain. The strength of pro-Ottoman feeling was demonstrated, much to Britain's surprise, in 1906 when the sultan claimed the Sinai peninsula as part of the empire and Britain claimed for Egypt a boundary stretching from al-ʿArīsh to the Gulf of ʿAqaba. The almost unanimous Egyptian support for the Ottoman cause in the so-called ʿAqaba incident came as a shock to Britain which believed that she was supporting a cause which would be popular in Egypt. In 1908 the Young Turk revolution put a question mark against the Ottoman link, but interest survived the dismissal of ʿAbd ül-Ḥamīd and in 1914 Britain still feared the effects of an Ottoman appeal to Egyptian sentiment.

Secular Egyptian patriotism and liberalism was a style of politics which was adopted from Europe by a small minority. Its ingredients were the romantic nationalism based on geography and history of Garibaldi and Mazzini and the political liberalism of Locke and Mill. It had no native Egyptian roots and its spread in Egypt owed much to the Syrian Christian journalists. It spread, however, to the People's Party where it became embedded in Egyptian nationalism. Arab nationalism was unknown in Egyptian politics except among Syrians such as Rashīd Riḍā. Muṣṭafā Kāmil showed no interest in supporting the Arabs of the Maghreb against French domination. Nevertheless, there was in Egyptian nationalism an Arabic cultural element through language and literature and the (diminishing) hostility towards the Turko-Circassian element in Egyptian life. It was during the British period that the Turko-Circassian element began to be absorbed into a common Egyptian élite as recruitment from the Ottoman lands fell off and military employment in Egypt was reduced. The Turko-Circassians eventually became merged in a common pasha/*efendi* class composed of all those whose power and wealth derived from government employment. Until 1914, however, the old Turko-Circassian élite continued to cultivate its Ottoman links.

Egyptian politics before 1914 was primarily concerned with political issues narrowly defined. Despite the great economic changes which had taken place in Egypt and the large economic choices which Egypt faced during the early twentieth century there was very little discussion of economic issues or any real attempt to formulate economic policies for Egyptian development. Only at the Heliopolis Congress of 1911 was there discussion of an economic programme, and it was left to the Bank

Miṣr group during and after the First World War to elaborate a programme for Egyptian economic development. There was more interest in social reform. All politicians were committed to a major development of education, which was variously seen as the key to the civilization of Egypt and to government jobs for students. The followers of ʿAbduh were keenly interested in legal reform and in other social problems including the position of women. One Islamic modernist, Qāsim Amīn, published two controversial books arguing the case for the emancipation of women.

The principal characteristics of Egyptian political expression in the years before 1914 were that it was confined to a tiny, Western-educated, urban élite and depended upon the support of a group of notables whose primary source of wealth was from the production of cotton. It was a modern system of politics, the work of men who were the product of the political, social and economic changes of the nineteenth century. Outside this group small numbers of students, minor public officials and artisans were brought into political activity in the towns but the bulk of the urban population and the great mass of the rural population remained outside the political arena. These last looked to the traditional modes of organization – guilds, orthodox Islam, Ṣūfī orders and family, tribal and village structures. None of these traditional institutions was politicized in this period. Many of them were very active; one of the striking features of Ṣūfī life in Egypt in the nineteenth century is its remarkable vitality and the extensive efforts at proselytism. But neither orthodox Islam nor the Ṣūfī orders nor the guilds sought to challenge the state. Egypt remained a Muslim country with a Muslim government; the khedive served the British control better than it served him. The British in Egypt never had to contend with the political danger which concerned them most: a popular Muslim uprising. Instead they assisted at the birth of what was after 1918 to develop into a more formidable danger, namely a modern nationalist movement, although as will be shown, what they feared most about the modern movement was that it was no more than a stalking-horse for a more traditional movement. It might be said of Britain in Egypt that to dispose of one myth she created another and made it real.

THE SUDAN AND THE MAGHREB

The Sudan

Egyptian rule in the Sudan was overthrown in 1885 by the Mahdist revolt. The revolt began in 1881, and for two years remained confined to the province of Kordofan; not until 1883 did the revolutionaries gain full control of the province and subsequently the revolt spread only slowly to the northern Sudan. In November 1883 the Egyptians made a major effort to crush the rising by means of a force under Hicks Pasha and it was after the annihilation of this force that the revolt spread rapidly. Since the summer of 1882 Egypt had been under the control of Britain, and Britain wanted no responsibility for the Sudan and wished to evacuate the Egyptian garrisons. Peaceful evacuation was impossible, however, and the British governor-general, Charles Gordon, elected to remain at Khartoum and endeavour to defeat the rebels. He failed, and on 26 January 1885 Khartoum fell to the Mahdist forces.

The Mahdist movement followed a pattern familiar in Muslim history. The Mahdi, Muḥammad Aḥmad ibn ʿAbdallāh, a religious leader with a reputation for asceticism, attracted a mixed group of followers; some joined out of religious conviction, some because they were discontented at Egyptian efforts to control slave-trading and some, like the Baqqāra nomads, because they disliked all government. A significant addition to the Mahdi's forces was the Beja tribes from the eastern Sudan; their adhesion severed connections between the Red Sea ports and Khartoum and made the mounting of a successful campaign against the Mahdi more difficult. It is evident that the rising was partly a response to the centralizing policy of the Egyptian government in the Sudan but it does not appear that the revolt was a simple reaction to perceived oppression; the rising did not take place in those regions which had experienced Egyptian government for the longest period but in marginal areas. One important factor was undoubtedly the weakening of Egyptian authority after the deposition of Ismāʿīl in 1879 and the consequent financial economies in the administration of the Sudan.

What sort of state might have been created by the Mahdi is unknown because he died only five months after the fall of Khartoum and control passed to one of his lieutenants, ʿAbdallāhi ibn Muḥammad al-Taʿāishī, who took the title of Khalīfat al-Mahdī (Deputy of the Mahdi) and established a regime of which the principal military support was his own Baqqāra tribe, excluding, for the most part, the more sophisticated Sudanese notables of the areas which had been longest under Egyptian rule although these men continued to staff the bureaucracy and the judiciary. The embryonic theocracy was, therefore, transformed into a tribal state and, subsequently, from about 1890 onwards, into a more familiar secular structure with a centralized administration, a paid army of 9,000 men loyal to the Khalīfa and new taxes to support it. The impulse of *jihād*, which remained powerful during the early years of the state and inspired campaigns into Darfur, Abyssinia and Egypt, also dried up after the defeat of 1889 in the last two areas and the inroads of famine and epidemics. In 1898 the state was destroyed following defeat by an Anglo-Egyptian expedition at Omdurman (1 September 1898).

The new government set up in the Sudan after 1898 was controlled and officered at the higher level by Britons, as governor-generals (notably Reginald Wingate, 1900–16), as provincial governors, commissioners and inspectors in districts. Although nominally a joint Anglo-Egyptian government (condominium) the Sudan government was wholly controlled by Britain, the Egyptian government was permitted no voice in its affairs and Egyptian officials were employed only at lower levels of administration.

The first task of the new government was pacification; the embers of Mahdist resistance were stamped out and other messianic movements suppressed. Subsequently, the southern (non-Islamic) provinces of the Upper Nile and Baḥr al-Ghazāl were also brought under the control of the Khartoum government. The second task was the provision of new institutions, notably a new legal system, a new system of taxation and rudimentary educational facilities, although little was done in education beyond the establishment of the Gordon Memorial College which provided for the sons of Sudanese notables who aimed at a career with government. A programme of economic development was also initiated, principally by the provision of railways. Between 1896 and 1898 the Sudan expeditionary force had carried forward the railway link to Egypt but a second rail link was built connecting Khartoum with the Red Sea, where Port Sudan was created in 1909 to replace Suakin. The improvement of communications permitted the development of export crops, notably cotton. The great Gezira scheme for the cultivation of cotton on irrigated land south of Khartoum was planned and a start on construction made before 1914. By 1914 order had been re-established in the Sudan and the country was experiencing considerable prosperity, to be enhanced by the boom conditions created by the First World War.

Libya

Ottoman government in Tripoli continued until 1911 when it was challenged by Italy. The Italian interest in Tripoli arose partly from an interest in acquiring a region which could be colonized with settlers from southern Italy, but principally from a desire to assert Italy's status as a Great Power and not to be left by Britain and France with no possessions in North Africa. On 28 September 1911 Italy presented an ultimatum to the Ottomans and hostilities began the following day. On 5 October Tripoli was occupied and on 5 November it was annexed to Italy. Considerable resistance to the Italian occupation was offered by the local Muslim population, with help from Ottoman officers, but the Ottomans were eventually obliged to cede their rights in Tripoli and Cyrenaica to Italy by the Treaty of Ouchy (15 October 1912). For the most part the Italian occupation was confined to Tripoli, however, and only the coastal towns of Cyrenaica were occupied by Italian garrisons; the interior was left to the Sanūsiyya until the 1930s. Following the Ottoman departure from Libya the Sanūsīs, under Sayyid Aḥmad al-Sharīf (1902–33, effectively until 1918) and Sayyid Muḥammad Idrīs (1933–69, effectively from 1918), provided the leadership of the resistance to the Italian occupation.

Tunisia

Tunisia was occupied by France in 1881. Tunis's bankruptcy had opened the way for European control but Anglo-French rivalries, as well as the reverses suffered by France in Europe, had prevented a French occupation and permitted the Ottomans to intervene to resume nominal control over Tunis's foreign relations in 1871. Under Khayr al-Dīn Pasha there were efforts to introduce reforms in Tunisia. However, in 1878, at the Congress of Berlin, Britain withdrew her opposition to French control and, amid great opposition from within France, a French expedition was sent to Tunis three years later. French control of Tunis was accepted by the Ottomans at the Treaty of Bardo (12 May 1881) but a popular uprising in Tunis took place against French rule. After the suppression of this opposition France established a protectorate in 1883.

Nominal authority in Tunis remained with the bey but France took effective control over the administration through the French resident-general. Local administration was, at first, left to local notables but French controllers gradually assumed more power in the provinces. The situation of Tunis was, therefore, similar to that of Egypt where Britain left in being the khedivate and exercised power through the consul-general. In practice French power in Tunis was stronger than that of Britain in Egypt for the establishment of the protectorate meant that she did not have the problem of Ottoman authority or of claims by other European powers. Further, in 1884, France abolished the system of international control over Tunisian finances and abrogated the extraterritorial rights of other Europeans. Nevertheless, the bey remained, like the khedive, a point of legitimacy around which opposition to colonial rule could rally.

In Tunisia France embarked upon a programme of economic development and modernization. Communications were developed, including roads, railways and ports; mining of phosphates and iron was developed; and there was a big expansion of trade, notably with France. Attention was also given to education and the press developed rapidly after 1904. A prominent feature of economic and social change was the introduction of a substantial European population. Settlement did not take the same pattern as in Algeria, although there were smallholding settlers. But for the most part French colonization in Tunis concentrated on the development of large French-owned estates specializing in the production of wine, wheat and olives. The concentration of ownership may be illustrated by the circumstance that two-thirds of all the land alienated to French settlers was held by a mere 100 people. The number of Europeans in Tunisia increased rapidly, especially after 1900. In 1881 there were 19,000 and in 1911 143,000 settlers.

The presence of European colonists in large numbers and the competition between settlers and notables for property gave a character to Tunisian political agitation different from that in Egypt. Opposition to French control came from a variety of sources, local, Muslim and nationalist – in 1911 opposition took a strongly pro-Ottomanist character. From the viewpoint of the future, however, the most interesting development was the establishment in 1907–8 (the same period when similar parties were established in Egypt), of the Young Tunisian Party, which called for the restoration of the authority of the bey, for democratic reforms, and especially, for an end to European colonization.

Algeria

Following the suppression of the Muslim revolt of 1871 Algeria experienced rapid economic development. Confiscation of tribal lands, followed by what were virtually forced sales in the 1880s, permitted the acceleration of European immigration, notably from Spain and Italy. The European population grew from 272,000 in 1870 to 681,000 in 1911, concentrated especially in the towns and coastal areas. The Muslim population, which had suffered severely during the early period of the conquest, also grew rapidly in the same years and by 1911 had reached 4.7 million. Large-scale economic enterprises were established. During the period after 1870 there was also major railway expansion; in 1870 there were 296 kilometres of line and in 1914 3,337 kilometres. Apart from agricultural expansion, there was also a growth of mineral exploitation (iron and phosphates) and a substantial growth of trade, mainly with France.

Political power passed from the military administration to a civil administration. At first an effort was made to rule Algeria directly from Paris; departments of administration in Algeria being placed under the corresponding ministries in France but this system was abandoned in 1896 and in 1900 Algeria was given administrative and financial autonomy. Within Algeria the settlers exercised an ever increasing influence over the administration.

French policy towards the Muslim population was changed after 1880. A new policy of assimilation was tried, but by 1900 it was decided that the attempt to turn Muslims into Frenchmen had failed and the policy was gradually abandoned in favour of a policy more attuned to local conditions. Only the Jewish population was assimilated, Jews being declared to be Frenchmen. However, the attempt to introduce French institutions was not abandoned and Algeria was still subjected to as much French law as it was thought would be tolerated. In 1912 it was also decided to impose conscription on the Muslim population in response to the desperate manpower situation which France found herself *vis-à-vis* Germany.

In Algeria more than any other part of the Near East profound changes were introduced by European agency which affected the lives of the Muslim peoples. But French penetration did not reach everywhere; although many Muslims were dispossessed of their land the Kabylie remained a stronghold of Muslim landholding. Algerians, however, perhaps because of the completeness of the destruction of their institutions, which removed all rallying-points except Islam, were slow to develop the constitutional opposition which became a feature of Egypt and Tunisia; only in 1912 did the Young Algerian Party form in opposition to the imposition of conscription.

IRAN

In 1906, there took place in Iran the so-called constitutional revolution, by which Iran acquired a written constitution. In the account of this episode which is most familiar to English readers, that published in 1909 by Edward Browne, the Iranian revolution appears like liberal versions of the French Revolution. A group of patriotic men, representing progress, freedom, tolerance and national independence, stood up against injustice and tyranny represented by the shah and his selfish supporters. By their efforts the reformers succeeded in forcing the concession of a constitution, but were eventually deprived of the full fruits of their efforts by the machinations of the reaction, abetted by Russia and, to some extent, by Britain. In this version the Iranian constitutional movement was ultimately a lost liberal revolution. It is the fate of Iran, however, to have deceptive revolutions; the Browne version bears little relation to the reality of the 1906 constitutional revolution.

In Chapter 3 the failure of Iran to carry out any programme of modernization in the nineteenth century was discussed. As a consequence of that failure the Iranian government remained weak and its situation deteriorated still further during the last quarter of the nineteenth century because of the fall in the real value of government revenues owing to inflation and the loss of silk revenues, and fresh burdens of public expenditure arising from the liking of Nāṣir al-Dīn and his successor, Muẓaffar al-Dīn Shāh (1896–1907), for expensive visits to Europe. Iranian governments attempted to balance the books by borrowing from abroad and by a reform of the tax system carried out through the agency of Belgian advisers, led by Joseph Naus, who were employed to superintend the customs collections which formed the major source of revenue still at the disposal of the Tehran government (the land tax receipts being spent almost entirely in the provinces in which they were collected). The customs revenues had been pegged at 5 per cent *ad valorem* since 1828 but under Naus yields were raised and a new tariff adopted in 1903. By 1905, when the new tariff was fully in operation, duties of 20 per cent were levied on exports, although this rate was applied principally to goods traded through the southern ports and therefore applied primarily to the trade with Britain and India. Naus became *de facto* minister of finance and produced a much more far-reaching plan for financial reform.

The financial policies of Naus led to considerable opposition, first from merchants and from courtiers, who believed that their pensions and other perquisites were threatened by the reforms. Hostility was magnified by the usual factional rivalries among courtiers and ministers and a number of factions coalesced in opposition to the chief minister, ʿAyn al-Dawla. The support of discontented courtiers and bureaucrats was an important element in the opposition to the shah in 1905–6 and they, as well as merchants, helped to finance the protests of those years.

The leading element in the opposition was the ulema. Among the ulema were supporters and opponents of the Qājārs. The attitude of members of the ulema was determined by several factors, including the sources of their income (whether contributions from the faithful, *waqf* grants, fees, pensions or property). Many members of the ulema held property without legal right and paid only a fraction of the appropriate revenue and these were especially concerned about the reforms. But ulema attitudes were also determined by ideological factors, including a hostility to foreign influence in Iran, and in this context the grant of concessions to foreigners, the foreign loans and the shahs' visits to Europe were all seen as opening Iran to outside influence. Hostility to non-Muslims was expressed in violent outbreaks against Christians, Jews and especially Bahā'īs (a branch of the Bābī sect regarded by Muslims as heretical) in 1902–3.

The virtual unanimity with which the ulema supported the constitutional movement in 1906, however, suggests that they perceived in the movement an issue which transcended sectional difference. Essentially, they saw it as a movement against government injustice and tyranny in which the interests of Islam and the people were to be best served by opposition to the policies of ʿAyn al-Dawla although that minister was noted for his strict personal adherence to Islam. Even those who, because of their links with the state, initially opposed the movement, were obliged to go along with it for fear of losing their following among the people. To that extent the movement may be seen as a popular movement into which the ulema were drawn to act as leaders. An important stage in the developing attitude of the ulema was the alliance formed on 23 November 1905 between two of the most prominent of the Tehran ulema, Sayyid Muḥammad Ṭabāṭabā'ī and Sayyid ʿAbdallāh Bihbihāni; thereafter their student followers acted in concert. Their need for money to maintain their students was an important factor in determining the course of events. The two leading *mujtahids* form an interesting contrast. Ṭabāṭabā'ī had the greater knowledge of European ideas, albeit only at second or third hand mainly via Ottoman sources: Bihbihānī, the more powerful, was less concerned with ideas and more with preserving his influence.

The muscle of the revolution was supplied by the urban crowd. A large constituent was the traditional bazaar, that is, the artisans and small shopkeepers of Tehran, who formed the principal group of supporters of the ulema, to whom they looked to represent their grievances. Another constituent was religious students. A third was new immigrants to Tehran. The number of urban dwellers in Iran doubled during the nineteenth century and the increase was most marked in Tehran, especially during the last quarter of the century. By 1900 the population numbered 250,000. The largest group of the new arrivals were peasants from surrounding areas but there were also men from the Caucasus and Transcaucasia and nomads or semi-nomads who were employed in unskilled occupations. Known as the "felt caps" this last group was a significant element in street violence during the revolution. To the general discontent in Tehran, which was directed against government financial policies and foreign influence, was added the especial resentment of attempts by rings of courtiers and bureaucrats to manipulate grain prices. There were bread riots in Tehran in 1903.

Caucasian influences were especially strong in the second city of Iran, Tabriz, which was also a major centre of the constitutional movement. From the 1890s onwards there was a considerable migration of workers to Russia, attracted by opportunities in the oil industry in Baku. Between 1900 and 1913 1.77 million Iranian nationals entered Russia legally and 1.4 million returned to Iran. Baku at this time was a violent, cosmopolitan city, noted for crime and the prevalence of secret societies. In this atmosphere Iranian workers were exposed to a number of ideas, which they brought back to Iran, notably during the Russian Revolution of 1905. The revolution in Russian Azerbaijan was marked by violent riots involving Christians and Muslims, and a number of Muslims from Azerbaijan fled to Tabriz during the autumn of 1905. There was also retaliation against Armenians in Iran in 1905. Tabriz, with its Turkish-speaking community, had natural links with Russian Azerbaijan and also close associations with the Ottoman territories. The Armenian school in Tabriz was also a source of new ideas.

The Turkish influence was especially pronounced among intellectuals. The whole vocabulary of reforming politics in Iran was drawn from Ottoman Turkish and the influence of the Tanẓīmāt was strong on all the early reformers. The newspaper *Akhtar* was published in Istanbul from 1876. Azerbaijanis were prominent among the radical theorists, notably Fatḥ ʿAlī Ākhūndzāda (1812–78) an outright Westernizer, who regarded religion as mere superstition and an obstacle to progress. These views were shared by his contemporary and one-time associate, Malkam Khān (1833/4–1908), the son of an Armenian convert to Islam, who argued that reforming ideas must be clothed in a garb of religion to be acceptable in Iran. From 1890 to 1898 Malkam Khān published a newspaper, *Qānūn*, modelled on the Young Turk publication, *Ḥürriyet*, in which he advocated the adoption of a constitution based upon the *Sharīʿa*. Another source of reforming ideas was

Jamāl al-Dīn al-Afghānī. Among his followers was Mīrzā Āqā Khān Kirmānī (1853/4–1896), who had a traditional education but rejected religion after becoming acquainted with Western ideas and who argued that Islam itself was alien to Iran. Kirmānī was opposed to the ulema and to the Qājārs and advocated a secular nationalism based upon a reformed Persian language, stressing the continuity of a Persian identity from the pre-Islamic period. Yet another source of new ideas was the Azalī Bābīs, many of whom concealed their perilous allegiance under a guise of Muslim orthodoxy. Some of the most influential participants in the constitutional movement were supposedly Bābīs, including Malik al-Mutakallimīn and Ḥājjī Mīrzā Yaḥyā Dawlatābādī, who played a critical role in linking with the Ottoman ambassador to present the ulema demands in 1906 and in drafting those demands.

In Browne's history much is made of the influence of the intellectuals, especially of Afghānī and Malkam Khān, but although their ideas had some effect, notably in the formulation of the constitutionalists' demands, it is plain that there was very little acquaintance with their ideas among the leading figures of the constitutional movement and no sympathy at all for the free-thinking element among the intellectuals. The tendency of modern research has been to play down the impact of these ideas and to look more closely at the views of those who played the leading role in the revolution. Just as in the case of the Young Turk revolution the emphasis has shifted from the relatively easily accessible ideas of the *émigrés* to the more obscure opinions of the direct participants. The dangers of assumptions about the transmission of ideas have become as obvious in the study of the Near East as they appeared to an earlier generation of sceptics who looked at the influence of the ideas of the philosophers on the French Revolution.

A still obscure element in the constitutional movement is the secret societies which flourished at the time. As with all such societies it is difficult to determine their strength and precise demands, as many of the sources are tainted. For example, one secret society established in May 1904 is reported to have had sixty members and to have put forward an eighteen-point programme of reform, but faith in this statement is reduced by the circumstance that the source for it is a historian (Malikzāda) who claimed that his father (Malik al-Mutakallimīn)), was a prominent member; other named members do not mention the society in their memoirs. For a second secret society, the Anjuman-i Makhfī of 1905, we are dependent upon the testimony of a contemporary historian, Nāẓim al-Islām Kirmānī. The programme of the Anjuman-i Makhfī, which mixes general statements of Muslim principle with detailed complaints concerning the grievances of bureaucrats and others, illustrates the oddity of the societies, and points to a situation in which a tiny membership put forward its specific individual complaints. Nevertheless, secret societies did exist and it is clear that they included members of the ulema, bureaucrats and some of the free-thinkers. They were a source of radical ideas and, occasionally, of action in 1905–6 and afterwards.

The event which sparked off the revolution was the physical punishment of merchants in Tehran on 12 December 1905. Members of the ulema gathered in protest at the principal Tehran mosque, the Masjid-i Shāh, whence they were ejected by the Imām Jumʿa, reputedly the wealthiest of the Tehran ulema and dependent on government patronage. From the Masjid-i Shāh the protesters went to a shrine on the outskirts of Tehran, named Shāh ʿAbd al-Āẓim, where they formulated a demand for a "House of Justice" (*ʿadālatkhāna*). The demand, which was accepted by the shah on 12 January 1906, was the first demand for a permanent device to regulate the activities of government. What is still uncertain is where the demand came from and what it signified. At the end of April 1906 the chief minister, ʿAyn al-Dawla, called a meeting to discuss what a House of Justice might be and it was at that meeting that a bureaucrat, Iḥtishām al-Salṭana, suggested that it should mean a popularly elected legislative council with power to control the shah and his ministers. This interpretation was quite unacceptable to the ministers. Subsequently, Ṭabāṭabāʾī himself launched a demand for a council (*majlis*) the powers of which he did not specify but which he appears to have seen as possessing legislative and financial powers. These ideas, however, were still indistinct and the concept of a House of Justice was still amorphous when there was a new clash on 10 July 1906 and the death of a member of the ulema. This event precipitated a much larger demonstration by the ulema. A thousand went to the religious centre of Qumm, 145 kilometres south of Tehran. This time the challenge to the ulema's standing was so plain that no member of the ulema could stand out and even those who had opposed the earlier demands were obliged to join. At the same time a large number of Tehran merchants and artisans went to the British Embassy where they took sanctuary. On 29 July the government gave way, ʿAyn al-Dawla resigned and on 5 August the shah issued a decree summoning a Majlis. On 18 August the ulema returned to Tehran.

During July the vague ideas of the demonstrators had taken much firmer shape. Exactly how this happened is still uncertain but several influences seem to have been at work. Through the British Embassy there may have been an input of constitutional ideas, because some members of the British legislation were known to be sympathetic towards the idea of an Iranian constitution. From the leading merchants and courtiers who helped to finance the demonstrations came fresh thoughts. And from the Ottoman ambassador and Dawlatābādī, who acted as intermediaries, seem to have come some crucial suggestions for changes in the drafting of the ulema demands. The effect of these influences on what was a relatively small group of the ulema, led by Ṭabāṭabā'ī who played the major role in presenting the demands, seems to have been ultimately to transform a series of precise complaints about individual cases of administrative abuse and vague yearnings for the rule of justice and the *Sharīʿa* into a demand for the resignation of the chief minister and for a constitution. It is inconceivable that the vast majority of the demonstrators had any such demand in mind when they began their demonstration in July 1906.

The most striking features of the Iranian constitutional movement are the small scale of the movement and its relatively non-violent character. The main technique of the demonstrators was to strike and seek sanctuary (*bast*), a traditional Iranian form of protest, although in 1906 practised on a mass scale. Several thousands of people were involved but it is impossible to think that such a movement could have prevailed against the Ottoman government. The demonstrators were able to succeed against the Iranian government because that government had no adequate coercive force at its disposal; the only effective unit, the Persian Cossack Brigade (which was in any case weak at that time) could not be employed. It is probably also true to say that an Iranian government would have been most unwilling to employ force against a movement so widely supported by the ulema, especially when the government was itself so divided about the appropriate response. A tiny movement therefore succeeded because it was pitted against a very weak government: although there are superficial resemblances between the Iranian constitutional movement of 1906 and the Young Turk revolution of 1908 the two movements are fundamentally different. One was the product of a modernizing society and the other of an unmodernized society.

The drafting of a constitution for Iran involved two stages: a preliminary law to enable the election of an assembly and a detailed fundamental law signed by Muẓaffar al-Dīn Shāh shortly before his death. It was inevitable that when men sat down to draft a constitution they should adopt the model of an existing constitution; no member of the ulema had any conception of what a constitution might look like with the result that the small number of intellectuals who had some acquaintance with Western political charters exercised an influence wholly out of proportion to their numbers. The Iranian constitution, therefore, was based, like so many others, on the Belgian constitution of 1831, but it possessed some features which indicated the doubts and aspirations of those who had led the movement which produced it. For the ulema the key question was the relation of the new document to the *Sharīʿa*. In the early discussions of a constitution there had, indeed, been some confusion about its nature, deriving from the similarity of two terms which were employed to describe it, namely *mashrūṭiyya* or government according to civilized principles, and *mashrūʿiyya*, or government according to the *Sharīʿa*. A second important cause of dispute concerned the location of sovereignty. The secularizers wanted a declaration that sovereignty belonged to the people but many members of the ulema believed this to be heresy; sovereignty belonged to God alone and God's law was already set out in the *Sharīʿa*. For men to arrogate themselves the right to make new law was to claim that they were equal with God. Although the secularizers triumphed in the matter of sovereignty the ulema forced the inclusion of an article which provided that all laws passed by the assembly required the agreement of a committee of five leading *mujtahids* that the laws were consistent with the *Sharīʿa*. The committee was never established, however, and the article remained inoperative. In the discussions over the constitution cracks began to appear in the united front which the ulema had presented in the summer of 1906. Ṭabāṭabā'ī and Bihbihānī continued to support the constitution but the orthodox began to group themselves around the figure of Fāżlallāh Nūrī, a leading Tehrani theologian who produced, in the summer of 1907, a series of penetrating criticisms of the constitution. Nūrī's influence was also able to win him the support of the leading *mujtahid* of Iraq. Nūrī also formed an alliance with the formidable minister, Amīn al-Sulṭān, who returned from exile to become chief minister in April 1907. For a time it seemed as if the Qājār government would successfully divide the opposition and recover control of events but these hopes ended with the assassination of Amīn al-Sulṭān on 31 August 1907.

From the beginning the assembly set itself in opposition to the government of the Qājārs, which remained in the hands of the old bureaucrats. The constitutionalists had perceived the need for haste in bringing the assembly into being and had, in consequence, very greatly over-represented Tehran which was given 60 of the 156 members of the assembly. Further, the quorum was set very low so that the assembly need not wait for the laborious elections to be completed in the provinces. When the assembly met it was dominated by Tehranis to which were soon added delegates from Tabriz and other major towns. Non-urban groups were hardly represented at all. The composition of the first

Majlis was also untypical. The largest group of deputies came from the bazaar – just over one-quarter and a further 15 per cent were merchants. Of the total one-fifth were ulema and another one-fifth bureaucrats. Only 13 per cent were classified as landowners. The Majlis was therefore predominantly urban and especially Tehrani. It represented the classes whose efforts had extracted the constitution from the shah and by no means what might be called the silent majority of the élite, let alone the vast majority of the rural inhabitants of Iran. The dominant feeling in the Majlis was hostility to government. The essential need of government was for money either by an increase of taxes or a foreign loan, but the Majlis refused to consent to either and instead demanded that economies should be made by the reduction of the shah's expenditure and of pensions. The constitutional revolution was showing itself to be an anti-modernizing revolution at heart, despite the genuine interest of the members in some features of modernization, namely the creation of a state-wide educational system, a national army and a national bank.

Government and Majlis were deadlocked, administration paralyzed. The new shah, Muḥammad ʿAlī, who, in Azerbaijan, had already acquired a reputation for a lack of sympathy with popular aspirations, began to contemplate forcible action against the Majlis in which notion he was encouraged by the Russian minister, Hartwig. Towards the end of 1907 it seemed possible that the shah might carry through a successful coup because at that time there was little enthusiasm left for the constitution. According to Nāẓim al-Dīn Kirmānī it was hard to find a thousand constitutionalists in Tehran in November 1908. Muḥammad ʿAlī, however, backed away from his projected coup in Decmber 1907 and continued to seek an agreement with the Majlis.

Agreement with the Majlis was made more difficult by the role of the Tehran mob and the secret societies. The proceedings of the assembly were open to the public and debates took place in the accompaniment of advice and threats from the audience. Members whose opinions did not find favour with the crowd went in fear of their lives and many moderates stopped attending the meetings. More and more the assembly came to be dominated by the irreconcilable opponents of the regime, including a small group of radicals among whom some of the Tabrizi delegates, led by Sayyid Ḥasan Taqīzāda, were especially prominent. The radicals were believed to be linked to the secret societies and the street groups.

The deadlock was finally broken by the shah in June 1908 when, with the aid of the Cossack Brigade, now reformed and strengthened, he closed the Majlis and suspended the constitution. Briefly, it seemed as though the shah had won but the weakness of Qājār government deprived him of complete victory, for he was unable to regain control in the provinces and, especially, in Tabriz, where the constitutionalists gained control of the government.

To write a history of Iran before the Pahlavi revolution of the 1920s is almost impossible for there was neither economic, social nor political unity. One writes about happenings in the capital, Tehran, as though they somehow represented a consummation of the national history but that assumption is a fiction. The constitutional revolution as described above was a Tehran affair. Similar upsurges had taken place in other urban centres but these had derived their character from the peculiarities of each area and, apart from links provided through newspapers, the telegraph and the mosque, they had followed their own directions. With the temporary extinction of the constitutional movement in Tehran, however, attention became focused on these provincial movements which now came to be seen as part of the national movement. In Tabriz the prosperous Shaykhī community with its strong commercial interests had adopted the constitutional cause, in opposition to the Qājār government and the larger but less well off Mustasharī community. The Shaykhīs employed their own military force consisting of a small group of men from Azerbaijan and Transcaucasia variously described as bandits, revolutionaries and patriots. This small group eventually took control of Tabriz, levied taxes on the inhabitants and supported the resistance against the besieging Qājār forces, themselves a heterogeneous collection of tribal and bandit groups paid mainly with promises of loot.

Muḥammad ʿAlī lacked money to raise troops to enforce his authority. The only possible source of quick funds was a foreign loan but this required British and Russian consent. Britain demanded the restoration of the constitution as a condition of the loan and since the signing of the Anglo-Russian agreement of 31 August 1907 the Russian Foreign Ministry was unwilling to move without British agreement. Hartwig had been dismissed and the British and Russian diplomatic representatives co-operated, in an effort to hold a balance between the constitutionalists and the shah and to force the contestants to agree to a peaceful compromise. In April 1909 it was a Russian army which finally saved Tabriz from surrender to the Qājār forces. It seemed that the Great Power tactics might succeed when on 10 May 1909 the shah agreed to restore the constitution, but the Anglo-Russian tactics misfired and the situation was resolved by a complete and unexpected victory for the constitutionalists in July 1909.

The July victory of the so-called constitutionalists derived from two further provincial movements. One took place in the north and centred in the province of Gīlān, which was both the centre of some of the most advanced agriculture, including silk cultivation, and the most open (except for Azerbaijan) to outside influence. In Gīlān an anti-landlord movement developed under the leadership of Caucasian revolutionaries and the nominal and reluctant headship of a prominent landowner, Muḥammad Wālī Khān, Sipahdār-i Aʿẓam, who had recently commanded the government forces against Tabriz, into a movement on Tehran to restore the constitution. At the same time an even more unlikely movement began in the south in the region of Isfahan among the Bakhtīyārī tribe of nomads. For long the Qājārs had successfully neutralized the Bakhtīyārīs by juggling candidates for leadership and one section of the Bakhtīyārīs had fought for the government in the siege of Tabriz. But divisions among the Bakhtīyārīs were now healed as they took advantage of the confusion to take control of Isfahan. The movement might have ended with the achievement of that traditional Bakhtīyārī objective but for the exertions of a Bakhtīyārī chief newly returned from Europe and full of enthusiasm for liberal ideas. Under the direction of Sardār Asʿad the Bakhtīyārīs advanced on Tehran in the name of the constitution. The small size of the two forces again indicates the absurd disproportion between ends and means in the Iranian revolution, greater even than in the contemporary revolution in Mexico which may afford a useful comparison. The Bakhtīyārī forces numbered only 2,000, the northerners about the same. But once again the weakness of the government forces betrayed the Qājār cause. The Gīlān and Isfahan groups united and occupied Tehran on 13 July, deposed Muḥammad ʿAlī who subsequently left for Russia, and replaced him with his nine-year-old son, Aḥmad Shāh, and a regency. The Sipahdār became the head of the new government, composed, as before, chiefly of Qājār bureaucrats. A new assembly was elected in October 1909.

Like the Young Turk revolution the Iranian revolution came in two stages; 1906 created a new arena and a conflict between government and assembly; only in 1909 was victory confirmed over the shah as it was also over the sultan. But they were very different victories. In the Ottoman empire it was an institution of the modernized state, the army which emerged as dominant in the new institution: in Iran it was a coalition of the traditional institution of the nomadic tribe and a heterogeneous collection of peasants and revolutionaries from the north which triumphed.

After 1909 attention is again focused on Tehran although the same unreality obtains; the provinces continued to have their development determined by different circumstances; for example the Bakhtīyārī victory in Tehran immediately persuaded their old nomad rivals the Qashqā'īs to assert control over the great province of Fārs, centred on the city of Shiraz. By the end of 1909 the real ruler of the south was the Qashqā'ī Īlkhān, Ṣawlat al-Dawla. In other areas similar situations obtained as local notables took effective control, exploiting traditional patron–client links. Sometimes they achieved power as nominal parts of the government apparatus and sometimes they worked outside it. Among the notables the Bakhtīyārīs were the largest gainers; for their services on behalf of the constitution they eventually secured seven governorships and two Cabinet seats. But in no way did they act as the servants of the central government.

Tehran became the scene of a struggle between the various factions which had won victory over Muḥammad ʿAlī. The leader of the Caucasian revolutionaries from the north, Yefrem Khan Davidiants, an Armenian Dashnak, became chief of police and gendarmerie in Tehran and mainly responsible for security. He eventually lost his life in operations against rebel groups in 1912. Most of the Bakhtīyārīs returned home after 1909, but came back in 1911 to play a more dominant role. The new Majlis had a different composition with a larger representation of landowners and a smaller number of Tehrani bazaar members. But the numbers of Majlis members were not significant because many did not attend and a small group of radicals tended to exercise, with the aid of the street mobs, a disproportionate influence. The most notable feature of the new political groupings was the eclipse of the ulema, who had dominated the revolution in 1906 and had played a leading role in the debates of 1906–8. Some of the leading figures were dead. Malik al-Mutakallimīn was killed after the June 1908 coup and Fażlallāh Nūrī was hanged after the 1909 victory of the constitutionalists. Bihbihānī was assassinated, probably by a radical group, and Ṭabāṭabā'ī, like many other members of the ulema, withdrew from political life leaving the field to the secular groups.

The situation after 1909 had some points of resemblance to that which obtained between 1906 and 1908. The great need of the government was for money to rebuild the administrative system and to support a modest military force which could preserve some order and assist in the collection of taxes. The obvious, immediate source of such money was a foreign loan but, as before, this required the agreement of Britain and Russia and therefore some compromise with those powers. Anglo-Russian co-operation continued but the Russian attitude began to harden against the constitutional movement, particularly after the murder of the Russian prime minister, Stolypin, and the replacement of

Izvolskii as foreign minister with Sazonov. The two great supporters of the entente with Britain had gone and those who regarded the agreement as a limitation on Russia's freedom to pursue an independent policy in Iran grew in influence. Whereas between 1908 and 1910 it had been Russia which had followed the British lead, from 1910 it was Britain which was obliged to accommodate itself to Russian policy. And between Russia and the Iranian government was the problem of the Iranian demand for the withdrawal of Russian troops which had occupied Tabriz in 1908. The Majlis was especially insistent that there could be no compromise over the Russian occupation.

There were, however, new features in the situation after 1909. With the defeat of the Qājārs the assembly was no longer so inclined to oppose the extension of government power and was disposed to support an increase of taxation and the raising of a military force to collect taxes. The search began for a friendly and disinterested foreign power which would assist Iran to carry through a programme of reform, with advice, money and possibly diplomatic help. Several possibilities were canvassed. Britain and Russia were unwilling to tolerate assistance to Iran from a major European power which ruled out France, Italy, Austria and Germany. Germany, through the 1910 Potsdam agreement with Russia, made it clear that she would not allow her Iranian interests to jeopardize her relations with Russia in Europe. Iran, therefore, turned to the minor powers. Belgian advisers were still present in the Treasury; the hated Naus had been dismissed after the revolution but a M. Mornard was in charge of the finances. Help was found in the United States. The US government was unwilling to involve itself directly in Iran but allowed the recruitment of a team of American advisers under the leadership of Morgan Shuster, a US banker, who, like many of his colleagues, had experience of colonial administration in the Philippines.

Shuster arrived in Tehran in May 1911 and quickly evolved a plan for financial reorganization and for the formation of a military force under his own control at the Treasury. The Treasury gendarmerie was planned to increase to 10,000–15,000 men and would have been, under European officers, a powerful force in Iran. Shuster, however, was quite unsuited to his situation. His knowledge of Iran was small and derived chiefly from Browne's misleading book. His contacts with Iranian notables were slight and conducted mainly through the intermediary of a Zoroastrian merchant. Shuster identified the situation in Iran as a conflict between the party of liberalism and progress represented by the radical element in the Majlis, a group of some ten to fifteen members, and the forces of reaction represented by most of the

Iranian notables, backed by Russia and Britain and ultimately linked to Muḥammad ʿAlī, who attempted to regain his throne with some unofficial Russian support in 1911. Once again it is useful to draw attention to the small size of the forces involved in the 1911 struggle. Muḥammad ʿAlī was estimated to have 2,000 Turkestan tribesmen and his brother in Kurdistan secured the support of perhaps as many Kurds. Government forces under Yefrem Khan numbered considerably under 1,000, including 500 Bakhtīyārīs, in the engagements against Muḥammad ʿAlī's forces.

Shuster offended almost everyone, but especially Russia which in November demanded his dismissal. The Majlis, which had been due to end its term in November 1911, prolonged its own life, supported Shuster and defied the Russian ultimatum. The Iranian government, disillusioned with Shuster and anxious to avert a yet more extensive Russian military occupation (which already extended to other provinces in the north), suppressed the Majlis on 24 December 1911 and dismissed Shuster the next day.

The closure of the Majlis marks the halting of the progress of the Iranian revolution. The constitution was in place but was temporarily suspended and the government was dominated by the Bakhtīyārīs and other notables. The power of the Tehran government was, however, severely limited, first on account of the Russian occupation of much of northern Iran, where government was carried on by local officials acting on the advice of Russian consuls backed by the Cossack Brigade under Russian officers and Russian troops; second, because of the much smaller number of British Indian forces which had been introduced to maintain order in parts of the south; and third, because of the power exerted by tribal and other elements in all the provinces of Iran. The government had no money and the only military force under its control was the Swedish-officered gendarmerie formed originally in 1911 to provide road guards and considerably developed with British encouragement after the abandonment of Shuster's proposed Treasury gendarmerie. The untrained gendarmerie, however, was no match for the powerful tribal groups which dominated the provinces. Politics in Iran did not begin again until the First World War.

ARABIA

In eastern Arabia the principal event of the early twentieth century was the recovery of the Saʿūdī state under the leadership of ʿAbd al-ʿAzīz ibn

Suʿūd. Saʿūdī rule had collapsed during the civil war which followed the abdication of Fayṣal ibn Suʿūd in 1865 and Najd had eventually fallen under the control of Muḥammad ibn Rashīd of Ḥāʾil, a former Saʿūdī vassal who became the leading figure in eastern Arabia in the late nineteenth century. After the death of Muḥammad ibn Rashīd in 1897 there was a scramble for power and in January 1902 ʿAbd al-ʿAzīz seized Riyāḍ and, during a series of campaigns against the Rashīdīs in the following years, made himself master of the whole of Najd, although nominal rule was in the hands of his father as imam until his death in 1928. In 1913 ʿAbd al-ʿAzīz extended his power to include al-Ḥasā, expelling the Ottoman garrison and thus gaining control of a fertile province with lucrative customs revenues and a position on the Gulf and raising the hope that he might be given British maritime protection. ʿAbd al-ʿAzīz also began to create a new instrument of power in the form of the Ikhwān settlements of which the first was established at Arṭāwiyya in 1912 by Ḥarb and Muṭayr tribesmen. The Ikhwān colonies were settlements of nomads who had adopted the Wahhābī code, taken up settled cultivation and opened religious schools and who were ready and willing to assist in the extension of Wahhabism by war (and also to derive some profit from raids).

To the Saʿūdī rulers the Ikhwān colonies offered an opportunity to weaken the tribal structure, control the nomads and harness their military power for war against their rivals, notably the Rashīdīs but also, eventually, the rulers of Hijaz and Kuwayt. The Ikhwān colonies became important settlements: at its peak Arṭawiyya was reported to include 10,000 inhabitants, which in eastern Arabian terms was a substantial agglomeration.

ʿAbd al-ʿAzīz now required some form of outside recognition in order to consolidate his position and provide a base for future expansion and he sought this from the two major powers of Arabia, the Ottomans and the British. From the Ottomans he sought appointment as the autonomous governor of eastern Arabia and from the British, to whom he made several applications from 1903 onwards, he sought protection against the Ottomans and a subsidy. Despite support from local British agents for his claims the British government was unable to accord ʿAbd al-ʿAzīz protection because this would run counter to the policy of treating the region as Ottoman territory and would jeopardize British relations with the Ottomans and so with other European powers. Britain preferred to seek agreement with the Ottomans on spheres of interest in Arabia.

The British sphere of Arabia remained confined to the arena of eastern and southern Arabia which had been marked out during the nineteenth century. Within the British sphere the objects were to limit British commitments to external protection, which could be exercised from the sea, and to avoid interference on land and in the internal affairs of the protected states. These objects were not wholly achieved. One tendency of British control was to freeze the existing political structure. The five Trucial shaykhs who were recognized as independent in 1914 were those who had signed the 1853 perpetual truce (Ajman, Abu Dhabi, Dubai, Umm al-Quwayn and Sharja). A sixth state, Ras al-Khayma was in practice acknowledged as independent, though in theory it was still subject to Sharja. Only two of the states which had signed the original 1820 peace had disappeared, an extraordinary example of durability. Although the endurance of the shaykhdoms may partly be attributed to the long and stable rule of some shaykhs, for example Shaykh Zayd ibn Khalīfa of Abu Dhabi (1855–1909), who was known as Zayd the Great, it may also be attributed to British weight thrown on the side of the status quo.

Another feature of British control in the years before 1914 was the tendency to interfere more in the internal affairs of the states. Even earlier in the nineteenth century this tendency had been noticeable, for example when Lewis Pelly was political agent in the Gulf (1862–73), but the tendency became more visible in the twentieth century and is especially noticeable in the case of Bahrayn. Once again pressure came from local British agents in opposition to the wishes of the Government of India, which, with the exception of the period of office of Lord Curzon, was opposed to the extension of British responsibilities in the Gulf and preferred to leave matters to the shaykhs. In Bahrayn, however, successive British agents pressed for reform of the customs administration and the appointment of a British adviser. In 1905, the Gulf Resident presented an ultimatum to Shaykh ʿĪsā and the process of encroachment culminated in the 1913 Bahrayn Order in Council which applied British Indian laws to Bahrayn and gave the political agent extensive control of the legal system, not merely as it applied to foreigners but also in relation to Bahrayni subjects. The operation of the order was suspended during the war and when it was eventually applied in November 1918 it led to a conflict between ʿĪsā and the political agent. In 1914 another agreement gave Britain control of oil development in Bahrayn.

Another example of British intervention may be supplied from Oman where the authority of the sultan in Muscat was increasingly challenged by a movement in the interior. In 1913 a tribal coalition, led by Shaykh ʿĪsā ibn Ṣāliḥ put forward a new claimant to the imamate and threatened to destroy the sultanate which survived in Muscat only by the help of British arms. Britain limited her intervention as in the past to the maintenance of the status quo on the coast and did not attempt to restore the sultan's authority in the interior of Oman, where it completely evaporated.

British control was also extended in southern Arabia. Concerned by the encroachments of the Ottomans and of European powers, in 1886 the Government of India put forward a scheme for controlling southern Arabia by formal protectorates over the various chiefs. In 1886 a protectorate treaty was signed with Socotra, in 1888–9 further treaties were negotiated with coastal rulers, and between 1895 and 1904 agreements were made with the chiefs of the interior. It was still the policy of the British government in London to avoid interference in the internal affairs of the region but this policy was opposed by the authorities in Aden and was menaced by the consequences of the arms traffic in the Red Sea which brought thousands of modern rifles into the region after 1880. The new weapons added a new, destructive dimension to traditional feuds and threatened the authority of the chiefs who appealed to Britain for support. Within Aden there was support for the ambitions of one chief, Sulṭān Aḥmad Faḍl of Lahej; indeed in the years before 1914 British policy in south-west Arabia was Laheji policy and Lahej became the chief beneficiary of the British presence. There were also advocates in Aden of a policy of ignoring the chiefs and moving towards direct British administration but London prevented the implementation of this policy.

Ottoman power in Arabia was declining in the years before 1914 when Ottoman resources were heavily committed in other areas of the empire. In the circumstances the attempt to impose authority by force which had characterized the years after 1870 was replaced by a policy of maintaining control by playing off against each other the various claimants to power in Arabia. In the long run the extension of the Hijaz railway towards Mecca would provide a stronger basis of Ottoman control in western Arabia and the development of the Baghdad railway would do the same for the east. In the meantime the Ottomans supported the Rashīdīs against the Saʿūdīs, and when the Rashīdīs proved unequal to the task encouraged Sharīf Ḥusayn of Mecca to extend his authority into eastern Arabia, as well as using him as an agent in an effort to recover Ottoman power in ʿAsīr. The Ottomans also sought a satisfactory arrangement with ʿAbd al-ʿAzīz ibn Saʿūd himself.

Ottoman authority was also challenged, on religious grounds, in Yemen, where Imām Muḥammad ibn Ḥamīd al-Dīn, opposed the innovatory Ottoman administration on the basis of the *Sharīʿa*. There followed a series of revolts and campaigns until, in 1911, by the Treaty of Da'an the Ottomans abandoned their effort to complete their control of Yemen by force and recognized the virtual autonomy of the Imām Yaḥyā in the northern Zaydī regions and gave him a subsidy. The Ottomans retained their position elsewhere and in 1914 still had about 2,000 troops in Yemen in addition to 4,000 Yemeni auxiliaries.

The principal threat to Ottoman control in Arabia was Britain and the two outside powers found it convenient to come to an agreement between themselves about spheres of influence in Arabia. The first area of agreement concerned the frontier between north and south Yemen, that is, between the areas of Ottoman claims and those of Britain from Aden. Between 1902 and 1904 the boundary between Yemen and the West Aden Protectorate was settled by a joint Anglo-Ottoman boundary commission. On 9 March 1914 a more general agreement was reached according to which Arabia was partitioned between the two powers by a line drawn from the eastern point of the 1902 Yemeni boundary line right across the desert to Qaṭar. Everything north of the line including al-Ḥasā and Najd, the territories of Ibn Suʿūd, was within the Ottoman sphere, and everything south of it was British. But this division, while it provided for an amicable settlement between the two principal powers, did not in itself affect the local powers of Arabia. Their relations with their suzerains were to be adjusted in dealings with them; all the agreement provided was that they could no longer play off one major power against another. In fact the ink was scarcely dry on the agreement than the outbreak of the First World War made it a dead letter and set the scene for a struggle between the two outside powers in which the local powers were completely involved.

NOTES

1. H. F. B. Lynch, *Armenia*, II, Beirut 1965, 84.
2. Quoted J. Gidney, *A mandate for Armenia*, Kent, Ohio, 36.
3. Quoted Z. N. Zeine, *The emergence of Arab nationalism*, Beirut 1966, 103.
4. E. W. Lane, *The thousand and one nights*, II, London 1839, 65.
5. Lord Cromer, *Modern Egypt*, II, London 1908, 334.
6. Afaf Lutfi al-Sayyid, *Egypt and Cromer*, London 1968, 8.
7. Quoted W. S. Blunt, *The secret history of the English occupation of Egypt*, London 1907, 149.
8. Cairns to Disraeli 29 Jan. 1876, quoted R. Blake, *Disraeli*, London 1966, 581.
9. Lord Dufferin: Report, in Dufferin to Granville No. 38 of 6 Feb. 1883, *Parliamentary papers*, HC 1883, vol. 133 (C. 3529), p. 39.

10. Cromer to Salisbury 6 Feb. 1897, quoted A. E. Mayer, "Abbas Hilmi II: the Khedive and Egypt's struggle for independence", unpublished Ph.D. thesis, I, Michigan 1978, 155.
11. Quoted Afaf Lutfi al-Sayyid, *Egypt and Cromer*, 78.
12. Quoted J. M. Ahmed, *The intellectual origins of Egyptian nationalism*, London 1960, 106.

CHAPTER FIVE
The Near East in the First World War

THE OTTOMAN ENTRY INTO THE WAR

The Ottoman decision to enter the First World War was the single most important event in the history of the modern Near East because it led directly to the destruction of the Ottoman empire and to the emergence of an entirely new political structure in the region. It could also be argued that the Ottoman decision was a major factor in the making of the modern world because it contributed largely to the prolongation of the war and thereby to the success of the Russian Revolution and to the political alignments of the twentieth century. Although this second, speculative aspect is outside the concerns of this book reflection upon the possibilities may help to direct attention towards the centrality of the Ottoman decision to make war.

The old view that the reason for Ottoman participation in the war was the dominance of German influence in Istanbul is mistaken. By 1914 Germany had lost interest in the Ottomans who approached the Entente for an alliance. The Ottoman–German alliance of 2 August 1914 was principally the outcome of Austrian pressure, it being the object of Austria to control Ottoman ambitions in the Balkans by tying the Porte into the Triple Alliance. On the German side only Wilhelm II was enthusiastic. For the Ottomans the alliance offered some measure of protection against Russia and the possibility of gains in the Balkans, North Africa or Transcaucasia. In fact the alliance was unknown to the majority of the Ottoman Cabinet and was the work of a small group composed of the prime minister, Saʿīd Ḥalīm, the minister of the interior, Ṭalʿat and the minister of war, Enver.

The conclusion of the alliance did not mean that the Ottomans would enter the war. A majority of the Ottoman ministers wished to remain neutral, at least until they saw who was likely to win. A minority believed that it was dangerous to wait; the war might finish quickly and neutrality might not protect the Ottomans from injury in a European peace settlement. Further, if the Ottomans could find a seat on the victor's side of the conference table they could make useful gains, either territorial (the Aegean Islands, or from Russia in eastern Asia Minor) or legal, for example by securing the abolition of the capitulations. The leader of this minority was Enver Pasha who was able to use his position as minister of war to draw the Ottomans into the war, first by taking the lead in the decision to admit the escaping German warships, the *Goeben* and the *Breslau*, into the Sea of Marmara and taking them and their crews into the Ottoman navy, and, second, by urging the bombardment of the Russian Black Sea ports, the event which declared the Ottoman entry into the war at the end of October 1914.

Although the Entente tried to keep the Ottomans out of the war they had not tried very hard. There appear to have been two reasons for the lack of Allied effort: first, it was thought that Ottoman participation would not greatly affect the issue; Italy was regarded as potentially a much more valuable ally and the principal efforts of the Entente were directed towards securing her support; and second, the prevailing impression in the British Foreign Office was that the Ottoman decision would be decided by the progress of the war. There was some merit in the second view; German successes against France and Russia in the early months of the war contributed to a drift of feeling in the Ottoman Cabinet towards a pro-German policy. Nevertheless, a majority still favoured neutrality and with more generous Entente offers to feed on might well have prevailed. There is nothing to be said for the first reason; the Entente completely underestimated the contribution the Ottomans would make to the war.

THE OTTOMAN EMPIRE AT WAR

Before considering the Near Eastern war in general it will be useful to examine the Ottomans at war. The CUP faction which had come to power in 1913 continued to dominate the empire throughout the war. The power of the sultan had been greatly abridged in 1909 and Sultan Meḥmed V was not the man to challenge the new order. A kindly old man, he contented himself with writing patriotic poems to encourage his soldiers. His successor, in July 1918, Meḥmed VI Vaḥīd al-Dīn, was a more ambitious figure who was ready to take advantage of the

Unionist disasters to recover some influence. It is impossible, despite Unionist dominance, to point to a single institution which governed the empire. The CUP party organization increased its influence through the war with the rise of its General Council, and individual party members achieved considerable influence although they did not hold government posts. The Ottoman Cabinet retained formal responsibility under the sultan for the conduct of government, but crucial decisions were often taken outside Cabinet as, for example, those concerning the Ottoman entry into the war. Saʿīd Ḥalīm remained as grand vizier until he was replaced by Ṭalʿat in February 1917, although his influence diminished after he lost his portfolio as foreign minister in October 1915 to Khalīl Bey, a supporter of Enver. The leading figure in politics, however, was Ṭalʿat, as minister of the interior until February 1917 and thereafter as grand vizier until the end of the war. But Ṭalʿat had little control over many areas of government. Between 1913 and 1918 the empire resembled a collection of mighty apanages held by the great Unionist factional leaders. Thus Enver ran the war telling his colleagues as little as he could of the situation. In so far as anyone controlled the ramshackle economy of the empire it was Ismāʿīl Ḥaqqī Bey, the general director of commissariat, and the principal rival of Enver. Others controlled geographical apanages: Raḥmī Bey controlled Izmir and even conducted his own independent negotiations with the Entente. So did Jemāl Pasha who became the dictator of Syria. Istanbul became increasingly the preserve of a man whose power base was in the Party, Kara Kemāl Bey; Kara Kemāl's job was to keep the Istanbul population contented and to accomplish this end he took extensive powers of ecônomic direction.

There is very little reliable information about the Ottoman economy during the war and the situation appears to have varied considerably from one region to another. From the government's point of view everything had to be subordinated to the needs of the war; as Enver remarked to a delegation of disgruntled businessmen, "we are fighting for our existence. We cannot be expected to think, at so vital a time, of secondary matters like agriculture and commerce."[1] At that time the Ottomans, like others, did not expect a long war and thought that they could get by without special measures. The first effects of the dislocation of trade and communications were to lead to a slump, but as demand increased and shortages made themselves felt this was succeeded by inflation. The government financed the war by savings from not having to pay interest on the largest part of the Public Debt which was held by Entente countries, by subsidies from Germany amounting to nearly £250 million, by internal loans which increased the Ottoman national debt from £T171 million in 1914 to £T466 million in 1918, and, especially, by printing paper money. According to the official figures the cost of living (taking 1914 as 100) rose to 400 at the beginning of 1917 and 2,500 at the end of 1918. The government attempted to control prices to reduce the impact on sensitive populations, such as that of Istanbul, but was only partly successful and those on fixed incomes were badly affected. Feeding Istanbul was a considerable problem. Although outside Istanbul the empire had been able to feed itself before 1914, Istanbul had always been partly dependent upon imported grain from France, Russia and Italy. These supplies were cut off by the war and the Ottomans were obliged to make a major effort to increase food production. It is very difficult to say how successful this effort was. The same problem existed with industrial production. The cessation of many traditional supplies forced the Ottomans to look to import substitution and efforts were made to encourage local industry. After the entry of Bulgaria into the war a direct line of communication with Germany was opened and trade revived. An export commission was established and the Ottomans exported quantities of wool, cotton, chrome, oil and leather to Germany for which they sought and received payment in cash which was used for essential imports.

The greatest pressure was on manpower. During the war the Ottomans conscripted about 3 million men, of whom some 325,000 were killed, 240,000 died of disease and an estimated 1.5 million deserted, although this last figure can never be better than a rough guess. At its peak the Ottoman army was probably never larger than 650,000; by October 1918 the paper strength was 560,000 of which the fighting strength was no more than 100,000. The abstraction of so large a number of people from the economy was a serious matter, the more so because the burden fell disproportionately on regions of the country which had already suffered during the wars of 1911–14.

Other regions of the empire suffered directly from military operations or through breakdown of communications or the pre-emption of inadequate, existing rail links and carriage systems for military purposes. The famine in Syria in 1915 was due in part to this circumstance, although it was charged that the effects were felt disproportionately in the Lebanon because that region was given a low priority on account of its Christian population and its supposed partiality for the Entente.

The war and the call for a *jihād* undoubtedly led to an increased sense of Muslim solidarity and an antipathy to Christians who were believed to support the Entente. The Greeks, concentrated in Izmir, and protected by Raḥmī Bey, escaped the worst effects of this animosity, but the Armenian population experienced the full force of Muslim resentment and suspicion caused by the disasters in eastern Asia Minor at the beginning of the war and the calls by Russian Armenians for Ottoman Armenians to join them in a struggle for freedom. Armenians were deported *en masse* from the eastern provinces and many (probably between a quarter and a half million) died, either from starvation and hardship or from massacre mainly at the hands of Kurdish tribesmen. No direct documentary evidence has ever come to light to show that the Armenian massacres of 1915 were the deliberate policy of the Ottoman government but local officials connived at the murders and took few steps to protect the Armenians. Possibly there was little the Istanbul government could have done to control events, but it is also possible that it believed that the Armenian presence in the eastern provinces was a constant threat to the integrity of the empire and was not sorry to see it removed. There is no doubt that the government endeavoured to conceal from enquirers what had happened.

The same xenophobia, visible in varying degrees among all the combatants, had an effect upon other areas of policy where it combined with the even stronger pressures towards centralization engendered by the needs of the war to produce discrimination in favour of Muslims and Ottomans and to some extent of Turks. The teaching of Ottoman history and the Ottoman language were made compulsory in all schools, that is, private as well as state schools; the use of Ottoman Turkish on signboards became compulsory; a law was passed obliging firms to keep their books in Ottoman Turkish; and the existing programme of teaching Ottoman Muslims to fill skilled jobs formerly the preserve of minorities, including foreigners, was extended and even taken to the lengths of encouraging prostitution among Muslim women on the grounds that otherwise Muslim money would go into the pockets of infidels. However, Muslim prostitutes were for Muslims alone; a great outcry was raised against any attempt by German soldiers to resort to them.

How far an ideology of Pan-Turkism, distinct from this inchoate Islamic sentiment, developed during the war is not easy to say. Fanned by the war against Russia and the possibilities of gains in Transcaucasia and even links with Turkestan, Turkism flourished at the level of ideological writing and may be discerned also in the policy of Enver. But the dominating impression of the Ottomans at war is of endorsement of former lines of development, especially in the realm of secularization despite the public Muslim fervour. In 1916 the power of the head of the Muslim hierarchy, the Shaykh al-Islām, was drastically reduced: he was removed from the Cabinet; his authority over *Sharīʿa* courts was transferred to the Ministry of Justice; he lost control of *waqf* administration; and he gave up authority over *madrasas* in favour of the Ministry of Education. In 1917 procedure in *Sharīʿa* courts was regulated by legislation; and civil courts were given control of family law, although the new code of family law was still largely a *Sharīʿa* code. Finally, the Gregorian calendar was introduced.

The Ottomans took the opportunity provided by the war to achieve a number of goals. The capitulations were abolished unilaterally on 8 September 1914 much to the annoyance of Germany which agreed only reluctantly as late as 11 January 1917. The Ottomans brought in a new discriminatory and protective tariff on 3 March 1916. Another object of Ottoman dislike was the limitations on sovereignty embodied in a number of international treaties including those of 1856 and 1878. These were all declared void on 1 November 1916, again in the face of German objections. The autonomous status of Lebanon, conceded reluctantly in 1861, was also abolished shortly after the outbreak of war.

In no way did the Ottomans fight the war as German puppets. Clashes with Germany occurred over many matters, including Egypt, Libya, Iran, Transcaucasia and the Balkans. Only over Bulgaria did the Ottomans give way to German wishes in a major matter. As part of the price of bringing Bulgaria into the war the Ottomans were obliged to surrender the left bank of the Maritsa to provide the Bulgarians with a direct rail link to the Aegean (22 September 1915). This concession was bitterly resented in Istanbul and in March 1918, during the negotiations involving the Russian treaty, the Ottoman government made a determined effort to recover the region, even threatening to withdraw from the war. The Ottomans refused to make similar concessions to the Greeks when Germany pressed them to do so in order to win over Greece. And the Ottomans were able to extract concessions from Germany. The 2 August 1914 treaty against Russia was replaced, at Ottoman insistence, on 11 January 1915 by a new, comprehensive treaty between the Ottomans and Germany. And in 1916, as the price of supplying Ottoman troops for use in the European theatre, Germany was obliged to agree not to make a separate peace without the Ottomans.

Many Germans disliked the Ottoman alliance, believing that the Ottomans were awkward and useless allies. In particular the Foreign Ministry view was that the Ottoman alliance, especially after the 1916 agreement, made the achievement of a separate peace with Russia much more difficult. It was mainly at the insistence of the German High Command that Germany held on to the Ottoman alliance. The generals believed and rightly that there could be no substitute for the Ottoman capacity to divert Entente resources. Accordingly, Germany steadily threw her weight in internal Ottoman politics behind those men, notably Enver, who were prepared to go on fighting. And the Ottomans fought on to the end, albeit at tremendous cost.

Indeed, the most remarkable feature of the Ottoman empire during the war was its endurance. After the heavy losses of the campaigns of 1915 and 1916 and the consequent strain on resources, the Ottomans hung on and in 1918 still could muster enough strength to attack Transcaucasia and to fight dogged defensive battles against greatly superior forces in Syria and Iraq. The Ottoman attitude is summed up by the spectacle of Fakhrī Pasha, the Ottoman commander in Medina, who fought on after the armistice because he refused to surrender to what he regarded as his contemptible Arab opponents. Medina only surrendered in January 1919 after General Fakhrī was removed by a coup. Under no worse a strain Russia collapsed through internal revolution; no such event overtook the Ottomans and those who argue that the fall of the empire was predestined through its internal dissensions must ask why the empire held on through the war.

THE CAMPAIGNS

The Ottoman entry into the war engulfed the Near East in strife. On 14 November the Ottomans issued a call to *jihād* aimed at spreading disaffection among Muslims in Entente territories. Although this call caused alarm, especially in Britain, it had relatively little effect, although it encouraged uprisings in Libya (autumn 1915) and Darfur in the Sudan which were duly suppressed. The Egyptian army (20,000 men) was employed almost exclusively on security duties in the Sudan. A further minor campaign took place in Aden where Ottoman troops took control of the West Aden Protectorate and besieged a British Indian force in Aden town. This action was partly offset by British support for Arabian rulers opposed to the Ottomans, notably in ʿAsīr and Najd, and, in 1916, in the Hijaz, which became the centre of the so-called Arab Revolt. But the most important operations were those in which Ottoman military forces confronted those of the Entente directly. These operations took place in Egypt and Palestine, Iraq, the Caucasus and at the Dardanelles.

On 3 February 1915 an Ottoman force which had crossed the Sinai Desert attacked British positions on the Suez Canal. The attack was repulsed and the anticipated Egyptian uprising did not take place.

However, reinforcements were sent to Egypt and the canal defences strengthened. The Ottoman attack was renewed in August 1916 and again defeated. By this time there was a large garrison of British and imperial forces in Egypt and it was decided to establish a forward defensive position in Sinai, based upon al-ʿArīsh. This line was occupied by December 1916. The new British prime minister, Lloyd George, now pressed for an advance into Palestine. This proposal was strenuously resisted by the principal military authorities on the grounds that such a campaign constituted a wasteful diversion from the main task of defeating Germany on the Western Front – a view which the military took consistently in relation to operations in the Near East. But Lloyd George continued to press his arguments and eventually prevailed. Although the British forces were repulsed at Gaza in March and April 1917, under a new commander, General Allenby, they captured Jerusalem on 9 December 1917. After consolidating his gains in southern Palestine Allenby renewed his advance in September 1918, broke the Ottoman resistance and by the end of October his advanced forces had reached Aleppo.

Planning for the British campaign in Iraq (better known as the Mesopotamian campaign) began before the entry of the Ottomans into the war when it was decided to prepare an expedition from India to secure the British position in the Persian Gulf. After the outbreak of war this expedition was directed to Basra which was captured on 22 November 1914. It was then decided to push forward from Basra so as to establish a suitable defensive line, and so successful was this advance that on 23 October 1915 the Cabinet at last agreed to the proposition, repeatedly advanced by the military in Mesopotamia, to advance on Baghdad. This advance was repulsed at Ctesiphon (22–24 November 1915) and the advance force fell back on Kūt where it surrendered on 29 April 1916. It was then deemed necessary to avenge the disaster and retrieve British prestige so the Iraq force was reinforced and under the command of General Maude captured Baghdad on 11 March 1917 and linked with Russian forces at Qizil Ribāṭ on 2 April. Thereafter, the tempo of the Iraq campaign slackened as resources were diverted to the Palestine campaign, but the advance continued and by the time of the Ottoman withdrawal from the war British forces were approaching Mosul which was occupied one week after the armistice.

The principal Ottoman campaign during the early months of the war was directed against the Russian frontier in Transcaucasia in the hope of inciting an anti-Russian uprising, but this venture ended in defeat and heavy losses for the Ottomans at Sarikamish in January 1915 and they were obliged to fall back upon the fortress of Erzerum.

Fighting continued through 1915, and on 15 February 1916 the Russians captured Erzerum and went on to inflict heavy losses on the Ottomans in the summer of 1916, when half of the Ottoman army was engaged by the Russians. Indeed, three-quarters of all casualties suffered by the Ottomans between November 1915 and March 1917 were sustained against the Russians and it is plain that Allenby's path in Palestine and Syria was made much easier by Russia's grinding down of Ottoman strength. Following the March 1917 Russian Revolution, however, Russian military efficiency began to decline and by the end of the year had disintegrated on the Transcaucasian front leaving local Georgian and Armenian corps to confront the Ottomans who launched a fresh campaign in the summer of 1918, swept through Armenian resistance and occupied Azerbaijan before the Ottoman collapse elsewhere forced them to withdraw.

Of all the Near Eastern campaigns during the First World War the best known is that of the Dardanelles. The object of the Dardanelles (Gallipoli) campaign was to force open the Straits, attack Istanbul, knock the Ottomans out of the war, open up a new supply route to Russia, and bring in all the Balkan states on the Entente side so as to permit an onslaught against Austria from the south. In this way, it was hoped, the deadlock on the Western Front might have been broken. The attempt to force the Straits was carried on by a naval assault in February and March 1915 and by troop landings in April and August. The campaign failed and the troops were eventually evacuated by January 1917. The Dardanelles campaign was especially important for its political consequences which will be considered shortly.

In terms of the war in general the main effect of the campaigns described above, together with those in Iran which will be considered later, was to tie down large numbers of Entente troops, supplies and shipping, resources which could otherwise have been used directly against Germany and Austria. In this way the very large manpower superiority which the Entente enjoyed on paper was offset at very little cost to Germany; in October 1918 there were still only 25,000 German officers and men in the Ottoman empire. In terms of the Near East the main result of the campaigns was to create military facts which had profound political implications for the future development of the region. It is now necessary to consider the political aspects of the struggle.

WARTIME AGREEMENTS AND PLANS

The Constantinople Agreement

During the first years of the war the central conviction of British strategy was that Russia was the key to victory. It was, therefore, essential that Russia should not be allowed to seek a separate peace and necessary to give her some worthwhile prize for which to fight. No major gain could be obtained by Russia at the expense of Germany or Austria but the entry of the Ottomans into the war made it possible to offer her Istanbul and the Straits, which were described later as "the richest prize of the whole war".[2] In November 1914 the British and French ambassadors in Moscow informed the Russian foreign minister, Sazanov, that the matter of Istanbul and the Straits would be settled in the manner Russia desired. Sazonov was overjoyed to receive this news which was more than Russia had expected for it is now clear that she would have been content with free passage through the Straits for Russian warships. In fact the generous wording of the Anglo-French offer may be misleading and it seems probable that the two Western powers believed that the matter might eventually be settled by internationalization of the Straits. Certainly, France never wished to concede so much to Russia but was obliged to go along with Britain. Such hopes were destroyed, however, by the decision to launch the Dardanelles campaign. The prospect of Anglo-French forces in Istanbul prompted Russia to seek firmer assurances which were given in an exchange of notes known as the Constantinople Agreement (March 1915). Russia now received a definite promise of the Straits and Istanbul in the event of a successful conclusion to the war. The qualification is important, however, because for most of the war it was believed that the end was likely to be some form of negotiated settlement in which all promises and agreements would merely constitute claims to be presented at a peace conference. The scenario commonly envisaged by British planners was of a post-war situation in which the dominant fact in the Near East would be the Ottoman–German alliance, a view shared by German planners. British plans were made with the notion of limiting the possible damage to their interests from such an alliance; the most obvious way was by limiting Ottoman authority over parts of the empire.

The Constantinople Agreement had two consequences. First, it made the achievement of a separate peace with the Ottomans much more difficult because such an arrangement would have involved the surrender by Russia of what she chiefly coveted. Promising peace feelers came to an end in March 1915 because Britain was no longer in a position to guarantee that Istanbul would remain in Ottoman hands. Only from the summer of 1917 onwards was there a real prospect of a separate peace, and by that time there were other parties involved and much larger questions of compensation to consider. Second, the agreement meant that France and Britain sought compensation for the great gains which Russia was promised.

French claims

The French claim was presented quickly: it was for Syria, apparently for the whole of Syria, although the position of Palestine was left unclear. France had not sought a partition; the great majority of Frenchmen were uninterested in colonial gains and even the supporters of colonies in France thought that France would lose in a division of the Ottoman empire. The strongest advocates of a partition were the officials on the spot: François Georges-Picot in Beirut and Albert Defrance in Cairo. Even before the entry of the Ottomans into the war Picot had discussed the possibility of an armed uprising with Maronite groups and he pressed for a French expeditionary force to be sent to Syria in order to forestall any British designs on the area. Picot found some support for this proposal in Paris although the support withered when the Dardanelles was chosen as the site of the main Entente expedition. France had not wanted the Dardanelles campaign but felt obliged to go along with Britain. However, the discussion of the campaign induced France to stake her claim to Syria on 8 February 1915. This claim was still by way of precaution for France yet hoped to avoid a partition, but the presentation of the Russian demand obliged France to come forward with a firm claim on 14 March. The government's weak resolve over Syria was subsequently strengthened by strong colonial party pressure to gain Palestine.

British claims

Britain was slower to present her main claim. There were certain obvious minor British gains from the war, for which she sought and received recognition. These included the removal of Ottoman sovereignty from Cyprus and Egypt and the extension of the British sphere in Iran to include most of what the 1907 agreement had placed in the neutral zone. But these were modest items and a committee under Sir Maurice de Bunsen was set up to consider more far-reaching objectives. Under the inspiration of one of its members, Sir Mark Sykes, the committee identified Iraq as the centre of British aspirations, seeing that region as a logical extension of the existing British position in the Persian Gulf. The implication of this reasoning was that Iraq was an extension of the British Indian sphere of interest in the Near East, but Sykes argued that it was desirable that the Iraqi position should be supported from the west, not from the east and, therefore, that it required a line of communications to a Mediterranean port which he suggested should be Haifa. The effect of this recommendation was to establish a British interest in Palestine, challenging the French claim, and to suggest a prospective division of the Near East into three spheres of influence – Russia in the north, Britain in the south and France in the centre. The committee did not, however, recommend a partition of the Ottoman empire, rather the establishment within it of spheres of influence. The continuation of the empire was still seen as desirable.

The Sykes–Picot Agreement

In the succeeding months Britain set out to achieve agreement on these lines with France and Russia. Negotiations with France did not begin until 23 November 1915. The French delegate, Picot, who had been left to write his own instructions, demanded the whole of Syria but did not expect to obtain so much and probably did not even want the whole. He wanted Cilicia, northern coastal Syria and a Greater Lebanon and this is what he achieved, although he was able to present his acceptance as a major concession. The British negotiator, Mark Sykes, was less skilful. However, he gained recognition of the British sphere in Iraq and the required Mediterranean outlet. The difficulty was with Palestine which was left in an uneasy compromise. By the so-called Sykes–Picot Agreement (3 January 1916). France was given *carte blanche* in Cilicia, coastal Syria and Lebanon and a sphere of influence stretching eastwards to Mosul in a projected independent Arab state or states. Britain received *carte blanche* in Basra and Baghdad and a similar sphere of influence in the southern region of the Near East. In Palestine Britain received Haifa and Acre, but the rest of Palestine was to be placed under an international administration with no indication of how that should be composed. The assent of Russia to these arrangements was sought and obtained in 1916, although when Russia observed the size of the Anglo-French claims she demanded and received further compensation for herself in the form of extensive territories in Armenia and Kurdistan abutting the Russian frontier in eastern Asia Minor (11–12 May 1916). Unknown to Sykes, Picot, while in Petrograd negotiating the Russian part of the deal, took the opportunity to secure Russian agreement (previously withheld) for the French claim to Palestine.

During the negotiations another claimant to the prospective spoils of the Ottoman empire appeared. This was Italy. The one major success of the Dardanelles campaign was that it persuaded Italy that she should throw in her lot with the Entente. Her principal ambitions were to be satisfied at the expense of Austria around the head of the Adriatic, but she did not wish to be left out of the Ottoman partition and by the Treaty of London (26 April 1915) it was agreed that Italy should retain the Dodecanese Islands which she had occupied in 1912 and that she should receive a sphere of influence in Adalia in western Asia Minor. Subsequently, this sphere was defined more closely in the Agreement of St Jean de Maurienne and increased to include Izmir and Konya (18 August 1917), but that agreement was made subject to ratification by Russia and since this ratification was never obtained Britain and France claimed that no further binding promise had been made to Italy. Indeed, this had been the object of the provision, for Britain had always opposed the Italian claims and had decided that the easiest way to dispose of them was to make them dependent upon a very unlikely Russian agreement.

Quite apart from these territorial dispositions the Entente powers also considered the Panislamic problem. In particular, Britain was concerned at the prospect of a hostile Ottoman sultan-caliph and the effect of his influence upon Muslims everywhere. Whether German or Russian influence prevailed at Istanbul it was desirable that there should be a pole of Muslim attraction which should be independent or in the British sphere. Accordingly, in all her negotiations with her allies, Britain insisted that Arabia should remain under independent Muslim rule and from an early time began to explore the possibility of an arrangement with a Muslim of standing. In this context attention was directed to the situation of Ḥusayn ibn ʿAlī, the sharīf of Mecca.

Ḥusayn–McMahon correspondence

Sharīf Ḥusayn had much to recommend him as a British ally. He was from the Prophet's own tribe of the Quraysh; as ruler of Mecca he would be able to keep open the pilgrim route for the benefit of Muslims from Entente countries; and a rising in the Hijaz would tie down Ottoman forces and make more difficult a renewal of the Ottoman attack upon Egypt. Further, Ḥusayn was already discontented with Ottoman attempts to curtail his power and his son ʿAbdallāh had sounded the British in Egypt in February and April 1914 about the chance of British support for Ḥusayn's pretensions. Accordingly, as it began to seem likely that the Ottomans would enter the war on the side of the Central Powers, the British authorities in Egypt were instructed to open contacts with the sharīf and, after hostilities commenced, to offer a guarantee that no intervention would take place in Arabia and promise assistance against external foreign aggression if the "Arab nation" assisted Britain. Also, a broad hint was given to Ḥusayn that Britain would welcome the assumption by the sharīf of the title of caliph. Contacts were established on this basis.

In the summer of 1915 the course of the Anglo-Hijazi discussions was radically changed by a demand, conveyed in a letter from ʿAbdallāh dated 14 July, for British approval of an Arab caliphate and British recognition of the independence of the Arab countries throughout the area from Cilicia in the north to the Indian Ocean in the south and from the Mediterranean to the Iranian frontier. The origin of this extensive demand is obscure. It is claimed that ʿAbdallāh's demand was based upon previous contacts between Syrian nationalists and the sons of Ḥusayn.

The British answer to these demands was hesitant: she would concede the demand for the caliphate but thought it premature to talk of frontiers for an independent Arab state. It was believed that ʿAbdallāh's territorial demands were merely extravagant bargaining counters. Britain was quickly disillusioned, however. In the next letter of the so-called Ḥusayn–McMahon correspondence Ḥusayn wrote himself to say that the territorial demands were the core of his requirements; further, that the demand was not his but that of the Arab people.

Britain then changed her position completely. In a letter of 24 October the British High Commissioner in Egypt, Sir Henry McMahon, agreed with certain important reservations, "to recognise and support the independence of the Arabs within the territories included in the limits and boundaries proposed by the Sherif of Mecca".[3] Before discussing the reservations it is necessary to account for his change of mind. There are three factors. First, a deserter from the Ottoman army, Lieutenant Muḥammad Sharīf al-Fārūqī, brought to Cairo a story concerning the existence of a vast secret society, to which 90 per cent of Arab officers in the Ottoman army belonged, and which aimed at creating an Arab caliphate in Arabia, Syria and Iraq. If Britain would support them the Arab nationalists would throw in their lot with her; if not, they would turn to Germany and the Ottomans. Although there were some question marks against Fārūqī's story and his own claims to be a spokesman, he made a deep impression on the British authorities in Cairo, the more so because his story appeared to confirm the claims of

Ḥusayn at several points. Second, the situation in the Dardanelles had reached a point of crisis. It seemed impossible that success could be achieved except at unendurable cost, yet evacuation was thought likely to end in a blood-bath (the loss of 35% of the troops was expected), an intolerable loss of Entente prestige throughout the East, and the release of Ottoman forces to threaten the Entente in Egypt, Iraq and Transcaucasia. Any Arab disaffection, mutiny or uprising would certainly diminish the effectiveness of the Ottoman army at the Dardanelles; also, in the event that it was decided to make a fresh Allied landing on the Syrian coast at Alexandretta, an Arab uprising would greatly assist such an operation. Even if Fārūqī's story was only partially true thousands of Allied lives might yet be saved. Third, there was a view among the British in Egypt that Britain could profit greatly in the future from becoming the patron of an independent Arab state, particularly in relation to French claims in the Near East.

British policy in the Near East was not monolithic. To the Cabinet the war in Europe and the dismal British showing at Loos filled the stage; the Near East was a side-show and the Arab question a mere stage-prop in that side-show. Ministers understood little of the situation and relied heavily upon the advice they received from men on the spot. To the Indian government and those connected with it the Near East bore a different aspect. India had long-established interests in the Near East in Aden and the Persian Gulf and was developing new concerns in Iraq. Plans for an independent Arab state or states were likely to embarrass those interests and British Indian officials opposed such projects. Britons in Egypt, however, were accustomed to dealing with a nominally independent government and saw how the extension of such a system into Arabia and Syria could secure British influence throughout the region and exclude that of France and Russia as well as that of Germany and the Ottomans. Since the outbreak of the war there had been much speculation on these lines in Egypt and there had come into being a group of knowledgeable British officials who followed the general views of the experienced Reginald Wingate (1861–1953), governor-general of the Sudan, and who were led by Captain (later General) Gilbert Clayton (1875–1929). This group was subsequently organized in the Arab Bureau (February 1916) and played a major role in British policy-making in the Near East. It was Clayton who interrogated Fārūqī and who recommended making the 24 October offer to Ḥusayn.

Britain did not concede all Ḥusayn's demands but made important reservations. Certain areas were excluded from the area of Arab independence on the grounds that they were not purely Arab. These were the northern districts of Mersina and Alexandretta and "portions of Syria lying to the west of the districts of Damascus, Hama, Homs and Aleppo". In the *vilāyet* of Baghdad and Basra it was stated that the British position and interests required that there should be "special measures of administrative control". It was also implied that the independent Arab state or states would be subject to British advice and assistance. Finally, a reservation was made in respect of existing treaties between Britain and other Arab chiefs and it was stated that the British promise related only to "those portions of the territories wherein Great Britain is free to act without detriment to her Ally, France".

The promises contained in McMahon's letter of 24 October 1915 have been the subject of great controversy. It has been complained, first, that they were incompatible with the agreement negotiated with France shortly afterwards and, second, that Britain failed to carry out her undertakings after the war. These complaints require consideration.

A comparison of the Sykes–Picot Agreement and the Ḥusayn–McMahon correspondence

Although the form of the two documents is very different the McMahon letter and the Sykes–Picot Agreement are broadly compatible, as, indeed, they were intended to be. Both propose that an independent Arab state or states should be established. Both stipulate that the area of coastal Syria and Lebanon should be excluded from the independent Arab area. There are however four evident differences between the two documents and these relate to Iraq, the degree of independence to be enjoyed by the independent Arab area, the position of Haifa and the status of Palestine.

Although both documents provide for a special position for Britain in Iraq the Sykes–Picot Agreement excludes Iraq from the area of Arab independence while the McMahon letter leaves it within. However, although the difference contributed to disputes at the time, the post-war decision to establish an Arab state in Iraq made the matter of no consequence.

In the Sykes–Picot Agreement it was laid down that the independent Arab area was to be divided into spheres of influence. In the northern sphere France was to enjoy rights of economic priority and of affording administrative assistance, and in the southern sphere Britain was to have similar privileges. No mention of such arrangements was made in the McMahon letter, although it was stated that Britain would offer advice and administrative assistance. Too much should not be made of this discrepancy; no one, Arab, Briton or Frenchman could have supposed that any Arab state would have been able to stand on its own without assistance and it was reasonable that Britain and France, the only two powers likely to be in a position to afford such assistance, should come to an agreement between themselves about who should provide help in order that they might avoid future squabbles. Such arrangements have subsequently come to be regarded as unacceptable in international relations, but they were not uncommon at the time and were generally considered to be sensible ways of avoiding conflict. A greater problem, which arose in 1920, was whether the Arab state had the right to refuse to accept advice and assistance.

In the Sykes–Picot Agreement Haifa and Acre were reserved for Britain but there is no mention of them in the McMahon letter. The discrepancy cannot be resolved but it need not detain us because, essentially, it forms part of the much larger dispute about the status of Palestine.

In the Sykes–Picot Agreement Palestine was to be placed under an international administration but the region is not mentioned in the McMahon letter and, therefore, unless it was excluded under some other provision, must be deemed to be part of the promised independent Arab area. The question which has been often debated is: was it so excluded?

When the question was asked some years later Britain's answer was that it was excluded under the provision relating to "portions of Syria lying to the west of the districts of Damascus, Hama, Homs and Aleppo". It was argued that the district or *vilayet* of Damascus in 1915 included the region which came to be known as Transjordan and that west of this region lay the sanjak of Jerusalem which was in effect Palestine. The difficulty with this ingenious argument is that if the word "*vilayet*" is understood to refer to the Ottoman administrative division usually translated as "province" the whole provision becomes meaningless because Hama and Homs were not provinces, and west of the *vilayet* of Aleppo was the sea. The phrase is only intelligible on the assumption that the term "*vilayet*" does not refer to an Ottoman province but is used in the common Arabic sense of an ill-defined area much as a Briton might say Huddersfield and district, meaning the town of Huddersfield and that area immediately surrounding the town which looked to it for its services. Used in that fashion the phrase makes apparent sense for the four towns mentioned lay in a more or less straight line and were joined by the railway and west of them lay coastal Syria and Lebanon, the very areas subsequently reserved to France in the Sykes–Picot Agreement. But Palestine does not lie to the west of this line but wholly south of the region so defined. Accordingly, if one interprets the phrase as being intended to indicate a region west of a vague line (and this interpretation is not unquestioned), it must be concluded that the British argument fails, that Palestine cannot be excluded from the independent Arab state by this reservation and that it is very difficult to believe that in 1915 anyone thought that it could so be excluded.

It has been argued, however, that Palestine was excluded by another provision, namely that which specified that the British promise applied only to those areas in which Britain was free to act without detriment to the interests of France. In October 1915, it was argued, Palestine was claimed by France as part of Greater Syria and, therefore, Britain was not in a position to make any promises relating to Palestine. There are objections to this argument also. The first need not detain us. It has been alleged that the French reservation was mistranslated into Arabic so as to convey a meaning opposite to that of the English and seriously mislead Ḥusayn. In fact, the Arabic translation appears to be correct and to convey the same meaning as the English. The second objection concerns the apparent purposelessness of, first, specifying the exclusion of coastal Syria and Lebanon on the grounds that they were not purely Arab, and then introducing a reservation of so broad a character that they would have been excluded anyway, for if there was some doubt in McMahon's mind whether Palestine was part of the area in which France was interested there was certainly no doubt that France was concerned about northern coastal Syria and Lebanon and he had been specifically told by London not to promise north-west Syria to the Arabs. In fact, by reserving French interests McMahon appears to have intended to keep open the possibility that, after all, France might claim Aleppo, Homs, Hama and Damascus, and not to have had other areas specifically in mind. It is this circumstance which appears to account for the peculiar form of his reservations, for in the light of what he understood to be Arab wishes it might have been sensible simply to have specified that the four towns should form part of the independent Arab state and left it at that. But by specifying an exclusion zone he did not close the possibility that other areas, not specifically excluded, might also be eventually withheld. The disadvantage of his approach, however, was that the listing of the four towns suggested a precise boundary only partly mitigated by the introduction of the vagueness of "districts". The third objection to the theory is that if it had been intended to exclude Palestine under the French reservation it is very odd that none of the participants, including McMahon, could subsequently remember that such had been the intention and that it was left to a clerk, some fifteen years later, to discover that Palestine was so excluded. Although none of these objections can constitute a conclusive rebuttal of the theory of the French reservation they do cast serious doubt upon its validity.

A fourth objection raises a fundamental question. It may be objected that an agreement which contains so large a reservation, the extent of which is quite unknown to one party and remains to be defined, to suit its own convenience, by the other, is hardly an agreement at all. And, of course, the McMahon letter of 24 October 1915 was not intended to be an agreement, only a declaration of intent contingent upon various uncertain factors and made at a particular stage in a long correspondence. London would have preferred no statement about the frontiers of the proposed independent Arab state: McMahon felt it necessary to make some statement but thought that he could make it sufficiently vague as to leave Britain and France a completely free hand. Plainly, he failed but he could not have foreseen, first, that it would be treated as a binding agreement, and second, that it would have been read not in the context of the French claims for which it had been intended to provide, but in the context of an Arab claim, inflamed by opposition to Zionism, to an independent Palestine. However, at the time there was no agreement because the correspondence between Ḥusayn and McMahon continued after the letter of 24 October, Husayn seeking to improve on the British offer, until the subject was dropped without agreement. It should be noted, however, that Ḥusayn and many Britons subsequently acted on the assumption that there was an agreement contained in the correspondence although they could not agree about what it was.

Did the British mean to exclude Palestine or not? If they had thought about the matter the answers of most ministers and officials in London would have been "yes". But there must be a possibility that those in Cairo had a different view. The inclusion of Palestine would have been consistent with their notion that a loose Arab confederation under British control offered the best means of securing British interests in the Near East. In that scenario exclusions should be kept to the minimum. Some concession had to be made to French claims in Syria and Lebanon and to Indian views about Iraq, but the concession should be small and the broadest area left for the British-controlled Arabs.

The second complaint is that Britain failed to carry out her undertakings after the war. As has been suggested there was no agreement about what those undertakings were. However, it is also plain that, whatever Britain was offering, she expected something in return. What did she expect and what was delivered?

There is little doubt what Britain expected in the autumn of 1915 and that was an uprising in Syria and a mutiny of Arab officers in the

Ottoman army. This is what Fārūqī had led them to expect and it appears to have been what Ḥusayn also expected. The uprising and mutiny did not take place. Arabs subsequently blamed Ottoman repression and the British failure to land at Alexandretta (although this had never been made a condition) for the failure of the uprising to materialize, but it seems more likely that the Arab Party in Syria was far from being as strong as had been represented to his interrogators by Fārūqī. Instead of the Syrian rising Britain was left with the Arab Revolt which commenced in the Hijaz on 5 June 1916. However, Britain did not specify that the Arab contribution should include a Syrian revolt and the Arab Bureau expressed satisfaction with the Arab Revolt that did take place. The Arab Revolt may have been a far cry from what had been hoped for, but it appears to have been accepted as a reasonable substitute.

The proclamation of the Arab Revolt provides an interesting contrast with the McMahon correspondence and gives some insight into Ḥusayn's attitude. Whereas in the McMahon correspondence Ḥusayn frequently adopted the language of Arab nationalism, presenting the Arab people as a very broadly defined group including Christians and Muslims, his proclamations of June 1916 were couched in much more traditional style, grounding his revolt not on secular nationalist aspirations but on the irreligion of the Young Turks and the tribal loyalties of the people of the Hijaz. The revolt, he stated, was against "the heedless ones who . . . took the religion of God as an amusement and a sport".[4] To regard Ḥusayn as a new style of Arab leader is wrong; he was in the style of Ottoman notables seeking to preserve a position of local autonomy and influence and for this purpose negotiating with Ottomans and Britons. It is interesting to note that he confined his quarrel to the CUP; the name of the sultan continued to be mentioned in Friday prayers in the Hijaz throughout 1917 and Ḥusayn continued to look for an arrangement which would establish Arab autonomy under Ottoman suzerainty. Ḥusayn's adoption, in his correspondence, of the style of modern nationalism was due partly to the circumstance that he was addressing Britons, to whom such discourse was more comprehensible than more traditional modes, and partly, it would seem, to the influence of his sons, who had imbibed a more modern notion of politics and wider ambitions. The British in Egypt misunderstood Ḥusayn. They believed him to have a wide appeal to Muslims and to Arabs when in fact he had neither; he was essentially an influential notable of Arabia; his ambitions were primarily in the Hijaz although he saw how, with British support, he could become a figure on a greater canvas. That canvas of the Arab nation had yet to be painted, however. The Arab

Revolt remained a very minor affair for some time; the Arabs took Jiddah (16 June 1916) and Mecca (4 July 1916) but could not capture Medina; and Britain declined to send British troops to assist them.

1917

In 1917 the war in the Near East began to take on a different character. There were four reasons for the change. First, the Ottoman armies, having performed with remarkable success for two years began to decline in efficiency. Losses at Gallipoli and in Transcaucasia took their toll, desertions increased, the pool of available manpower began to dry up, and the strain on Ottoman resources became greater. Second, the new government of Lloyd George in Britain began to take a much more considerable interest in the Near East, partly in response to the failure to achieve any gain on the Somme during the summer and autumn of 1916; the easier, Ottoman target might provide cheap, glamorous victories to cheer up a depressed war-weary public in Britain. Third, Russia progressively dropped out of the war and left behind a vacuum in the Near East which had to be filled by Britain. France was fully occupied in the west and in the Balkans although her fears of British designs on Syria persuaded her to send token forces to the Hijaz and with Allenby to Palestine. Italy had no resources to spare, and in any case Britain was wary of giving her any role in the Red Sea. Accordingly, Russia's withdrawal had the effect of making Britain the dominant Entente power in the Near East. The Russian withdrawal also opened another possibility, namely a negotiated peace with the Ottomans, and some interest in this possibility was shown in the summer of 1917, but so long as there was a hope that Russia might stay in the war the chance was not pursued with conviction and the prospect of Russia leaving the war made the Ottomans less inclined to respond to peace proposals since it seemed that the Central Powers were winning and that the Ottomans might do better by waiting. Further, so many interests had by then been built into the defeat of the Ottomans that it was difficult to harmonize these into acceptable peace proposals. Also, there was, among many members of the British government, an emotional distaste for the Ottomans and a desire to destroy their empire. Nevertheless, from September 1917 onwards there was a strong British disposition towards a separate peace with the Ottomans on the basis of autonomy for the non-Turkish areas. Finally, the Russian collapse opened the possibility, which continued to haunt Britain until October

1918, of a drive by the Central Powers using Panislamic and Pan-Turanian propaganda, against India. Fourth, the entry of the United States into the war (although she remained at peace with the Ottomans) gave a different gloss to the concept of war aims by emphasizing the notion of self-determination. The idea implicit in the Constantinople and Sykes–Picot Agreements that Great Powers arranged the disposition of territories without much regard to the wishes of their inhabitants fell out of favour: a peace settlement, it came to be accepted, must be based upon the wishes of the people affected and this idea was enshrined in the proclamations issued in 1917 and 1918.

IRAN

Russia's withdrawal had a major effect in the eastern part of the region. Although Iran had declared her neutrality when the Ottomans entered the war her declaration had been to no avail because the Ottomans had refused to recognize her neutrality while Russian and British troops were stationed in Iran, and Ottoman troops had entered the province of Azerbaijan. Within Iran a powerful movement grew up under the leadership of the Democratic Party in opposition to Anglo-Russian pressure and this group looked to the possibility of an alliance with the Central Powers. By the autumn of 1915 the German–Iranian discussions had reached an advanced stage and to preserve Entente influence Russian troops advanced towards Tehran. As a result of this action Entente dominance over the Iranian government was confirmed, but armed resistance sprang up throughout Iran fostered by German agents such as Wassmus in the south, and in the west a rival government was established by the Democrats under Ottoman patronage. In the summer of 1916, after Ottoman troops were released by the British surrender at Kūt, a new Ottoman offensive into Iran was launched.

The Entente sought to retain its influence through these years by subsidies, by the direct use of force (chiefly by Russian troops) to crush the rebels, and by making an agreement with the Iranian government which would give the Entente effective control over Iran's armed forces or, more precisely, would enable the Entente powers to raise forces in Iran and employ them under Entente control, for Iran's tiny forces had disintegrated during the war. In August 1916 such an agreement was secured but the Entente found it impossible to get it ratified. In the meantime Russia continued to control the Persian Cossack Brigade and Britain raised the South Persia Rifles.

The effect of the war on Iran was to turn the country into a number of unofficial battlefields. The authority of the central government broke down completely over most of the country, there was widespread tribal raiding, autonomous regimes were established in areas such as Azerbaijan and Gīlān, there was famine, especially in the north-west which had seen the greatest part of the fighting, and, at the same time, there were pockets of tranquillity which enjoyed untroubled prosperity.

So long as the principal burdens of military operations were borne by Russia there was little that Britain could do but to follow Russia's lead in her dealings with Tehran. The fading of Russia in 1917 imposed new burdens on Britain while it also supplied new opportunities to pursue her own policy. The threat from the side of Iraq was diminished by the British capture of Baghdad in March 1917, but a new danger appeared of the movement of forces and agents of the Central Powers through Transcaucasia and Iran into Russian Turkestan and Afghanistan, where they might join with released prisoners of war and discontented Afghans to threaten the Indian frontier. To prevent this eventuality Britain extended her occupation of south-east Iran northwards to establish a cordon, took up a position on the Caspian Sea, and pushed a small force from Iraq through north-west Iran into Transcaucasia, as well as continuing her efforts to reduce tribal opposition in southern Iran with the aid of the South Persia Rifles. The Iranian government resented these British actions on Iranian territory but Britain did not alter her policy to try to reach an understanding with Iran; rather she continued to hope that a better disposed government would be formed in Tehran. But this did not happen until the autumn of 1918, when the collapse of the Central Powers ended Iranian hopes that succour might come from that source. By the end of the war Britain was in a dominant position in Iran with no rival.

PALESTINE

The main area of British operations in the Near East in the latter part of 1917 and 1918 was Palestine and Syria. Lloyd George had urged an offensive in this region since December 1916 but it was not until autumn 1917 that Allenby broke the Ottoman defences and occupied southern Palestine including Jerusalem. Before this event there had been important developments in British policy towards Palestine. In the Sykes–Picot negotiations Britain had been principally concerned to avoid recognizing a French right to Palestine; in April 1917 a committee set up to consider British territorial desiderata concluded that Palestine was of such strategic value as a buffer to Egypt and as a link between the British position in Egypt and that which was now adumbrated in Iraq that it should, if possible, be secured for Britain. The committee's views (which appear to have been largely the opinions of its secretary, Leo Amery) were merely noted as an indication of objectives and did not become part of British policy. Nevertheless, there was serious concern lest the war should end with a German-controlled Ottoman empire in charge of Palestine on the borders of Egypt.

Britain's strategic interest in Palestine ran in seeming tandem with the aims of the Zionists to secure future arrangements for Palestine which would permit unrestricted Jewish immigration.

Enlightenment ideas, the pressure of modernization, discrimination and occasional persecution had had a disturbing effect upon Jews in central and eastern Europe and during the latter part of the nineteenth century a great emigration took place. The favourite destination was the New World, many went to western Europe and a few to Palestine. Among those in central and western Europe a feeling grew up that Jews could never be accepted as equal citizens of the states in which they resided and that they should create a state of their own. This was the argument of Theodor Herzl, the founder of modern political Zionism. The Zionist Congress Party, founded at Basle in 1897, chose Palestine as the site of this state and sought support among the Great Powers for their aim. They received some sympathy but little support because it was plainly unacceptable to the Ottomans that there should be another state planted in their territory and the Zionist substitution of the word "homeland" for "state" did not change their ultimate goal. Nor did the Zionists obtain widespread support from the Jewish communities of Europe and the United States. By 1914 they had made little progress either in obtaining diplomatic support or in settling emigrants in Palestine. At that time there were no more than 100,000 Jews in Palestine, numbering a little over 10 per cent of the total population and less than half of these were Zionists. The outbreak of the First World War added to the Zionists' troubles because it left them divided between the Central Powers and the Entente.

It was in these circumstances that a remarkable political leader emerged in Britain. This was Dr Chaim Weizmann (1874–1952). He became the dominant force in British Zionism (being elected president of the English Zionist Federation on 11 February 1917), circumvented the efforts of Jews opposed to Zionism, developed contacts with influential Britons in public life and persuaded many to support his aims, and, by 1917, found himself negotiating with the British government for official endorsement of Zionist hopes. The outcome was the Balfour Declaration of 2 November 1917.

The Balfour Declaration

The Balfour Declaration was contained in a letter addressed by the foreign secretary, Lord Balfour, to a prominent Zionist, Lord Rothschild. By it Britain promised to use her best endeavours for the establishment in Palestine of "a national home for the Jewish people" subject to two provisos: that nothing should be done which might prejudice either the civil and religious rights of existing non-Jewish communities in Palestine or the rights and political status of Jews in any other country.

The Balfour Declaration was virtually meaningless and committed Britain to nothing. "A national home for the Jewish people" was a deliberately vague formulation which might mean no more than a cultural centre. And if the provisos were taken seriously there was very little that could be done without affecting the rights of non-Jewish communities in Palestine or of Jews outside Palestine. The first proviso was included to meet the objections of those who opposed the Balfour Declaration on the grounds that it would arouse Muslim opinion against Britain and the second was designed to placate those assimilationist Jews who feared that Zionism would damage their own position as citizens of other countries by the implication that their proper home was in Palestine. In fact, neither group was satisfied.

Why did Britain issue the Balfour Declaration? There is no simple answer. The British strategic interest in Palestine was clear but the link between that interest and Zionism is much less obvious. Those who argued that there was a link pointed to the value of having within Palestine a community loyal to Britain or to the circumstance that a British commitment to Zionism would attract the support of Jews everywhere for post-war British rule in Palestine. But an Arab commitment might also have supplied a loyal community and in that case Britain could have rested her claim on self-determination. Further, Britain already had a convenient buffer for the Suez Canal in Sinai. Realistically, it was evident that any British position in Palestine was likely to depend primarily on the fact of military occupation and on a bargain with France. In fact, although the strategic argument was prominent in earlier stages of the long discussion which preceded the issue of the Balfour Declaration, in the last period it was less to the fore than political arguments.

The political arguments concerned the attitudes of Jews in Russia and the United States and the possibility that Germany might pre-empt the Entente with a similar declaration. It was argued that the most powerful movement among Jews in those countries was Zionism, and the espousal of Zionism by Britain would induce Jews in Russia to press for Russia to remain in the war and Jews in America to demand a more active role by the United States. These arguments had a powerful effect on the Cabinet but subsequent events cast some doubt upon their validity, for Russia left the war and there was no discernible change in US policy. In fact, the strength of Zionist feeling at that time among both Jewish communities seems to have been exaggerated, as was President Wilson's own enthusiasm for Zionism. And Germany, because of her Ottoman alliance, was in no position to make a pro-Zionist declaration.

Lastly, one cannot disregard personal motives. Although some ministers hotly opposed Zionism, others, and notably Lloyd George and Balfour, plainly felt a personal interest in the success of what they saw as a great historical movement. Similar feelings seem to have existed among several of the officials closely concerned with the negotiations which led to the Balfour Declaration. The prevalence of these favourable dispositions among individuals must be accounted a triumph of Zionist persuasion and particularly a tribute to the skill of Weizmann.

Much of the labour which has gone into explaining the origins of the Balfour Declaration was perhaps unnecessary. The belief that the declaration was a momentous event has exposed the motives of those involved to the closest scrutiny. But it was not the declaration which was important but the subsequent adoption of the Zionist programme; to those who issued it, the declaration was simply one more item in a long catalogue of wartime documents; and no sooner was it published than it was virtually forgotten by all except the Zionists.

THE ARAB POLICY

The incorporation of a Zionist element into British policy in the Near East did not mean the abandonment of the Arab element introduced in 1915. The Arab card had been a disappointment; no uprising in Syria or Iraq had occurred; and the revolt in Arabia made little progress after its early successes. But there was still interest and this was enlivened in the summer of 1917 when a son of Ḥusayn, Fayṣal, accompanied by

T. E. Lawrence, led an Arab force northwards, linked with tribes in Transjordan, captured ʿAqaba and began to harass Ottoman supply lines, particularly by attacks on the Hijaz railway which linked Damascus with the Ottoman garrison in Medina. The presence of this force was of assistance to Allenby's operations in Palestine and Syria and Arab forces took part in the Syrian campaign of September–October 1918 and in the capture of Damascus on 1 October 1918. Taken in conjunction with the Ḥusayn–McMahon correspondence and with subsequent declarations the role of Fayṣal's force provided the basis for arrangements which placed the temporary administration of the interior of Syria in his hands. These arrangements have also been seen as an attempt by some Britons around Allenby to use the Arab claims to exclude France completely from the area.

Members of the Arab Bureau remained committed to a picture of a post-war Arab Near East composed of various Arab states, chiefdoms or principalities, bound loosely together under sharifian leadership and under British control exercised locally and through Ḥusayn. Such an arrangement was seen as the most effective means of excluding Ottoman and German influence in the event that the war ended in a negotiated settlement and of keeping out France. Although this scenario had received a setback through the modest Arab performance in 1916, it was strengthened again by four factors: the glamour of the Fayṣal/Lawrence operations; the decline of the Indian government as a factor in Near Eastern policy-making after the dismal revelations of its mismanagement of the Mesopotamian campaign; the increasing British unhappiness with the Sykes–Picot Agreement; and the introduction of the concept of self-determination.

Advocates of the Arab policy achieved an early success after the conquest of Baghdad when, in opposition to the views of the British in Iraq and of the Indian government, it was decided that Baghdad should be developed as an Arab state under British control. The success, however, was only partial for the chief advocate of the Arab policy in London, Mark Sykes, had wanted a largely autonomous Basra and Baghdad, whereas the government decided that Basra should be British and that control over Baghdad should be as tight as necessary and that there was no commitment to the effect that Baghdad should form part of a single Arab state.

The Arab policy was also kept warm by a series of assurances offered to Ḥusayn during 1917–18. These assurances related to the Sykes–Picot Agreement, the Balfour Declaration, the British occupation of Palestine and other matters. In none of these assurances was the possibility of a united Arab state under the rule of Ḥusayn excluded, although no undertaking was given to him and Britain still refused to grant his wish to be recognized as king of the Arabs. It is evident that Ḥusayn derived encouragement from these assurances as was intended.

Somewhat contradictory assurances were given to a group of seven Syrians living in Cairo who had asked for an assurance that Syria would be autonomous after the war, free, that is, not only from Ottoman control but also from sharifian. The British reply, known as the Declaration to the Seven, dated 16 June 1918, was intended as a broad statement of British policy towards the Arab Near East. The British answer dealt in Arab generalities rather than Syrian specifics and is chiefly notable for the prominence which it gave to self-determination. It divided the Arab Near East into four categories of areas: those independent before the war, those freed from Ottoman control by Arab action during the war, those occupied by Allied armies and those still under Ottoman control. In the first two categories Britain would recognize "the complete and sovereign independence of the Arabs inhabiting these areas" and in the third category Britain desired that "the future government of these regions should be based upon the principle of the consent of the governed".[5] Britain desired that areas in the fourth category would achieve their freedom and independence. The implications of the assurance concerning areas freed by Arab action was apparently that the Arabs had a claim to complete independence in those parts of Syria which they liberated themselves. It has been argued, although the evidence is far from conclusive, that British forces in Syria were deliberately restrained so as to allow the Arabs to liberate Damascus and thereby strengthen their claim to independence *vis-à-vis* France. The Declaration to the Seven can be seen as another way of undermining the Sykes–Picot Agreement. Its importance should not, however, be overrated; very few Britons took any notice of it at the time.

The clearest expression of the notion of self-determination occurs in the Anglo-French Declaration of 7 November 1918, a statement intended to further undermine the Sykes–Picot Agreement. The declaration began with a piece of humbug as sickening as it was false:

> The end which France and Great Britain have in view in their prosecution in the East of the war let loose by German ambition is the complete and definitive liberation of the peoples so long oppressed by the Turks and the establishment of national Governments and Administrations drawing their authority from the initiative and free choice of indigenous populations.

It went on to promise disinterested assistance to governments established in Syria and Mesopotamia, but any impression that the two powers were promising independence is mistaken, for the gilded phrases were qualified by the reservation to Britain and France of the right "to assure by their support and effective aid the normal working of the Governments and Administrations".[6]

The Arab Near East experienced some striking changes during the war. In Arabia Ottoman rule was broken. In the Hijaz this was accomplished through the Arab Revolt, although Medina did not surrender until January 1919. In central Arabia ʿAbd al-ʿAzīz ibn Suʿūd (Saud) threw off his Ottoman allegiance and signed a treaty with Britain on 26 December 1915. ʿAsīr also became independent of Ottoman authority, although Ottoman garrisons remained on the coast until May 1919. Only Yemen retained its Ottoman allegiance. The Hijaz, Najd and ʿAsīr had all been drawn into alliance with Britain. So also had Qaṭar. What remained to be determined was the outcome of the rivalries between the Arabian states and the attitude which Britain would take towards their contests.

Ottoman authority was also broken in Syria which, by the end of the war, was under British military occupation, although for administrative purposes it was divided into three Occupied Enemy Territory Administrations (OETAs), controlled by France in the north, Britain in the south and Fayṣal in the east. These administrations corresponded roughly to the scheme of the Sykes–Picot arrangement, with Britain in possession of the international administration of Palestine. They were, however, temporary administrations only, pending a peace settlement. It remained for the people of Syria to adjust themselves to their loss of the familiar Ottoman umbrella and to the new possibilities opened up by the prospects of peace.

Basra and Baghdad had been occupied by British Indian forces. At the beginning of October 1918, the Cabinet, foreseeing an Ottoman collapse, ordered the British commander to advance on Mosul which was eventually occupied one week after the armistice. The decision to take Mosul was justified on military grounds and by the need to preserve law and order, but in the minds of the British authorities in Iraq Mosul was required to make a viable state of Iraq in the future. But no decision had been taken in London that there should be a state of Iraq. It had been decided that Basra should be British, that Baghdad should be under an Arab government with British control and no decision had been taken about Mosul. In the meantime there was taking shape in Iraq a British-controlled administrative system staffed in the higher reaches by Britons and Indians with very little place for Iraqis. The future of Iraq was very much an open question.

EGYPT

Egypt remained the key to the British position in the western part of the Near East as the Persian Gulf, backed by India, was in the eastern part. At the outbreak of war Egypt was still part of the Ottoman empire and its ruler, Khedive ʿAbbās Ḥilmī II, long unhappy with British control, was in Istanbul where there were also members of the Egyptian Nationalist Party wholly opposed to the British occupation. ʿAbbās was persuaded to put his name to a proclamation calling upon Egyptians to rise against British rule.

Britain responded by declaring a protectorate (18 December 1914), terminating Ottoman authority and deposing ʿAbbās, putting in his place his uncle, Ḥusayn Kāmil, who was given the title of sultan. At the time London wanted to annex Egypt but was persuaded not to do so by representations from the British in Egypt who feared that such an act would jeopardize Egyptian co-operation with Britain. In 1917 the situation was reversed. At that time the British high commissioner in Egypt, Wingate, proposed that Egypt should be annexed, partly to legitimize the extensive additional control over Egypt which Britain had come to exercise during the war and partly as a safeguard in the event that a negotiated peace left Germany dominant in Istanbul. The government in London refused on the grounds that the new movement towards self-determination made annexation inappropriate and that it would have had a bad effect throughout the Near East and in India, where British policy had moved in the opposite direction. Instead, Britons began work on designing a new system of government for Egypt within the protectorate. This involved the abolition of the capitulations and the replacement of the Kitchener constitution with a two-chamber parliament dominated by non-Egyptians. In the same year the complaisant Ḥusayn Kāmil died and was replaced by his brother, Ahmad Fu'ād, a much more ambitious personality, who aspired to play an independent role in politics, endeavoured to recover the power to choose his own ministers and began to talk the fashionable language of nationalism.

Apart from the facilities offered by the Suez Canal to Britain Egypt was important during the First World War (as during the Second) as the main base for operations in the Near East. In 1915 Egypt was the principal regional centre supporting the Dardanelles campaign; in 1917–18 it was the base for operations in Palestine and Syria. Accordingly, there were at all times substantial numbers of troops and large quantities of supplies in Egypt. Further, the perennial shipping problems made it desirable to draw on Egyptian resources as much as possible. In particular, there was a heavy demand for Egyptian labour which was met by measures which were barely distinguishable from forced labour. There was also a considerable demand for Egyptian grain, cotton and industrial products.

The Egyptian economy underwent a transformation during the war. In the early months, with the fall-off in demand from traditional markets and the lack of shipping, there was a slump but from 1915 onwards there was a boom led by soaring cotton prices. Egyptian landlords did very well out of the war; the position of peasants is less easy to gauge and varied from one region to another. Granted the critical labour shortage, it seems probable that agricultural labour was able to command a higher price for its services. There was also a new demand for locally produced industrial products; light industries – textiles and food processing – grew rapidly during the war. On the heels of this development there came into being something which could be called an Egyptian business class, of which the best-known representative was Talʿat Ḥarb who gathered around him a group who advocated the establishment of a native Egyptian bank – the Bank Miṣr. This group began to challenge the monopoly of financial and industrial power formerly enjoyed by non-Egyptians: Europeans, Syrians and Greeks.

The external financial position of Egypt was also radically changed during the war. In 1914 the whole of Egypt's visible trade surplus had been consumed in paying interest to overseas stockholders; the very large surplus earned by Egypt during the war enabled Egypt to repatriate her foreign debt and left her in a strong position at the end of the war.

The war also imposed considerable hardships on Egypt. Apart from the pressure on labour the war led to shortages of many goods formerly supplied from Europe and elsewhere. Also, the large amount of money available for spending in Egypt, combined with the shortages, led to inflation which was especially felt by bureaucrats who were already discontented by the influx of Britons into the administration and concerned by the prospect of the establishment of closer British control under the proposed new regime in Egypt.

The war contributed to a rapid politicization of Egypt. Bureaucrats, industrialists and workers became more conscious of the effects of governmental decisions upon their livelihoods and more responsive to the appeals of pre-war politicians. The politicians themselves were concerned that the changes proposed in the constitution of Egypt would curtail their own power and influence. Lawyers practising in the Mixed Courts were worried about the proposed judicial changes and the religious classes by the extension of infidel control and the threat to the *Sharīʿa*. Finally, the popularity of the new ideas of self-determination, contained in various wartime speeches and proclamations, encouraged Egyptians to demand greater control over their own affairs. Although Egypt had been neutral during the war she had played an important role in the struggle and this circumstance became the basis of a claim to state her case at the peace conference.

THE END OF THE WAR

The last year of the war saw the fortunes of the combatants in the Near East change rapidly. The withdrawal of Russia from the war and the signature of the Treaty of Brest-Litovsk opened new possibilities for the Ottomans in Transcaucasia. By March 1917 the Russian forces had penetrated far into Ottoman territory in eastern Asia Minor. As the Russians were withdrawn in 1917 their places were taken by Transcaucasian volunteers. The Ottomans remained on the defensive throughout 1917, expecting to recover this territory together with areas lost in 1878 at the peace settlement. In 1918 Ottoman ambitions increased and an offensive against Transcaucasia was launched in February. As Russian authority collapsed the three countries of the region, Georgia, Armenia and Azerbaijan bound themselves together in the hastily constructed Federated Transcaucasian Republic (22 April 1918). Their resources were small, however, and their differences great. To Georgians freedom also meant the opportunity to throw off Armenian control of their economic life and relations quickly deteriorated between the two countries. Disputes also occurred between Armenia and Azerbaijan over territory. When the Ottomans turned their forces against Transcaucasia the federation fell apart (22 May 1918). Azerbaijanis welcomed the Ottomans as fellow Muslims and Turkish speakers: the Georgians took cover in an alliance with Germany and the Armenians were left to face the Ottomans alone. By September 1918 the Ottomans were in control of much of Transcaucasia.

The Ottoman strategy was what it had always been: to ride on the back of Germany. By the summer of 1918 the Ottoman military situation was desperate although the Ottoman government was unaware how desperate because the true facts were concealed from them by Enver. However, the shape of the peace settlement would not be determined by the fortunes of war in the Near East but by what happened in Europe. Until the 1918 German spring offensive in France and Belgium finally ran out of steam it was always possible that the war would end in a negotiated settlement resting upon the fact of an undefeated German army's superiority in Europe. In the early part of 1918 the Ottomans might have been able to obtain a separate peace based upon the grant of independence to Arabia and autonomy to other areas, but Ṭalʿat and Enver still believed they could do better with Germany. Not until August 1918 did the tide turn in Europe and still it was generally believed that the war would continue through 1919. As the Ottomans saw it they should continue to establish facts on the ground which would be the basis for claims at the peace. Despite the heavy defeats in Syria in September and October 1918 they could go on fighting so long as they could still draw on German support. Allenby's advance had far outrun his supplies and a further advance into Anatolia could scarcely be mounted before the spring of 1919.

It was the collapse of Bulgaria which sealed the fate of the Ottomans, partly because it broke the line of communications with Germany but mainly because it left Istanbul unprotected. Bulgaria had entered the war in October 1915 when the price of her support seemed right and the fortunes of the Entente were at a low ebb in the Near East following the failure at the Dardanelles. Part of the price was paid by the Ottomans through the concession of Thrace west of the Maritsa, but Bulgaria also looked to recover what she had lost to Serbia. The adhesion of Bulgaria and the Ottomans to the Central Powers determined the fate of the Balkans during the war. Serbia was crushed, Romania was easily defeated when she entered the war in August 1916 and Greece accomplished little. One party in Greece, led by King Constantine, sympathized with the Central Powers and favoured neutrality; the other, led by the magnetic prime minister, Venizelos, wanted to enter the war on the side of the Entente, seeing in this action the opportunity to secure gains at the expense of the Ottomans. The result was confusion until the deposition of Constantine in June 1917, after which Greece entered the war. By then a mixed Entente force had been established in Salonika (late 1915) where it was immobilized by malaria and a smaller Bulgarian army until 15 September 1918, when it broke out of the Salonika bridgehead, completely defeated the Bulgarian forces and forced Bulgaria to sue for an armistice (29 September 1918). One part of the force then wheeled right and advanced on Istanbul. On 1 October Germany informed the Ottomans that they were seeking peace and on 5 October the Ottomans asked for US help in arranging peace. The CUP government resigned on 13 October: a new government under Aḥmed ʿIzzet Pasha, composed mainly of politicians hostile to the CUP, sought an armistice.

The Ottoman collapse took Britain by surprise; less than a month earlier she had been planning fresh campaigns for 1919. British interest in a separate peace with the Ottomans had diminished; although Lloyd George favoured a quick peace he bowed to the military views that Britain should leave the final settlement to a peace conference and seek only a speedy armistice. France and Italy were also strongly against a peace in the autumn of 1918, no doubt fearing that British military predominance in the Near East would give Britain a preponderant voice in the settlement.

The Armistice of Mudros

The Cabinet were divided over what should be the terms of an armistice. Some, like Curzon and Austen Chamberlain, wanted hard terms – as the influential official, Ronald Graham, put it: "It is absolutely essential for us, if we wish for future peace and order in India, Egypt and the Moslem world, to show with unmistakable clearness that the Turk is beaten and is forced to accept such terms as we choose to offer".[7] Others, supported by the chief of the imperial general staff, Henry Wilson, wanted to offer the Ottomans mild terms. Still under the impression that the Germans and Austrians would go on fighting into 1919, Wilson was prepared to pay a high price to get the Straits open immediately so that Entente forces could be brought through Romania against Austria. In any case, it was argued, once in control of the Straits Britain could obtain whatever else she wanted.

The doves won the argument despite the strong expression of support for severe terms by the French and the Italians. Although a long list of demands was sent to the British negotiator, Admiral Gough-Calthorpe, he was told that he need obtain only the first four, of which by far the most important was the opening of the Straits. Indeed, to sweeten the pill Calthorpe was permitted to offer some guarantees about the future peace settlement if necessary. The remaining twenty suggested clauses Calthorpe could drop if he wished. These clauses included those suggested by the advocates of the hard line, notably the all-embracing clause seven, suggested by Italy, according to which the Allies were to have the right to occupy any strategic point. This clause, the Italians thought, might enable them to remedy, by introducing their own troops, some of the legal deficiencies of their own claims in Asia Minor.

The negotiations opened at Mudros on 27 October. The Ottoman delegation was inexperienced and unable to communicate with Istanbul. The delays in starting the negotiations also worked against the

Ottomans because it was becoming plain that the German and Austrian will to continue was flagging and, therefore, the importance of opening the Straits less than had appeared. Even so, if the Ottomans had understood the Allied eagerness to open the Straits they could have sold themselves more dearly. As it was they were obsessed with keeping the Greeks out of Istanbul and for promises concerning this they conceded everything on Calthorpe's shopping list. The armistice was signed on 30 October 1918. The Cabinet was delighted at the unexpected bonus. The Ottomans had thrown themselves on British mercy; they were to discover that this was a commodity in short supply.

NOTES

1. Quoted Ahmed Emin, *Turkey in the World War*, New York 1930, 109.
2. British memorandum to the Russian government, 27 Feb./12 March 1915, in J. C. Hurewitz (ed.), *The Middle East and North Africa in world politics*, II (1914–45), New Haven, Conn. 1979, 18.
3. Sir Henry McMahon to Sharif Ḥusayn, 24 March 1915, in Hurewitz, *Middle East and North Africa*, 50.
4. Quoted C. E. Dawn, *From Ottomanism to Arabism*, Urbana, Ill. 1973, 77.
5. Declaration to the Seven, 16 June 1918 in Hurewitz, *Middle East and North Africa*, 112.
6. Anglo-French Declaration, 7 Nov. 1918 in Hurewitz, *Middle East and North Africa*, 112.
7. Quoted V. H. Rothwell, *British war aims and peace diplomacy*, Oxford 1971, 240.

CHAPTER SIX:

The Remaking of the Near East 1918–1923

The defeat of the Ottoman empire and the prostration of Iran meant that the European powers, for the first time, had a free hand to impose what settlement they liked upon the Near East. Further, whereas in the past the European powers had been restrained by their own rivalries, the removal of Russia, Germany and Austria from the scene left only Britain, France and Italy directly concerned, and of those powers the position of Britain was dominant because of her military strength in the Near East. It seemed that, if she chose to exercise her power, nothing could prevent Britain from rebuilding the Near East in whatever style she preferred. In fact, Britain did not impose the settlement which she desired and the structure of the Near East which emerged by 1923 was the consequence of compromises between Britain and other European states and between Europe and a resurgent Near East. The subject of this chapter is the manner in which those compromises were achieved and the significance of the new pattern which appeared.

In contemplating the approach of the European powers to the Near East settlement it is necessary to bear in mind certain background factors. First and foremost was an unwillingness to consider fresh military exertions. Europeans were tired of war and there was a general desire for demobilization and reconstruction. Throughout the peace settlement one of the major preoccupations of military planners was to find the troops to police any settlement. Faced with this problem the British chief of the imperial general staff, Henry Wilson, identified three priority areas – Ireland, India and Egypt. Anything else was expendable. Against this calculation could be set an economic proposition; a favourable Near Eastern settlement might help to restore European economies by providing zones for future trade and investment. Such ideas played a considerable part in French and Italian thinking and a smaller role in British considerations.

A second factor is the European order of priorities. The main enemy had been Germany and the main task of the peace settlement was to try to ensure that Germany would not again disturb the peace of Europe. Accordingly, the first and largest efforts of the peacemakers were bent towards achieving a peace with Germany and a comprehensive settlement in central Europe. Such a settlement also had to take account of other factors, notably the threat posed by Bolshevism in Russia which was to be dealt with partly by direct intervention in Russia and partly by surrounding Russia with a ring of buffer states. Bolshevism was also the most prominent element in another major concern of the peacemakers, namely how to avoid revolution within their own countries. France escaped it, Britain confined revolution to Ireland, although it was feared that Britain itself might succumb, and Italy did eventually fall victim to the revolution of Mussolini's Fascists. The Near Eastern settlement had a lower priority than these matters. Once the chance of a quick agreement was let slip it was evidently going to be a long time before the Entente could give its mind to the region.

A third factor was the principles which had to be seen to underpin any settlement. The war had seen a drift of opinion away from the notion of multinational empires and towards that of the recognition of the general principle of nationality and of the rights of nations to self-determination as soon as they were thought fit to exercise that right. Partly, this development had been due to the circumstance that the three Central Powers had all been multinational states and therefore nationalism was a convenient weapon to use against them, the more so after Russia dropped out of the war. Partly, it was due to the advent of the United States; knowing little of foreign affairs Woodrow Wilson found it convenient to construct his foreign policy from first principles, and if nationality was not the first among principles it was a fashionable leader of the parade. Partly, it was a response to agitation within the colonial empires of the Entente, notably in India, where Britain committed herself in 1917 to a movement towards responsible government. And, partly, it was a reflection of a genuine conviction that self-determination offered a better way forward in political organization. Translated into the terms of the peace settlement this factor showed itself in a disposition to favour the emergence of small states corresponding as closely as possible to nations (albeit tempered by the need to reward friends and punish enemies), and to avoid annexations. It followed that if the needs and ambitions of Great Powers were to be satisfied new devices must be found to disguise their gains. Accordingly, there came into prominence the concepts of spheres of influence, of treaty arrangements with independent states and, above all, of mandates, an invention designed to reconcile the wants of Great Powers with the hopes of aspirant nations or, as some cynics put it, to cast a garb of respectability over the desire of the Great Powers to get their teeth into their former enemies' colonies. Although the latter proposition often more justly represented the reality it would be wrong to discount the element of moral fervour in those who made and carried out the settlement. The apparatus of international organization and the code of human rights which were established, the commitment to small nations and the notion of obligation, all represented a feeling which could not be discounted; deals had to be sold to people who believed in morality.

The last factor, and perhaps the most important, was prestige. The Entente had won a long and bitter struggle and it was important to demonstrate that it had won, both to convince people that the sufferings had been worth while and to persuade potential enemies that they would be very ill-advised to try their fortunes against such invincible foes. Rewards and punishments were not only part of a moral order and of a political reorganization but they were the outward and visible signs of power. In no area was this concept of prestige stronger than in the Near East. An Asian power had challenged the might of Europe and it had called upon Muslims everywhere to rise against their European rulers. It was of great importance to show that this attempt had failed miserably and that condign punishment awaited those who might try to emulate the Ottomans. Panislamism was to be taught a lesson.

PROBLEMS OF PEACEMAKING

It is now time to turn to the general problems involved in the Near Eastern peace settlement and to observe how they were influenced by the factors outlined above. Punishment of the transgressor and security against Panislamism were to be achieved primarily by weakening the Ottoman empire through detaching territory from it and by imposing upon the remainder some form of control; the alternative of reconstructing the Ottoman empire as an element of stability in the area was excluded. In this decision there was undoubtedly mixed a degree of hostility to Turks as such; the nineteenth-century liberal dislike for the Turk, inflamed by the war, found expression in the policies of Lloyd George and others.

The destruction of the Ottoman empire could be defended on the principle of nationality. Further, the invocation of the demands of the nationalities could also supply an answer to the problems of policing the settlement because the nations who gained would be expected to fight for the privileges bestowed upon them. And again, the creation of small national states could provide a basis for the continued influence of the European powers because these states could hardly stand alone and would require the protection and assistance of Great Powers. By their wartime declarations, notably the Fourteen Points (Point Twelve) and Lloyd George's Caxton Hall speech of 5 January 1918, the Allies were committed to the support of the claims of certain nationalities. There was broad agreement that Armenia, Syria, Mesopotamia, Palestine and Arabia should be separated from the Ottoman empire, and Kurdistan was later added to this list. There was no agreement, however, on the boundaries or the status of these countries.

The greatest problem in the Near Eastern peace settlement was that of the Straits. The Russian solution had now gone; control of the Straits could not be left to the Turks; the choice, therefore, was between one of the Entente powers, a new state or an international regime. As the mutual suspicions of the powers were too great to permit the adoption of either of the first two possibilities, there remained the creation of an international regime which, in its turn, linked with ideas of a new international order.

The key to a settlement of the Near Eastern problem was the adjustment of differences between the European powers themselves. It was plain that if Britain and France could agree on any course of action that course would prevail because Italy was in no position, legal or military, to object, and the United States could not or would not do much to affect the Near Eastern settlement. Subsequently it was claimed that the principal reason for delay in the Ottoman peace was the inability of Wilson to commit his country to the acceptance of mandates in the Near East and the need to wait for some final decision on this point. But there would have been no need to wait for the USA if Britain and France had been in agreement; the USA had not been at war with the Ottomans.

Britain and France already had in the Sykes–Picot Agreement the basis for a settlement of the Near East. If they could quickly agree on a suitable modification of that agreement to take account of the withdrawal of Russia and of other new factors a rapid Near Eastern settlement was possible. In December 1918 it seemed that Lloyd George and Clemenceau had achieved the basis of such an agreement. But, thereafter, Britain and France became divided and, although the eventual settlement did derive from a bargain made between them in December 1919, a year had been lost in which other crucial decisions had been made and the situation in the Near East had changed materially. In particular, by the time their settlement was presented at Sèvres they were no longer the only European powers who mattered because the return of Russia to the scene in 1920 represented a new factor which had to be taken into account in the final settlement of the Near East. The containment of Bolshevism was a significant factor in the British design for peace in the Near East.

At the end of 1918 France's chief aim was to reach agreement with Britain on the Near East. Clemenceau was uninterested in the region; his concern was with the Rhine and he was willing to buy British support in the German settlement with concessions in the Near East. The colonial party, on the other hand, was concerned to hold on to Syria which they saw as likely to slip away from France into the grasp of Britain; for them the best solution was confirmation of Sykes–Picot but if this could not be obtained they wanted at least confirmation of the French position in northern Syria and Lebanon. In December 1918 Clemenceau met Lloyd George and came to the understanding mentioned above; it was not written down in any formal agreement. The arrangement was that France would surrender her claim to Mosul to Britain and also allow Britain to undertake the administration of Palestine. In return she would have confirmation of her position in Syria, a share of the oil of Mosul and possibly other concessions in Africa, as well as support in Europe. It subsequently became clear that the British and French were not in agreement about what had been decided at this meeting and, in particular, about the degree of control France should have in Syria.

In coming to this verbal understanding with Clemenceau, Lloyd George had gone outside the formal machinery of British policy-making. During the course of 1918 policy-making for the Near East had been drawn together in an interdepartmental committee known as the Eastern Committee. The chairman and dominating personality in this committee was Lord Curzon. The Eastern Committee had spent much of its time in considering the settlement of the eastern part of the region – Iran, Transcaucasia, Turkestan and Iraq – but it had also looked at the western areas and had concluded that the Sykes–Picot arrangement was not a suitable basis for a settlement. In the Near East Allenby and his staff were also opposed to the Sykes–Picot Agreement and within that group were strong advocates of the Arab solution. Until there was peace or some other arrangement, Allenby, as the Allied commander in the theatre, was in charge of temporary arrangements and he refused to hand over more than local administrative control in coastal Syria and Lebanon to France. British troops remained in the area and final powers of decision with Allenby.

There was then no agreement within Britain on the policy to be followed and no disposition in Paris to follow up the Lloyd George–Clemenceau understanding. Although a proposal for the division of oil interests in Mosul was worked out between the two countries, Lloyd George refused to confirm it. Instead, the peacemakers in Paris listened to numerous submissions from the claimants to a share of the Ottoman inheritance.

When the peacemakers assembled in Paris in January 1919 there was no more than a very rough agreement on the outlines of an Ottoman peace with disputed wartime arrangements and tentative understandings to cover the details. Most of the peace was still to play for; indeed when the Ottoman delegation came to submit its own proposals in June 1919 these took the form of a plan for the continuation of the Ottoman empire, conceding only local autonomy to the Arab provinces and expressing a willingness to negotiate with Britain about the future of Cyprus. These proposals, however, were treated as absurd; the Ottomans would have to surrender much more than this to satisfy the claims upon them.

The principal claimants in Paris were the Armenians, the Greeks, the Arabs, the Zionists and the Iranians. Some of these groups were represented by more than one delegation; for example, the Armenian claims were presented by one delegation speaking for the Ottoman Armenians, another acting for the Republic of Armenia formed out of Russian territory and by some forty individual spokesmen. The claims of these various groups and individuals were in conflict. The practice of the Supreme Council was to refer the claims to specialized committees composed principally of officials. In some cases commissions were sent to examine the situation on the ground. While these investigations proceeded the council discussed various possible arrangements for the Near East. At the same time they were obliged to take decisions which, although they were said not to prejudice the final settlement, inevitably had an influence upon it.

The examination and discussion of Near Eastern questions went on during the first half of 1919 while the main attention of the council was devoted to the European settlement. At the time the council broke up in July 1919 no decisions on the Near East had been reached. The plans which had been sketched out were dependent upon the acceptance by the United States of mandates for Armenia and the Straits. By November 1919 it was apparent that the United States would not accept any responsibilities in the Near East. Britain and France, having patched up some of their differences over Syria by the Deauville Agreement of September 1919 (see below, p. 324), decided to discuss the basis of an

Ottoman peace treaty. These discussions took place in London in December 1919 and were followed by the Conference of London (February–April 1920) when Italy and other parties were drawn into the discussions and detailed drafts prepared which were adopted with modifications at the Conference of San Remo (April 1920) and embodied in the Treaty of Sèvres reluctantly signed by the Ottomans on 10 August 1920. That part of the Sèvres settlement which related to the non-Turkish parts of the Ottoman empire became the basis of the final settlement of the Near East in those areas, but that part which related to Anatolia and Thrace was successfully challenged by the Turkish Nationalists and remodelled in the Treaty of Lausanne, 24 July 1923. Simpler than describing the process of the negotiation and partial undoing of the Treaty of Sèvres as a whole, will be to examine the various parts of the settlement relating to different countries of the Near East. It should be remembered, however, that the treaty represented a package in which certain elements were traded off against others by the Great Powers.

ANATOLIA AND THRACE

One major factor in the Anatolian settlement was the role of Greece. In Paris the Greek claims were presented by the prime minister, Eleftherios Venizelos (1864–1936). Venizelos was a man of great ability who made a lasting impression upon all who encountered him. After his first meeting with Venizelos in December 1912 Lloyd George remarked: "He is a big man, a very big man."[1] Lloyd George's faith in Venizelos was to be a significant factor in the Near Eastern settlement. During the war Venizelos had committed himself wholly to the Entente and finally had brought Greece into the war on the side of the Allies. He had the reputation of a moderate but there was nothing moderate about the Greek claims he presented and which included southern Albania, the whole of Thrace, all the islands of the eastern Mediterranean and western Asia Minor.

The Greek claims produced a mixed reaction and considerable opposition within many delegations. While they were still being considered, however, it was decided, in May 1919 to send Greek troops to Izmir, nominally to preserve order but actually to administer a rebuff to Italy. Italy, discontented with proposed arrangements for the disposition of Fiume, had walked out of the council. Further, under the provisions of Article 7 of the Armistice of Mudros Italian troops had moved into the province of Adalia and threatened to pre-empt council decisions on Asia Minor. The establishment of Greek troops in Izmir would check Italian ambitions. But, although there is no direct conclusive evidence on the point, there is also a strong suspicion that some of those concerned in the transaction were principally concerned to provide the Greek claims with some substance on the ground. Although it was agreed, at Clemenceau's insistence, that the decision to send in Greek troops would not prejudice the eventual settlement, it soon became clear that it had done so. In the hands of so skilful a debater as Venizelos the Greek action came to constitute a moral claim on the council.

The Greek landing at Izmir on 15 May 1919 had three main effects. First, it contributed to a resolution of the differences between Italy and Greece who contrived an agreement about their conflicting claims in Thrace, Albania, the Mediterranean and western Anatolia in July 1919. Second, it provided strong support for the Greek claim to part of Asia Minor. A Greek administration was established in Izmir and a Greek army assembled which was available for further expansion or for policing the eventual settlement. For the time being it was decided to limit the extent of Greek-controlled territory, but other proposals to replace the Greek force with an international Allied force were not implemented. Third, the Greek intervention was the decisive event in launching the Turkish armed struggle against the Allied attempt to impose a settlement on the Near East. Immediately after the Greek landing there were reports of Greek atrocities against Muslim civilians, which were later substantiated by a committee of inquiry (October 1919). These Greek actions fuelled an already strong detestation of the Greeks in Anatolia and Thrace.

Among Ottomans there was a great variety of opinions concerning their ultimate goals and the means of obtaining them. Two main currents of opinion may be discerned in 1919. The first, which was followed by the sultan and many members of the old Liberal Party, held that the Ottomans were in no condition to resist the Allies and that the best hope lay in blaming members of the CUP for past sins and persuading the Allies (Britain or the United States) to become the protectors of the empire. Those who followed the second current, who included many former members of the CUP, believed that it was useless to look for mercy from the Allies and that such a policy would only expose the empire to dismemberment for the benefit of the European powers, the Greeks and the Armenians. In their hostility to the claims of the Greeks and Armenians the members of this group could appeal to powerful Muslim sentiments within the empire. They advocated resistance to Allied and other demands, if necessary by arms. From December 1918 scattered local resistance groups, known as Societies for the Defence of Rights, appeared in many areas and defied both the Allies and the official Ottoman government in Istanbul, although it was plain that they had sympathizers within the government. But a more concerted resistance had to depend upon organized Ottoman forces and these survived in considerable numbers only in eastern Asia Minor where they offered some protection to the local inhabitants against the claims of the Greeks and Armenians. It was the object of the Allies and the official Ottoman government to exercise fuller control over these forces and to carry out the demobilization which had been agreed. For that purpose and to restore order in May 1919 General Muṣṭafā Kemāl was sent to eastern Asia Minor as inspector-general of the Ninth Army.

In eastern Asia Minor Muṣṭafā Kemāl assumed leadership of what became known as the Nationalist movement. At a meeting at Amasya in June 1919 it was agreed to set up a national resistance movement and in July–August at the Congress of Erzerum a declaration was issued proclaiming the goals of the movement for the defence of the eastern provinces. Similar congresses were held in other regions and representatives of all the groups came together at Sivas in September 1919 and amalgamated to form the Society for the Defence of the Rights of Anatolia and Rumelia. The goals of the movement were set out in what became known as the National Pact and which reproduced most of the Erzerum formula. All territories within the national boundaries at the time of the armistice which were inhabited by a Muslim majority were declared to be an integral part of the state. The society set up an executive committee under the leadership of Muṣṭafā Kemāl and this committee assumed the direction of the campaign.

In 1919 the Nationalist movement was weak and divided. The strongest impulses were those of loyalty to Islam and the sultan and of hostility to infidel domination. Accordingly, Muṣṭafā Kemāl first sought agreement with the sultan based on the replacement of the government of Damad Ferīd Pasha with one better disposed to the Nationalists and more willing to stand up to Allied demands. In this he was successful. After failing to secure Allied aid in crushing the Nationalist movement Damad Ferīd resigned and the new government of ʿAlī Rižā Pasha included members sympathetic to the Nationalists. On 22 October an uneasy agreement between government and Nationalists was reached at Amasya. Elections to the Ottoman Parliament were then held and a Nationalist majority was the result. The new Parliament met in Istanbul in January 1920 and promptly adopted the National Pact. Violent resistance continued in the provinces.

Anatolia in the Sèvres settlement

In their plans for an Ottoman peace treaty Allied leaders took little account of the emergence of a Nationalist movement in 1919. It is true that the plans for the wholesale partition of Anatolia, adumbrated in discussions during the early part of 1919, were dropped in November 1919, but this was largely to suit the convenience of Britain and France. In early 1919 it had been envisaged that Thrace and Anatolia would have been divided into territories under the control of France, Italy, Greece and the United States through the mandate device, but the withdrawal of the United States and the desire of the other powers to restrict Italy led to a decision that there should be no mandates in Anatolia but only spheres of influence for Italy and France. Italy and France would have liked full economic and administrative control in their respective spheres, but because of British opposition their claims were eventually reduced until the spheres of influence consisted of areas within which other powers would observe what was called a self-denying ordinance. This arrangement was formalized in an elaborate Tripartite Treaty. Second, it was decided that there should be no independent state at the Straits. Lloyd George and Curzon had wanted to exclude the Ottomans from Istanbul and persuaded France to agree, but they were forced to reverse their position when their colleagues in the British Cabinet decided, under the influence of arguments about the evil effects which Ottoman expulsion from Istanbul would have in India and the greater ease with which the Ottomans could be controlled if they were given Istanbul, that the Ottomans should be left in control of Istanbul. This decision also ruled out the possibility that Istanbul might have been given to Greece, although such a move would have been strongly opposed by France and Italy which were coming to perceive Greece as an arm of British influence in the Near East. In place of an independent state in the area, it was decided that control of the Straits should be vested in an international commission with extensive powers. Military occupation of the Straits zone was to continue.

Greece was, however, given extensive territories including the whole of Thrace (apart from a small area around the Straits) and Izmir. The arrangement for Izmir caused much controversy and was a compromise. Izmir was to remain under Greek control but Ottoman sovereignty for two (later increased to five) years, at the end of which time the inhabitants would be free to choose to unite with Greece if they so wished. The arrangement was virtually an incitement to Greece so to conduct the administration of Izmir as to induce Muslims to depart and Greeks to settle and to ensure the required majority. No part of the settlement aroused greater opposition than this acquiescence in Greek claims to Izmir; indeed supporters of the arrangement were few and it may be said that the Greeks would not have been given Izmir but for two circumstances: the unfailing support of Lloyd George for Greece and the fact that the Greeks were already there. The Allied representatives in Istanbul all protested against this element in the settlement and said it would make it impossible for them to form a moderate party in Istanbul which would be willing to work the settlement. The effect of the cession of Izmir to Greece would be to play into the hands of the Nationalist opponents of the Allies and would mean that the Allies would have to enforce the treaty with forces provided by themselves. The Allied leaders refused to make any change in the terms of the treaty.

Armenia received rather different treatment. The more extensive Armenian claims for a Greater Armenian state stretching from the Black Sea to the Mediterranean were dismissed. Quite apart from the thinness of the Armenian population in the western area of Cilicia that region was intended to constitute a French sphere. It was decided that Armenia should consist of a nucleus of the former Russian Armenian territories together with an area of Ottoman eastern Asia Minor. There was dispute about the size of this area. The Armenians wanted it to be as large as possible and to include Erzerum and an outlet to the Black Sea. They found some support among the Allies, but Lloyd George opposed the gift of Erzerum to the Armenians and urged that Armenia should be confined to a much smaller area. In the end it was decided to refer the dispute to President Wilson for solution and Wilson awarded the Armenians the larger territory including Erzerum and Trebizond on the Black Sea. The United States, however, would not help the Armenians to conquer and keep this territory and none of the other powers would offer military assistance, so it was left to the Armenians to implement this part of the settlement themselves. It was made plain to the Armenians that they should expect no military aid, but the Armenian delegation of Ervatis Aharonian stated that they looked for no such help and would manage with financial help and the assistance of volunteers who were expected to come forward, especially from the Armenian community in the United States.

A second political unit was also projected in eastern Asia Minor. This was Kurdistan. It had been anticipated by Britain that an independent state of Kurdistan would be created both as a way of disposing of the Kurdish territories and as a means of weakening the Ottomans.

Three main difficulties were encountered. First, there was the problem of separating the Kurdish from the Armenian lands as the same lands were claimed by both groups and the populations were still intermingled even after the massacres of Armenians. In any case the Armenians always took the view that it was unreasonable to allow the circumstance that the Armenian inhabitants had been murdered or expelled to influence the decision on the future government of these lands against the Armenian claim; to do so would be to allow the criminals to profit from their crime; rather, the murders and expulsions constituted part of the moral claim of the Armenians to these lands. It was suggested that the problem might be solved by appointing the United States mandatory for both Armenia and Kurdistan, but that project collapsed and no one else wanted the dual burden. Nor could there have been easy agreement between Britain and France about which of them might take a mandate for Kurdistan. At one time a Franco-British condominium was proposed but Britain rejected this solution as a recipe for trouble.

The second problem was that many Britons, notably those connected with the administration of Iraq, had no wish to see assigned to Kurdistan territories which they believed were necessary for the viability and defence of Iraq. If there was to be a Kurdistan it could not include Mosul, but a Kurdistan without Mosul would be a disturbing presence in the region. A further problem concerned the possible effect of a Kurdistan upon the Kurdish areas of Iran.

The third and greatest problem was the difficulty of finding representative Kurdish leaders. In Paris were a group of Western-educated Kurdish intellectuals, led by Sharīf Pasha, who talked Kurdish nationalism but who could not show that they had followers in Kurdistan. In Istanbul was a so-called Kurdish Club under Sayyid ʿAbd al-Qādir, which negotiated both with the British and the Ottoman government in search of the best deal. And in Kurdistan was a puzzling group of local tribal leaders among whom some Britons affected to find the true spirit of Kurdish nationalism and others to discern no more than Muslim and tribal loyalties. It is also true that very many Kurds fought on the side of the Turkish Nationalists, regarding themselves not as Kurds but as Ottoman Muslims. In the absence of convincing Kurdish leaders it was impossible to say that there should be a Kurdish state. Accordingly, it was determined by the Treaty of Sèvres that Kurdistan should remain under Ottoman sovereignty (the Ottoman government having indicated its willingness to concede a measure of autonomy), but the possibility of a Kurdish state was kept open by the provision that within a year the Kurds could petition the League of Nations for recognition of their independent statehood.

Shorn of Armenian territories and of Thrace, Izmir and possibly Kurdistan, and with very limited authority over the Straits region the surviving Ottoman state, now almost wholly confined to Anatolia, was to be kept in order through French and Italian influence in their spheres, by financial controls imposed on the new state, by the new arrangements for the Ottoman Public Debt which for France was a major interest, by special provisions for the treatment of minorities and the continuation of the capitulations, and by the reduction of its armed forces to no more than 15,000 plus a gendarmerie of about 35,000. It was understood that this harsh settlement would be resisted and the military authorities calculated that 27 divisions would be required to police the settlement. Once it was decided to offer no assistance to the Armenians the requirement was reduced to 23 of which the Allies were to produce 19 and the Greeks 3, leaving 1 division unprovided.

Having decided on a harsh peace the Allies were determined to show that they were resolved to uphold it. Accordingly, when news was received during the Conference of London of a massacre of Armenians by resistance forces at Marash and this event was placed alongside other evidence of Nationalist assertiveness, it was decided to demonstrate Allied indignation by some signal measure of retaliation. On 16 March 1919 Istanbul was formally occupied, the government thought to be sympathetic to the Nationalists forced to resign, Damad Ferīd restored to power, several Nationalists arrested and deported and the Parliament suspended and shortly dissolved. The new government denounced the Nationalists and the Shaykh al-Islām issued a *fetvā* against them, proclaiming it a religious duty for Muslims to slay them. Muṣṭafā Kemāl and other leaders were sentenced to death in their absence.

The Nationalist recovery

The occupation of Istanbul in March 1920 was a crucial event in the post-war history of the Near East because it ended the possibility that some compromise might have been found between the moderate group around the sultan and moderate elements among the Nationalists and a block formed which would have been willing to implement the Treaty of Sèvres in something like the form in which it was drafted. The division between the sultan's government and the Nationalists also posed problems of legitimacy for the latter. In the short run the Nationalists employed traditional arguments, arguing that their allegiance to the sultan was unimpaired but that the sultan was in captivity, and persuading leading members of the ulema to issue *fetvās* against the government in Istanbul which was held to be executing the will of the infidel. But in the longer term the Nationalists had to develop new modes of legitimizing their actions and an important step in this direction was the summoning of a new assembly to meet at Ankara. This assembly, opened on 23 April 1920, was known as the Grand National Assembly and it embodied a claim to authority based upon the will of the people as represented by itself. Even so, the assembly proceeded slowly and reluctantly along this revolutionary course; its first session was preceded by an elaborate religious ceremony and a proclamation which made no mention of Turkey or of Turks but referred only to the need to save religion's last country.

The Grand National Assembly was very divided. It was composed of 92 deputies who had previously been elected to the Istanbul Parliament, 14 who had returned from exile and 232 deputies newly elected to the Ankara Assembly. There was then a majority of new men but they were still drawn from the old ruling class of the Ottoman state and consisted of former government officials, army officers, professional men and ulema. In no sense were they radicals; there was only a single worker and no peasant, although there were five Kurdish chiefs. Their strongest impulses were to preserve as much as possible of the old Ottoman system that they knew and they perceived the sultan and Islam as pillars of stability. Notions of popular sovereignty were suspect because they seemed to point in the direction of the Bolshevik Revolution and neither the ulema nor the Westernizers (many of them former members of the CUP) wished to travel along that path. To most of the delegates Turkish Nationalist doctrines appeared as an unwelcome leap in the dark when applied to politics. They wished to regard their own assumption of authority as merely temporary and destined to cease when the sultan was freed from bondage. Not until January 1921 did Muṣṭafā Kemāl persuade the assembly to recognize that sovereignty resided in the nation and in the Grand National Assembly as the representative of the nation: executive power was then delegated to a Cabinet under its president Muṣṭafā Kemāl.

In 1920 the Nationalists were in a critical position. Apart from the Greeks in the west, the French in the south and the Armenians in the east they had to contend with the army of the caliphate, a heterogeneous force sent against them by the Istanbul government, and with numerous rebellions which were essentially responses to the religious call from Istanbul. The anti-Nationalist forces included Circassian bandits, peasants, local religious leaders, tribal forces, local notables and conservative townsmen. Against these religiously inspired uprisings the regular army of the Nationalists was unreliable and to crush the opposition Muṣṭafā Kemāl was obliged to rely on similar irregular forces composed mainly of ex-bandits and led by a Circassian, Ethem Bey. Ethem became the principal military support of the so-called Green Army, formed in the spring of 1920. The Green Army was a political rather than a military organization and included elements of radical socialism (represented by members of the newly formed Turkish Communist Party), Muslim fervour and nationalism. The growth of the Green Army was an index of the strength of what was known as the Eastern ideal within the Nationalist ranks. Hostility to the West as the author of Sèvres led to a turning to the East and an idealization of the Bolshevik Revolution as representing a new pattern of development which could be harmonized with Islam. During 1920 the radical Left came more and more to dominate the Green Army, which began to appear as a challenge to the authority of Muṣṭafā Kemāl.

For the time being Muṣṭafā Kemāl temporized with the Left and attempted to control them by manœuvre. In October 1920 he established his own, loyal Communist Party as a rival magnet for radicals, and strengthened the laws and began propaganda against undesirable communism. By the end of 1920 the civil war was won and Muṣṭafā Kemāl was able to adopt stronger measures against the radicals and the wild irregular forces. In January 1920 he defeated Ethem, who fled to join the Greeks, and the so-called disloyal Communist Party of Turkey was closed down. The irregular forces were incorporated into the regular Nationalist forces. By the end of 1920 the Nationalists were in a much stronger position: the divisions within their own ranks were reduced and the forces of the sultan were defeated.

The return of Russia as a factor in the Near East also aided the Nationalists. As early as 26 April 1920 the Nationalists had appealed to Soviet Russia for assistance and in the summer of the same year sent a mission to Moscow. The Nationalists sought an offensive and defensive alliance but the Bolsheviks were less enthusiastic because of mistrust of Nationalist aims in Transcaucasia and a conviction that an alliance with the Nationalists would make it more difficult to obtain the agreement with Britain which they sought. No alliance was then signed and in the autumn of 1920 relations between the Nationalists and the Soviet state became very strained because of the Nationalist attack on Armenia. Continued concern about Armenian ambitions and activities and irritation at the Armenian refusal to allow supplies to pass through Armenia from Russia to the Nationalists led to a Nationalist invasion of Armenia in the autumn of 1920, the defeat of the Armenians and the acceptance by them of the Treaty of Alexandropol (2 December 1920). The treaty was never ratified because the Bolsheviks seized control of Armenia and the continuation of disputes about the frontier and other matters soured relations between the Nationalists and the Russians.

An alliance between Soviet Russia and the Nationalists was finally concluded on 18 March 1921 (Treaty of Moscow, dated 16 March 1921). Both sides would have preferred a satisfactory agreement with Britain but finding that impossible to obtain they settled for each other. Their alliance continued to be an uneasy one and little assistance reached the Nationalists from Soviet Russia during most of 1921. The Bolsheviks disliked Muṣṭafā Kemāl's treatment of the radical Left elements in the Nationalist ranks and for some time believed that he might be overthrown by groups loyal to Enver Pasha. However, the Nationalist success at the Sakarya in the summer of 1921 (see below, p. 318) persuaded the Russians to deal with Muṣṭafā Kemāl, and the Treaty of Kars (13 October 1921) settled the issues at dispute between the Nationalists and the Transcaucasian states and fixed the eastern frontier of Turkey. The possession of Kars and Ardahan, lost by the Ottomans in 1878, recovered in 1918 and lost again in 1920, was now secured to the future Turkish republic. After the signature of this agreement and a separate treaty with the Ukraine (2 January 1922) relations between Russia and the Nationalists rapidly improved and supplies of arms and other equipment were an important factor in the re-equipment of the Nationalist forces ready for the successful campaign of the summer of 1922.

The alliance of the Nationalists and Soviet Russia caused much concern in Britain, where it was seen as an alliance of Bolshevism and Panislamism which could menace British interests throughout the Near East and India. It was argued that Britain must break the alliance by detaching one party or the other. The Indian government and the War Office favoured an attempt to win over the Nationalists and create in Islam a solid barrier to Bolshevism in the East. Winning over the Nationalists required the abandonment of Sèvres. Lloyd George, however, appears throughout to have favoured an agreement with Soviet Russia making the abandonment of anti-British activities in the East a condition of recognition of the Soviet regime, the cessation of British support for the White Russian forces and a trade treaty. An Anglo-Russian agreement, it was thought, would leave the Nationalists isolated and make possible their defeat and the confirmation of the Sèvres settlement. The result would turn on the outcome of the conflict between the Nationalists and the Greeks.

The Greco-Turkish War (1920–2) and the Lausanne Settlement

The Ottoman reaction to the rigour of the Treaty of Sèvres made it clear that if the Allies would not moderate its severity they would have to enforce the treaty by arms. The successes of the Nationalist forces at Bursa and Pandorma created a threat to Istanbul itself. At Ismid, on 15 June 1920, the Nationalists clashed with British forces. France and Italy would have accepted a modification of Sèvres but Britain insisted on upholding the treaty by the use of Greek troops. Their employment was sanctioned in June 1920 and the Greek forces quickly dispersed the Nationalist forces in north-west Asia Minor. At that moment, if the Greek forces had pressed on against the main Nationalist strongholds in central Anatolia they might have achieved a complete victory because the Nationalists were at their most vulnerable. Venizelos, however, had agreed to stop the Greek advance at Pandorma and, instead, he turned the Greek forces against Eastern Thrace, with the result that the next Greek campaign in Anatolia was postponed until 1921 when the Nationalists were stronger. Also, by that time Venizelos himself had fallen from power.

The death of King Alexander on 25 October 1920 turned the Greek election in November into a struggle between Venizelos and his old enemy ex-King Constantine. Venizelos lost and in December 1920 Constantine returned to the throne. These events had a considerable effect upon the place of Greece in Allied strategy in Asia Minor because while Venizelos had a claim on Allied gratitude Constantine had none and for those who wanted to drop the Greeks his return provided a fine opportunity. France, Italy and many Britons wanted to take the chance that was offered but Lloyd George held firm; there would be no modification of Sèvres although there would be no financial support for Greece either – henceforth Greece was on her own apart from the hints of encouragement which Lloyd George continued to offer.

In 1921 Greece had a choice; she could withdraw from her advanced positions, remain on the defensive and hope to negotiate a settlement with the Ottomans, or she could advance and stake all on defeating the Nationalists with the possible prize of a much larger share of Asia Minor and, perhaps, Istanbul itself if she were successful. She chose to advance. At the London conference held in February 1921 the Greeks argued that the Nationalists were very weak and could be defeated in three months. They were not interested in a negotiated settlement with the Nationalists who were also represented at the conference. It seems unlikely, however, that a negotiated settlement would have lasted because the Ankara government subsequently made it clear that it would accept no modification of the National Pact despite the indications to the contrary offered by the Nationalist representative, Bekir Sāmī. Britain remained officially neutral and refused to join France and Italy in pressing for a renegotiation of Sèvres. The Greeks were left with the impression that they had been encouraged by Britain to attack.

The Greek offensive was launched on 23 March but was held at the second battle of Inönü and obliged to withdraw to its start line. This was the first serious setback suffered by Greek forces in Asia Minor (the repulse of their attempt to take Eskishehir in January 1921 at the first battle of Inönü was not a significant test) and it prompted the Greeks to re-examine their position. The future dictator, Ioannis Metaxas, argued in favour of the abandonment of Asia Minor and concentration in Thrace, but the government decided that its position demanded a victory and planned a second offensive for the summer of 1921 after the army had been reinforced. Britain, however, was also concerned by the Greek failure because, if the Greeks withdrew unilaterally to Izmir, Istanbul and the Straits would be left uncovered as they had been in the summer of 1920 and the Nationalist attack might fall on the Allied forces there. Accordingly, Britain offered mediation on the basis of a Greek withdrawal and an autonomous Izmir. The Greeks refused and began their summer offensive on 10 July. The Greek summer offensive of 1921 enjoyed considerable initial success, but the Nationalists retreated in good order and took their stand in front of Ankara on the River Sakarya, where the Greek advance was held, and in September 1921 the Greeks fell back to Eskishehir. The battle of the Sakarya was a turning-point in the struggle for it represented the defeat of the Greek hopes of a military solution. Their hopes now rested on the ability and willingness of the Allies to salvage something for them by diplomatic negotiation. In the meantime they elected to stay in their positions so that they had territory with which to bargain.

France and Italy were also seeking a political solution to their difficulties. They had never liked the Greek gains in the peace settlement and suspected that the Greeks were no more than the agents of a British design for the mastery of the eastern Mediterranean. From the summer of 1920 the two Continental powers had been willing to throw over the Greeks and make an agreement with the Nationalists. They wanted, however, to retain other gains from Sèvres, and this desire made agreement difficult. In March 1921 both had negotiated agreements with Bekir Sāmī only to find that the Ankara government would not accept them. But, on 20 October 1921, France did succeed in negotiating an agreement with the Nationalists (the Franklin–Bouillon Agreement) by which France agreed to withdraw from Asia Minor and the frontier of Syria was settled. Nationalist negotiations were also conducted with Italy, although these failed to result in agreement.

The reluctance of France and Italy to offer any support for Greece made it difficult for Britain to achieve a negotiated settlement. Throughout the autumn and winter of 1921–2 Curzon strove to open a negotiation on the basis of an autonomous Izmir and a Greek Thrace. In the meantime the Greek plight grew more desperate and they began to contemplate a unilateral withdrawal. Still they hung on in the hope that something would come out of the negotiations. Eventually, in March 1922, Curzon assembled a conference of Allied foreign ministers in Paris and produced an offer of a Greek withdrawal from Asia Minor without guarantees for the Christians of Asia Minor, and a compromise frontier in Thrace. But the negotiations broke down over the Nationalist demand that the Greeks should begin their withdrawal before the peace agreement was signed. The offer was chiefly important as pointing the way towards the eventual settlement at Lausanne.

After the failure of the March negotiation the obvious course for the Greeks was to withdraw to defensible lines around Izmir but at this point fantasy began to direct Greek policy; the Greeks stayed in their positions and planned a seizure of Istanbul, although this latter project was abandoned in July in the face of Allied opposition. In the meantime the Nationalists prepared the offensive which they launched on 26 August 1922 near Afyon Karaḥiṣār. The Greek front collapsed and a disastrous retreat did not end until the Greek troops left Asia Minor. On 9 September the Nationalists entered Izmir which became the scene of murder and destruction.

The Greek collapse re-created the situation of 1920 in a much more serious form. With the Greek shield gone nothing stood between the victorious Nationalist forces and Istanbul and Thrace except for the Allied garrison in the Straits zone. Would the Allies fight? On 15 September Britain called upon the Dominions to help but only New Zealand agreed. On 19 September Poincaré said France would not fight and the Italians made it clear that they would not do so either. Britain apparently had the choice between fighting and ignominious surrender to the Nationalists with the dreaded loss of prestige throughout the East. The Cabinet decided to fight and ordered that the Nationalists should be given an ultimatum. But the crisis was in the end averted; restraint by the local military commanders saved the day and on 11 October the Convention of Mudanya provided a compromise. The Greeks withdrew from Eastern Thrace and the path was open for a full renegotiation of Sèvres. There was one important casualty of the so-called Chanak crisis, however, and that was Lloyd George. The Conservative Party had been so incensed at what was seen as the foolhardy policy of Lloyd George in risking war without support that they voted to withdraw from the Coalition which fell from power. Lloyd George was replaced as Prime Minister by Bonar Law at the head of a Conservative Cabinet.

The Near Eastern settlement was renegotiated at the Conference of Lausanne (December 1922–July 1923). The conference involved all the parties to the Near Eastern question except one, the official government of the Ottoman empire. Since the end of 1920 the Ottoman government had been powerless to affect the course of events but it had remained the only government recognized by the Allies and was therefore invited to the conference along with the Nationalists. It was plain to Muṣṭafā Kemāl that the presence of two Ottoman delegations which could be played off against one another was intolerable and the invitation precipitated a crucial decision by the Grand National Assembly, namely the abolition of the sultanate on 1 November 1922, thereby clearing the way for the later establishment of the Turkish republic. Only one Turkish delegation appeared at Lausanne, that of the Nationalists led by ʿIṣmet Inönü.

The leading figure on the Allied side at Lausanne was the British foreign secretary, Lord Curzon. Until October 1922 Curzon had worked in the shadow of Lloyd George carrying out a policy in which he did not believe. Nevertheless, he had supported Lloyd George principally through a conviction that the greatest issue at stake in the Near East was Allied prestige. The Allies could not afford to bow to force; any change in the Sèvres settlement must be one properly negotiated and agreed by all parties. Accordingly, throughout the period 1920–2 he had devoted his main effort to trying to hold together Britain, France and Italy in support of an agreed policy, although in the face of the search by France and Italy for a separate agreement with the Nationalists he had found the achievement of that end increasingly difficult. Before the Lausanne Conference opened, however, he was successful in establishing among the principal Allied powers broad agreement on the policy they should pursue, despite the fact that his own government was tired of the Near Eastern business and inclined to surrender to the Nationalists on several issues. At the conference Curzon was able to secure most of the points he thought essential. His success was due to his diplomatic skill and to the circumstance that the Nationalists were willing to meet him more than half-way.

Some features of the Near Eastern settlement were left intact at Lausanne, in particular those affecting the Arab provinces. Although many Nationalists wished to continue the struggle to liberate other parts of the Ottoman empire, Muṣṭafā Kemāl saw that any attempt to challenge the arrangements for the Arab provinces would precipitate war with Britain and France and jeopardize all the gains so painfully won by the Nationalists. Other features of the old settlement had already sunk into oblivion and were not resurrected, including the proposals relating to Armenia and Kurdistan. The eastern settlement was left as it had been agreed by the Nationalists and the Soviet Union. The fate of the Greek claims in Asia Minor had already been decided by war, France and Italy had abandoned their projected spheres of influence in Asia Minor, and the southern frontier of the Turkish state had been agreed with France. Alexandretta had been left in an ambiguous position in that settlement but that issue was not raised at Lausanne. What remained to be determined, therefore, was the frontier of Turkey with British-controlled Iraq (involving the disposition of Mosul), the frontier of Turkey with Greece in Thrace, the future arrangements for the Straits, and a number of questions involving the capitulations, the treatment of minorities and finance.

The territorial questions were quickly settled by agreement. Britain and the Nationalists could not agree on who should have Mosul but they did agree a procedure for settling the matter by negotiation and reference to the League of Nations. The Thracian frontier was settled by confirming the Maritsa as the frontier between Turkish Eastern Thrace and Greek Western Thrace; Edirne was left to Turkey. The question of the Straits threatened great problems because the Nationalists had agreed in March 1921 with the Soviet formula that the arrangements for the Straits were a matter for the Black Sea powers alone, and the Soviet delegate, Chicherin, wanted the Straits closed to all warships except those of Turkey. It was claimed a great success for Curzon that he broke the Soviet–Nationalist alliance on the Straits, but in fact the Nationalists' concern was to establish Turkish sovereignty and control in the Straits and they had no wish to share this with the Soviet Union. Allied support for such a Straits arrangement was a valuable support for the Turks and Curzon was pressing on a half-open door. The new regime for the Straits provided for the passage of warships through the Straits subject to certain restrictions, a small demilitarized zone along the Straits, an international commission to superintend the operation of the convention and permission for Turkey to garrison Istanbul.

The non-territorial questions caused greater difficulties and their solution prolonged the conference to July 1923, a period of sustained tension because it seemed possible that at any time the Nationalists might seize Istanbul, clash with the British garrison and precipitate war. Cool nerves enabled those concerned to get through without a breakdown although the atmosphere may have contributed to Turkish victory on almost all the outstanding points. The capitulations were abolished, an Allied face-saving formula adopted on the treatment of minorities (a matter which was solved chiefly by an exchange of populations between Greece and Turkey), and the Sèvres plans for Allied economic and financial control were all dropped.

By 1923 a significant part of the Entente plan for the remodelling of the Near East had failed. There were four reasons for this. First, the Allies were unwilling or unable to implement their solution themselves. This circumstance was due to the divisions between them and the general reluctance of their peoples to accept new burdens in the Near East. Second, the Greeks and the Armenians were too weak to undertake the main duty of policing the settlement themselves. Third, the return of Russia to the scene was a major factor operating against the Entente scheme. And, fourth, the determination of the Nationalists and the military, political and diplomatic skills of their leaders were ultimately decisive.

SYRIA AND LEBANON

In Paris during the early months of 1919 appeared several Arab delegations with different proposals for the future of Syria, Lebanon and Palestine. Some of these represented Christian groups. One, the Central Syrian Committee of Shukrī Ghānim, who had lived in France for many years, proposed a large Syria under French mandate; a Maronite delegation which included Émile Eddé asked for a Greater Lebanon under French protection; another Maronite delegation under the Maronite patriarch asked for a Lebanese state within its "historic and natural frontiers". The majority Sunnī Muslim community was represented principally by Fayṣal ibn Ḥusayn who demanded independence for all the Arab states south of the Taurus mountains. He did not, however, maintain a claim for a single Arab state. The Arab people were one, he declared on his return to Syria, but the time was not ripe for one government; Syria, Iraq and the Hijaz should each enjoy their separate independence. Later, for tactical reasons, he reopened the idea of a single state of Syria and Iraq, but in Paris he asked for an independent Syria including Lebanon and Palestine within which he offered concessions to minorities and privileges to the European powers.

The council was divided. France wished to stand by the Sykes–Picot arrangement, which she now translated into a demand for a mandate over all Syria. Britain sought assurances that the Arab state would be left substantial independence in the interior. In an effort to break the deadlock Woodrow Wilson proposed that a commission of inquiry should be sent to discover the wishes of the people of the area. This scheme was approved on 25 March but France did not want it and for a time Britain supported France. As Lloyd George put it, "For us, the friendship of France is worth ten Syrias."[2] Also, Britain believed that the commission would be rendered unnecessary by agreement between Fayṣal and the French. But no agreement appeared and it was decided that, after all, the commission should go. But France refused to take part unless Britain evacuated Syria and Britain and Italy would not take part without France. So the King–Crane Commission became purely an American venture. In fact it is doubtful if even Wilson wanted it; his purpose seems to have been to use the threat of the commission to extract concessions from France, and Britain seems to have regarded it in the same way. The commission did visit Syria in the summer of 1919 and submitted a report on 28 August to the effect that only the Catholic community was in favour of French rule; the majority of the people wanted independence and if they had to have a mandatory wanted only one for the whole area, preferably the United States or Britain, but not France. However, the report was not published and was ignored.

While waiting for a report which it did not want the council had taken no decision on the future of Syria. Certain negative decisions had been taken, however. Wilson had tacitly admitted that the United States would take no mandate for Syria and Italy had never been a candidate. Britain had stated explicitly that she would not accept a mandate for Syria. Assuming that there would be no independent Arab state in the interior of Syria, the only possible mandatory was France. What remained to be determined was the manner in which France would conduct such a mandate and the attitude of the Arabs to French claims.

During the summer of 1919 feeling ran high in France concerning her treatment by Britain in the Near East. She had not wanted the inquiry and believed that Allenby's staff in Syria was busily rigging the results so as to achieve a verdict unfavourable to France. Although Clemenceau remained indifferent to Syria he could not take the same view of French prestige when that was made into the issue by the colonial party. Relations between Britain and France deteriorated so badly during the strong French newspaper denunciations of British greed in the Near East that eventually even Lloyd George decided that a deal must be struck and France conciliated. Also, it was desirable for reasons of economy to reduce British military commitments.

Britain and France reached agreement at Deauville on 15 September 1919. Lloyd George offered to evacuate British troops from Syria and Cilicia, handing over to France and to the Arabs, in the regions of their respective OETAs, but tried to impose certain conditions on France concerning her policy towards the Arabs. Clemenceau accepted the evacuation but refused the conditions and Lloyd George did not insist on them. Fayṣal protested but his complaints were disregarded. The British evacuation began immediately and was completed by the end of November 1919. The effect of the British decision was to give France a free hand in the settlement of Syria and Lebanon. In October Britain told Fayṣal to make what arrangements he could with France. All that remained for Britain to do was to negotiate with France on the borders which should separate the British-controlled areas in Palestine and Iraq from those of France in Syria and Lebanon and to agree the terms of the various mandates. This was largely accomplished by the end of 1920.

During the course of 1919 a great change took place in the attitudes of Syrian Arabs. Until the end of the war the vast majority of Syrian notables had been loyal Ottoman citizens. Syrians had played little part in the Arab Revolt; only nine joined the Arab army and six others engaged in anti-Ottoman activities. Much has been made of the executions of pre-war Syrian Arab nationalists by Jemāl but only thirteen suffered in this way and two others were imprisoned. Most of the pre-war proponents of Arabist ideas had co-operated with the Ottomans. Very shortly after the war it became apparent to the notables that the Ottoman empire had gone and would not return and that Syria must find a place somewhere along a spectrum of which one pole was independence and the other rule by European powers. Muslim Syrian notables did not want French rule because they believed it would result in domination by favoured Christian minorities. Many Greek Orthodox Christians took a similar view, anticipating that French rule would favour Catholics. The only credible rallying-point against French rule in 1919 was Fayṣal who was responsible for the government of OETA East with its centre at Damascus. But the Syrian notables would not accept Hijazi rule. Accordingly, they adopted the vocabulary of Arab nationalism with its links to the fashionable doctrines of self-determination and endeavoured to assume the government of Syria, reducing Fayṣal to the position of agent of their ambitions. Political societies such as al-Fatāt grew rapidly. The speed of the transition in political orientation was astonishing and may be attested from the case of Sāṭiʿ al-Ḥuṣrī, who was to become the most sophisticated and lucid ideologist of Arab nationalism between the two world wars. Al-Ḥuṣrī was an Ottoman official and the son of an Ottoman official. He spoke

Ottoman Turkish as his first language and until the armistice had been indistinguishable from other Ottoman bureaucrats. Within months of the end of the war he had joined Fayṣal in Syria and was speaking the language of Arab nationalism, albeit with a thick Turkish accent.

Fayṣal's administration in Damascus was recruited primarily from Syrians, often former Ottoman officials, supported by a few Iraqis and Egyptians. His administrative system was the old Ottoman system but on to it he endeavoured to graft a political element, a parliament in Damascus. This parliament, or the General Syrian Congress as it came to be known, included members drawn from all of Greater Syria (including Lebanon and Palestine) and not merely from OETA East, but it was dominated by the old Damascus notables, men who had been pro-Ottoman during the war; pre-war Syrian Arab nationalists were not prominent and formed a majority only in the army command. The congress met on 20 June 1919 and passed a number of resolutions calling for a sovereign, independent Greater Syria under the rule of Fayṣal.

In introducing a political element into the government of Syria Fayṣal and the Syrians hoped to influence the report of the King–Crane Commission and the decisions of the Supreme Council in Paris. Their actions, however, ran counter to British views which were that Fayṣal was only a temporary administrator under Allenby's military government and that political action was out of place. Allenby tried to prevent the development of political institutions and the apparatus of a civil government in Damascus, the effects of which extended outside Damascus to affect the views and aspirations of Arabs in Palestine and Iraq. Also, Allenby was increasingly concerned about the prevalence of disorders in Damascus and the tendency of disorder to spill over from the Arab zone into the British and French zones.

The British withdrawal in the autumn of 1919 led to an increase in violence. Bands of irregulars raided the French zone and there was fighting between French and Arab forces in northern Syria. Attacks took place on communications and on French posts. Part of this disorder was undoubtedly due to the inadequacy of Fayṣal's administration to control the situation; he lacked skilled officials, disciplined forces (conscription was introduced in December 1919) and he lacked money. His financial situation was made worse when first Britain and then France ended their subsidies to Damascus early in 1920.

Fayṣal was in an increasingly difficult position. He wanted to rally political support to assist him in bargaining with the European powers but the demands of the Syrian notables limited his own freedom of manœuvre in any negotiations. In Paris in the spring of 1919 he had undertaken to try to persuade the Syrians to accept a French mandate but he confessed to Clayton that he could not do so in the face of the bitter hostility of the Syrians. He had called the congress into being in June 1919 in order to mobilize Arab opinion to impress the council. This manœuvre had achieved little and after the Deauville Agreement Fayṣal accepted British advice to settle with France. On 27 November 1919 he agreed to recognize French occupation of coastal Syria and Lebanon in return for French recognition of an Arab state in the interior. Following this agreement he dissolved the congress in December 1919. However, there was still no agreement over the extent of French authority over the Arab state and Fayṣal still had not lost hope that an international conference might yet establish a large Arab state. Fayṣal still needed political support and in February 1920 he was forced to recall the congress in order to obtain an endorsement of his stand before his new visit to Europe. Feeling now was running very high in Syria, encouraged by the successes of the Nationalists in Asia Minor, and supported by powerful religious sentiments. Once again Fayṣal could not control the congress which on 7 March 1920 offered him the throne of Greater Syria. The new kingdom was proclaimed on 8 March and a constitution was quickly drafted and adopted. A government was formed under ʿAlī Riḍā al-Rikābī, a supporter of Fayṣal, but after the announcement of the San Remo decisions this government was replaced by a more radical uncompromising government under Hāshim al-Atāsī, the president of the Greater Syrian Congress.

The establishment of the United Kingdom of Syria was unacceptable to France, which was awarded a mandate for Syria and Lebanon on 28 April 1920. Nor was it acceptable to Britain which had been awarded a mandate for Palestine. Further, Iraqis in Damascus had also proclaimed ʿAbdallāh ibn Ḥusayn as king of Iraq and help was sent from Syria to Iraqi rebels against British rule. France had now reorganized her administration in Syria; Picot had gone and was replaced with a military governor, General Gouraud, whose chief political adviser was Robert de Caix, the leading expert of the Syrian group within the colonial party in France. De Caix had argued steadily that France should neither abandon her interests in the Near East nor attempt to maintain the large claims of the Sykes–Picot Agreement. Rather, she should confine her interests to Syria and Lebanon, reach agreement with Britain and with the Nationalists in Anatolia and then deal with the Arabs. Agreement with Britain had been obtained and in May 1920 de Caix led a mission to Ankara which opened a series of negotiations which culminated in the Franklin–Bouillon Agreement. On 14 July 1920 Gouraud presented Fayṣal with an ultimatum demanding unqualified acceptance of the French mandate, adoption of the French currency system, an end to anti-French activities, the abolition of conscription and the reduction of the Arab army and the handing over to French control of the railway from Aleppo to Rayyaq, which would have involved the establishment of French military garrisons in several Syrian towns.

The Syrian Arab kingdom came to an end in July 1920. Fayṣal accepted the French ultimatum on 20 July, three days after it expired, having first dismissed the congress which wanted to reject the ultimatum. Gouraud refused to stop his advance unless several further conditions were met. These were not met and the French continued their advance, defeated the Syrian forces at Maysalūn on 24 July and occupied Damascus the following day. Fayṣal had tried desperately to retain some control over the situation and to make a bargain with France which would leave intact some element of Arab authority in Damascus but he failed to prevent Syrian resistance. On 1 August Fayṣal left Syria for Palestine.

PALESTINE

Claims to Palestine were presented in Paris in the early months of 1919 by Fayṣal for the Arabs and by Weizmann for the Zionist Organization. For Fayṣal Palestine was, by implication, part of the Arab lands for which he demanded independence and in this view he reflected what was known of Palestinian Arab sentiment, for statements by Palestinian Arabs all emphasized the idea of Palestine as part of a Greater Syria. The Zionist claim was for the establishment of a Palestinian state under British mandate and incorporating the programme of the Jewish national home which, through Jewish immigration and close settlement on the land, would develop into an autonomous commonwealth. The Zionist claim was carefully composed (the much more extreme claim (the so-called National Demands) which the Jewish community in Palestine (the Yishuv) had wished to present was suppressed) and effectively delivered; Weizmann, like Venizelos, made a strong and favourable impression on the Supreme Council. There was, in the wings, a third claim, namely that by Britain to be the mandatory authority, but this was still subject to the agreement of other members of the council and especially of France. The council made no decision on these claims at the time but postponed any decision pending the report of the King–Crane Commission.

The history of the post-war settlement of Palestine, however, begins at the end of 1917 after the conquest of Jerusalem and the establishment of a British military administration in Palestine. To the Zionists this was the opportunity to realize their dreams and the Zionist Organization sent a commission under Weizmann which arrived in Palestine in April 1918 to examine ways in which the Zionist programme could be implemented. The Zionists were disappointed to discover a reluctance on the part of the military administration to co-operate in their aims and disillusioned also by the evidence of hostility among the Palestinian Arabs. After a confrontation with certain Arab notables in May 1918 Weizmann more or less abandoned hope of conciliating the Palestinian Arab leaders and instead, at the suggestion of Clayton, who was chief British political officer in Palestine, attempted to reach an agreement with Fayṣal. The two men met on 31 May 1918 and established a basis for the agreement concluded in January 1919 between Fayṣal and Weizmann by which Fayṣal, on behalf of the Arab kingdom of the Hijaz, accepted that Palestine should not form part of the projected Arab state and also that the Zionist programme, in some part at least, should be implemented there. In return Weizmann promised for the Zionists to provide economic assistance to the Arab state and to respect certain Palestinian Arab rights. However, Fayṣal made the agreement conditional on the fulfilment of his own demands for Arab independence, a condition which, of course, was not fulfilled and which was unlikely to be fulfilled.

British plans for Palestine were still not fully conceived in early 1919. In 1917 Britain had contemplated control of Palestine as a means of excluding Ottoman, German or French influence but there was no conviction in 1918 that Palestine should be British. Clayton favoured the incorporation of Palestine in an Arab state with Britain as adviser. When the Eastern Committee reviewed the position of Palestine on 5 December 1918 Curzon concluded that it was promised to the Arab state, believed that Britain should be the mandatory, but kept open a United States option. But even if Britain undertook the administration of Palestine it was still a question what place the Zionist programme would have in Palestine; the Balfour Declaration, as has been shown, committed Britain to very little, and the administration in Palestine was now strongly opposed to the more far-reaching aspects of the Zionist programme; relations between the British and the new head of the Zionist Commission, Menachem Ussishkin, were very poor.

The confirmation of the British commitment to control of Palestine and to the Zionist programme was the work of Lloyd George and Balfour. There was no reason why the two points should have been linked; if France agreed that Palestine should be British, Zionist support was of no importance. Alternatively, Britain could have linked her claim to Palestine to self-determination, in which case, as the results of the King–Crane Commission showed, she could have achieved control of an Arab state. The requirements of Near Eastern strategy may explain the British desire to control Palestine, but they cannot explain the linking of control to support for Zionism, particularly when the Palestine administration had repeatedly warned that adoption of the full Zionist programme would make the government of Palestine much more difficult. The motives of Lloyd George and Balfour remain a mystery. Guilt, sentiment and a sense of history have all been brought forward as explanations. Explaining why Palestine was excluded from the application of self-determination Balfour said that Palestine was wholly exceptional: "that we consider the question of the Jews outside Palestine as one of world importance, and that we conceive the Jews to have an historic claim to a home in their ancient land".[3] Another explanation stresses the situation in eastern Europe; in the spring of 1919, it is argued, the British delegation in Paris became alarmed at the prospect of revolution consuming all of Europe and saw Zionism as a means of drawing the radical enthusiasms of the Jews of eastern Europe away from Bolshevism.

By the summer of 1919 the decision was made in favour of the Zionist policy. Clayton, who had urged an Arab policy combined with a cautious and modest Zionist programme, was replaced as chief political officer by Richard Meinertzhagen, a committed Zionist, at the end of July 1919 and in the same month work was begun, in conjunction with the Zionist leaders, on drawing up the mandate. Until the end of its life on 30 June 1920 the military administration continued to be hostile to the Zionist programme on the grounds that it was unacceptable to the Arab population and a major cause of unrest in Palestine. But the administration failed to influence British policy.

The Anglo-French bargain of December 1919 effectively secured Palestine for Britain and Britain was duly awarded a mandate for Palestine at San Remo in April 1920. It was decided to take the opportunity to bring the military administration to an end and to establish a civil government with Herbert Samuel as first high commissioner. The new civil administration began work on 1 July 1920. The drafting of the mandate was an act of far greater importance than the drafting of the Balfour Declaration but it received far less attention at the time and has attracted much less interest subsequently. The mandate was drafted by relatively junior officials on the basis of a Zionist draft and incorporated the Zionist programme. Although it was regarded with distaste when it was scrutinized at a higher level in the Foreign Office and was amended, the substance of the original was left intact. The negotiation of the frontiers of Palestine and Syria and Lebanon also took place on the basis of Zionist proposals which were aimed at securing control of the headwaters of the Jordan and the Līṭānī and extended much further north than those envisaged in the Sykes–Picot Agreement. On these proposals Britain was obliged to compromise; she obtained the headwaters of the Jordan but had to give way to France over the Līṭānī. The eastern frontiers of Palestine were fixed along the Jordan; the area east of the Jordan came to form the amirate of Transjordan.

TRANSJORDAN

Britain gave little thought to the future of the lands beyond the Jordan before the summer of 1920. Before 1914 the region had been ruled from Damascus; in 1917–18 it had been the region in which Fayṣal's Northern Arab Army operated; and at the end of 1918 it was placed in OETA East, part of the Arab administration under Fayṣal. Although most of it lay in the region allocated to Britain as a sphere of influence under the Sykes–Picot Agreement Transjordan's future was regarded as being part of the Arab state. It was the collapse of Fayṣal's Syrian kingdom in 1920 which raised the question of what should be done with Transjordan. It was generally recognized that there could be no question of the region falling to France and two possibilities were canvassed: to attach it to Palestine or to leave it independent. Samuel, in Palestine, advocated placing it under direct British administration from Palestine, although he did not necessarily assume that it should become part of the region in which the Jewish national home was to be established. The Zionists also wished Transjordan to be included in Palestine. The Foreign Office decided otherwise. Transjordan was too great and expensive a burden for Britain to administer and, therefore, only a handful of British political officers should be sent to the region to encourage the establishment of local self-government. The officers were sent in August 1920 and work was commenced on setting up local institutions including a small force of gendarmerie. The officers had only modest success in the troubled region and in November 1920 they were confronted with a new problem in the form of ʿAbdallāh ibn Ḥusayn who arrived at Maʿān on 11 November with 500 bedouin from the Hijaz following an appeal from the people of Damascus to Ḥusayn for help against the French. France asked Britain to control him and Samuel proposed to send a military expedition from Palestine to establish complete British control over Transjordan. The British government was unwilling to sanction such an expedition and decided to try for agreement with ʿAbdallāh. Accordingly, at the Cairo Conference of March 1921 it was decided to separate Transjordan from Palestine and ʿAbdallāh was offered a British subsidy to rule Transjordan. The arrangement was thought by both sides to be a temporary expedient: ʿAbdallāh hoped to become ruler of the whole of Syria and Britain thought that eventually Transjordan would come under direct rule from Palestine. ʿAbdallāh's initial appointment as governor of Transjordan was for six months only. But at the end of six months T. E. Lawrence recommended that the arrangement should be continued and a statement issued excluding Transjordan from the Zionist provisions in the mandate. Against the continued opposition of Samuel this was agreed and the Transjordan arrangement was launched on the path to permanence. In 1923 a formal Anglo-Transjordanian agreement was signed.

IRAQ

Another new state to emerge in the Near East as a result of the peace settlement was Iraq. In Iraq as in other parts of the Near East it is necessary to distinguish two separate problems in the peace settlement: the physical, geographical delineation of the state and the nature of its political system.

The major influence on the physical shape of the Iraqi state was the vision of two political officers, Sir Percy Cox and Arnold Wilson, and one politician, Lord Curzon. It was Cox who pressed for the original advance on Baghdad, Wilson who later argued for the occupation of Mosul and Curzon who laid the basis for the retention of Mosul at Lausanne in 1923. None of these decisions was required by British imperatives: by the occupation of Basra in 1914 Britain had secured all her objectives in the Gulf region cheaply and economically and there was no military justification for the advance to Baghdad which tied up troops which could have been better employed elsewhere. Again, in 1918 there was no military reason to advance on Mosul; it was unnecessary for the defence of Baghdad and tied down no Ottoman forces. And in 1923 the Cabinet was opposed to any major effort to retain Mosul and would have given way to the Turkish Nationalists on this point. It was Curzon who insisted that Mosul should not be surrendered.

It had been argued that Britain's real interest in Iraq was economic and that she desired to secure control of supplies of wheat, cotton and oil. The vision of Iraq as an imperial granary, derived from the pre-war Willcocks irrigation plans, appears in the de Bunsen Committee Report of 1915 and in 1918 the argument was pressed by Percy Cox. There is no evidence that such notions affected British decisions, however; rather they are arguments adduced to persuade others to agree to a proposal advocated for different reasons and they were two-edged; in 1918 and in 1922 there was concern that the case for British control of the region would be weakened if it was thought that Britain sought economic gain and especially if the gain was to be reaped primarily by private interests. This consideration applied especially to the oil factor which appeared during the latter part of the war. In a paper written by Admiral Sir Edmund Slade on 29 July 1918 it was argued that Britain had become over-dependent upon oil from the United States and that she should seek to diversify her sources of supply. Slade mentioned Iranian and Mesopotamian oil as possible sources. His arguments were supported by oil interests and made one important convert, Sir Maurice Hankey, the Cabinet secretary, who wrote (30 July 1918): "The retention of the oil-bearing regions in Mesopotamia and Persia in British hands, as well as a proper strategic boundary to cover them, would appear to be a first class British war aim."[4] Hankey urged Lloyd George to advance to Mosul to secure the oil and Balfour to include the acquisition of oil in his statement of war aims to the Imperial War Cabinet. Balfour opposed the idea of making oil a war aim on the grounds that it was too imperialist an objective so Hankey widened the argument to include water as well as oil. In the end the Mesopotamian field commander, General Marshall, was asked to take the matter into consideration, together with other factors, in deciding whether to advance further up the Tigris. Oil was, therefore, one factor in the decision but only one, and to the acting chief political officer, Arnold Wilson, its significance was not so much that Britain might obtain supplies of oil but that oil revenues might make the Iraqi state he envisaged more viable. Similarly, Curzon's support for the advance to Mosul in the Eastern Committee was not based on oil but on the need to weaken the French claim to Mosul under the Sykes–Picot Agreement; he used the argument of oil because of its appeal to Lloyd George.

In the immediate post-war period there was no attempt to develop Iraqi oil, principally because Curzon took the view that Iraqi development must await the peace conference's decisions on the future of Iraq. There was much greater interest in Iraqi oil by France and the United States. France made the obtaining of a share in Iraqi oil a condition of giving up her claim to Mosul and this was quickly agreed in the Long–Berenger Agreement of February 1919. Although this agreement was disowned by Lloyd George it was not because he objected to the division of oil but because of his other differences with France, and when Britain and France were reconciled at the end of 1919 and the oil deal renegotiated the new arrangement followed the lines of the Long–Berenger Agreement. It is fair to conclude that oil was not an important bone of contention between Britain and France. The United States was concerned that Britain was gaining control of too large a proportion of world oil supplies and claimed a share. It was the Americans who argued that British policy at Lausanne over Mosul was dictated by a desire for control of oil. Curzon denied that this was the case and the documents support his contention. For Curzon the main issue was prestige and for the Iraq Committee in London it was the future defence of Iraq. Nor was oil the main consideration for the Turks; they were willing to offer the United States a generous share of the oil in return for support for their claim to Mosul and they declined a share of oil offered by Britain. In fact, for all the parties primarily concerned, the great issues were territories and prestige; oil was no more than a bargaining counter.

The Treaty of Lausanne provided for further negotiations about the future of Mosul between Britain and Turkey, and if these failed for a reference to the League of Nations. Negotiations did fail and the matter was referred to the league in 1924. The league rejected Turkey's request for a plebiscite and decided to send a commission of inquiry to Mosul. The commission's report favoured the Iraqi claim to Mosul. There is little doubt that the existence of Anglo-Iraqi control was a major factor; pro-Ottoman feeling in the region was strong but witnesses who testified to the commission were anxious to appear to be loyal to the government which actually controlled Mosul. Oil was a major factor in the Mosul Commission's decision only in so far as it accepted the view that oil revenues were important for the viability and economic development of Iraq and that it was important that the matter should be settled and oil production should begin. The league was concerned that without Mosul Britain might find the financial burden of Basra and Baghdad too great and throw up the mandate. Mosul, therefore, stayed with Iraq.

Iraq was a consequence of what may be termed a series of logical accidents. Basra was required for prestige and the defence of India, Baghdad for prestige and the defence of Basra, and Mosul for prestige, the defence of Baghdad and the viability of the whole. But, having acquired each element in such fashion, there seemed no reason why they should be held as one state and post-war planning envisaged a different result. Basra, it was commonly agreed, should be retained under British control but Baghdad, and consequently Mosul, were not essential to British purposes. Baghdad, it was thought, might become an Arab state under British protection, a view strongly advocated from Cairo; and Mosul, it was argued, could become part of a Kurdish state. It was, above all, Arnold Wilson who demanded that Basra and Baghdad should be retained as a single unit and that Mosul should be retained to make the state viable both from the viewpoint of defence and from that of economics. That view triumphed partly through accident – the failure of Kurdish leaders to emerge, the troubles of Arab politics and the problems with France – and partly through the persistence of Wilson.

But what sort of state should Iraq be? Wilson's view was that it should be a showpiece of British imperialism. The associations of imperialism are now commonly with the idea of economic exploitation, but Wilson represented a quite different notion of imperialism as the white man's burden; the duty of Europe to provide disinterested good government over many years in order to raise the moral and material conditions of the subject people. In India and in Egypt Wilson believed there were examples of the success of British imperialism, but in Iraq he thought the mistakes of the past would be avoided and the country remodelled in a fashion that would show the world what Britain could achieve as well as confer great benefits upon the people of Iraq. This end could only be accomplished through a long period of British rule. "Having set our hands to the task of regenerating Mesopotamia we must be prepared to produce the men and the money for a period of years at least as long as the period of our tenure of Egypt."[5] He had no time for devolution; the sort of administration he envisaged may be seen by its composition in 1920 when, of the holders of higher administrative posts, 507 were British, 7 Indian and 20 Arab.

Wilson's view ran counter to the fashionable notion of self-determination which was represented by the Cairo demand that Basra and Baghdad should be part of the Arab state or states. It was the Cairo view which came to prevail in London and from 1917 to 1920 Wilson fought a constant battle to maintain his notion of how Iraq should develop against pressure from London for a devolved system of government. What might have been the eventual result of this contest if other events had not supervened is difficult to say; it may be that Wilson would have contrived to carry on his British system of administration under an Arab façade or he might have had to give way. After Britain was awarded the mandate for Iraq at San Remo in April 1920 serious consideration was given to the constitutional development of Iraq, and London decreed that there should be a real measure of self-government in the Arab state of Iraq. Wilson was to be replaced by Sir Percy Cox. But Cox at that time supported Wilson's policy and the chief impulse behind London's Arab policy, namely the desire to use it to control France in Syria, was very shortly to lose its point when France asserted complete control in Syria in July 1920. The future of Iraq was still open. But, in any case, Wilson's system was brought tumbling down by the Iraqi uprising of 1920.

The Iraqi uprising which lasted from July to the end of October 1920 was a turning-point in the post-war history of Iraq. The disturbances began among the tribes of the lower Euphrates at the end of June and spread to engulf about one-third of Iraq. The principal areas involved were the tribal areas of the upper, middle and lower Euphrates and to a lesser extent the upper Tigris. The towns, the lower Tigris and Kurdistan were mainly quiet. To bring them under control required large troop reinforcements, fierce fighting and an expenditure of £40 million. The exertions were such as to call into question the worth of Iraq to Britain.

Various interpretations of the rising were offered. According to one school of thought, popularized by T. E. Lawrence, it was a nationalist uprising; the Iraqis, having thrown off their Turkish oppressors had now turned against their British overlords. But the Iraqis had not thrown off Ottoman rule and the areas which had displayed nationalist activity before the war, namely the towns, were quiet in 1920. Nevertheless, there was a nationalist element associated with the propaganda and aid forthcoming from Syria, and its effects were perceived among the Sunnī tribes of the upper Euphrates.

A second explanation points to the role of religion and especially of Shiʿism. The hostility to British, infidel rule on the part of the Shīʿī *mujtahids* of Najaf and Karbalāʾ was clearly stated and their influence on the Shīʿī tribes of the middle and lower Euphrates strong. Disturbances among the Muntafiq Arabs were especially prolonged. This interpretation, however, runs counter to the nationalist interpretation, because the Shīʿī theologians with their leanings towards Iran and Panislamism and their dislike of Sunnī rule from Baghdad, were in no way attracted to Arab nationalist ideas.

A third explanation emphasizes more traditional tribal attitudes. The possibilities of loot and the opportunities provided by British troop withdrawals, tax demands after the tax holiday of the war, the demands for labour for irrigation works, inflation and the ending of jobs provided by British military spending during the war all seem to have contributed to the rising.

No single explanation can account for the Iraqi uprising; it was a mixture of nationalism, religion and tribalism with the latter impulse predominating. Most of the men of wealth and property, the traditional notables, townsmen and tribal shaykhs stayed aloof from the business. In British eyes, however, the uprising seemed to confirm the opinion that Wilson's system was doomed to failure and that a nationalist solution was required to avert similar problems in the future. The effect of the uprising, therefore, was to speed up the process of creating an Arab government in Iraq and to lead to the devolution of more power to it.

The task of creating the new system fell to Sir Percy Cox, who set up an interim government under the *Naqīb* of Baghdad at the end of 1920 while he worked out a permanent solution. This solution, which was to install Fayṣal as head of an Arab government, was adopted at the Cairo Conference of March 1921. Alternative solutions which were canvassed included a republic, another Hashemite ruler (possibly ʿAbdallāh ibn Ḥusayn), and Sayyid Ṭālib, the pre-war nationalist from Basra and possibly the ablest politician in Iraq. These possibilities and many more, including the Aga Khan and an Iraqi notable, were considered. All were dismissed in favour of Fayṣal who had the merits of being opposed to the Ottomans and likely to be able to form an army more quickly than any other candidate. ʿAbdallāh was given Transjordan, Sayyid Ṭālib was arrested and deported and no Iraqi notable wanted the job. Indeed, it is interesting to note that the traditional Sunnī notables of Baghdad still looked back fondly to the departed Ottoman rule; they took longer to adjust to the new realities than did the notables of Damascus. In the summer of 1921 a referendum, judiciously managed, resulted in a claimed 96 per cent of the population of Iraq expressing their willingness to accept Fayṣal as king and he ascended the throne on 23 August 1921.

It remained to settle the terms of Britain's relationship with Fayṣal's Iraq. Fayṣal, supported by Cox, wanted to abrogate the mandate and replace it with a treaty. The Cabinet would not accept this solution. Prestige demanded that the mandate should remain but to a large extent it was replaced by the Anglo-Iraqi Treaty of 10 October 1922. The treaty left Iraq in control of her own affairs subject to overriding British control exercised through finance, defence, foreign policy and administrative advisers and with guarantees for foreigners, missionaries and minorities. On paper Britain had full control: in practice the Cairo Conference had taken a crucial decision on defence which effectively meant much greater autonomy for Iraq. This was the decision to replace British ground forces in Iraq by Royal Air Force units.

The decision to employ the RAF in Iraq was taken for two reasons, neither of them fundamentally to do with Iraq. The first reason was to find some unique role for the RAF which would safeguard its existence and avoid its reabsorption by the army. The second was the desire for economy; a few aeroplanes were much cheaper than ground troops and the new colonial secretary, Winston Churchill, was anxious to achieve economies in his new job. In the event, although the RAF patrols were excellent for protecting Iraq against the attacks of desert tribesmen from Arabia, they could not do the ordinary work of internal security which perforce fell to the hastily created Iraqi army. The consequence was that the Iraqi state quickly assumed the ordinary coercive powers of a state and with them a much greater control over civil government.

ARABIA

As a result of the war Britain was in a strong position in Arabia. She had protected her own sphere of interest and strengthened her control by new treaties with Kuwayt, Qaṭar and Najd. Through the use of naval and military power, alliances and subsidies she had weakened Ottoman control over northern and western Arabia and completed its destruction by her military defeat of the empire. And she had contrived to exclude other powers – France, Italy and Japan – which might have gained a foothold in the region.

In the post-war settlement Britain had no plans for radical changes in her own sphere and sought to re-establish the system which had existed prior to 1914 rather than to acquire the position of complete dominance envisaged by Curzon. In the Persian Gulf Britain controlled the sea, maintained maritime peace, avoided, as far as possible, interference on land, and endeavoured to exclude outside powers from the region. By the treaty of Sīb (1920) Britain helped to negotiate a settlement between the sultan of Muscat and the tribes of interior Oman. In south-west Arabia there was more disagreement about the future: in India Aden was viewed in traditional fashion as an expensive and not particularly valuable imperial outpost; in London it was seen as part of the Arab future. In practice the two views cancelled each other out and Aden remained much as it was. In the Aden Protectorate Britain concentrated on rebuilding the pre-war system of working through friendly chiefs, notably the ruler of Lahej; the more radical alternative of abandoning the area to the imam of Yemen was not pursued.

The main problem concerned the future of the former Ottoman sphere in Arabia. Different views were propounded in Iraq, India and

London. In Iraq the problem was seen as one of safeguarding the frontiers of the Iraqi state from tribal inroads: in India as preserving the British sphere and dealing with each individual Arab ruler on his merits: in London it was hoped that an independent confederation of Arabia would emerge under the direction of an Arab ruler who would look to Britain for guidance and support. In 1918 it was thought that Ḥusayn ibn ʿAlī might be that ruler and there was support for his claims against those of Sayyid Muḥammad ibn ʿAlī al-Idrīsī in ʿAsir and against ʿAbd al-ʿAzīz ibn Suʿūd in Najd. India, concerned with Gulf affairs, was more inclined to look to Ibn Suʿūd.

In the years after 1918, the power of Ibn Suʿūd, aided by a British subsidy until 1924, steadily increased. From 1918 the Ikhwān became an important military factor, replacing the cultivators and townspeople who had formerly constituted the main coercive force at Ibn Suʿūd's disposal. In 1920 Saʿūdī power was extended into the highlands of ʿAsīr, in 1921 to the Rashīdī capital of Ḥāʾil, and in 1922 the capture of Jawf opened the way into Transjordan. By that time Ibn Suʿūd was clearly the dominant force in Arabia and presented a problem to Britain because of his pressure upon the British-controlled sphere. In 1922, by the Conference of ʿUqayr, agreement was reached with Ibn Suʿūd on the definition of the frontiers of Najd, Iraq and Kuwayt and of the neutral zone (actually the pasture lands of the Ẓāfir nomads) which separated Kuwayt and Najd. Other boundary problems remained. In defining the territorial boundaries of states in this way Britain was continuing the process of imposing European notions of state organization and international relations on the Near East.

Britain's main concern was still with Ḥusayn who was seen as an actor in a wider Arab and Muslim context. As ruler of the Hijaz he controlled the pilgrimage and as head of the Hashimite family he was a component of the settlement of Palestine and Transjordan, where he could be used to control ʿAbdallāh. Ḥusayn regarded himself as king and Fayṣal and ʿAbdallāh merely as his viceroys in the Arab lands and he did not approve of their independent policies. Within the Hijaz Ḥusayn was not a popular ruler. He controlled only the towns and after the loss of his British subsidy he tried to improve his finances by heavy taxation of merchants and pilgrims. Ḥusayn's major concern, however, was with Ibn Suʿūd in Arabia.

The rivalry between Ḥusayn and Ibn Suʿūd first led to violence in July 1918 when Ḥusayn's forces were defeated at Khurma, a village in central Arabia claimed by Ḥusayn on political grounds and Ibn Suʿūd on religious grounds. In May 1919 Ḥusayn sustained a heavier defeat at the neighbouring village of Turaba, when his broken troops were slaughtered by the Ikhwān and he suffered a major blow to his prestige. The loss of the two villages was important because with them went the allegiance of the Ṣubay tribe and all its pastures extending for 200 kilometres. Ḥusayn responded by attempting to form alliances with Kuwayt, Ḥā'il and other anti-Saʿūdī forces but these failed him. He also appealed to Britain and found support in Cairo. But Britain limited her help to pressure on Ibn Suʿūd not to follow up his advantage and refused Ḥusayn the military support which he requested. In December 1919 Britain offered to mediate between the two rulers and to try to settle the frontier between their lands. The suggestion had come from Ibn Suʿūd and in January 1920 Ḥusayn agreed to meet the Najdī ruler. But the meeting did not take place and Britain tended to blame Ḥusayn for what was seen as his obduracy. In fact, as the hopes of the Arab policy waned, Britain's disinclination to involve herself in Arabia in support of the pretensions of any Arab ruler became stronger.

In 1921 Britain made a further attempt to reach agreement with Ḥusayn. In July T. E. Lawrence was sent to offer Ḥusayn a subsidy of £100,000 a year, together with British support for his position in the Hijaz, if he would accept the position which had emerged in the Arab areas following the events of 1920 and the 1921 Cairo Conference. Ḥusayn refused to recognize the Palestine settlement and the negotiations dragged on for years without success. The episode tended to confirm the growing British view of Ḥusayn as a nuisance. Finally, in December 1922, a British effort to settle the Arabian dispute by negotiation at the Kuwayt Conference failed; Britain then decided to wash her hands of the business and to leave the matter to be settled between Ibn Suʿūd and Ḥusayn.

The post-war settlement of Arabia owed something to British intervention; Britain maintained her influence in her old sphere and also interposed her authority to draw boundaries in the interior. But her hopes of becoming the general arbiter of Arabia broke down through her inability to find a suitable local agent and her unwillingness to put in the resources required to form and maintain a British-directed system. Diplomacy, subsidies and supplies could ensure some influence but only a very limited power to control events. It was also true that there was never agreement in Britain about what the purposes and shape of a British system should be. In the end Britain had little control over the three principal local powers, Yemen, Najd and the Hijaz. Her main success was in excluding outside powers.

EGYPT

On 13 November 1918 a delegation (*wafd*) of Egyptian politicians, led by Saʿd Zaghlūl Pasha, asked the British high commissioner for permission to go to London to present Egyptian demands. Zaghlūl was one of the most prominent Egyptian politicians. He had fallen into disfavour immediately before the war and the delegation may be seen as part of his attempt to recover his position. Equally, it may also be seen as part of an attempt by his rivals to discredit him if he failed or to exploit his success if the delegation was accepted. The delegation was a typical assembly of Egyptian politicians; ten of the fourteen were big landowners and a third of the delegation were lawyers. A majority were members of the Umma Party.

When London refused to receive the delegation there followed a campaign of petitions in support of the group and the prime minister, Ḥusayn Rushdī Pasha, resigned. In March 1919 Zaghlūl was arrested and deported. There followed a series of demonstrations, strikes and riots in Cairo and other towns and what amounted to armed revolt in the provinces and these troubles were not finally quelled until May 1919.

The Egyptian insurrection of 1919 had a profound effect upon the British attitude towards Egypt and upon British policy in that country. It was not the urban aspects which dismayed Britons but the revelation of widespread agrarian discontent and violent hostility. As in other colonial territories the British in Egypt had supposed that while British rule might be unpopular with a class of aggrieved politicians, frustrated bureaucrats, malcontent students, ambitious lawyers and unregenerate upholders of the old order, it was welcomed by the mass of peasants whom it had relieved from exploitation and to whom it had brought some measure of prosperity. The discovery that they were in error and that British rule still rested not on consent but on force was an important factor in deciding Britons to seek a new path in Egypt which would disentangle them from involvement in Egyptian government. The British interpretation of the uprising was, therefore, central to the evolution of Egypt.

The disturbances began on 9 March with student demonstrations in Cairo. These demonstrations were quickly organized by groups within al-Azhar, although not by the orthodox Muslim hierarchy which held aloof from the troubles. The Azhar was able to muster its traditional artisan following and from about 12 March the urban poor from the new slums also began to take part, although their role was less significant than that of the students. On 12 March the disturbances also spread to Alexandria and Tanta where students again took the lead. In each case the pattern was similar with civil servants and artisans joining the demonstrations and remaining the leading element even though much of the damage was done by the urban poor. On 15 March a novel development was the strike of Cairo railway workers from the working-class quarters of Bulaq and Muski. Judging from the composition of the urban groups and their demands it is fair to say that the urban movement was basically political and nationalist although it had religious and class aspects.

The rural disturbances, which began after the urban disturbances had been largely brought under control, were quite different in character and had little connection with the urban disturbances. There has been much controversy about the nature of the rural troubles, but there is a consensus that no single explanation fits the rural disturbances but that they took a different character in different areas.

In many areas a leading role was taken by the provincial notables, the same class which had formed the backbone of support for ʿUrābī but which had suffered a considerable decline in their local influence since 1882. Often, such local notables took over administration in their areas, seeing the disturbances as an opportunity to regain some measure of local autonomy. Government servants and the *efendi* class generally also took a prominent part in the disturbances in the provinces and formed tactical alliances with provincial notables in some areas but their aims remained quite distinct; they wished to retain the system of control which had been developed and looked to Cairo and national politics. The role of the peasants was different again. Broadly speaking they were against all government, whether central or local, and directed their attacks against government establishments. Beyond this their aims varied considerably from one area to another. In the Delta provinces the aim was village autonomy and in the big cotton-growing provinces of the Delta periphery they turned violently against all landlords. Bedouin also took a hand in the western provinces from 19 March. Their aim was purely tribal plundering and they clashed with notables and peasants. In Upper Egypt, on the other hand, peasants and bedouin often combined in attacks upon big provincial centres, notably at Minya where there were also attacks upon urban Copts (the large community of Copts in the countryside was not singled out in this fashion suggesting that the motive was less religious than class). In Asyut slogans such as "there is no government", and "we want bread", appeared. The area around Minya and Asyut witnessed some of the most severe and bloody fighting of the whole uprising; historically it was always the region most prone to violent disturbances. In the regions further south towards the Sudan border yet another pattern emerged with alliances of notables, *efendis* and peasants.

The insurrection had political, economic and religious aspects. Politically, those whose interests were tied up with the state tended to look to the nationalist lead, but those who saw the state as the enemy opposed it either in the interests of local autonomy or of no government at all. Economically, there is some link with the cotton economy. In those areas where it was most developed the movement decidedly took on an anti-landlord aspect. An interesting feature is the association of the areas of greatest violence with what might be called the marginal areas of the cotton economy. The high price of cotton during the war had led to a considerable extension of the cultivation of high-yielding varieties of cotton which required large quantities of water to succeed. At one time it was suggested that the fall in the price of cotton was a direct cause of the rural disturbances, but the timing of price movements and the disturbances makes this explanation unacceptable. What does seem to be the case, however, is that those areas which had recently adopted heavily irrigated cotton production included some of the most disturbed areas and this may be explained by reference to the circumstance that these areas were the ones which found difficulty in maintaining their new-found prosperity because they were insufficiently equipped to sustain high levels of production, particularly as they were often inadequately equipped with drainage. Those areas which were long established in cotton and those which had not adopted the new varieties were less affected.

None of the contemporary British explanations of the rural disturbances quite fits the facts either in terms of timing or distribution. The arguments that the British had bought up the cotton crop in 1919 below market price, that wartime requisitions of fodder had caused much discontent and that the forced recruitment of many of the 500,000 Egyptians required for the Labour and Camel Transport Corps had led to widespread rural hostility all fail on these grounds. The British may have been nearer the mark in their interpretation of the urban disturbances which they saw as the product of *efendi* and worker resentment of wartime inflation and foreign control of government employment and the economy. But here again they missed the point that the very nature of the structure of Egyptian government under the protectorate meant that these groups had to look primarily to Egyptian politicians for their future.

The uprising exposed the inadequacies of the British authorities in Cairo. Wingate had previously been called to London after his disagreement with the Foreign Office refusal to allow the delegation to come to

London and the conduct of British policy fell into the hands of the acting high commissioner, Milne Cheetham. Cheetham was taken completely aback by the extent of the disturbances and more or less lost his head. Only a determined effort by the military authorities restored order and control of British affairs in Egypt was quickly given to Allenby as special commissioner. Consideration of the future of Britain in Egypt devolved on London, however, and fell into the hands of Lord Milner, who led a commission of inquiry to Egypt (December 1919–March 1920).

Unlike Cheetham, who blamed the disturbances on Bolshevism and nationalism, Milner saw the root cause of the problem in a departure from the Cromer principles through the elaboration of British controls and personnel. He wished to draw back from the close supervision of Egyptian affairs implied in the protectorate and adopt a system which would safeguard British strategic interests but detach Britain from too intimate a connection with Egyptian government. These ideas were formed before his delayed departure for Egypt and from the beginning he was less concerned with determining what had happened in Egypt than in working out an agreement for the future. For this purpose he hoped to talk to the Egyptian moderates, but was frustrated because the complete boycott of his mission prevented him from reaching anyone with whom he could discuss the future of Egypt. Nevertheless, he recommended that Britain should scrap the protectorate and restore autonomy to Egypt, reserving only British control of foreign affairs and the Sudan and a British garrison.

Milner now had to persuade Egyptian politicians and his own Cabinet to accept an Anglo-Egyptian agreement on this basis. The work proved to be long and tedious and only partly successful. From June to August 1920 Milner negotiated in London with Zaghlūl and ʿAdlī Yegen Pashas and produced a declaration of intent embodying the idea of an independent Egypt in alliance with Britain and provisions for the protection of British strategic interests. Unfortunately, this declaration was received in totally different ways by the Egyptians and by the Cabinet. To the Egyptian nationalists it was merely a starting-point of a negotiation in which they looked for further concessions and for the Cabinet it represented a dangerous and unacceptable concession to Egypt.

From the autumn of 1920 until February 1922 the attempt to reconcile the British and Egyptian viewpoints proceeded through a variety of negotiations. The view adopted by Allenby and Curzon was that, although they disliked Milner's declaration and wished it had never been made, there was no going back on its main notion of an Anglo-

Egyptian alliance to replace the protectorate. The Cabinet was still determined to try to strengthen the provisions to safeguard British interests, in particular the size of the British garrison, and the Egyptians were equally anxious to whittle the same provisions down; indeed the internal conflicts of Egyptian politics made it impossible for either ʿAdlī, Fuʾād or Zaghlūl to make concessions lest they be denounced by the others for betraying Egyptian interests.

By November 1921 the negotiations were deadlocked and Allenby and his advisers in Egypt were brought to contemplate the complete breakdown of Anglo-Egyptian co-operation and the possibility of having to construct a purely British government of Egypt and to enforce its will by force on an insurrectionary population. The only alternative appeared to be a unilateral British declaration of Egyptian independence and Allenby threatened to resign if this policy was not adopted. At that point the Cabinet gave way and on 28 February 1922 Britain issued a declaration announcing the end of the protectorate and, therefore, the independence of Egypt subject to reservations on four points to be the subject of future agreement. These points were the control of Egyptian defence and foreign policy, the security of the Suez Canal, the government of the Sudan and the future of the capitulations.

The British declaration of 28 February 1922 was an important event in the post-war settlement of the Near East. No other position in the Near East had the same strategic importance for Britain as the Suez Canal, not even the Straits. It had come to be accepted that to control the canal it was necessary to control Egypt and, since 1882, there had been a steady growth of British influence in Egypt culminating in the establishment of the protectorate in 1914 and the wartime proposals for annexation. The uprising of 1919 was a watershed in this process, marking the point at which the movement for closer control was reversed. It can be argued that Britain gave up nothing that mattered in 1922 because she reserved the points which affected her vital strategic interests and retained control of the canal. But this view depends upon the assumption that Britain could possess the same freedom of strategic manœuvre in Egypt without direct control of Egyptian government as she did when she could control the appointment of ministers and the policies of that government. Time was to prove that she could not enjoy the same freedom as in the past just as the majority of the Cabinet had supposed. The year 1922 did mark a real retreat by Britain from her position of dominance in the Near East by weakening her strength in the most vital area.

The British retreat was not a voluntary withdrawal but was imposed upon her by her appreciation of the strength of opposition to British control in Egypt. British control of Egypt was seen to rest on Egyptian consent and willingness to co-operate, and that consent and co-operation were apparently withdrawn in 1919 and never restored. Whether the British diagnosis of the situation was correct is uncertain. The identification of the 1919 disturbances as a fundamentally anti-British politica movement drawing on a variety of grievances was probably mistaken; there was little connection between the rural disturbances and the urban political movement; having suppressed both of them, the latter quite easily, Britain could have resumed her former course. But once the identification was made and Britain began to look for a political solution by negotiation with the nationalist leaders there was no going back; facts were created by the identification of them as facts and the prominence which Britain gave to Zaghlūl changed the face of Egyptian political life.

IRAN

As a consequence of the war Britain was left dominant in Iran. German, Ottoman and Russian influence had all departed and there was no challenge from France as there was in the western areas of the Near East. British or British-controlled forces dominated the main centres of Iran in the south and east and British forces were pushed forward into Transcaucasia. In Tehran a government sympathetic to Britain was in power. The questions which were discussed in the Eastern Committee concerned whether Britain should aim at perpetuating her control of Iran and by what means.

Two views were presented. The view of the Indian government was that Britain should aim at an agreement with moderate nationalism in Iran. The alternative, of maintaining close control over a pro-British government, was thought to be too expensive in money and resources and the Indian government was unwilling to meet the bill. The opposing view, maintained by Curzon, was that Britain should consolidate her predominance by a long-term agreement with the pro-British faction in Iran. A protectorate and a mandate were dismissed because of international complications and because they ran contrary to the prevailing ideas of self-determination, but it was intended to secure by the agreement the strategic advantages which might have been procured by the other devices.

Curzon's view prevailed and, unlike the situation in the Ottoman territories, he was allowed to implement his policy with little interference from other members of the Cabinet. The result was the Anglo-Persian agreement of 9 August 1919 which provided for the reorganization of the Iranian army, finances and customs duties under British supervision and for the construction of railways. In return Britain was to lend Iran £2 million. "A great triumph", wrote Curzon, "and I have done it alone."[6] To the Cabinet he explained that the agreement would ensure British predominance and safeguard British India, the Gulf and oil interests.

The agreement failed for three reasons: Iranian opposition, British reluctance to do what was necessary to support it and the return of Russia to the Near East.

Placed as Iran was between Britain and Soviet Russia her foreign policy had followed one of three paths: to try to play one power off against another, to seek the help of a third power or to make an agreement with one or other of her great neighbours. In 1919 she had no choice but to adopt the third course but she hoped to secure some advantages from her decision, in particular to secure an indemnity for her losses during the war and to acquire territory from the Ottomans, Russia and Afghanistan. The discovery that Britain would not help to secure these goals for Iran quickly weakened the position of those who had negotiated the agreement, a position already damaged by the widespread and accurate rumours that they had personally received money for their part in the transaction. Further, Britain was unwilling to assist in quelling disturbances in Iran which led to a loss of government control over Azerbaijan, Khurāsān, Gīlān and Māzandarān. In the last two provinces the radical, Panislamic movement of Kūchik Khān proffered a threat to Tehran itself, the more so when the radicals received assistance from Soviet Russia. As more and more of the Democrats who had fled during the war drifted back to Iran the opposition to British control grew stronger.

During 1919 pressure within Britain and India for a reduction of British military commitments in the Near East grew. At first, the controversy focused on Transcaucasia. Curzon argued that it was important to maintain British forces in Transcaucasia in order to give some support to the infant Transcaucasian republics so that they might in time come to constitute a solid barrier against the penetration of Ottoman or Russian influence into the southern areas of the Near East and towards India. It seems likely that he also had in mind that once British troops were removed from Transcaucasia the arguments for retaining them in Iran would become less strong. It was also hoped that British troops on the eastern frontiers of Iran could be available to support movements for independence within Turkestan if required.

But neither London nor India were willing to provide the forces for these adventures and first the forces on the borders of Turkestan were withdrawn and then those in Transcaucasia. Their withdrawal assisted the reassertion of the power of Russia in these regions.

On 18 May 1920 Bolshevik forces landed in Gīlān province and gave their assistance to the rebels under Kūchik Khān. The Soviet government also made a powerful bid for an agreement with Iran. Already, in January 1918, the Bolshevik government had formally renounced tsarist policies, agreements and concessions limiting Iranian sovereignty, and during the subsequent months made several efforts to persuade Iran to negotiate a treaty to settle the future relations of the two states. Whilst Iran had hoped for gains from the Anglo-Iranian Agreement she showed no interest in any arrangement with Soviet Russia, but with the decline of hopes of British help and the evident power of Russia to create or compound disturbance in Iran she changed her view and opened negotiations in May 1920. In August a delegation was sent to Moscow and the negotiations were carried on in that capital. By the end of the year a treaty was ready for signing; this eventually became the Soviet–Iranian Treaty of 26 February 1921. The treaty confirmed the cancellation of tsarist concessions and financial claims, and in April 1921 Soviet forces left Iran.

The prolonged character of the Russo-Iranian negotiations was the consequence of the persistent Iranian hopes that something useful might yet come from the agreement with Britain and of fears that Iran might lose by transferring her allegiance to Soviet Russia. The acid test was the willingness of Britain to offer protection against Soviet Russia but this Britain would not do. Curzon was alone in his belief in the importance of Iran to Britain; his Cabinet colleagues did not think Iran worth any great expenditure of resources and certainly not worth a war with Soviet Russia. In fact, Lloyd George was himself looking for an agreement with Soviet Russia, which was achieved on 16 March 1921 by the Anglo-Russian Trade Agreement. When it was announced that British troops were to be withdrawn from Iran by April 1921 British influence in Iran, or at least in Tehran, was greatly weakened.

The 1919 agreement achieved little. Under its provisions a new customs tariff was drawn up, a plan for railway construction devised and a scheme for a unified Iranian army, built around the South Persia Rifles, worked out. But very little was accomplished and the financial reorganization made no progress. One reason for this lack of success was that the agreement was never ratified. The British had failed to realize the significance of the provision in the 1906 Iranian constitution which declared that all treaties must be submitted for ratification by the

Iranian Parliament (Majlis). By the time the necessity for ratification was admitted it was clear that there would be great difficulty in assembling a parliament which would ratify the agreement in the face of nationalist opposition. During the latter part of 1920 there was a fruitless search for a government which would get the agreement through the Majlis or would agree to implement it without parliamentary approval. The end was that the agreement was abandoned and in the process the government of Iran was reduced to a few disputing factions.

The situation was resolved by a *coup d'état* on 21 February 1921 of which the chief instrument was the reorganized Cossack Brigade led by Colonel Riżā Khān. The Cossack Brigade had virtually disintegrated in 1920 after defeat at the hands of Kūchik Khān. Britain had secured the dismissal of its White Russian officers and had undertaken the task of reorganization with the aid of British officers. It was subsequently claimed that during this reorganization Britain decided to solve her problems by assisting Riżā to carry out the military coup but there is no good evidence to support this contention. It is quite apparent that nothing was known of such a scheme in London and it is probable that the British minister, Herman Norman, knew nothing of it either. There is some suggestion that individual members of the British mission might have had a hand in the events of February 1921 and it is certainly the case that they had contact with Riżā's co-conspirator, Sayyid Żiyā al-Dīn Ṭabāṭabā'ī, a radical Iranian reformer with pro-British sympathies. But while it seems likely that some Britons may have had knowledge of what was planned and done nothing to obstruct it, seeing a coup as perhaps the only salvation for Iran at that time, there is no worthwhile evidence that they helped to organize it.

In Iran, as elsewhere in the Near East, Britain had lost her predominance during the post-war settlement. Britain was still a significant factor in Iran by virtue of her position in the Gulf, her oil interests and her links with chiefs and tribes in southern Iran. But her dominance in Tehran was gone. Like other countries in the Near East, Iran, in 1921, was setting out on a new course, not wholly independent but with substantial power to determine her own destiny.

THE NEW NEAR EAST

The new Near East which came into being between 1918 and 1921 was radically different from the Near East which had existed in 1914. The major change was the destruction of the Ottoman empire, an event which was the result not of any inexorable internal disease but of a hasty decision to enter a war on what proved to be the wrong side. The war had witnessed many plans drawn up on a variety of principles for the reconstruction of the Near East, but the end of the war saw Britain dominant in the Near East and in a position to enforce a settlement largely to suit her own convenience. But the pattern of the new Near East was not enforced by Britain but represented a compromise between British desires, the fears and ambitions of other European powers and the hopes and passions of the people of the Near East.

The most striking feature of British policy is the divisions among the policy-makers. For most of the war the pace had been made by the men on the spot: the Arab Bureau in Cairo, Percy Cox and Arnold Wilson in Iraq, Mark Sykes in London and everywhere. They were the men who produced the plans and strategies which became embodied in British policy. In the latter stages of the war and after the war the initiative passed to London where individual members of the Cabinet – Lloyd George, Balfour, Churchill, Milner and, above all, Curzon – attempted to devise some broad design for a British-dominated Near East. They came up against the circumstance that the will was lacking in Britain to sustain a dominant role in the Near East and that compromises were necessary in order to meet the requirements of the doctrine of self-determination, the demands of Britain's allies and the lack of available resources of manpower in Britain. The compromises sought were through the employment of agents or collaborators with whom Britain could share power in the Near East. This strategy was generally unsuccessful. In Asia Minor the Greeks proved unable to support the burdens they had undertaken; in Transcaucasia and Turkestan the movements of independence could not support themselves against internal dissension and the Russian challenge; in Egypt and Iran the moderate pro-British groups with whom it was hoped that a deal could be struck proved not to exist; and in Arabia the British protégés fell to fighting among themselves. Only in the Fertile Crescent was there some small measure of success after the Arab strategy was abandoned.

The role of other European powers was significant in the new shape of the Near East. In the Levant France's refusal to be levered out of Syria and Lebanon and her unwillingness to accept any significant restrictions upon her freedom of action were key factors in determining the future shape of Syria and Lebanon. In the northern and eastern areas it was the return of Russia which was a decisive factor. Soviet Russian help for the Turkish Nationalist forces for the victorious campaign against the Greeks in 1922 and Russia's return to Transcaucasia, after the defeat of the White Russians, signalled the end of the hopes of independence cherished by the small states of the region. Similarly, in the East, Soviet forces, joining with those of the Russian settlers in Turkestan, were able to complete the destruction of the rebel Muslim movements of Turkestan. It was in Iran, however, that Soviet Russia played an especially notable role, providing the reason and the opportunity for Iran to escape from the British embrace, but at the same time refraining from pushing her advantage to the point of endangering the unity of Iran. The Soviet-Iranian Treaty of 26 February 1921 was an important factor in ensuring that the Iranian state would retain its existing configuration, just as the British refusal to support Iran's expansionist claims had also contrived to produce the same result.

The third factor which shaped the modern Near East was the internal forces of the Near East itself. Violent resistance to European domination was a feature of the post-war settlement in Asia Minor, Syria, Palestine, Iraq and Egypt. In the cases of Asia Minor, Iraq and Egypt it had a decisive influence on the form of government which eventually emerged in those countries. It has been the usual practice to describe this resistance as "nationalist" although it has always been recognized that the movements concerned contained elements which were not nationalist. It would be true to say that nationalism, in the sense of a commitment to a belief that members of an identified ethnic group had the right to an independent state, was a minor element in the movements. The predominant features of the armed disturbances were older: Islam, tribal bonds and ambitions, and peasant discontents: and it was these features which made the disturbances so dangerous. What frightened Europeans most about the disturbances in Anatolia were their Muslim implications and what alarmed the British most in Egypt in 1919 was the movement of the bedouin. Yet there was a nationalist element in the leadership of each of the movements concerned: Muṣṭafā Kemāl and his associates in Anatolia, Fayṣal in Syria and Iraq, the Wafdists in Egypt – for each of them there was a reality in the notion of a Turkish, Arab or Egyptian nation – and it was the nationalist element which profited most from the disturbances. The foot-soldiers of the uprisings fought for religion, loot or some older sentiment, usually one which was opposed to any form of state authority, but what they got was eventually an embryonic national state which bore on them much more heavily than any colonial regime.

Why did nationalism win? First, Europeans made errors in their identification of the opposition and greatly overestimated the role of nationalism in it. To some extent they were the victims of their own propaganda of the last years of the war which had depicted an enemy world full of nations in swaddling clothes ready to emerge in leading strings under the banner of self-determination. But perhaps more importantly the Europeans wanted nationalism to be the most prominent element; nationalism they understood – it was a modern European doctrine and those who professed it talked the language of debating chambers. Islam and tribalism, on the other hand, seemed dark and dangerous factors, elemental passions rather than doctrines; and their leaders, if they could be discovered, were hard, uncompromising men uncorrupted by reason. Second, the nationalist leaders were well placed to exploit the situation in which they found themselves. They were the product of the long process of modernization which the Near East had undergone since 1800. They were familiar with European institutions and could use them; Muṣṭafā Kemāl was produced by the greatest of all the European-style institutions exported to the Near East before 1914, namely the Ottoman army, and although it was irregular forces which supported the Nationalist resistance in Anatolia in 1919 and 1920, it was the rebuilt army led by old Ottoman officers which dominated the situation in 1922. Former Ottoman officers were also the chief props of Fayṣal in Syria and later in Iraq. Fayṣal, like Zaghlūl, was also familiar with another Western-style institution, the deliberative assembly; the techniques and the language of politics acquired in the pre-1914 Assemblies of Istanbul and Cairo served the nationalists in good stead, as a similar experience in Tehran also served those Iranian politicians who sought to obstruct the operation of the Anglo-Iranian Agreement. These men had also learned the most central lesson of modernization, namely the necessity of organization, and they were able to create institutions which could harness the forces they rode and direct them on the paths they had glimpsed. The shape of the new Near East owed much to ancient forces but it owed more to its modernization experience.

NOTES

1. Quoted M. Llewellyn-Smith, *Ionian vision: Greece in Asia Minor, 1919–1922*, London 1973, 18.
2. Quoted P. C. Helmreich, *From Paris to Sèvres*, Columbus, Ohio, 1974, 70.
3. Lord Balfour, Memorandum on Syria, 11 April 1919 in *Documents on British Foreign Policy*, Series I, IV, 340–49.
4. Maurice Hankey, Diary, 29 July 1918. Quoted in S. Roskill, *Hankey: man of secrets*, I, London 1970, 583.
5. Quoted J. Marlowe, *Late Victorian*, London 1967, 199.
6. Quoted H. Nicolson, *Curzon: the last phase*, London 1934, 138.

Bibliographical Guide

NOTE

The following guide is intended only to illustrate the range of source material available for the study of the Near East in the nineteenth and early twentieth centuries and to direct attention towards the more important books and a few of the articles on the subject. To economize on space the subtitles of books are normally omitted as are the number of volumes, the publishers and the place of publication if it is London. The list of books is confined to works in English apart from a few important books in French and German. Readers who wish to investigate further the range of articles on the subject are recommended to begin with the *Index Islamicus* and its *supplements* (1958–   , edited by J. D. Pearson *et al.*) which is available in major libraries. The titles of journals mentioned have normally been abbreviated and page numbers of articles omitted: a list of more important journals dealing with the modern Near East is given below, together with abbreviations.

Asian and African Studies (*AAS*)
Archivium Ottomanicum (*AO*)
Bulletin of the School of Oriental and African Studies (*BSOAS*)
International Journal of Middle Eastern Studies (*IJMES*)
Journal of the American Oriental Society (*JAOS*)
Middle East Journal (*MEJ*)
Middle East Studies (*MES*)
Maghreb Review (*MR*)
Studia Islamica (*SI*)

1. PRIMARY SOURCES

The principal source for the history of the Near East during the nineteenth and early twentieth centuries is the government archives of the states of the Near East. So far these archives have been very incompletely examined by historians and most of the history of the modern Near East has been written from other sources which will be described in due course. When the archives of the Near Eastern states have been fully exploited the history of the modern Near East, it is fair to predict, will look very different from the version presented in this and other books. It is also true that the revision will be the work of many years and even generations.

The largest and most important of the archives of the Near Eastern states is that of the Ottoman empire which contains material relating to all of the regions which once formed part of the empire as well as documents relating to foreign states with which the Ottomans had dealings. Not all of the imperial archives are open to scholars; in particular, the records of the Ministry of the Interior, so important for the study of provincial affairs, are unavailable. And of those records which are open many are ill-sorted and inadequately listed and some are more open in theory than in practice. The most important collection and that most used by scholars is the Prime Ministers' Archives (Başvekalet (Başbakanli̊k) Arşivi) in Istanbul. The material in these archives affords a view across a very wide range of activities and includes the archives of the Finance Ministry and the Yi̊ldi̊z Palace Archives, that is to say material relating to the reign of ʿAbd ül-Ḥamīd II. Another important archival collection is the records of the Foreign Ministry (Hariciye Vekaleti Arşivleri) also in Istanbul. Whereas most of the material in the Ottoman archives is in Ottoman Turkish, the Foreign Ministry records include translations of many documents into French. A third valuable collection of material is the Topkapi̊ Palace Archives which contains additional information relating to the operation of the sultanate. And there are a number of other archives containing material relating to other departments of Ottoman government. The principal guides to these records are in Turkish but three articles by Stanford J. Shaw will be helpful to English readers. These are "Archival sources for Ottoman History: the archives of Turkey", *JAOS*, lxxx, 1962; "The *Yi̊ldi̊z* Palace archives of Abdülhamit II", *AO*, iii, 1971; and "Ottoman archival materials for the nineteenth and early twentieth centuries: the archives in Istanbul", *IJMES*, vi, 1975. There are, of course, also many collections of Ottoman provincial records in the archives of the states which once formed part of the Ottoman empire; in recent years much work has been done on such records in Damascus, Belgrade and in Bulgaria.

Documents and information from the Ottoman archives were published during the life of the empire and further material has been published since 1922. Of particular note is the collection of imperial *sālnāmes* or gazetteers which were published annually from 1847 until 1908 and irregularly thereafter. In addition similar provincial *sālnāmes* were published, containing detailed information relating to particular provinces. These provincial *sālnāmes* were published irregularly and some have been lost. The Ottomans also published much material relating to finance and trade as well as substantial collections of legislation. Translations of Ottoman laws include G. Aristarchi Bey, *Legislation ottomane, ou recueil des lois, reglements, ordonnances, traités, capitulations et autres documents officiels de l'empire ottoman*, 7 vols, Constantinople 1873–88, and G. Young, *Corps de droit ottoman*, 7 vols, Oxford 1905–6.

The second most substantial collection of state archives is that of Egypt. These extensive and varied materials in Turkish, Arabic, French and other languages are in process of being brought together and rehoused in the Egyptian National Archives (*Dār al-wathāʾiq al-qawmiyya*) in Cairo. The material relates to all aspects of Egyptian life – social, economic and political – and is now being used extensively by scholars to provide quite new insights into Egyptian history.

No other state archives rival the Ottoman and Egyptian records for the nineteenth and early twentieth centuries, but important collections of archival materials exist in the Sudan in the Central Records Office in Khartoum where the surviving records of the Mahdist state and of the condominium are deposited. There is no state archival collection as such in Iran. Individual ministries, notably the Ministry of Foreign Affairs, do possess nineteenth-century documents which, although not generally available, have been used by privileged scholars. In Iraq are archives of the Ottoman provincial governments. The archives of Saudi Arabia are not generally available to scholars. In all regions there are records of local government. In general it must be said that pride, suspicion, bureaucracy and lack of money have constituted serious obstacles to the proper preservation, arrangement and utilization of archival materials throughout the Near East and the situation will not improve until governments appoint scholars to manage archives and give them a free hand.

European archives have been widely used for the study of the history of the Near East. Various departments of European governments preserved records relating to the Near East but the most important are those of Foreign Ministries. These records are primarily of use for the history of diplomatic transactions and foreign policy and, inevitably, tell readers more about the European powers concerned than about the history of the Near East. Nevertheless, they contain a great deal of information about aspects of Near Eastern life including politics and areas of economic activity, notably trade and finance. The tsarist archives are not normally available to scholars from outside the USSR but those of France (Archives du ministère des affaires étrangères in Paris), of Austria (Haus-, Hof-, und Staatsarchiv in Vienna) and Germany (Auswärtiges Amt in Bonn; earlier records in Potsdam with microfilms of the later records in London and Washington) are often used. The British Foreign Office records in the Public Record Office in Kew constitute a valuable collection which may be supplemented for certain areas of the Near East (Arabia, Iraq and Iran) by the India Office records in the India Office Library in London. The British records are especially important for the history of Egypt since 1882.

During the nineteenth and twentieth centuries all the European states published, from time to time, material from their archives relating to the Near East; the British publications were usually in the form of Parliamentary Papers, the so-called Blue Books; and the French Foreign Ministry documents as *Documents diplomatiques*. In addition all have published special collections of documents on foreign policy which include information concerning the Near East. For Russian dealings with Transcaucasia and relations with Iran and the Ottomans during the first half of the nineteenth century *Akty sobrannye kavkazskoj archeologicheskoj komissiej*, Tiflis 1866–78, is a treasure-house of information. Soviet publications include the incomplete *Mezhdunarodnye otnosheniya v epokhu imperializma* (1930 onwards; partial German edition by Otto Hoetzsch, *Die Internationalen Beziehungen im Zeitalter des Imperialismus*, Berlin 1931–6, which may be supplemented by E. D. Adamov (ed.), *Die Europäischen Mächte und die Türkei während des Weltkrieges*, Dresden 1930–2). Among current projects are *Vneshnaya Politika Rossii*, Moscow 1960 onwards, and *Dokumenty Vneshnej Politiki SSSR*, Moscow 1959 onwards which covers the period since 1917. The principal collections of French documents are *Les origines diplomatiques de la guerre de 1870–71*, Paris 1910 onwards, and *Documents diplomatiques français 1871–1914*, Paris 1929–60. For German documents see *Die Grosse Politik der Europäischen Kabinette*, Berlin 1922–7, which covers the period from 1871 until 1914; and for Austrian documents there is *Österreich-Ungarns Aussenpolitik, 1908–1914*, Vienna 1930. The collection of United States' documents, *Foreign relations of the United States*, is especially useful for the history of the Ottoman empire during the war years. British documents are published in *British documents on the origins of the war*, 1927–38, and *Documents on British foreign policy*, 1947 onwards, which covers the period since 1919. Convenient shorter collections of documents on diplomacy are J. C. Hurewitz (ed.), *The Middle*

East and North Africa in world politics, I and II (1535–1945), New Haven, Conn. 1975–9, and M. S. Anderson, *The Great Powers and the Near East, 1774–1923*, 1970.

The correspondence of European consuls in the Near East is often useful for social and economic developments and for local history. A large collection of French material relating to Lebanon has recently been published under the title, *Documents diplomatiques et consulaires relatifs à l'histoire du Liban*, Beirut 1975 onwards.

Business, personal and other non-governmental archives are being increasingly used to rewrite Near Eastern history. The habit of Iranian politicians of preserving their papers has proved of much benefit to historians in recent years, while in Egypt the papers of the Bakri family enabled F. de Jong to throw new light on the activities of Ṣufi orders (*Turuq and Turuq-linked institutions in nineteenth century Egypt*, Leiden 1978). T. Walz, "Family archives in Egypt", in *l'Égypte au XIXe siècle*, Paris 1982, is a preliminary survey. European and United States' missionary archives have been exploited for information on the spread of modern education in Syria but they also contain information on other aspects of social life. In European countries there are large collections of private papers relating to the Near East and a list of such papers in the United Kingdom exists in J. D. Pearson (ed.), *A guide to manuscripts and documents in the British Isles relating to the Middle East and North Africa*, 1980. The principal collections are in London but important archives also exist in Oxford (St Antony's College) and in Durham (the Sudan Archive).

The amount of memoir literature available for the nineteenth and twentieth centuries is considerable. Often such memoirs were published in newspapers and periodicals which themselves become an important source of information, especially after the 1860s. The national libraries of Near Eastern countries are the principal repositories of newspapers although the conditions in which they are stored often leave much to be desired. Some valuable collections of newspapers and periodicals exist in other countries; the Library of Congress has useful runs of certain periodicals and the Browne Collection in Cambridge University has a number of rare Persian newspapers relating to the years before the First World War. Memoirs were also published as books. Among the more important Iranian memoirs are those of Mirzā ʿAlī Khān Amīn al-Dawla, *Khāṭirāt-i sīyāsī*, Tehran 1962, and Muḥammad Ḥasan Khān, Iʿtimād al-Salṭana, *Rūznāma-yi khāṭirāt*, Tehran 1967. For the Ottoman empire we have the memoirs of Saʿīd Pasha, *Khāṭirāt-i Saʿīd Pasha*, Istanbul 1912; Aḥmed Jevdet Pasha, *Teẕākir*, Ankara 1953–67; Kāmil Pasha, *Khāṭirāt-i Ṣadr-i Esbaq Kāmil Pasha*, Istanbul 1913, as well as those of several prominent Young Turks including Jemāl Pasha, *Memoirs of a Turkish statesman, 1913–1919*, 1922, and Ismāʿīl Kemāl, *The memoirs of Ismail Kemal Bey*, 1920, which have both been translated into English.

The borderline between memoir, contemporary history and chronicle is one that is not always easy to draw. During the nineteenth century, chronicles, the staple source of the historian of earlier periods of Near Eastern history, merge into genuine history writing. The great work of the Egyptian historian, ʿAbd al-Raḥmān al-Jabartī, *ʿAjāʾib al-āthār fiʾl-tarājim waʾl-akhbār*, Cairo 1880, which covers the beginnings of our period, is primarily a chronicle and a collection of biographies. An indifferent French translation, Chefik Mansour *et al.*, *Merveilles biographiques et historiques ou chronique du Cheikh Abd-El-Rahman El-Djabarti*, Cairo 1888–96, exists. The Qājār chronicles of the first half of the nineteenth century, notably Muḥammad Taqī Kāshānī, Lisān al-Mulk Sipihr, *Nāsikh al-tawārīkh*, 1857, and Riżā Qulī Khān Hidāyat, *Rawżat al-ṣafā-i nāṣirī*, Qum 1920/21, also belong to the old chronicle tradition, but later works, for example Muḥammad Ḥasan Khān Iʿtimād al-Salṭana, *Mirʾāt al-buldān*, Tehran 1877–80, and *Tārīkh-i muntaẓam-i nāṣirī*, Tehran 1881–3, are complex mixtures of chronicle, history and administrative handbook. They invite comparison with the enormous and unclassifiable work of ʿAlī Mubārak Pasha, *Al-khiṭaṭ al-Tawfīqiyya al-jadīda*, Cairo 1888, a compound of twenty volumes of history, geography, memoir and gazetteer which contains a vast amount of information concerning Egypt in the middle of the nineteenth century. A similar transition is discernible in Ottoman history writing: the chronicle of ʿAṭāʾullāh Meḥmed Shānīzāde, *Shānīzāde Tārīkhi*, Istanbul 1873–4, is in the Ottoman court chronicle tradition (although the author uses European language sources) and describes events during the early nineteenth century; the lengthy work of Aḥmed Jevdet Pasha, *Tārīkh-i devlet-i ʿaliyye*, Istanbul 1854–83, although following in general the chronological style of the chronicle, includes also an essentially historical treatment of certain episodes. Those who are interested in the development of Near Eastern historiography are recommended to consult B. Lewis and P. M. Holt (eds), *Historians of the Middle East*, 1962. The examples given, however, may serve to illustrate the great amount of source material of a traditional kind which exists for the Near East during the nineteenth century.

A much used source which is also in great abundance for the nineteenth and early twentieth centuries is the writings of European travellers. These writers are habitually described as travellers and many of them were precisely that but others were long resident in the Near

East. The great merit of their work, of course, is that they were writing for Europeans and therefore asked questions about matters on which Europeans wanted information and classified their information in categories familiar to Europeans. The information which they provide is, therefore, usable by historians in ways in which information supplied by some Near Eastern writers is not. Although some Near Eastern writers adopt the categories and causal relationships of Europe many do not and the information which they supply is often whimsical in its variety and apparently inconsequential in its connections. The major demerit of the European travellers is the counterpart of their merit: that is that they tended to push information into a European mould and to draw inferences about links and causes which were alien to the societies which they described and often outrightly misleading to the historian. Further, they often ignored areas of Near Eastern activity, notably social and religious life, taking the false view that these were dying relics of the past of little interest to Europeans. Having said this it should also be said that the best European writers were very good indeed and that without their work the history of the Near East in the modern period would be a good deal thinner than it is.

Among the best European writers on the Ottoman empire were Adolphus Slade, whose *Records of travels in Turkey, Greece, etc.*, was published in 1854 and M. A. Ubicini, whose *Letters on Turkey* were published in 1856. An excellent source for the history of Syria in the mid-nineteenth century is C. H. S. Churchill, *The Druzes and the Maronites under Turkish rule*, 1862. For Iran S. G. W. Benjamin, *Persia and the Persians*, x, Boston 1887, is a good collection of information excelled only by G. N. Curzon (i.e. the future Lord Curzon), *Persia and the Persian question*, 1892. For the earlier nineteenth century the writings of J. B. Fraser, James Morier and John Malcolm help to illuminate the situation of Iran. The history of Arabia would be much poorer if we did not have the accounts of a number of European travellers from Burckhardt through Richard Burton to Charles Doughty and W. H. Shakespeare. And in his *Manners and customs of the modern Egyptians*, 1836, E. W. Lane produced one of the most attractive and informative of all accounts of Near Eastern society. Europeans also produced major compendia of information. First in time and fame is the great French *Description de l'Egypte: état moderne*, Paris 1809–22, the product of the work of the scholars whom Bonaparte took to Egypt. And at the other end of the century are the major works of V. Cuinet, *La Turquie d'Asie*, and *Syrie, Liban, Palestine*, Paris 1890–8 which included much information drawn from Ottoman archives. Students of the history of the Persian Gulf would have a more difficult task without the aid of the

Gazetteer of the Persian Gulf, Calcutta 1908–15, compiled from British records by J. G. Lorimer.

2. SECONDARY SOURCES

General

Of general histories of the Near East S. N. Fisher, *The Middle East: a history*, New York 1959, and G. E. Kirk, *A short history of the Middle East*, 1964, emphasize contacts with the West. C. Brockelmann, *History of the Islamic peoples*, 1960, gives more weight to indigenous factors but is severely factual and its treatment of the modern period is slight. The most comprehensive work is P. M. Holt, Ann K. S. Lambton and Bernard Lewis (eds), *Cambridge history of Islam*, 1970. For the modern period P. M. Holt, *Egypt and the Fertile Crescent, 1576–1922*, 1966, is a very reliable guide but it deals only with the Arab Near East. W. Yale, *The Near East: a modern history*, Ann Arbor 1959, is concerned with the nineteenth century and primarily with international relations. A useful introduction is Peter Mansfield, *The Ottoman Empire and its successors*, 1973. W. R. Polk and R. L. Chambers, *The beginnings of modernization in the Middle East*, Chicago 1968, contains some important essays on a theme which is central to the present book, and another fertile collection of articles is Albert Hourani, *The emergence of the modern Middle East*, 1981, which is principally concerned with the nineteenth century. Hourani's *Arabic thought in the liberal age, 1798–1939*, 1962, together with Hamid Enayat, *Modern Islamic political thought*, 1982, will serve as reliable guides to the history of ideas. The European impact on the region is the subject of B. Lewis, *The Middle East and the West*, 1964. Education is covered in J. S. Szyliowicz, *Education and modernization in the Middle East*, Ithaca, NY 1973, and law in N. Coulson, *A history of Islamic law*, Edinburgh, 1964, and M. Khadduri and H. Liebesny (eds), *Law in the Middle East*, Washington 1956. I. M. Lapidus (ed.), *Middle Eastern cities*, Berkeley, Calif. 1969, is one of the very few works to deal with the topic of urbanization. Carleton S. Coon, *Caravan*, 1952, the progenitor of the "mosaic" concept, still provides an excellent introduction to the social structure of the traditional Near East. Those who are little acquainted with Islam will wish to consult H. A. R. Gibb, *Mohammadanism*, 1969, and *Modern trends in Islam*, Chicago 1947. The latter book deals with the modernist movement. Other aspects of the same movement may be investigated with the aid of Nikki R. Keddie,

Sayyid Jamal ad-Din "al-Afghani", Berkeley, Calif. 1972, Elie Kedourie, *Afghani and Abduh*, 1966, and M. H. Kerr, *Islamic reform*, Berkeley, Calif. 1966, which is concerned with the work of ʿAbduh and Rashīd Riḍā.

Those in search of general statistical information should see Justin McCarthy, *The Arab world, Turkey and the Balkans (1878–1914)*, Boston 1982, which presents statistics derived mainly from Ottoman sources. McCarthy has also written on nineteenth- and twentieth-century population problems basing his work on the Ottoman archives. See *Muslims and Minorities*, New York 1983, and "Nineteenth century Egyptian population", *MES*, xii, 1976. For the population of Syria see Haim Gerber, "The population of Syria and Palestine in the nineteenth century", *AAS*, xiii, 1979. A major recent study on the effect of the plague is D. Panzac, *La peste dans l'empire Ottoman, 1700–1850*, Louvain 1985. There are three useful economic histories of the Near East dealing with the nineteenth and twentieth centuries. These are Z. Y. Herschlag, *Introduction to the modern economic history of the Middle East*, Leiden 1964, R. Owen, *The Middle East in the World Economy, 1800–1914*, 1981, and C. Issawi, *An economic history of the Middle East and North Africa*, 1982. Issawi has also produced three books of source extracts, readings and commentary relating to the economic history of the region. These are *The economic history of the Middle East, 1800–1914*, Chicago 1966, which deals principally with the Arab world, *The economic history of Iran, 1800–1914*, Chicago 1971, and *The economic history of Turkey, 1800–1914*, Chicago 1980. A good descriptive geography is W. B. Fisher, *The Middle East*, 1963, and three historical atlases are H. W. Hazard, *Atlas of Islamic history*, Princeton 1954, R. Roolvink, *Historical atlas of the Muslim peoples*, Amsterdam 1957, and William C. Brice, *An historical atlas of Islam*, Leiden 1981. Francis Robinson, *Atlas of the Islamic world since 1500*, 1982, is rather more than an atlas as it contains many pictures and a substantial text.

The Eastern Question

By far the best general survey is M. S. Anderson, *The Eastern question, 1774–1923*, 1966. On the period of the Revolutionary and Napoleonic Wars see F. Charles-Roux, *Les Origins de l'expédition d'Égypte, Paris 1910*; V. J. Puryear, *Napoleon and the Dardanelles*, Berkeley, Calif. 1951; T. Naff, *Ottoman diplomacy and the Great European Powers, 1797–1802*; and P. F. Shupp, *The European powers and the Near Eastern question, 1806–7*, New York, 1931. The rivalry of Britain and Russia during the post-1815 period may be traced through J. H. Gleason, *The genesis of*

Russophobia in Great Britain, 1815–1914, Cambridge, Mass. 1950; E. Moseley, *Russian diplomacy and the opening of the Eastern Question in 1838 and 1839*, Cambridge, Mass. 1939, which uses Russian archival material; and H. L. Hoskins, *British Routes to India*, New York 1928. M. E. Yapp, *Strategies of British India*, Oxford 1980, discusses rivalry in the eastern part of the region. A more general account of eastern rivalries, especially good on Russian aspects, is D. Gillard, *The struggle for Asia, 1828–1914*, 1977. The background to the Crimean War is described in V. J. Puryear, *International economics and diplomacy in the Near East*, Stanford, Calif. 1935, which places stress on economic factors in eastern rivalries, and his *England, Russia and the Straits question, 1844–1856*, Berkeley, Calif. 1931. H. W. V. Temperley, *England and the Near East: the Crimea*, 1936 is still the best general account of Crimean War diplomacy. It may be supplemented by G. B. Henderson, *Crimean War diplomacy*, Glasgow 1947, a helpful collection of essays.

The following period may be studied through W. E. Mosse, *The rise and fall of the Crimean system*, 1963. More attention has been given to the Eastern Crisis of 1875–8 than to any other episode prior to the First World War. A reliable account of the general background is provided by W. Langer, *European alliances and alignments, 1871–1890*, New York 1950. For the opening of the crisis see D. Harris, *A diplomatic history of the Balkan crisis of 1875–8*, Stanford, Calif. 1936, and for the whole episode there is no sounder work than M. D. Stojanovic, *The Great Powers and the Balkans, 1875–1878*, Cambridge 1938. Russian policy may be followed through B. H. Sumner, *Russia and the Balkans 1870–1880*, Oxford 1937, and Charles and Barbara Jelavich (eds), *Russia and the East, 1876–1880*, Leiden 1959. R. Millman, *Britain and the Eastern Question, 1875–1878*, Oxford 1979, is a detailed account of British Cabinet views of the crisis. An older, much quoted account of the developing role of British interests in the Near East is D. E. Lee, *Great Britain and the Cyprus Convention policy of 1878*, Cambridge, Mass. 1934. The end of the crisis is the subject of W. Medlicott, *The Congress of Berlin and after*, 1938, and the same author has also written an account of the subsequent years in *Bismarck, Gladstone and the Concert of Europe*, 1956. W. Langer, *The diplomacy of imperialism, 1890–1902*, New York 1951, provides information about the crises of the 1890s, notably the Cretan episode. Although several recent articles and monographs deal with aspects of the Anglo-Russian entente of 1907 the only full-length study is the now old R. P. Churchill, *The Anglo-Russian Convention of 1907*, Cedar Rapids, Ia. 1939. For the last great crisis before 1914 see E. C. Helmreich, *The diplomacy of the Balkan Wars*, Cambridge, Mass. 1938.

Economic aspects of European rivalries in the East may be studied first in D. C. M. Platt, *Finance, trade and politics in British foreign policy, 1815–1914*, Oxford 1968, and H. Feis, *Europe the world's banker, 1870–1914*, New Haven, Conn., 1930. Most work has been done on the period after 1870. On the Suez Canal C. W. Hallberg, *The Suez Canal*, New York 1931, is a good introduction but D. A. Farnie, *East and west of Suez*, Oxford 1969, is the fullest study of the ramifications of the canal problem. On rivalries in Asia Minor H. S. W. Corrigan, *British, French and German interests in Asiatic Turkey, 1881–1914*, 1954, provides a broad basis which may be amplified through the exhaustive Jacques Thobie, *Intérêts et impérialisme français dans l'empire ottoman (1895–1914)* Paris 1977; C. Ducruet, *Les capitaux européens aux Proche Orient*, Paris 1964; and W. O. Henderson, "German economic penetration in the Middle East, 1880–1914", *Economic History Review*, xviii, 1948. D. C. Blaisdell, *European financial control in the Ottoman empire*, New York 1929, is a good account of the Ottoman Public Debt Administration. J. Wolf, *The diplomatic history of the Bagdad railroad*, Columbia 1936, is probably the most useful treatment of its subject and the other well-known railway in the Near East is the centre of the interest of W. Ochsenwald, *The Hijaz railroad*, Charlottesville, Va. 1980.

The Ottoman Empire

H. A. R. Gibb and H. Bowen, *Islamic society and the West*, 2 pts, 1950–7, is a good account of the institutions of the empire at the beginning of the period. It should be read with N. Itzkowitz, "Eighteenth century Ottoman realities", *SI*, xvi, 1962. K. Karpat, "The transformation of the Ottoman state, 1789–1908", *IJMES*, iii, 1972, is an interesting overview of change. The best written general history of the process of Ottoman reform is B. Lewis, *The emergence of modern Turkey*, 1961. Other general accounts worth study are N. Berkes, *The development of secularism in Turkey*, Montreal 1964, and S. J. and E. K. Shaw, *History of the Ottoman Empire and modern Turkey*, II, Cambridge 1977. S. J. Shaw, *Between old and new*, Cambridge, Mass. 1971, is a valuable account of the reforms of Selim III. F. E. Bailey, *British policy and the Turkish reform movement*, Cambridge, Mass. 1942, gives an outline of the early Tanẓīmāt period and R. H. Davison, *Reform in the Ottoman Empire 1856–1876*, Princeton 1963, is an excellent account of the later period.

The bureaucratic aspects are delineated in C. V. Findlay, *Bureaucratic reform in the Ottoman Empire*, Princeton 1980, and critics of the Tanẓīmāt form the subject of S. Mardin, *The genesis of Young Ottoman thought*, Princeton 1962. R. Devereux, *The first Ottoman constitutional period*,

Baltimore 1963, is the most detailed account of the making of the 1876 constitution. There is no good biography of ʿAbd ül-Ḥamīd II in English; Joan Haslip, *The sultan*, 1958, has at least the merit of being readable. The *émigré* opponents of ʿAbd ül-Ḥamīd are studied in E. F. Ramsaur, *The Young Turks*, Princeton 1957, and the best account of the 1908 revolution and its aftermath is in F. Ahmed, *The Young Turks*, Oxford 1969. D. Quataert, *Social disintegration and popular resistance in the Ottoman Empire, 1881–1908*, New York 1983, provides some information about background factors of a socio-economic character. Two useful articles on the 1909 counter-revolution are D. Farhi, "The Şeriat as a political slogan – or the incident of the 31st Mart", *MES*, vii, 1971, and V. R. Swanson, "The military rising in Istanbul, 1909", *Journal of Contemporary History*, v, 1970. Ideological aspects of the period are described in D. Kushner, *The origins of Turkish nationalism*, 1977.

The Balkans

By far the best starting-point is L. S. Stavrianos, *The Balkans since 1453*, New York 1958, which has an excellent bibliography. Other general accounts include C. and B. Jelavich, *The Balkans in transition*, Berkeley Calif. 1963, B. Jelavich, *The establishment of the Balkan national states, 1804–1920*, Seattle 1977, B. Jelavich, *History of the Balkans, I: Eighteenth and nineteenth centuries*, Cambridge 1983, and R. Clogg (ed.), *Balkan society in the age of Greek independence*, 1981. D. Djordjevic and S. Fischer-Galati, *The Balkan revolutionary tradition*, New York, 1981, deals with a familiar feature of Balkan life and death. The best history of Serbia is now M. B. Petrović, *A history of modern Serbia, 1804–1918*, New York 1976, and of Greece R. Clogg, *A short history of modern Greece*, Cambridge 1979. Also on Greece see C. W. Crawley, *The question of Greek independence*, 1952, and D. Dakin, *The Greek struggle for independence, 1821–1833*, 1973, which deal with the origins of the state. A collection of documents on the same topic is in R. Clogg (ed.), *The struggle for Greek independence*, 1973. For Romania it is still necessary to go back to R. W. Seton-Watson, *A history of the Roumans from Roman times to the completion of unity*, Cambridge 1934, although this may be supplemented by G. J. Babango, *The emergence of the Romanian national state*, New York, 1979, the old, but excellent, T. W. Riker, *The Making of Rumania*, Oxford 1931, and B. Jelavich, *Russia and the formation of the Romanian national state, 1821–1878*, Cambridge 1984. The history of Bulgaria during the Ottoman period is a problem. M. Macdermott, *A history of Bulgaria, 1393–1885*, 1962, is rather uncritically sympathetic to the Bulgar cause. For those who can read German, A. Hajek, *Bulgarien unter der Turkenherrschaft*, Berlin 1925, is much better and M. Pinson, "Ottoman Bulgaria in the first Tanzimat period – the revolts in Nish (1841) and Vidin (1850)", *MES*, xi, 1975, is a valuable article. For the post-1878 period we now have the sound book by R. J. Crampton, *Bulgaria 1878–1918: a history*, New York 1983, which is based mainly on Austrian archival sources. On the origins of Albania there is the excellent S. Skendi, *The Albanian national awakening, 1878–1912*, Princeton 1967. For Macedonia see E. Barker, *Macedonia: its place in Balkan power politics*, 1950; D. Dakin, *The Greek struggle in Macedonia, 1897–1913*, Salonika 1966; and D. Slijepcević, *The Macedonian question*, Chicago 1968. On Balkan economic developments during the period see J. R. Lampe and M. R. Jackson, *Balkan economic history 1500–1950*, Bloomington, Ind. 1962, and I. Berend and G. Raki, *Economic development in East Central Europe in the nineteenth and twentieth centuries*, New York 1974. A valuable recent revisionist study which challenges those theories which stress the role of commerce as a factor of change is B. McGowan, *Economic life in Ottoman Europe: taxation, trade and the struggle for land, 1600–1800*, Cambridge 1981.

Anatolia

As remarked in the text no one has ever thought it worth writing a history of Ottoman Anatolia and information has to be sought in general works, unpublished theses and a few articles of which A. Gould, "Lords or bandits? The Derebeys of Cilicia", *IJMES*, vii, 1976 is a useful example. What writing has been done has concentrated mainly on the problems of eastern Anatolia. W. E. D. Allen and P. Muratoff, *Caucasian battlefields*, Cambridge 1953, provides a general account of Russo–Ottoman wars and H. Pasdermadjian, *Histoire de l'Arménie depuis les origines jusqu'au le traité de Lausanne*, Paris 1949, A. O. Sarkissiaṇ, *History of the Armenian question to 1885*, Urbana, Ill. 1938, and L. Nalbandian, *The Armenian revolutionary movement*, Berkeley, Calif. 1963, between them cover the Armenian problem. On the Kurds the most penetrating study is M. van Bruinessen, *Agha, shaikh and state*, Utrecht 1978.

Syria (including Lebanon and Palestine)

For a general outline see A. L. Tibawi, *A modern history of Syria*, 1969, and K. S. Salibi, *The modern history of Lebanon*, 1965. The Tanẓīmāt in Syria is the subject of M. Ma'oz, *Ottoman reform in Syria and Palestine*,

Oxford 1968, and the same scholar has edited a collection of essays entitled *Studies on Palestine during the Ottoman period*, Jerusalem 1975. For Lebanon in the period down to 1860 see I. Harik, *Politics and change in a traditional society: Lebanon 1711–1845*, Princeton 1968; W. R. Polk, *The opening of south Lebanon, 1788–1840*, Cambridge, Mass. 1963; and Y. Porath, "The Peasant Revolt of 1858–61 in Kisrawan", *AAS*, ii, 1966. Two French studies must be noted: D. Chevalier, *La Societé du Mont Liban à l'époque de la révolution industrielle en l'Europe*, Paris 1971, and T. Touma, *Paysans et institutions féodales chez les Druses et les Maronites du Liban du XVIIe siècle à 1914*, Beirut 1972. On the missionary impact are two studies by A. L. Tibawi, *British interests in Palestine, 1800–1901*, Oxford 1961, and *American interests in Syria, 1800–1901*, Oxford 1966. For Russian interests see D. Hopwood, *The Russian presence in Syria and Palestine, 1843–1914*, Oxford 1969, and T. Stavrou, *Russian interests in Palestine, 1882–1914*, Thessaloniki 1963. Two important recent studies on social and political change from the mid-nineteenth century are L. K. Schilcher, *Families in politics*, Stuttgart 1965, and P. Khoury, *Urban notables and Arab nationalism*, Cambridge 1983. Both these works contribute to a new understanding of the rise of Arab nationalism and follow a line of argument previously elaborated in essays by C. E. Dawn, *From Ottomanism to Arabism*, Urbana, Ill. 1973. For earlier interpretations see C. Antonius, *The Arab Awakening*, 1938, and Z. N. Zeine, *The emergence of Arab nationalism*, Beirut 1966. On the last period before 1914 see R. I. Khalidi, *British policy towards Syria and Palestine, 1906–1914*, 1980, and J. R. Spagnolo, *France and Ottoman Lebanon, 1861–1914*, 1977, which also provides a detailed account of the politics of Lebanon in this period, and W. Shorrock, *French imperialism in the Middle East: the failure of policy in Syria and Lebanon 1900–1914*, Madison, Wis. 1976.

Iraq

Two books by S. H. Longrigg, *Four centuries of modern Iraq*, Oxford 1925 and *Iraq, 1900–1950*, 1953, provide a useful outline of events although they are short on analysis. The latter quality is provided by T. Nieuwenhuis, *Politics and society in early modern Iraq*, The Hague 1982, and by H. Batatu, *The old social classes and the revolutionary movements of Iraq*, Princeton 1979, of which the first section provides a comprehensive delineation of the main features of Iraqi society and politics. For the period immediately before the First World War there are several studies, including S. A. Cohen, *British policy in Mesopotamia 1903–1914*,

1976, and G. R. Atiyah, *Iraq 1908–1921*, Beirut 1973. H. Mejcher, *Imperial quest for oil*, 1976, and M. Kent, *Oil and empire*, 1976, are principally concerned with the role of oil in the shaping of British policy in Iraq.

Egypt

Of the several good general histories of Egypt during the modern period the most useful is P. J. Vatikiotis, *The modern history of Egypt*, 1969. A stimulating collection of essays is P. M. Holt (ed.), *Political and social change in modern Egypt*, 1968. For the situation of Egypt at the beginning of the period an indispensable background study is A. Raymond, *Artisans et commerçants au Caire au XVIIIe siècle*, Damascus 1973–4. A recent study of Muḥammad ʿAlī is Afaf Lutfi as-Sayyid Marsot, *Egypt in the reign of Muhammad Ali*, Cambridge 1984. The work certainly brings the pasha alive, but it has not completely replaced H. H. Dodwell, *The founder of modern Egypt*, Cambridge 1931. Both books must be supplemented by more specialized studies. The diplomatic background to the rise of Muḥammad ʿAlī is described in S. Ghorbal, *The beginnings of the Egyptian question and the rise of Mehemet Ali*, 1928, and J. Marlowe, *Perfidious Albion*, 1971. H. Rivlin, *The agricultural policy of Muḥammad ʿAlī in Egypt*, Cambridge, Mass. 1961, is a very hard read but it has much information. We still lack good studies of the reigns of ʿAbbās I, Saʿīd and Ismāʿīl, although valuable books concerned with particular aspects of the period have appeared, notably F. Robert Hunter, *Egypt under the khedives, 1805–1879*, Pittsburgh 1984, a study of the emergence of a bureaucratic élite, and D. Landes, *Bankers and pashas*, Cambridge, Mass. 1958, which looks at the seamy side of Ismāʿīl's borrowings. P. Crabitès, *Ismail, the maligned khedive*, 1933, is still the best defence of Ismāʿīl's policies. Jacob Landau, *Parliaments and parties in Egypt*, Tel Aviv 1953, has useful information about Ismāʿīl's constitutional experiments.

The ʿUrābi revolt has attracted much attention. The best account of British policy is in R. Robinson and J. Gallagher, *Africa and the Victorians*, 1961, which may be contrasted with the older accounts by Lord Cromer in *Modern Egypt*, 1908, and W. S. Blunt, *The secret history of the English occupation of Egypt*, 1907. But on the internal history of the revolt the best study is A. Schölch, *Egypt for the Egyptians*, 1981. There are several good studies of the British period including Afaf Lutfi as-Sayyid (Marsot), *Egypt and Cromer*, 1968, R. Tignor, *Modernization and British colonial rule in Egypt, 1882–1914*, Princeton 1966, and Jamal Muhammad Ahmad, *The intellectual origins of Egyptian nationalism*, 1960. I respect much of what I think I understand of J. Berque, *Egypt: imperialism and revolution*, 1972, but as a book it defeats me. P. Mellini, *Sir Eldon Gorst*, Stanford, Calif. 1977, is a valuable study of Cromer's successor.

On economic developments see A. E. Crouchley, *The economic development of modern Egypt*, 1938; E. R. J. Owen, *Cotton and the Egyptian economy, 1820–1914*, Oxford 1969; and P. Gran, *The Islamic roots of capitalism, 1760–1840*, Austin, Tex. 1979. On legal changes see J. Y. Brinton, *The Mixed Courts in Egypt*, New Haven, Conn. 1968 and F. J. Ziadeh, *Lawyers, the rule of law and liberalism in modern Egypt*, Stanford, Calif. 1968 which also focuses on the Mixed Courts. G. Baer has written many valuable socio-economic studies concerning Egypt, including *A History of landownership in modern Egypt*, 1962, *Egyptian guilds in modern times*, Jerusalem 1964, *Studies in the social history of modern Egypt*, Chicago 1969, and *Fellah and townsman in the Middle East*, 1982, which also deals with Syria. On the development of ideas, see C. A. Wendell, *The evolution of the Egyptian national image*, Stanford, Calif. 1972, and N. Safran, *Egypt in search of political community*, Cambridge, Mass. 1961.

North Africa

P. M. Holt and M. W. Daly, *The history of the Sudan*, 1979 provides a good outline of events which may be supplemented for the earlier period by R. Hill, *Egypt in the Sudan, 1820–81*, 1959, and for the Mahdist uprising by P. M. Holt, *The Mahdist state in the Sudan, 1881–1898*, Oxford 1970, and A. B. Theobald, *The Mahdiyya*, 1951. On the British period M. Shibeika, *British policy in the Sudan 1882–1902*, 1952, and M. Abd al-Rahim, *Imperialism and nationalism in the Sudan*, Oxford 1963, are valuable, but M. Daly, *Empire on the Nile*, Cambridge 1986, an extremely full account of the years 1898–1934, has largely replaced previous studies of this period of Anglo-Sudanese history. For North Africa at the beginning of the period there is Charles-André Julien, *History of North Africa*, 1970.

For Libya we now have a good general history: J. Wright, *Libya: a modern history*, 1982, which can be used alongside the older A. J. Cachia, *Libya and the second Ottoman occupation, 1835–1911*, Tripoli 1945. W. C. Askew, *Europe and Italy's acquisition of Libya, 1911–1912*, Durham, NC 1942 deals with the diplomatic background to the end of Ottoman rule. Two specialized studies on the Sanusiyya are E. E. Evans Pritchard, *The Sanusi of Cyrenaica*, 1949, and N. A. Ziadeh, *The Sanūsīyah*, Leiden 1958.

For French North Africa we lack good studies in English although the situation is now rapidly improving. There is a useful survey of the literature in M. Brett, "The colonial period in the Maghrib and its aftermath: the present state of historical writing", *Journal of African History*, xvii, 1976. The same author has edited a collection of papers entitled *North Africa: Islamization and modernization*, 1973, which will introduce readers to some recent research. Although old, S. H. Roberts, *A history of French colonial policy, 1870–1925*, 1929, is still useful. J. Abun-Nasr, *A history of the Maghrib*, Cambridge 1975 and M. Morsy, *North Africa, 1800–1900*, 1984, are general histories; the latter includes Egypt in a despondent account of North African development. A similar gloom enshrouds the valuable work of L. Valensi, *On the eve of colonisation: North Africa before the French conquest, 1790–1830*, New York 1977.

For Tunisia see L. Carl Brown, *The Tunisia of Ahmad Bey, 1837–1855*, Princeton 1974; G. S. Van Krieken, *Khayr al-Din et la Tunisie (1850–1881)*, Leiden 1976; and J. Ganiage, *Les origins du protectorat français en Tunisie, 1861–1881*, Paris 1959. Arthur Marsden, *British diplomacy and Tunis, 1875–1902*, 1971, inevitably stands on the outside of events. The role of Islam in Tunisia may be studied in A. H. Green, *The Tunisian ulama, 1873–1915*, Leiden 1978, and in Algeria in A. Christelow, *Muslim law courts and the French colonial state in Algeria*, Princeton 1985.

A general history of Algeria is G. Esquer, *Histoire de l'Algérie, 1830–1881*, Paris 1960, and attention should be drawn to articles by P. von Silvers in *IJMES* and *MR*.

Morocco lies outside the scope of this book but readers might like to note the existence of the massive work of J.-L. Miège, *Le Maroc et l'Europe (1830–1894)*, Paris 1961, and the recent study by Edmund Burke III, *Prelude to protectorate in Morocco*, Chicago 1976.

Iran

Not many years ago there were few modern studies of Iranian history but the situation has now greatly improved. P. Avery, *Modern Iran*, 1965, provides a good outline which has largely displaced Sir P. Sykes, *History of Persia*, 1915 and later editions. Edmund Bosworth and C. Hillenbrand (eds), *Qajar Iran*, Edinburgh 1983, is a valuable collection of essays as is also M. Bonine and N. R. Keddie, *Modern Iran*, Albany, NY 1981. Nikki Keddie has also produced a collection of her own essays in *Iran: religion, politics and society*, 1980. An essay of fundamental importance is E. Abrahamian, "Oriental despotism: the case of Qajar Iran", *IJMES*, v, 1974. For a detailed account of the early nineteenth century one must still go back to R. G. Watson, *A history of Persia*, 1866, but the subsequent reforming period is dealt with in the monographs by S. Bakhash, *Iran: monarchy, bureaucracy and reform*, 1978, and G. Nashat, *The origins of modern reform in Iran, 1870–80*, Urbana, Ill. 1982.

E. G. Browne's *The Persian revolution*, Cambridge 1910, is still valuable for its detailed information but a better overview of the movement is provided by E. Abrahamian, *Iran between two revolutions*, Princeton 1982, and R. A. McDaniel, *The Shuster mission and the Persian constitutional revolution*, Minneapolis 1974, is a well-balanced account of its aftermath. H. Algar, *Religion and state in Iran 1785–1906*, Berkeley, Calif. 1969, is a well-informed study of the role of the ulema although the author tends to exaggerate the extent to which they were opposed to the state. He has also written a valuable biography of one reformer, *Mīrzā Malkum Khān*, Berkeley, Calif. 1972. N. Keddie, *Religion and rebellion in Iran*, 1966, is an account of the role of the ulema in the tobacco concession dispute. M. Bayat, *Mysticism and dissent*, Syracuse 1982, is another study of the relation between religion and politics and Abd al-Hadi Hairi, *Shiʿism and constitutionalism in Iran*, Leiden 1977, considers the same problem in the period after the 1906 revolution from the viewpoint of those *mujtahids* who supported the constitution. Much has been written on Iranian foreign policy. An overview is provided by R. K. Ramazani, *The foreign policy of Iran, 1500–1941*, Charlottesville, Va. 1966. Studies of special periods include M. Atkin, *Russia and Iran, 1780–1828*, Minneapolis 1980; F. Kazemzadeh, *Russia and Britain in Persia 1864–1914*, 1968; R. L. Greaves, *Persia and the defence of India, 1884–1892*, 1959; and four articles on the subsequent years down to 1914 in *BSOAS*, xxviii, 1965, and xxxi, 1968; D. McLean, *Britain and her buffer state*, 1979; and B. G. Martin, *German–Persian diplomatic relations 1873–1912*, The Hague 1959. Although several useful articles on aspects of Iranian economic life have appeared we still lack any comprehensive account for the nineteenth century. A. K. S. Lambton, *Landlord and peasant in Persia*, 1953, has much valuable information about agrarian conditions and J. Bharier, *Economic development in Iran 1900–1970*, 1971, provides a general survey of economic conditions at the end of the period.

Arabia

We have nothing like a general history of Arabia during the nineteenth and early twentieth centuries and it is necessary to piece together histories of particular regions. On the Gulf region an outstanding book is J. B. Kelly, *Britain and the Persian Gulf, 1795–1880*, 1968. R. Kumar, *India and the Persian Gulf region, 1858–1907*, 1965, and B. C. Busch,

Britain and the Persian Gulf, 1894–1914, round off the story. Oman is covered in R. G. Landen, *Oman since 1856*, Princeton 1967, and J. E. Peterson, *Oman in the twentieth century*, 1978. For south-west Arabia we have a good general history of Aden, R. J. Gavin, *Aden under British rule 1839–1967*, 1975, which may be supplemented for the early years by Z. H. Kour, *The history of Aden*, 1981. T. Marston, *Britain's imperial role in the Red Sea area, 1800–1878*, Hamden, Conn. 1961, has much information but needs to be used with care. On the Yemen, Husayn b. Abdullah al-Amri, *The Yemen in the 18th and 19th centuries*, 1985, provides a true insider's view of Yemen; E. Macro, *Yemen and the Western world since 1571*, 1968, is a much more general account. On ʿAsīr there is the old study by Sir Kinahan Cornwallis, *Asir Before the First World War*, Cambridge 1976, and for the Hijaz some specialized studies of which may be mentioned Salah Muhammad al-Amr, *The Hijaz under Ottoman rule, 1869–1914*, Riyadh 1978, and R. Baker, *King Husain and the kingdom of the Hejaz*, Cambridge 1979. H. St John Philby's *Saudi Arabia*, 1955, is still useful for the history of eastern Arabia, but for the nineteenth century we have a detailed account by R. B. Winder, *Saudi Arabia in the nineteenth century*, New York 1965, which is based upon Arabic chronicles. G. Troeller, *The birth of Saudi Arabia*, 1976, has been criticized but it is a helpful work based upon British archival material. John S. Habib, *Ibn Saʿud's warriors of Islam*, Leiden 1978, and C. M. Helms, *The cohesion of Saudi Arabia*, 1981, deal with aspects of the twentieth century history of the state. Finally, it should be noted that valuable essays on Arabian history appear in *Arabica* and *Arabian Studies* and scholars associated with those journals have also produced volumes of useful essays, including R. L. Bidwell and G. R. Smith (eds), *Arabian and Islamic studies*, 1983.

The First World War

H. S. Sachar, *The emergence of the Middle East, 1914–1924*, New York 1969, is a general account of the war and the peace settlement but is not wholly reliable. On the internal history of the Ottoman empire during the period the only book in English is Ahmed Emin, *Turkey in the World War*, New Haven, Conn. 1930. We badly need an account of the war from the Ottoman point of view which makes use of the mass of recent Turkish work on the subject. German policy is the subject of U. Trumpener, *Germany and the Ottoman Empire, 1914–1918*, Princeton 1968, and Austrian of F. G. Weber, *Eagles on the Crescent*, Ithaca, NY 1970. For Russia see M. B. Petrovich, *Russian diplomacy and eastern Europe, 1914–1917*, New York 1963; for France C. M. Andrew and A. S. Kanya-

Forstner, *France overseas*, 1981; and for the United States L. Evans, *United States policy and the partition of Turkey, 1914–1924*, Baltimore 1965. There is an excellent collection of essays surveying the interests and policies of the major powers in the Near East in M. Kent (ed.), *The Great Powers and the end of the Ottoman Empire*, 1984. Z. A. B. Zeman, *A diplomatic history of the First World War*, Oxford 1971 has useful information relevant to the Near East. Most attention has concentrated on British policy and the wartime agreements. H. N. Howard, *The partition of Turkey*, Norman, Okla. 1937 provides a suitable introduction to the subject which may be pursued in more detail in E. Kedourie, *England and the Middle East*, 1956, and *In the Anglo-Arab labyrinth*, Cambridge 1976, a study of the Ḥusayn–McMahon correspondence based on British archives. A. L. Tibawi, *Anglo-Arab relations and the question of Palestine, 1914–21*, 1977, looks at the same subject and the same material but comes to very different conclusions and I. Friedman, *The question of Palestine, 1914–1918*, 1973, presents a Zionist view of the same topic. The Indian dimension of British policy may be studied in B. C. Busch, *Britain, India and the Arabs, 1914–21*, Berkeley, Calif. 1971, which gives most attention to Arabia and Iraq. For the attempts to make peace with the Ottomans see V. H. Rothwell, *British war aims and peace diplomacy*, 1971. One of the main architects of British policy is the subject of a recent biography, R. Adelson, *Mark Sykes*, 1975. W. J. Olson, *Anglo-Iranian relations during World War 1*, 1984, provides the most complete study in English of changes in Iran during the war. For British policy it may be supplemented for the period after 1917 by F. Stanwood, *War, revolution and British imperialism in central Asia*, 1983. Still the best study of the Balfour Declaration is L. Stein, *The Balfour Declaration*, 1961, although a good recent account of the making of the decision to support Zionism in Palestine is R. Sanders *The high walls of Jerusalem*, New York 1983. The only work worth reading on the armistice of Mudros is a two-part article by G. Dyer, "The Turkish armistice of 1918", *MES*, viii, 1972.

The Peace Settlement

H. W. V. Temperley (ed.), *A history of the Peace Conference of Paris*, VI, 1924, contains a good outline of the Ottoman peace. A detailed study of the formation of the Sèvres treaty is in P. C. Helmreich, *From Paris to Sèvres*, Columbus, Ohio 1974. There is no similar study of the transformation of Sèvres into Lausanne; H. Nicolson, *Curzon, the last phase*, 1934, and S. R. Sonyel, *Turkish diplomacy 1918–1923*, 1975, present two differing interpretations of the latter conference. R. Davison,

"Turkish diplomacy from Mudros to Lausanne", in G. A. Craig and F. Gilbert (eds), *The diplomats 1919–31*, Princeton 1953, is also a good account of its subject. A useful account of the rise of the Kemalist movement is in E. D. Smith, *Turkey: origins of the Kemalist movement and the government of the Grand National Assembly 1919–1923*, Washington, DC 1959: it may be supplemented by Lord Kinross, *Ataturk*, 1964. For Greek activities see M. Llewellyn-Smith, *Ionian vision*, 1973. Still worth reading on the struggle in Asia Minor is A. Toynbee, *The Western question in Greece and Turkey*, 1922. A more modern study is H. J. Psomiades, *The Eastern question: the last phase*, Thessaloniki 1968. There are some useful studies of Transcaucasia, including Armenia. F. Kazemzadeh, *The struggle for Transcaucasia 1917–1921*, New York 1951 provides a general account which may be supplemented for Armenia by the writings of R. Hovannissian, *Armenia on the road to independence 1918*, Berkeley, Calif. 1967, and *The Republic of Armenia*, I, II, Berkeley, Calif. 1971, 1982, and by J. B. Gidney, *A mandate for Armenia*, Kent, Ohio 1967, and A. Nassibian, *Britain and the Armenian question, 1915–1923*, 1984. There is much material dealing with the settlement of the fate of the Arab provinces of the Ottoman empire. S. H. Longrigg, *Syria and Lebanon under French mandate*, 1958, describes the establishment of French control following the bargain between Britain and France studied by J. Nevakivi, *Britain, France and the Arab Middle East, 1914–1920*, 1969. On the same subject H. H. Cummings, *Franco–British rivalry in the post war Near East*, New York 1938, is still worth reading. An Arab view is presented in Z. N. Zeine, *The struggle for Arab independence*, Beirut 1960. Several books describe the early years of British rule in Palestine including J. J. McTague, *British policy in Palestine 1917–1922*, Lanham 1983; D. E. Knox, *The making of a Near Eastern question*, Washington, DC 1981, and B. Wasserstein, *The British in Palestine*, 1978. P. Sluglett, *Britain in Iraq, 1914–1932*, 1976, is the most recent study of the settlement in Iraq but P. W. Ireland, *Iraq*, 1937, is still valuable and J. Marlowe, *Late Victorian*, 1967, is an instructive biography of one of the principal architects of the state, Arnold Wilson. For the Kurdish question see C. J. Edmunds, *Kurds, Turks and Arabs*, 1957. The Cairo Conference of 1921 is the central concern of A. S. Klieman, *Foundations of British policy in the Arab world*, 1970.

The course of British wartime policy towards Egypt may be followed in Lord Lloyd, *Egypt since Cromer*, 1933, but the best book on the post-war settlement is J. Darwin, *Britain, Egypt and the Middle East*, 1981, which should be accompanied by study of a major essay by E. Kedourie, "Saʿd Zaghlul and the British", in *The Chatham House version*, 1970, a collection of essays of considerable value in any examination of

British policy in the Near East. V. Chirol, *The Egyptian problem*, 1921, presents the Milner Commission version of the causes of the 1919 uprising and Mahmud Y. Zayid, *Egypt's struggle for independence*, Beirut 1965, presents an Egyptian nationalist view, but by far the most interesting analysis of the 1919 uprising which has appeared recently is R. Schulze, *Die Rebellion der ägyptischen Fallahin*, Berlin 1981. In addition to works mentioned in previous sections the post-war settlement of Iran may be traced in N. S. Fatemi, *Diplomatic history of Persia, 1917–1923*, New York 1952, and the very thorough W. Zürrer, *Persien zwischen England und Russland, 1918–1925*, Berne 1978. There are no studies of the peace settlement in Arabia worth noting apart from those previously described. It remains only to mention two general studies of British policy in the Near East at the end of the war. The first is B. C. Busch, *Mudros to Lausanne*, Albany 1976, which is an account of the gradual contraction of British responsibilities throughout the whole region and is based upon British archival sources. The second is A. P. Thornton, *The imperial idea and its enemies*, 1959, a study of the same process in which the emphasis in explanation is upon loss of will rather than lack of resources.

Glossary

The terms in this glossary are Slavonic, Turkish, Persian and Arabic although the great majority have their origin in the last language. The form of transliteration and the meaning assigned to them relate to their use in the nineteenth and twentieth centuries.

ʿAbā A coarse woollen cloth also termed *kasā*.

ʿAdālatkhāna House of justice.

ʿAdl Justice.

Agalîk Landed estate.

Agha (also *aga*: Persian *āqā*) Chief, master, landowner. In the nineteenth-century Ottoman empire (OE) used to denote army officers who were not college trained.

ʿĀlim A graduate, lit. one who has knowledge (*ʿilm*), that is, Islamic-based knowledge.

Amīr Military commander, governor, minor ruler. *Amīr al-muʾminīn* Commander of the faithful = caliph.

Amīra Term applied to Armenian notables linked to Ottoman state.

Anjuman Society, council.

Aʿyān Plural of Arabic *ʿayn*. Used in OE to signify local notables.

Bāb Gate. *Bāb-i ʿĀlī* The high or exalted gate = the Sublime Porte. The office of the Ottoman grand vizier used as a synonym for the government of the OE.

Bābī A member of a heterodox sect in nineteenth-century Iran, a follower of Sayyid ʿAlī Muḥammad of Shiraz (1819–50), who was known as the *Bāb*.

Bahāʾī Follower of Bahāʾallāh, leader of a branch of the *Bābī* sect.

Bayrakdar (*bayraqdār*) Standard-bearer. An Ottoman title.

Beg (*bey*) Lord, title used for high officials and tribal leaders. Turkish equivalent of Arabic *amīr*. *Beglerbeg* (*Beylerbeyi*) Originally commander-in-chief, later a provincial governor and by the nineteenth century a title.

Beglik A landed estate.
Berāt Order, patent, grant or deed of protection. Arabic *barāʾa*.
Boyar (Slavonic) Lord, master, notable.
Caliph (Arabic *khalīfa*) Deputy or successor (sc. of the Prophet). In the nineteenth century the Ottoman sultan claimed authority over all Muslims on the basis of his alleged succession to the ʿAbbasid caliphs.
Capitulations Grants or treaties establishing a system of extraterritorial jurisdiction and tariff limitation in the OE.
Chiftlik (occasionally *jiftlik* or *chiflik*) A farm, later a landed estate.
Chorbaji Janissary officer commanding a regiment (*orta*). A Bulgarian notable.
Dār al-Ḥarb "House of War", that is, territories outside Muslim rule.
Dār al-Islām "House of Islam", that is, territories under Muslim rule.
Dawla The state.
Defterdār One who keeps a register (*defter*), a treasurer.
Derebey Valley lord. Term employed to denote rural notables in Anatolia.
Dervish (Arabic *Darwīsh*) A member of a Sūfī fraternity or *ṭarīqa*.
Dey (*dayi̊*) Literally maternal uncle. Title of Janissary or corsair leader of North Africa.
Dhimmī A non-Muslim belonging to a monotheistic community (Christian or Jew).
Dīwān Court, council, department of government, ministry.
Dūnum (Turkish: *dönüm*) A measure of land area corresponding to 919 square metres (in Iraq 2,500 square metres).
Efendi Ottoman title of Greek origin used in this period to denote members of the civil bureaucracy and more generally to describe literate townsmen, more particularly those educated in secular style.
Faddān A measure of land area in Egypt corresponding to 4,201 square metres from the time of Muḥammad ʿAlī. Used also in Syria with a very wide range of meanings.
Fallāḥ (plural *fallāḥīn*) A farmer or cultivator, especially in Egypt.
Farmān Decree, command, order.
Fatwā (Turkish, fetvāʾ) A legal opinion given by a *muftī*.
Fiqh Islamic jurisprudence.
Ghāzī A fighter in the holy war (*ghazwa*), a hero (of Islam).
Ḥadīth Sayings of the Prophet, forming one of the principal sources of the *Sharīʿa*. Among Shīʿīs also the sayings of the *imāms*.
Haiduk A bandit (Serbian).
Haidut A bandit (Bulgarian).
Hājjī (Turkish, Arabic = Ḥājj) One who has accomplished the pilgrimage to Mecca, one of the five prescribed duties of Muslims.

Ḥākim Governor.
Hümāyūn Imperial.
Ikhwān Brethren. In early twentieth century applied to members of religious/agricultural settlements in central Arabia.
Iltizām Tax farm.
Imām Prayer leader in mosque. In Shīʿī usage one of the divinely guided successors of the Prophet beginning with his son-in-law ʿAlī ibn Abī Ṭālib.
Iqṭāʿ Assignment of revenues, usually land, in return for military or bureaucratic services. Loosely, a fief. Cf. Persian *tiyūl*, Turkish *tīmār*.
Janissaries (*Yeni-cheris*) Regular Ottoman infantry.
Jarīb A measure of land area in Iraq corresponding to approximately 3,723 square metres.
Jihād The struggle against evil or unbelief, in particular the holy war against unbelievers.
Jizya Poll tax paid by a *dhimmī*.
Kâhya bey General deputy of the Ottoman grand vizier.
Kāriye (Arabic = *Qāriya*) Ottoman local government division.
Khalifa See caliph.
Kharāj Property tax usually levied on land.
Khaṭṭ Edict.
Khuṭba Friday sermon, including a prayer mentioning the name of the ruler.
Klepht Greek bandit.
Livā Ottoman local government division.
Madrasa Muslim college of higher education.
Majlis Council, parliament.
Maktab Muslim primary school.
Mamlūk Slave imported into Muslim territory normally for military service.
Mashrūʿiyya Government according to the *Sharīʿa*.
Mashrūṭiyya Constitutional government.
Mejelle Ottoman code of civil law.
Millet Religious community, nation.
Mīrī Appertaining to the state, state land.
Muftī Muslim jurist qualified to give opinions on matters of legal interpretation.
Mujtahid Jurist qualified to give authentic opinions on the interpretation of the *Sharīʿa* especially among the Shīʿa.
Mulk State.
Mülkiye Appertaining to civil government, Ministry of the Interior, Ottoman college for education of state servants.

Mullā Lesser member of religious classes, cf. Persian *ākhūnd*.
Multazim One who holds an *iltizām*, a tax farmer.
Mustawfī A revenue official, an accountant.
Müteşarrif A government official. In OE the district officer immediately below the governor.
Mütesellim Ottoman provincial official with responsibilities for collection of revenues.
Muqāṭaʿajī Holder of an estate privileged for tax purposes. By the nineteenth century indistinguishable from the holder of an *iqṭā*.
Nāḥiye Ottoman local government division.
Nāʾib Deputy.
Naqīb al-Ashrāf Leader of the descendants of the Prophet in a particular locality.
Pasha Ottoman official title, usually born by those with rank of minister, governor or equivalent.
Qabīla Tribe.
Qaḍā Ottoman local government division.
Qāḍī Muslim judge appointed by the state with administrative as well as judicial duties.
Qāḍī-ʿasker Army judge. In the OE a high judicial official.
Qāʾim maqām Deputy, especially of a high official; in Iran the chief ministers of a provincial governor; in OE official in charge of a district.
Qanāt Underground channel constructed to convey water for drinking or irrigation.
Qānūn Ordinance, law.
Qāt Narcotic shrub grown in Yemen.
Reʾis efendi In OE deputy to the grand vizier in charge of foreign affairs.
Ṣadr-i aʿẓam Title of the Ottoman grand vizier.
Sanjak Ottoman administrative division.
Sayyid A descendant of the Prophet; pl. *sāda*.
Ser-ʿasker Commander-in-Chief of the army, minister of war.
Sharīʿa Islamic law.
Sharīf (pl. *Ashrāf*) A descendant of the Prophet, especially the sharīf of Mecca, cf. *Naqīb al-Ashrāf*.
Shaykh al-balad Village headman.
Shaykh al-Islām Religious official. In OE the chief muftī and leader of the religious hierarchy.
Shīʿī One who regards ʿAlī ibn Abʿ Ṭālib and certain of his descendants as divinely guided leaders of the Muslim community.
Shūra Council.
Sipahi Ottoman cavalryman.

Sipahsālār Commander-in-chief of the army.
Ṣūfī Religious mystic, member of a *ṭarīqa*.
Sulṭān Muslim title derived from the word for power, literally one who holds power.
Sunnī One who follows the *Sunna* or traditions of the Prophet, a member of the largest Muslim sect..
Ṭarīqa Path, the mystic path of the Ṣūfis, a Ṣūfi order or brotherhood.
Ṭā'ifa Corporation, an organized group of people pursuing the same occupation, etc.
Tanẓīmāt Reforms, name given to nineteenth-century Ottoman reform movement.
Ṭapu Register, land registered in accordance with the 1858 Ottoman land law.
Timar Assignment of revenues (usually land) in return for services (usually military) in OE.
Ulema (Arabic *ʿulamā'*) Plural of *ʿālim*, those with religious knowledge.
ʿUmda Village headman.
Umma The Muslim community.
ʿUrf Customary law.
ʿUshūrī Form of land tenure in Egypt.
Uṣūl Sources or principles (of law).
Vālī (Arabic *wālī*) Governor.
Vilayet (Arabic *wilāya*) Ottoman province (district).
Vizier (Arabic *wazīr*) Minister.
Wafd Delegation.
Waqf Charitable endowment.
Waṭan Place of origin, fatherland.
Zadruga Serbian extended household.
Zakāt Muslim tax prescribed in Qur'ān.

Genealogical Tables

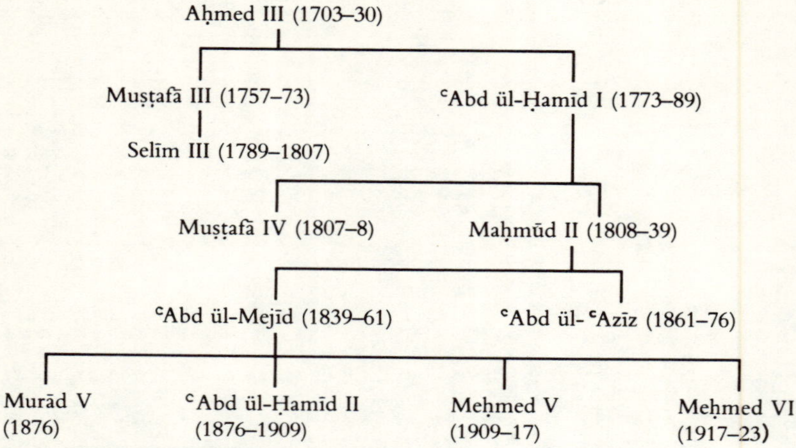

1. Ottoman Sultans with Regnal Dates

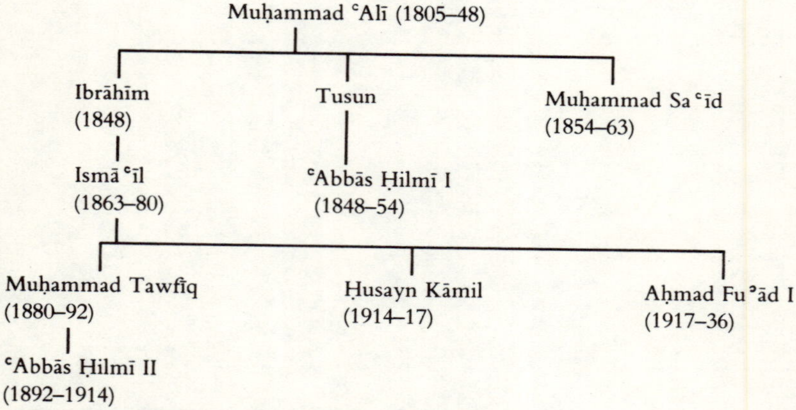

2. The Muḥammad ᶜAlī Dynasty with Regnal Dates

Maps

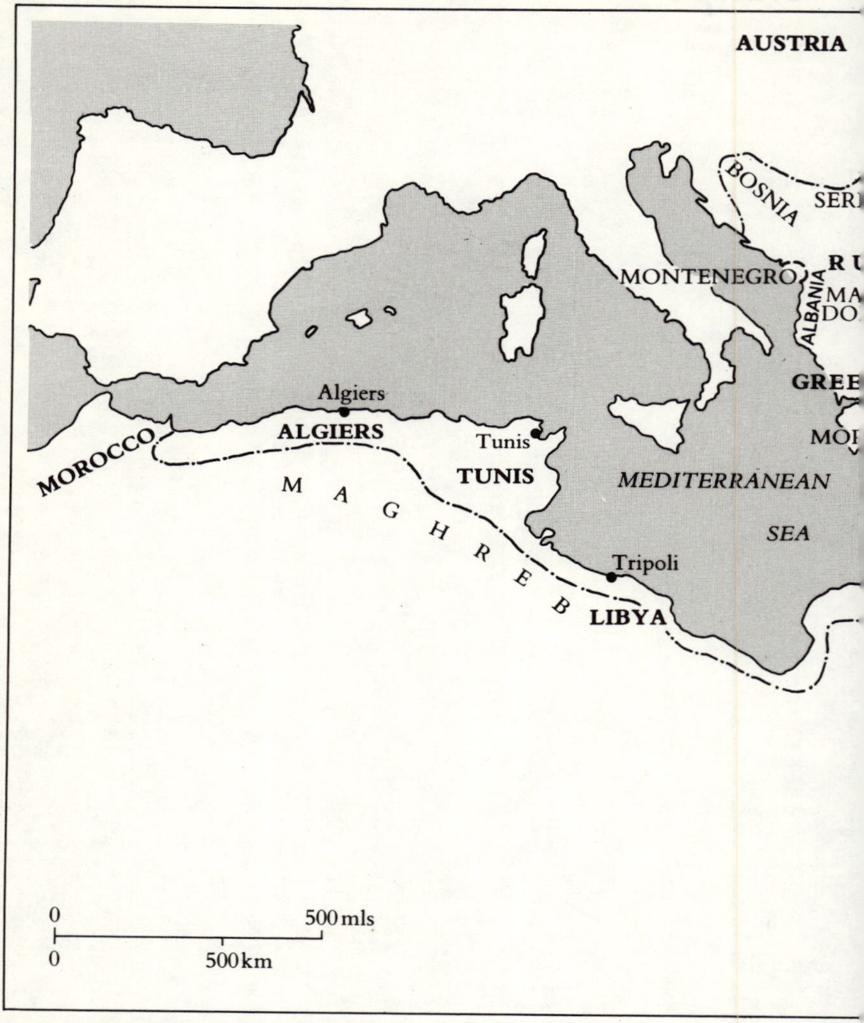

1. The Ottoman Empire in 1792

RUSSIA
OLDAVIA
NCIPALITIES
CRIMEA
LACHIA
CASPIAN SEA
CAUCASUS MTS.
GARIA
BLACK SEA
GEORGIA
TRANSCAUCASIA
I A
Trabzon
Istanbul
ARMENIA
RACE
Erzerum
AZERBAIJAN
Ankara
Bursa
ANATOLIA
Kurds
Diyarbakr
Izmir
Konya
CILICIA
Mosul
IRAN
IRAQ
Aleppo
Baghdad
CYPRUS
ETE
Beirut
Damascus
Acre
SYRIA
Basra
Jerusalem
Alexandria
Kuwayt
Persian Gulf
Cairo
'Anaza
EGYPT
NEJD
RED SEA
HIJAZ
Medina
Aswan
ARABIA
Jidda
Mecca

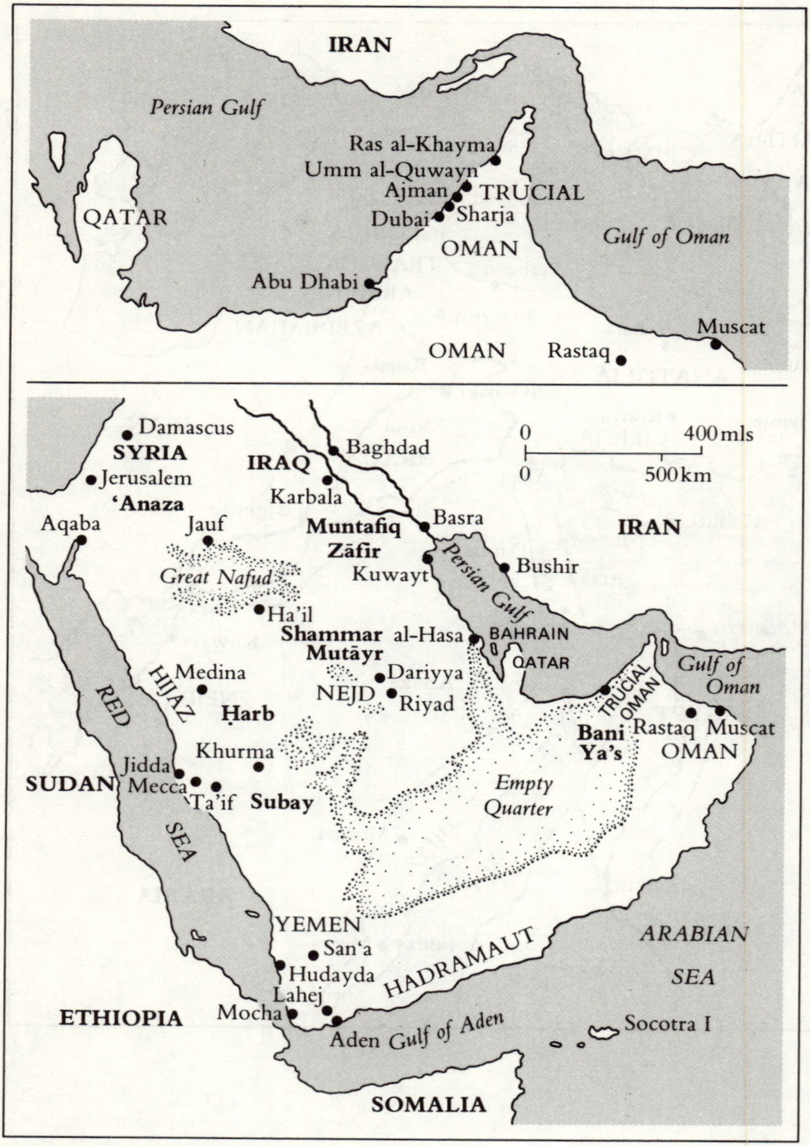

2. Arabia in the Nineteenth Century

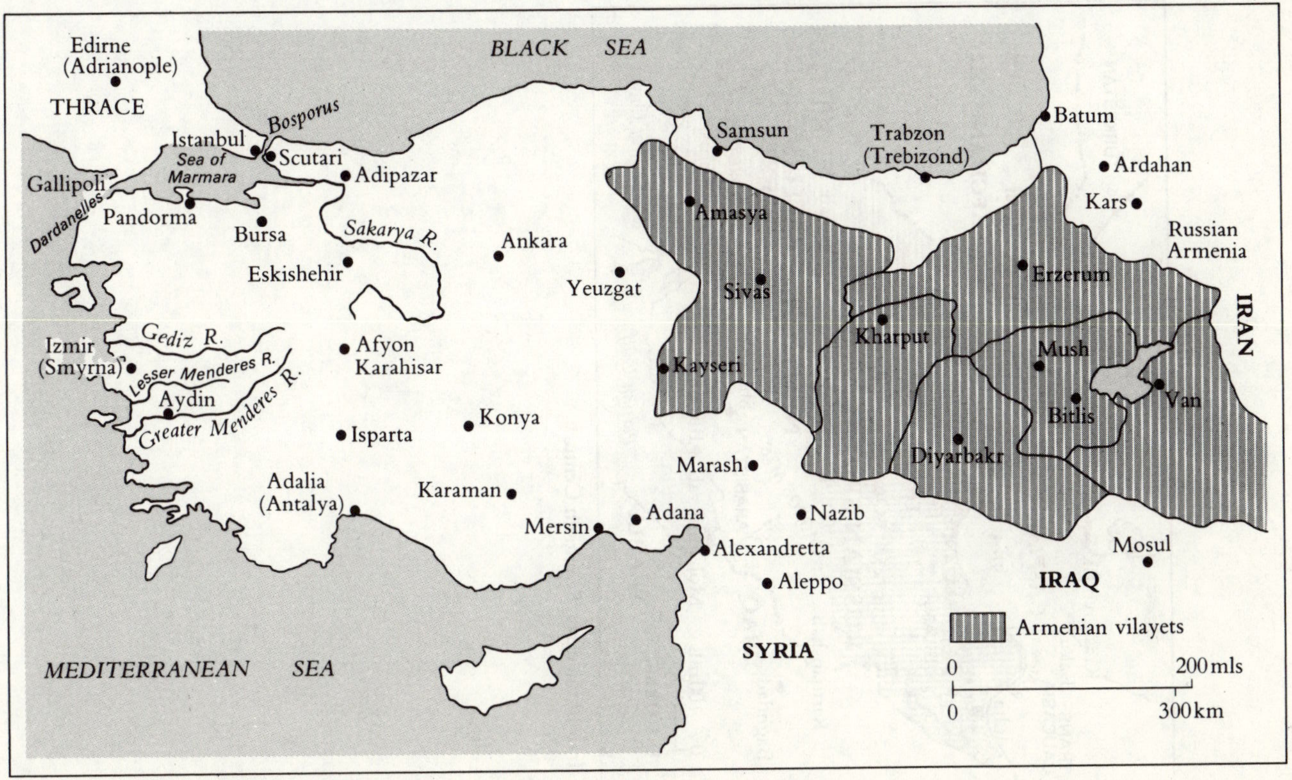

3. Antolia in the late Nineteenth Century

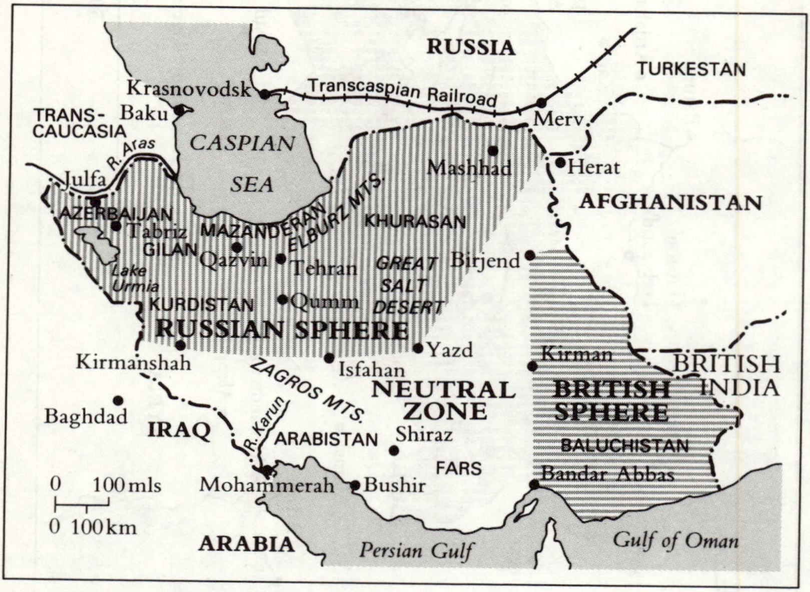

4. Iran in the early Twentieth Century

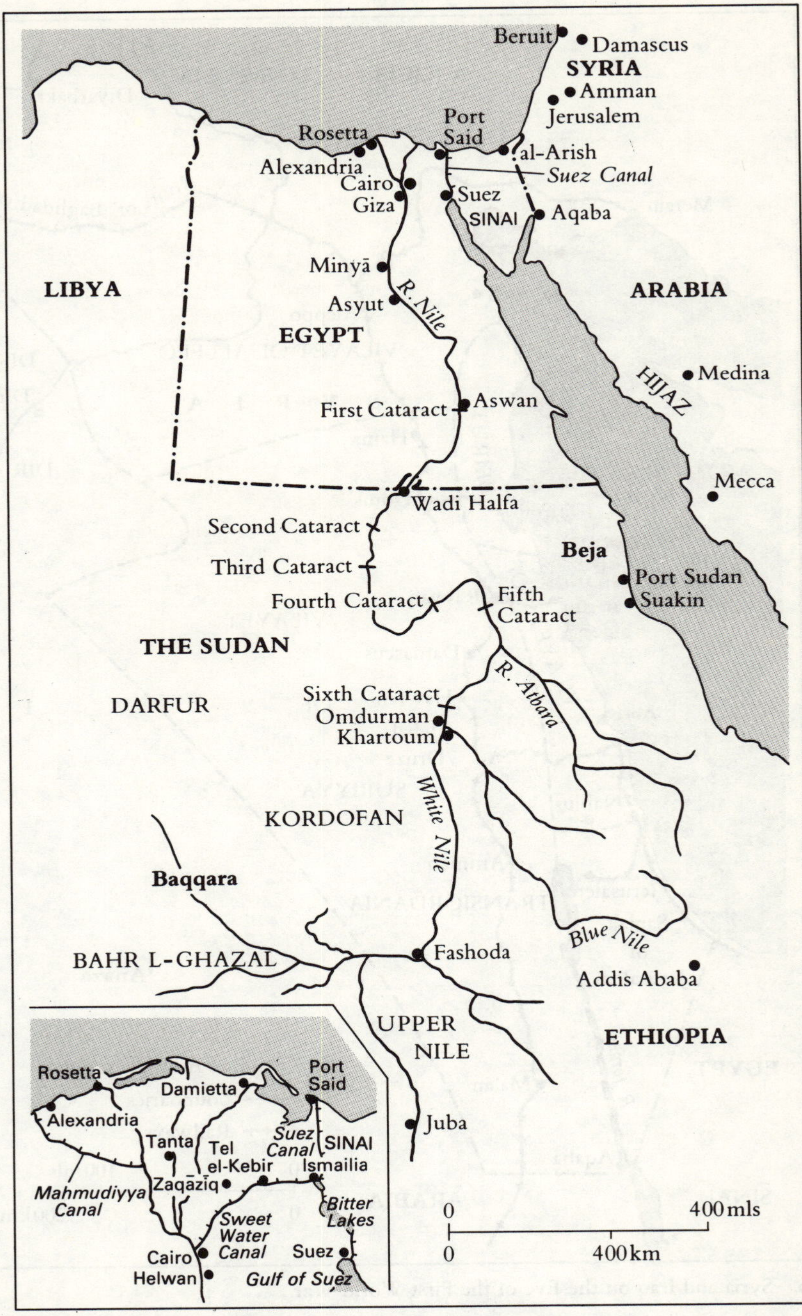

5. Egypt and the Sudan in the early Twentieth Century

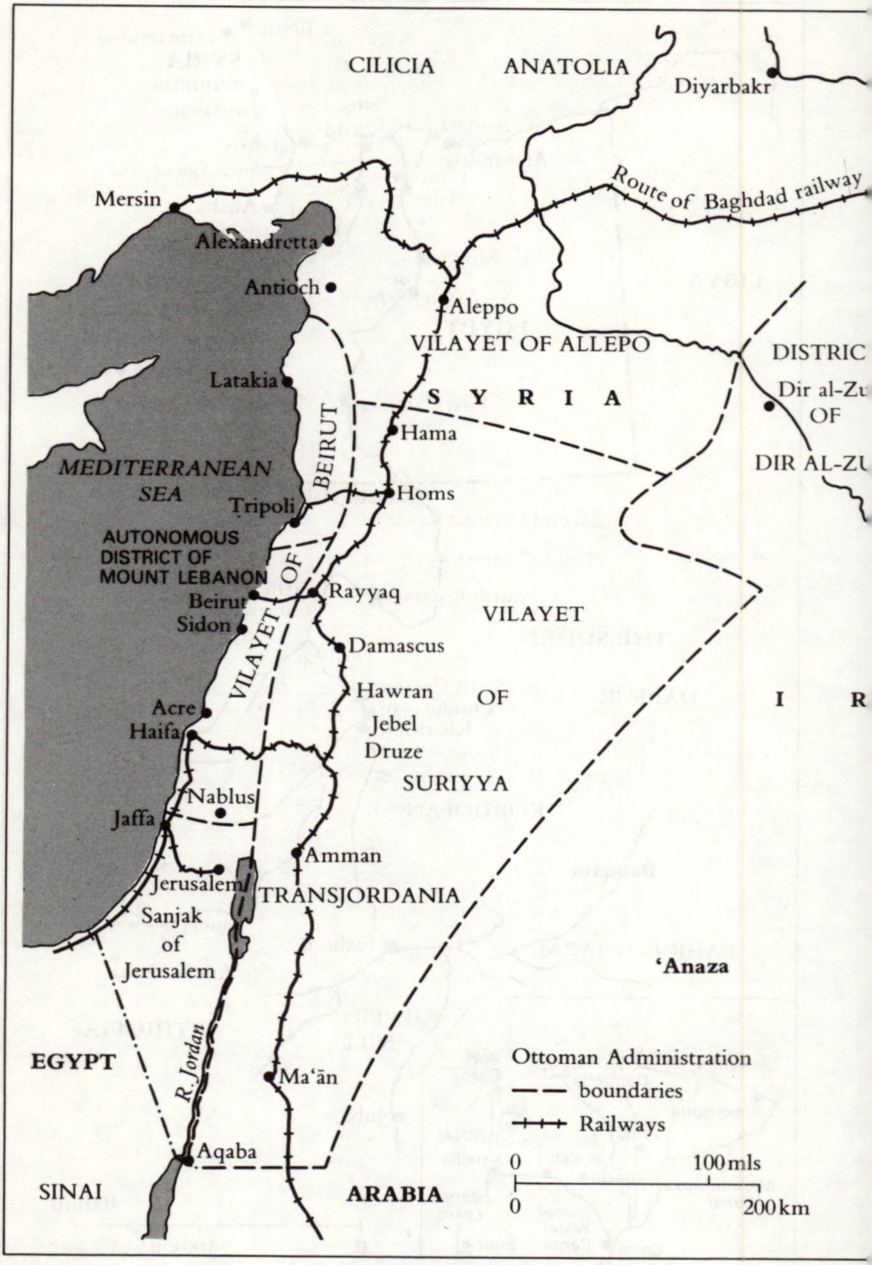

6. Syria and Iraq on the Eve of the First World War

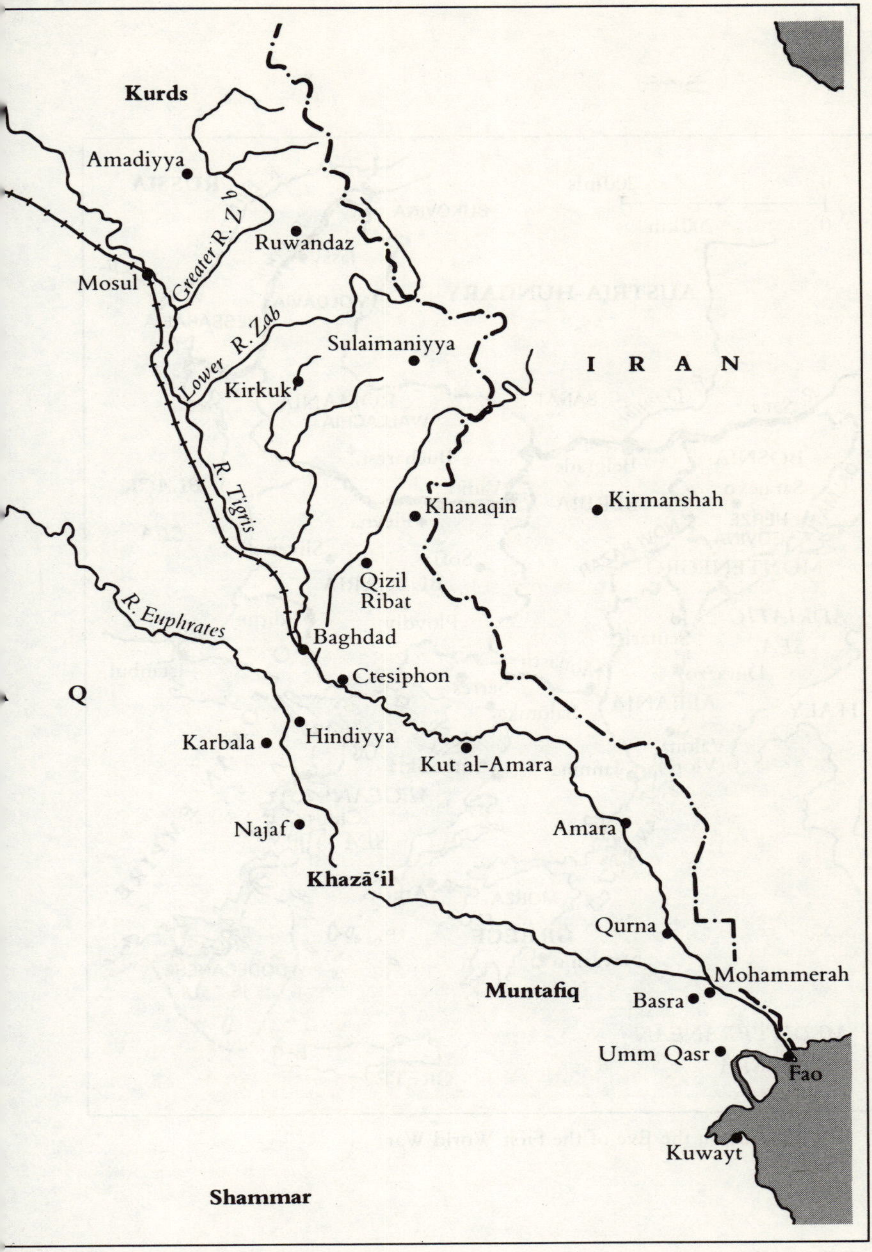
Kurds
Amadiyya
Ruwandaz
Mosul
Greater R. Zab
Lower R. Zab
Sulaimaniyya
Kirkuk
I R A N
R. Tigris
Khanaqin
Kirmanshah
Qizil
Ribat
R. Euphrates
Baghdad
Ctesiphon
Q
Hindiyya
Karbala
Kut al-Amara
Najaf
Amara
Khazā'il
Qurna
Mohammerah
Muntafiq
Basra
Umm Qasr
Fao
Kuwayt
Shammar

7. The Balkans on the Eve of the First World War

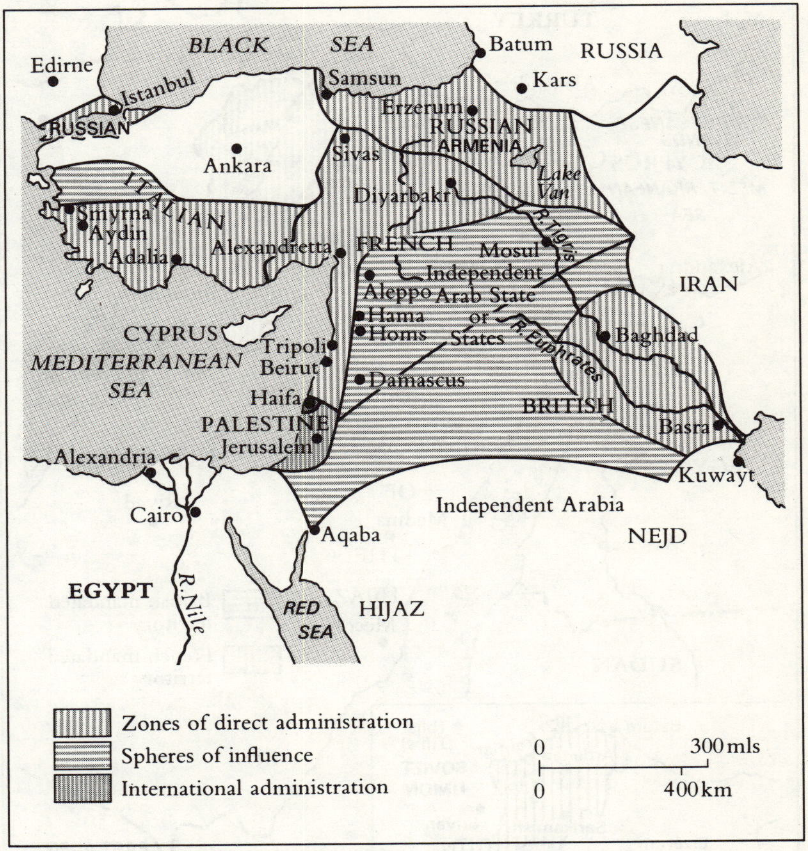

8. Entente Partition Schemes 1915–17

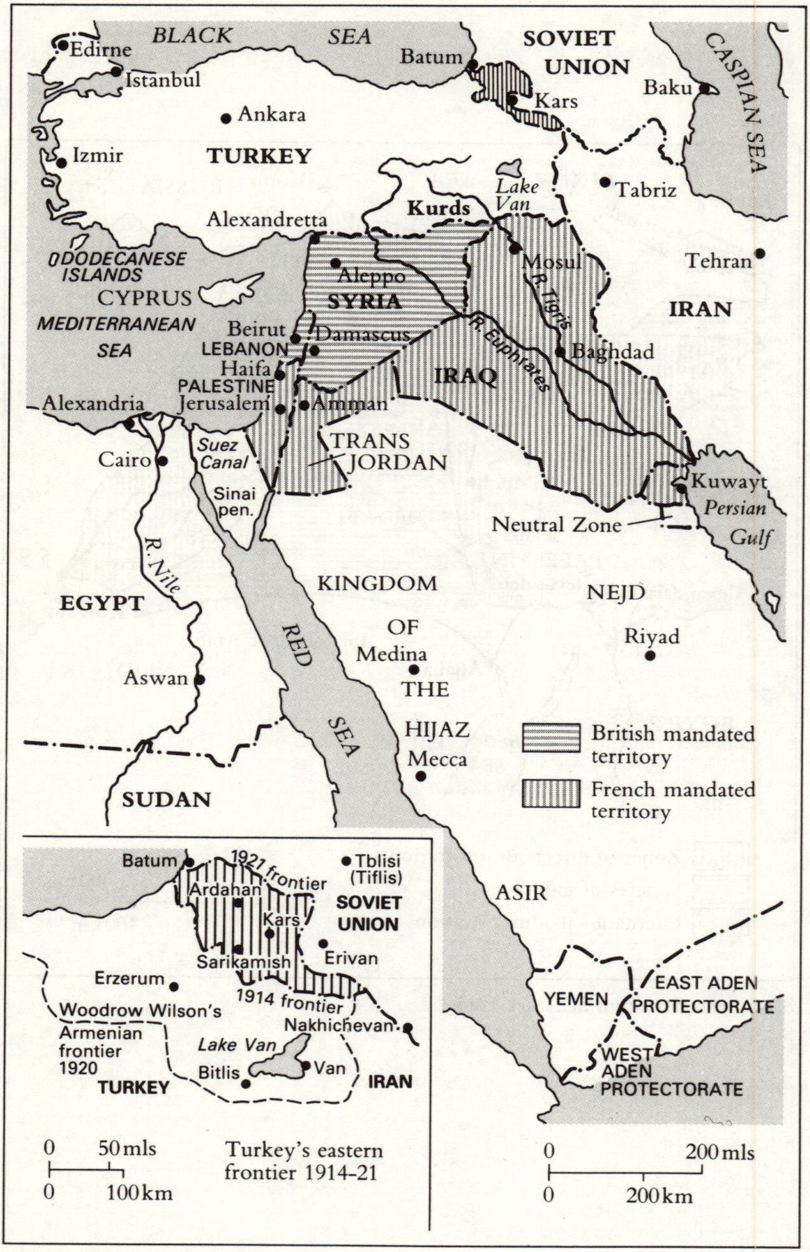

9. The Near East in 1923

Index